STUDIES IN TEXT GRAMMAR

FOUNDATIONS OF LANGUAGE

SUPPLEMENTARY SERIES

VOLUME 19

STUDIES IN TEXT GRAMMAR

Edited by

J. S. PETÖFI *and* H. RIESER

D. REIDEL PUBLISHING COMPANY

DORDRECHT-HOLLAND / BOSTON-U.S.A.

Library of Congress Catalog Card Number 73–75766

ISBN 90 277 0368 X

Published by D. Reidel Publishing Company,
P.O. Box 17, Dordrecht, Holland

Sold and distributed in the U.S.A., Canada, and Mexico
by D. Reidel Publishing Company, Inc.
306 Dartmouth Street, Boston,
Mass. 02116, U.S.A.

Printed in The Netherlands by D. Reidel, Dordrecht

TABLE OF CONTENTS

FOREWORD

If we consider how theoretical operations belonging to the methodological inventory of linguistics are carried out (i.e. the way linguistic theories are set up), three main criteria suggest themselves for classifying them:

(1) Both, nature and type of the *aims of the scientific knowledge applied* which allow to specify the epistemological interests as well as the theoretical impact constituting the purpose of linguistic operations;

(2) the nature of the intellectual *procedures* in connection with which a set of intersubjectively acceptable operations should guarantee that current postulates of the theory of science be maintained;

(3) the *set of data* serving as an empirical basis for the theories to be established on the one hand and as a correlate for the further development, the testing and the evaluation of theories on the other hand.

It is to be considered a basic concept (as well as a motive) of current text-linguistic research that due to the linguistic analysis of discourses a further *development of linguistics* has set in or is still to be achieved as regards the three criteria mentioned above.

Therefore, if we want to estimate text-linguistic approaches (or concepts), works (methods), or knowledge (results) we should take the view allowing for the general *valuation of the linguistic discipline* or one of its sub-disciplines. This should be done with respect to the contributions gathered in this volume as well.

Considering that the different steps and research-programs should be judged above all according to their *global perspective*, such a suggestion does not seem to be out of place. The following passages try to make this perspective clearer and to specify it by way of investigating the criteria mentioned more closely, namely the aims, the set of theoretical operations, and the problems of the empirical basis.

It has been mentioned already that the linguistic analysis of texts changes *the aims of linguistics* as regards their nature and their type. Granted that this assumption can be accepted, this implies the following: the type of epistemological interest changes because the linguist now deals with objects (i.e. discourses) which have to be considered embedding structures (frames) for linguistic phenomena constituting the domain of the various sentence-grammatical approaches. The fact that discourses themselves may be described by means of theoretically determined complex embedding operations is, of course, no valid objection against the textlinguistic approach. It is quite clear, however, that the epistemological interest is now concentrated on objects and relations between objects of a much more inclusive kind. Therefore the categories of the structural descriptions used, the rules of grammar, and the corresponding diagrams try to mirror the structural properties of these objects and the relations between them.

From this it follows that the *type* of epistemological interest changes as well: objects (i.e. sets of discourses) have to be treated, the description of which requires *more dimensions* than sentence-grammatical descriptions. This is due to the fact that the linguistic construct 'text' denotes the structure and the manifestation of linguistic objects observed in verbal communication. Only those objects which are not reduced by the various abstracting or idealizing methods of scientific analysis show all the various functions tied up with language in its ordinary use. Precisely these functions may then be considered as the legitimate objects of linguistic investigation and theoretical reconstruction.

This 'multi-level-dimensionality' of the text-analytic tools to be developed corresponds closely to the plurality of disciplines involved, if pragmatic and other functions of discourses should receive an adequate theoretical treatment. Some characteristics of this development may be inferred from the fact that logico-semantic languages are used for the description of the semantics of discourses, that the semantic analysis of discourses is – at least sometimes – linked up closely with the theory of literature and, that the interest in rhetoric, psychology etc. is still growing. It should be taken into consideration, however, that the participation of the various disciplines mentioned rests upon the delimitation of disciplines established and accepted thus far, i.e. disciplines like linguistics, logics, psychology, theory of literature etc.

Especially two characteristics are closely linked up with this development in linguistics as outlined above: In the first place it is more and more recognized that elaborate linguistic operations play a basic role as regards the semantic analysis of discourses, therefore the interest in developing adequate heuristic procedures is still going on. Discourses are regarded as objects the complex treatment of which has to be developed before the process of theoretical idealization (reduction, formalization) can be carried out successfully. In other words: Sound hypotheses about the complex properties of the set of objects/phenomena in question have to be established first, then it will be possible and reasonable to select subsets constituting the main (although preliminary) domain of scientific investigation. In the second place a growing interest for the different *domains of application* of text-grammatical research can be observed. The reason for this is the fact mentioned above that language is normally used in communication, discourses are therefore to be considered as the primarily observable empirical data. Consequently, their investigation will be of immediate relevance for solving the basic theoretical questions of an empirically founded pragmatics.

The changes within the domain of operations used in linguistic methodology closely correspond to the current trends of the development of the linguistic intentions as it has been briefly outlined above. Roughly, intellectual procedures of scientific importance may be classified into *procedures belonging to the proper treatment of the objects in question* and into *procedures leading to the controllable acquiring of empirically founded results*, in other words, into *analytic (mainly inductive) procedures* and *(mainly deductive) procedures, allowing for the set-up of hypotheses to be tested and evaluated* such that some decision as to the empirical validity, the equivalence of theories etc. can be achieved. The first group is intended to serve the aims of structural analysis, it contains operations such as segmentation and identification, the comparison of objects, classification, the set-up of classes of relational properties etc. The second group permits the description and systematization of the outcome of the structural analysis by means of some well-defined descriptional or theoretical language, it contains operations such as symbolizing, the proper set up of hypotheses, of definitions, the classification of hypotheses according to the theoretical status of the descriptional language they are formulated in, the rules of inference and deduction to be used etc. From the methodological point of view the theoretical status of the operations enumerated clearly remains the same, it should be noticed, however, that the *domain* is changed: text-linguistic research requires classificatory procedures and operations different from those applied in sentence-grammatical research. Above all, classes of elements and semantic functions of a different kind have to be discovered and to be formulated, e.g. the semantic relations *between* sentences, sequences of sentences and discourses. In addition to this, operations originally belonging to the methodological inventory of other disciplines are used, e.g. operations adopted from logics, psychology, sociology, communication theory, cybernetics etc. In this connection such questions have to be solved as whether a specifically set up *text grammar* is necessary, and if so, how it should be established, how *textual coherence* should be described and explained, which classes (e.g. syntactic, semantic referential, ontological) it is determined by etc.

The reason for the changes mentioned, which partly even necessitate methodological revaluations and improvements, may be seen in the fact that due to the linguistic analysis of discourses the *empirical basis* of linguistics has been changed, more precisely, expanded. Therefore not only theoretical statements, i.e. statements in some theoretical language based upon the expanded set of objects under investigation, have to be developed and evaluated but also statements with respect to different and so far neglected properties of linguistic acts become possible and necessary. Some remarks concerning the heuristics necessary to achieve this aim have already been given. It is important to maintain, however, that this approach will permit to regard the properties and structures of *observable linguistic acts* as the empirical basis of linguistic theories and as the legitimate domain of objects submitted to the various scientific procedures. In other words: These procedures are focussed on the *communicative aspects of linguistic acts.* The demonstration that linguistic methods which already exist and the application of which turned out to be successful as regards restricted domains may even be applied to the expanded domain of objects will constitute an interesting and valuable by-product of this approach.

One consequence already to be observed is, that – apart from deeper insight as regards the various functions of language – the problems of semantics, especially the semantics of individual elements (terms etc.) can be treated with greater accuracy and in a more general manner. Thus questions regarding the contextsensitivity, i.e. the intensional and extensional restrictions of elements have to be treated and solved in connection with *all the possible verbal and non-verbal contexts.* It should be clear then, that the problems of the internal and the external reference of discourses can be handled with better prospects. If we consider that the problems of intensional semantics and of interpretations related to presupposed worlds or models are given greater attention, it is to be assumed that formal instruments can be developed which permit the consistent analysis of literary texts as well as the description of the reception of texts. At the same time domains of objects are discovered such as e.g. the production of texts showing extreme properties, say 'concrete poetry' and 'visual poetry', where the methods of linguistic analysis cannot succed any longer, and where different and even more powerful analytical instruments will be needed.

To put it briefly: As regards the criticism and the evaluation of the articles gathered in this volume, they are to be estimated, first of all, with reference to the main perspectives connected with the linguistic analysis of discourse, text grammar etc. as they have been touched upon above, then, according to the special approaches, methods, proposals etc. tied up with the topics chosen. A rough outline of the contents of the articles contained is given – tied up with some introductory and completing remarks – in the subsequent overview.

University of Constance
Fachbereich Sprachwissenschaft

P. HARTMANN

JÁNOS S. PETÖFI AND HANNES RIESER

OVERVIEW

0. It is the aim of this volume to present some pieces of recent linguistic research which aim at the description of discourses and at the development of a formal theory, called *text grammar,* which should permit the enumeration of abstract objects, called *texts.*

The selection of the articles contained in this book was guided by two considerations: On the one hand, we thought it worthwhile to publish some essays concerned with the heuristic and the methodological foundation of such a theory, as might be seen from the articles of Irena Bellert, Teun van Dijk, Wolfram Köck, and Werner Kummer, on the other hand we wanted to present some papers dealing with questions of the formal set-up of an empirically adequate text grammar, as might be seen from the articles of János S. Petöfi and Hannes Rieser. In addition to methodological questions, the papers of Ihwe, Petöfi, and Rieser deal with some aspects concerning the evaluation of a text-grammatical theory relative to some given domains of application.

Although the theoretical points of view of the different contributors are certainly not identical, not to say controversial, which prevents the discussion of the problems enumerated within *one* homogeneous theoretical frame, the essays do show one important common feature: they argue that many relevant phenomena of natural languages such as the structure of sequences of connected sentences, definitivization, definite descriptions, pronominalization, co-textual referentialization, semantic relations like synonymy, co-hyponymy, hyperonymy, presupposition, entailment, natural inferences, etc., can only be treated successfully (if they can be treated successfully at all) within the frame of a text grammar, whereas the existing sentence grammars cannot account for such phenomena in a sufficient general and consistent way.

Another argumentation common to most of the articles is, that text grammars can provide relevant contributions to the solution of problems put forward by empirical sciences or arts which in some way or other are concerned with discourses. Especially the papers of van Dijk, Ihwe, and Petöfi provide detailed formal and empirical arguments along this line.

It can be maintained with good reason that the development of linguistics from a more or less sentence-grammatical orientated to a text-grammatical directed theory, as it is presented in this book, is mainly due to science-

J. S. Petöfi and H. Rieser (eds.), Studies in Text Grammar, 1–16.

theoretical considerations, concerning above all the empirical adequacy of a linguistic theory, its confirmation, and its supposed applicability. Therefore the foundation of this direction of linguistic research is closely connected with an intense discussion of methodological questions. Especially the set-up of adequate descriptional and theoretical languages (text grammars), the consistency (homogeneity) of partial theories, the generalization of sentence grammars, the integration of types of sentence grammars into text grammars, and the formal and empirical results of such procedures receive great interest.

Besides these interests concerning the set-up of a linguistic theory as an empirical theory most (text) linguists share the view that linguistic phenomena should be discussed within the frame of a homogeneous theory, however provisional and tentative such a frame may be, and that the mere accumulation of empirical 'facts' (examples taken from natural languages) will certainly not lead to a consistent theory. It is claimed that such a tentative theoretical frame determines the inductive heuristic work to be done and the formal set-up as well as the testability of parts of the theory and the application of the theory itself. In other words: even pre-theoretical heuristic steps leading to the construction of a theory must be guided by methodological considerations, they are in fact dependent upon tentatively set up (meta-) theoretical postulates and general epistemological interests, e.g., the type of explanation to be aimed at, the specification of the questions such a theory should answer, the compatibility conditions it should fulfil with respect to other theories etc.

This does not mean, of course, that the work done on the different types of sentence grammars has had no influence upon text linguistics; on the contrary, all the articles contained in this volume show that their authors have greatly benefitted from recent research done in linguistics, especially from the discussion context-free phrase structure grammar vs transformational grammar, interpretative semantics vs generative semantics as well as from current logics, philosophy of language and communication theory.

1. Thus van Dijks paper *Text Grammar and Text Logic* is intended as a contribution to the logical analysis of texts of natural languages, a topic which has received considerable attention during recent years. He discusses the relations between logics and linguistics and tries to show which of the descriptive tools provided by current logical systems can be used for the description of natural texts.

The starting point for his argumentation is provided by the analogy between the principles according to which proofs are derived in formal languages and theories and those strategies which determine the successful set-up of coherent texts in natural languages. As a basically sound working hypothesis he assumes that sentences which constitute the texts of a given object language have to be regarded somehow as premisses or conclusions of a natural syllogism. This hypothesis determines the formal (and still very tentative) set-up of the text grammar he proposes.

According to the meta-theoretical postulates given in the introductory passages of his paper it is the main task of a text grammar to reconstruct the semantic relations existing between sequences of sentences and to explain because of which semantic properties natural texts have to count as coherent. An elaborate comparison of formal logics and natural logics shows that logical systems established so far are not yet rich enough to guarantee an adequate and empirically acceptable description of the global semantic information of natural texts. This tentative evaluation of logical systems leads to a catalogue of phenomena of natural languages for which specific classificatory procedures and adequate notations have to be established, if a natural logic is to be developed, e.g. for quantification in natural languages, the use of intersentential connectives, negation, the use of modalities etc. He arrives at the conclusion that due to these shortcomings and because of the fact, that logical systems lack a sufficiently elaborated and empirically relevant semantic component as well as a well defined pragmatics their application would not only lead to a rather fragmentary description of natural texts but also to an empirically inadequate one.

On the basis of this comparison of logical systems and of what he calls 'natural logic' the tentative tasks of a text logic are laid down. This text logic is conceived of as a part of a generative grammar enumerating sets of theoretical objects, called 'texts'. The admissible formulas provided by the text logic serve as an input to other grammatical (especially transformational) rules. The text logic proposed will permit the explanation of more or less intuitive semantic notions like ambiguity, synonymy, paraphrase, coherence, presupposition, and entailment, therefore it has to contain a set of basic predicates, a set of derived predicates, meaning postulates, construction rules and specific constraints mapping the properties of the object language onto the descriptional language. It is intuitively clear that such a text logic is a far more general and therefore a much weaker system than a formal logic which is supposed to permit the derivation of acceptable proofs, i.e. 'inferential texts', without regard to any specific object language. In opposition to a formal logic which is supposed to generate specific texts only, i.e. proofs which have to count as valid, a natural logic has to admit interpretations which are empirically relevant, because such a system is conceived of as part of an empirical theory.

Now, it is certainly the case that the analogy between proofs in formal languages and natural texts cannot be taken in too strict a sense, although it must be admitted that it may very well serve as a promising heuristic instrument. Therefore the notions of inference and logical entailment have to be weakened to some degree such that they may be applied to natural texts, i.e. a natural logic has to specify under which conditions an arbitrary following sentence is admissible, given an ordered set of preceding sentences. To say this is equivalent to saying that texts of natural languages are constructed in such a way that the constituting sentences are conceived of as theorems derivable within the text logic.

In order to describe the semantic relations between preceding and following sentences a Modal Predicate Calculus is proposed first. However, this calculus is modified gradually such that it can be used for a more adequate description of the semantic relations within natural texts. Especially those phenomena are discussed which intuitively determine the coherence relation in natural texts, e.g. restricted quantification and identity, partial identity and inclusion on the one hand, presupposition, entailment and different types of strong and weak consequences on the other hand. The discussion of these intensional relations leads to the interesting hypotheses, 'that a sentence of a text is derivable only if its presuppositions have been previously derived, which makes presupposition a well-formedness condition for texts" and "that the set of presuppositions must be consistent". One of the most remarkable relations introduced in addition to presupposition and entailment is that of 'possible consequence'. This relation is assumed to be the weakest coherence relation in natural texts. The discussion about semantic relations to be introduced for the consistent description of texts is closed by a tentative list of the derivational principles of text logic. This list is not assumed to be exhaustive. It may very well serve as a sound basis for discussions which should permit the further precision and elaboration of a working text logic.

2. Irena Bellert's paper *On Various Solutions of the Problem of Presuppositions* is intended as a contribution to the analysis of semantic relations in natural texts. In our opinion, such analyses are considered to be necessary preconditions for the establishing of a text grammar, especially for the construction of a lexicon and the definition of a set of (possibly) transformational rules which determine the admissible positions of sentences in a text, granted that a canonical logico-semantic deep structure can be established which contains the necessary semantic information (cf. the contribution of Petöfi to this problem in opposition to that of van Dijk, who proposes the somewhat different approach of introducing the semantic information step by step, thus reconstructing the conditions which must be observed if a coherent text should be produced).

According to Bellert's argumentation Frege's proposal for the solution of the presupposition problem does not meet the tasks of a linguistic theory.

The same holds true for Russell's treatment of the problem. Then Strawson's definition of presupposition is introduced. It is shown that the concept of presupposition necessarily has to play an important role in the description of the semantics of natural languages. However, the question of the adequate treatment of this semantic relation within the framework of different linguistic theories has led to a series of confusions and controversies, especially as far as the question is concerned which propositions have to count as presuppositions, which as implications or entailments. The same holds true for the decision of whether presuppositions belong to the semantic or to the pragmatic component of a linguistic theory. We think that, apart from terminological controversies, many of these problems result from the fact that most linguistic theories are not developed thus far as to permit the consistent treatment of the presupposition problem. The solutions given are more or less *ad-hoc* solutions depending on the pieces of object language under discussion. Naturally, if not even rough outlines of the set-up of a linguistic theory are provided, and if the tasks of the different components of the theory remain vague, the question which component has to account for presuppositions cannot be answered seriously at all.

Subsequently Austin's interpretation of the terms 'presuppose', 'imply' and 'entail' is presented, especially Austin's notion of implication receives some serious criticism. If the result of this discussion can be accepted, this is of considerable importance for the establishing of a linguistic theory: According to Bellert's opinion, Austin's analysis of implication leads to ontological problems, the treatment of which goes far beyond the theoretical possibilities of a linguistic semantics. The linguist should concentrate his interest on such implications which can be treated with reference to the utterance in question and the truth of which can be decided by purely formal means.

Bellert does not accept the differentiating criteria Austin proposes for 'imply' and 'entail'. She tries to show that the presupposition relation can be described conveniently as a special case of the implication relation. The relation of implication plays a central role in Bellert's concept of a theory accounting for the semantics of a natural language. This is demonstrated in connection with the discussion of the various solutions of the presupposition problem proposed by linguists thus far.

3. In contrast to Bellert, Werner Kummer tries to give an account of 'pragmatic presupposition' in his contribution *Pragmatic Implication*. His analysis starts from the definition of 'pragmatic presupposition' as given by Robert Stalnaker in his paper *Pragmatics*. He assumes that the determination of the meaning of the operators *believe* and *know* is one of the basic problems if the

notion of 'pragmatic presupposition' be defined. Following Bellerts distinction between 'real belief' – 'purported belief', the proposes that the notions 'purported belief' and 'purported knowledge' can either be treated as undefined basic terms in a pragmatic language or they can be reduced to the notions 'doxastic implication' and 'epistemic implication'. First it is shown that this reduction is possible, then it is argued that 'pragmatic presupposition' can be explained in these terms too, if it can be successfully proved that the definiens in the definition of this concept can be reconstructed in terms of doxastic and/or epistemic implication. In order to achieve this aim, a concept of 'pragmatic implication' is developed from the notions of 'doxastic implication' and 'epistemic implication'. 'Pragmatic implication' may serve as an explicatum of the notion 'pragmatic presupposition'' as given by Stalnaker. It is suggested that the notion of 'pragmatic implication' be accepted as one of the basic terms in a pragmatic language.

4. The difficulties of establishing an adequate heuristics for an empirically valid text grammar (text theory) are discussed by Wolfram K. Köck in his article *Time and Text: Towards an Adequate Heuristics.*

Linguistics has only recently developed tendencies to investigate the syntactic and semantic mechanisms of discourses (texts) rather than those of utterances which can be described by the theoretical construct 'sentence'. In various publications dealing with some aspects of discourses, both traditional and modern, the basic importance of 'tense' is emphasized repeatedly and, in fact, declared a crucial problem for any text theory.

The article has grown out of primarily heuristics-oriented research on precisely this problem. It summarizes in rather abstract form what the author thinks to be the adequate science-theoretical orientation for all research on textual matters as well as for the solution of various particular problems implied by them such as, e.g. the role of 'tense'. Therefore he presents a global heuristic framework which should allow the proper isolation of individual problems to be dealt with in search for an adequate text theory. As a matter of fact, it is quite impossible to evade dealing with the basic questions of a text theory when trying to find out about the particular position of just one, however, essential, constituent, 'tense'. It seems equally impossible and even misguided to attempt any specific investigation of isolated problems without proper theoretical, or at least, pre-theoretical orientation. This seems to be especially the case with the intricate subject of time in language.

According to Köck, the question of tense in discourses first demands a clarification of the meaning of both 'tense' and 'text'. Naturally such a definition cannot be achieved outside the framework of some adequate theory of language. A necessary precondition for such a framework is, of course, that the general science-theoretical principles of the construction of adequate (empirical) theories are taken into consideration and sorted out according to the type of explanation the theory of language is supposed to meet. Köck postulates that such a theory in order to be adequate, must represent a specific range of phenomena in such a way as to allow their explanation according to an established set of general empirical hypotheses. His meta-theoretical postulates thus go far beyond those claimed and accepted by van Dijk, Petöfi and Rieser, for, according to his opinion, the theory should also permit the manipulation of the objects in question in all the various fields of practical application, e.g. as far as linguistics is concerned, the control of the meaning of utterances wherever they play a dominant role, e.g. in politics, law, theology, journalism, mass media etc. This would imply that the theory be stated according to the accepted standards considered to be valid for empirical sciences, so as to admit of intersubjective testing of all sorts, and not only to the much narrower concept of testability as it is proposed by Petöfi and Rieser. If this should be achieved, naturally, the basic epistemological facts concerning all attempts to attain knowledge of whatever kind, have to be taken into account.

Köck proposes to use the formal model developed in cybernetics to represent the basic structure of the feedback system man/mind – environment. This model should serve as a tool for the set-up of the outline of what would have to count as an adequate theory of language. It is further supposed to provide the adequate framework for any study of discourse as well as for that something called 'time' and its representation in/by language.

The author of *Time and Text* claims, that in terms of such an anthropo-cybernetic model (the model is supposed to be strongly motivated by empirical anthropological evidence) the shortcomings of certain concepts of 'text' may be shown conveniently. Such shortcomings may result from an impermissible reduction of the phenomenon (often called 'idealization') for the purpose of some pre-established methodology. Köck stresses that most recent research in textual matters so far has been concerned with a 'reduced' phenomenon, usually the written/printed and necessarily impoverished representation of some verbal utterance. He argues that what is needed is abstraction and not reduction and that – in order to comply with the requirements of applicability as outlined above – full and unimpaired functional systems must at least first be sketched within which language or verbal utterances are possible and actualized respectively, before a well-motivated and more specialized line of research may be taken up. It is argued that the acceptability of a discourse has to be illuminated sufficiently, before its grammaticality can be profitably studied. However, acceptability can only be characterised within an appropriate functional model of language. Such a model is briefiy outlined in terms of the mentioned anthropo-cybernetic model man – environment (ACM).

The ACM allows to handle some features of 'time' and their representation in natural languages. It is shown that tense is only *one* linguistic means of referring to time. According to the author's opinion it would be hopelessly inadequate (and even impossible) to say anything relevant when not taking into account all the other forms of time reference or temporal meaning. Subsequently some basic problems, connected with the topic of 'time and text' are discussed, among others e.g. implicit temporal semantics (covering the temporal components which are inherent features of lexemes, i.e. part of their meaning) and explicit temporal semantics (the traditional categories like tense, time adverbials, and all other word classes expressly or implicitly denoting time). Further the question is touched of whether temporal elements play a distinctive role as regards different types of text.

5. A presentation of an inclusive text grammar is given in János S. Petöfi's contribution *Towards an Empirically Motivated Theory of Verbal Texts.* In the first section of this paper the tasks are enumerated which are regarded as tasks of an empirically motivated grammatical theory. The set-up of the text grammar is based on the hypothesis that text grammars can and should be regarded as generalized (and expanded) sentence grammars. Their expansion depends on the empirical aims of the theory.

Because of this main working hypothesis it is, of course, necessary to establish a typology of sentence-grammatical conceptions, i.e. to build up a hierarchy of sentence grammars the differentiating criteria of which are provided by their theoretical power, especially by their empirical adequacy. This attempt is restricted to an expanded version of the Chomsky Grammar and to generative semantics.

The Chomsky Grammar (CKP-model) generates deep structures which, on the one hand, semantic representations are assigned to by a semantic interpretative rule system, on the other hand these deep structures serve as an input for syntactic transformation rules and phonological interpretative rules transducing them into surface structures. How linear manifestations are brought about is considered to be a question of performance. The tasks of the semantic component of the CKP-model can be specified as follows: determination of both the number and the meaning of the possible readings of the sentences in question, determination of semantic anomalies, determination of the paraphrase relation between given sentences.

It is argued by Petöfi that the semantic rule system can at most solve the first and the second task. Moreover, even those tasks can only be solved within the boundary fixed by the syntactic component. More precisely: the possible readings can just be assigned to deep structures. It is quite impossible to explain syntactical ambiguity and the notion of paraphrase within the CKP-model in general. This type of sentence grammar is labelled conception type *A*.

Conception type *B* is provided by a sentence grammar as it has been outlined thus far within generative semantics. According to this conception the base component of the grammar immediately generates semantic representations. Therefore no semantic interpretative process exists and consequently no semantic interpretative rules apply. The adherents of conception type *B* do usually not treat the question of 'generation'. As a notational tool they use an extended predicate calculus which is more or less adapted to the particular features of natural languages. They try to develop a representation which determines the linear manifestation non-ambiguously.

Considering the directedness of the sequences of the different operations within conception type *A* and *B* respectively, the difference between them can be stated as follows: The sequence of operations within *B* is unidirectional, it leads from semantic representations to surface structures. This model will in principle be able to generate paraphrases, it cannot explain, however, whether the linear manifestation arrived at the intended meaning only or whether it represents other meanings too. In other words: it does neither account for syntactical ambiguity nor for the possible readings of the linear manifestation.

Consider, that the sequence of operations within *A* is not unidirectional, it leads, on the one hand, from deep structures to the semantic representation and, on the other hand, from deep structures to the surface structures. This model accounts for the possible readings of the deep structure, but it does not explain the syntactical ambiguity of the linear manifestation nor does it allow to enumerate the admissible paraphrases of the semantic representation.

Consequently, a text grammar resulting from the generalization of either *A* or *B* would be inadequate, if it is demanded that this same text grammar be used for the synthesis, the analysis and the comparison of arbitrary texts. Therefore Petőfi first tries to set up a complex sentence grammar which combines the defining characteristics of *A* and *B*.

On the basis of the typology of sentence grammars types of text grammars are defined. It is assumed that basically two types of text grammars can be distinguished, namely *fixed linearity text grammars* and *not fixed linearity text grammars*.

The following basic types of text grammars are known so far ('+' indicates fixed linearity and '−' indicates not-fixed linearity) (see Table I).

Thus far text grammars of Type I and of Type IV have been investigated

TABLE I

	Type I	Type II	Type III	Type IV
Text base	+	–	+	–
Integrated sentence grammar	+	+	–	–

more closely. It is assumed that there are a lot of other types in between Type I and Type IV the formal properties of which are not yet known. A text grammar of Type I is then to be considered a generalized context-free phrase structure grammar using fixed linearity *both* within the text base and within the integrated sentence grammar. Such a text grammar has been proposed by Rieser in various publications. Petöfi developed a text grammar of Type IV which results from the generalized not-fixed linearity sentence grammar mentioned above.

Let us briefly consider the set-up of a Type I text grammar. It is the aim of a Type I text grammar to provide a formal explanation for the notion "text of a natural language $\mathscr{L}$", i.e. to establish a formal device which permits the general definition of texts and classes of texts (= texts showing similar structural properties). A Type I text grammar is supposed to assign at least one syntactic-semantic description to a text (= string of terminals) of a theoretical language $\mathscr{L}^1$. It further has to permit the derivation of texts of unbounded length and to account for the fact that texts can be embedded into other texts. This grammar does account for the explanation of *linear grammatical coherence,* i.e. it determines the syntactic-semantic connexions between sequences of sentences and sentences within the derived texts. It is supposed to account for the syntactic-semantic connexions between different texts too and it is considered to permit a formal classification of these connexions. A Type I text grammar thus enumerates texts of a theoretical language which can be mapped into the set of the discourses of a natural language. For such a grammar strategies have been developed which permit both, the synthesis and the analysis of linear coherent texts, i.e. on the one hand they allow texts to be generated, on the other hand arbitrary strings of graphemic elements can be submitted to them and then they permit the decision as to whether the strings belong to the theoretical language determinable by the grammar. The synthesis component of a Type I text grammar is developed such that a string of abstract syntactic categories a string of semantically interpreted terminal elements is assigned to. As hinted at above, such a grammar contains an explicit sentence grammar consisting of a syntactic level, a semantic level and a graphematic level as well as a lexicon. In addition to these levels a hypersyntactic component compatible with the sentence-grammatical component was developed. The semantic component used and its sub-component, the lexicon, are built up such that they allow for the integration of pragmatically interpretable indices (reference indices, selectional restrictions).

The formal devices developed so far are supposed to permit the construction of a text typology. A text type is considered to be a set of texts, the elements of which show common formal properties (e.g. as far as the syntactic-semantic mechanisms of the linear coherence are concerned). According to the sketchy information given above, clearly a Type I text grammar must contain a set of rules determining the hypersyntactic text base, a set of unordered, sub-indexed syntactic rules, a set of semantic rules (functions) relating terminals with nonterminals, a well-defined lexicon, and a set of transformation rules (of a very restricted kind) determining linear grammatical coherence.

It has been assumed during recent years (especially by Petöfi) that Type I text grammars prove to be empirically inadequate, mainly because of their fixed linearity base (s). These assumptions have been guided by theoretical considerations concerning the set-up of different sentence grammars. The empirical proofs for these intuitively reasonable assumptions still have to be provided (for a first and surely very tentative attempt along this line cf. the contribution of Rieser to this volume). Petöfi distinguishes between co-textual and contextual aspects/properties of texts. According to this basic separation two classes of systematic arguments/hypotheses concerning the given domain of objects (=discourses) can be distinguished: The co-textual aspects are defined as those components of text structures which are intersubjectively inferable by means of explicit theories. The communicative (i.e. pragmatic) aspects of texts are included among those structures which make up the set of the contextual properties of texts. It is argued that an adequate text theory must treat both aspects. Therefore a text grammar is considered to be only one, although necessary and basic component of a text theory. Its task is the description of the grammatical aspects of the co-textual structures inherent in texts. Under optimal conditions its set-up can be made such that certain compatibility requirements be preserved. This implies that a theory accounting for the contextual aspects of texts can be integrated into or (which is more likely) joined to the text grammar proposed. Petöfi maintains that only a text grammar of Type IV can meet those compatibility requirements as well as certain empirical requirements concerning e.g. the theoretical reconstruction of the intuitive comparison of texts, of the building up of paraphrases etc. The tasks of a Type IV text grammar are formulated as follows: A Type IV text grammar is supposed to assign to a given text (=linear manifestation) all admissible syntactic-semantic representations

(=text bases), i.e. to analyse texts, it must further generate all types of text bases, i.e. enumerate texts, and, finally, it has to determine the syntactic-semantic relations between any two given texts, i.e. it has to permit the comparison of texts.

With reference to text grammars not-fixed linearity means that the text base consists of a text-semantic representation, i.e. a semantic representation containing the whole semantic information of the text and of an information block. It must be stressed that *the semantic representation is indifferent with respect to the linear manifestation.* The information block contains all *those informations which are necessary for transducing the semantic representation into an admissible linear manifestation.*

Clearly the above-mentioned tasks can only be carried out if a lexicon of a rather special kind and a bidirectional system of formation rules and transformation rules are developed. In addition to that algorithms for the analysis, the synthesis and the comparison of texts must be set up and these three algorithms must meet the compatibility condition. As elementary units within the lexicon, the rule systems and the algorithms so-called predicate functions are used. It is obvious that because of the predicate functions used the semantic representation of the text sentences and the semantic representation of the text can be formulated within one homogeneous theoretical language.

6. Hannes Rieser's paper *Sentence Grammar, Text Grammar, and the Evaluation Problem* is intended as a contribution concerning the theoretical set-up and the empirical adequacy of text grammars. The basic assumption is that the theoretical power of a text grammar depends to some extent (if not completely) on the sentence grammar generalized. If it can be proved that the sentence grammar integrated into a text grammar is in some way empirically inadequate then it can be concluded that the resulting text grammar will show empirical inadequacies as well. It is further maintained that the explanatory adequacy of a text grammar does not only depend on the sentence grammar integrated but also on the practical interests leading to its construction, i.e. on its supposed domain of application and the nature of the practical problems to be solved.

The domain of application of the text grammar proposed is provided by the legal texts valid for some stateable time interval. It is argued that the test of the empirical adequacy of text grammars and the decision as to whether two given text grammars are equivalent to each other must be carried out with respect to the tasks the grammars in question should fulfil *and* with respect to the solution of some practical problems.

These topics are treated with respect to a context-free phrase structure grammar. The generalization of such a grammar leads to a text grammar of Type I. First a context-free phrase structure grammar G_{d_i} is set up in this paper ('d' denotes that the grammar is intended to reconstruct some sub-language of German) which can be given a semantic interpretation and which generates a language L_d^1. It is shown that this grammar must be restricted as far as its syntactic and its semantic component is concerned if a language ${}_jL_d^1$ is to be generated, i.e. a language which can be mapped onto the language of jurisdiction ${}_jL_d^0$. This restricted grammar ${}_jG_{d_i}$ is considered a formally delimitable sub-grammar of G_{d_i}. For G_{d_i} an additional (auxiliary) formal device is introduced. This device permits that sets of synonymous and hyperonymous sentences be derived with respect to a distinguished sentence ${}_j\mathrm{SAT[IMP](1)}_1^1 \in {}_jL_d^1$. It is shown, however, that these sets are incomplete if compared with the sets of synonymous and hyperonymous sentences which are proper sub-sets of ${}_jL_d^0$. Therefore, G_{d_i} and ${}_jG_{d_i}$ cannot be considered empirically adequate sentence grammars the generalization of which leads to empirically adequate text grammars. Nevertheless, it is maintained that the investigation of fixed linearity sentence grammars and of fixed linearity text grammars is a necessary precondition for establishing a hierarchy of text grammars. Subsequently a sentence grammar ${}_jG_{d_k}$ is outlined. ${}_jG_{d_k}$ is supposed to provide a better basis for the derivation of a complete set of synonymous and hyperonymous sentences. The set-up of ${}_jG_{d_k}$ is discussed in connection with an intuitive logico-semantic analysis of ${}_j\mathrm{SAT[IMP](1)}_1^0$.

7. We suppose that Jens Ihwe's contribution *On the Validation of Text Grammars in the Study of Literature* will be of considerable interest both to the linguist and to the literary theoretician. He starts from the plausible premise that the estimation of which tasks linguistics is supposed to fulfil within the study of literature depends on the delimitation of the domain of a theory of literature.

Here, in our opinion, a more general remark does not seem to be out of place: It should be observed that due to the stage of development of text grammars no sharp separation line between (what might be called) theoretical text linguistics and applied text linguistics can be drawn. Such a clear-cut division analogous to, say, that of theoretical linguistics and applied linguistics does not seem to be appropriate in any case if it is accepted that a text-grammatical theory must be set up as an empirical theory meeting the rather strong postulates of current scientific explanation. Most of the text grammars set up so far have been constructed with respect to some special interest concerning its supposed application. Therefore statements concerning the empirical adequacy and the evaluation of a text grammar are explicitly or implicitly given with respect to some special tasks formulated by the investigator. Naturally these tasks are not always the tasks mentioned within the theoretical frame of the grammar under investigation. It is trivial (but not always observed) that a Theory T explaining a set of states of affairs A can only explain a set B if it was intended to do so, i.e. if $B \subset A$ or the like.

This rather unsatisfactory state as far as the possibility for a reasonable and intersubjectively testable evaluation of text grammars is concerned could only be brought to an end if a formally defined hierarchy of text grammars could be set up along the lines sketched above. If such a hierarchy could be established sound arguments concerning the theoretical power of text grammars could be given quite easily.

It is argued by Ihwe that the set-up of an adequate theory of literature has to take into consideration the results of the work done by the Russian foralists, the results of modern theory of science, empirical linguistic theory, the theory of communication, the analysis of ordinary language, and logics. A model containing the parameters which are assumed to permit the explanation of the specific status of literary texts presupposes the existence of a well-established model of verbal communication and verbal interaction. The natural domain of a theory of literature consists of those specific properties of linguistic objects which are considered to have a so-called differentiating function. This implies that it is possible to assign to different linguistic objects different functions according to their contexts of use. Therefore it follows that the objects to be considered as literary texts and, hence, as belonging to the proper domain of a theory of literature cannot be determined on the basis of inherent properties of some kind. On the contrary, it is maintained, that the estimation of whether some arbitrarily chosen text must be regarded as belonging to the set of literary texts depends on the socio-cultural norms accepted and developed in a particular society or in a particular social group. Therefore the demarcation line between literary and non-literary texts cannot be drawn on the basis of two grammars G_i and G_j only, where G_i generates a theoretical language corresponding to the standard language and G_j generates a so-called poetic language, deviating in some respect from standard language. This, however, does not exclude that there *is* a subset of the set of defining properties which can be reconstructed by means of a grammar G_j. G_j is supposed to be a grammar resulting from an extension or a comprehension – as the case may be – of the different sets of rules belonging to G_i.

A necessary precondition for such an approach, however, is, that the domains of G_i and G_j respectively are not sentences but texts. The task of a G_i to be successfully used in the theory of literature is considered to be the determination of those regularities which allow the connection of well-formed sequences of sentences. A G_j corresponding to G_i must be able to define the notion of 'narrative structure'. Besides these more general claims concerning the theoretical tasks of text grammars, Ihwe makes a quite important claim concerning the formal set-up of G_i. Because of the fact that – as far as heuristics is concerned – narrative structures can be described only by means of a descriptional language set up according to an extended predicate calculus, both G_i and G_j have to be formulated in a theoretical language which is itself either an extended predicate logic of some kind or which can be translated into such a logic. In addition to this, G_i and G_j have to meet certain compatibility conditions. Assuming that the theory of non-verbal behaviour can be set up as an empirical theory, then G_i and G_j have to be compatible with such a theory. This claim naturally results from the explanatory adequacy a theory of literature is supposed to meet. It is argued that these claims result from the more or less observable fact that literature has to be regarded as a complex social phenomenon. Therefore a set of differentiating 'formal' features is at most a sufficient but certainly not a necessary condition for the 'literaricity' of texts.

It is quite obvious that not all interesting heuristic and methodological problems concerning text grammars could be treated within this volume. The reader interested in these problems is referred to the introductory study of Teun A. van Dijk, *Some Aspects of Text Grammars,* The Hague: Mouton 1972, where many current problems of text grammars are discussed. Various sentence-grammatical and text-grammatical models (both traditional and modern) are treated in János S. Petőfi's, *Transformationsgrammatiken und eine ko-textuelle Texttheorie*, Frankfurt: Athenäum 1971 (*Linguistische Forschungen* **3**). The semantic relations of presupposition and entailment are treated in János S. Petőfi and Dorothea Franck (eds), *Präsuppositionen in Philosophie und Linguistik/Presuppositions in Philosophy and Linguistics,* Frankfurt: Athenäum 1973. The text grammars of Type I and Type IV, as briefly outlined above, were described in Teun A. van Dijk, Jens Ihwe, János S. Petőfi, Hannes Rieser, *Zur Bestimmung narrativer Strukturen auf der Grundlage von Textgrammatiken*, Hamburg: Buske 1972 (*Papiere zur Textlinguistik/Papers in Textlinguistics* **1**). A short version of this paper appeared in *Foundations of Language* **8**, 499–545 ('Two Text Grammatical Models'). Some further problems concerning the application of text grammars are discussed in Peter Hartmann und Hannes Rieser (eds.), *Angewandte Textlinguistik I*, Hamburg: Buske 1973 (*Papiere zur Textlinguistik/Papers in Textlinguistics* **2**). Several aspects of the methodological foundation of text grammars are discussed in Martin Rüttenauer (ed.), *Konstanzer*

Textlinguistikkolloquium 1972, Hamburg: Buske 1973 (*Papiere zur Textlinguistik / Papers in Textlinguistics* **3**). Some problems of the con-textual component (problems of the set-up of a partial text theory consisting of a text grammar and an extensional semantic component) are discussed in János S. Petöfi and Hannes Rieser, *Probleme der modelltheoretischen Interpretation von Texten*, Hamburg: Buske 1973 (*Papiere zur Textlinguistik / Papers in Textlinguistics* **7**). The relation between linguistics and the theory of literature is described in great detail in Jens Ihwe, *Linguistik in der Literaturwissenschaft. Zur Entwicklung einer modernen Theorie der Literaturwissenschaft*, München: Bayerischer Schulbuchverlag 1972 (*Grundfragen der Literaturwissenschaft* **4**). An English version is to appear in the series *De Proprietatibus Litterarum*, Mouton, The Hague.

The work of the contributors to this volume Jens Ihwe and Wolfram Köck as well as the work of the editors was supported by the 'Deutsche Forschungsgemeinschaft' DFG (German Research Foundation), Bonn-Bad Godesberg.

October 1972

JÁNOS S. PETÖFI
University of Bielefeld
Fakultät für Linguistik und Literaturwissenschaft

HANNES RIESER
University of Constance
DFG-Projekt 'Textlinguistik'

TEUN A. VAN DIJK

TEXT GRAMMAR AND TEXT LOGIC*

1. INTRODUCTION

1.1. This paper is intended as a contribution to the recent developments in the logical analysis of natural language. In particular, it investigates some of the logical properties of so-called TEXT GRAMMARS, i.e. grammars formally describing the structure of texts in natural language. Our main working hypothesis will be that the base of a grammar contains, or is identical with a (natural) logic, and that such a 'logic' should most appropriately take the form of what might be called a TEXT LOGIC. Besides a more general discussion of the relations between logic and linguistics and of the present status of logical systems in grammatical research, we will specify some of the main tasks and requirements of a text logic. Special attention will be given to the abstract structures underlying description, quantification and identity in texts. These problems are also relevant in standard sentence grammars, but it will be argued that they can be better formulated in the framework of a text grammar and its corresponding text logic, thus leading to a number of interesting generalizations. It must be underlined that our attempt is provisional and often highly speculative, and that the treatment of the different problems will remain rather informal.

1.2. One of the ideas that have led to the renewed attempts to bring to bear logical systems in the description of natural language is the hypothesis that the abstract or underlying structure of sentences may be identified with their LOGICAL FORM. Although in a somewhat different sense, this suggestion, to be found primarily in the writings of philosophers and logicians, has been taken up in recent work on generative grammar, especially by those propagating its variant known as 'generative semantics'.[1] As is well-known by now,

* This is a slightly revised version of a paper contributed to the symposium 'Zur Form der Textgrammatischen Basis', University of Konstanz (W.-Germany), September 3–9, 1972. I am indebted to the participants of the symposium for many useful comments, which regrettably could not be fully accounted for in this version. Many points of the global framework we intended to sketch here require separate and detailed treatment.

[1] 'Generative semantics' is not a homogeneous direction within the theory of generative grammars. Its main propagators defend rather different views. See McCawley (1968) and the other papers in Bach and Harms (1968) and especially the programmatic article of Lakoff (1971a). One of the most serious attempts in this direction has been Rohrer (1971). For criticism, see Chomsky (1970, 1971) and Katz (1971).

J. S. Petöfi and H. Rieser (eds.), Studies in Text Grammar, 17–78. *All Rights Reserved.*

the scattered attempts in this direction have, in a sense, put Chomsky's model upside down by abolishing syntactic deep structure and substituting for this deep structure the semantic representation or logical form of the sentence. Several sequences of transformations would then assign lexical, syntactic and phonological structures to this underlying semantic representation. We will at present ignore the properties of such transformations, which in general may be viewed as local and global derivational constraints upon finite sequences of phrase markers. We are also aware that little is understood at present of the nature of the (transformational) rules relating semantic representations with abstract and more superficial syntactic structures, and that from the point of view of explicitness generative semantics cannot (yet) be considered to be a serious alternative to the standard, syntactically based grammars. Nevertheless, we take our discussion below as lending support to a grammar having semantical (or 'logical') structures as its base structures. We will see in particular that these contain some important properties which are main conditions for the transformations to operate, e.g. the famous 'identity'-condition determining definitivization, pronominalization, reflexivization and relativization. Thus, we share the view of many linguists and logicians who consider the elaboration of an explicit semantic theory as a task that is preliminary to our understanding of many syntactical (and lexical) rules and transformations. In order to arrive at a satisfactory degree of explicitness, such a semantic theory is assumed to have a non-trivial formulation (and ensuing formalization) in terms of (an) existing system(s) of modern logic, e.g. a MODAL PREDICATE CALCULUS, provided some important extensions and alterations are made, in order that such a calculus may adequately account for the abstract structure of sentences in natural language. Some of these extensions will be discussed below.

1.3. The ideas which, more specifically, have elicited the present paper have evolved from other's and our work on generative text grammars. As we will briefly indicate in the next section, such grammars – besides a description of the structure of sentences – must formulate conditions and transderivational rules relating sentences in a grammatical ('coherent') text. It has been assumed that such rules are based on the semantic structure of textual sequences of sentences. Many of these relevant intersentential relations seem to invite

---

Although the scattered generative semantic studies do not at present have a well-defined grammatical basis which would be a serious alternative to Chomsky's syntactically based (extended) standard model (1965, 1970) we think it should be recognized that they have at least undertaken to treat a number of highly interesting semantic problems, neglected or inadequately treated in the standard model. Moreover, relations between logic and grammar are to be found especially in these semantic approaches.

to serious logical analysis, the more so while at least some of them appear to be identical with genuine logical principles. A (natural) text logic has as its main task to formulate these principles of intersentential relations, as well as the constraints which these put on the logical form of sentences in a text.

It is not strange that we claim that a logic of natural language should be a text logic, not only for empirical and grammatical reasons, but also for the simple reason that logical systems themselves are in fact formal text logics. Derivations (proofs) constructed by the rules and categories of such systems are also 'discourses', consisting of coherent (consistent) sequences of sentences. We will argue below that there are certain non-trivial analogies between the structures and principles of formal proofs and systems (theories) on the one hand and the structures and principles of texts in natural language on the other hand. More in general we assume, then, that the most relevant application or elaboration of logic for natural language pertains to the abstract constructs we call 'texts', such as they must be generated by text grammars, even when, e.g. speaking of (complex) sentences, we merely refer implicitly to texts.

Before we begin our preliminary remarks to support these claims and hypotheses, let us first briefly and informally recall the main characteristics of the grammar we have in mind.

2. The hypothetic form of text grammar[2]

2.1. In general we adopt the main principles of current generative transformational theories, i.e. those defining a grammar recursively specifying an infinite set of abstract underlying structures and a set of transformations mapping these structures onto an infinite set of surface structures. The difference with sentential grammars, however, is that derivations do not terminate as simple or complex sentences, but as ordered n-tuples of sentences ($n \geqslant 1$), that is as SEQUENCES. The intuitive idea, then, is that the text grammar must formulate derivational constraints such that certain sequences are

[2] For detailed discussion of the forms, properties, aims and applications of text grammars, or of text theories in general, cf. van Dijk (1971, 1972), Ihwe (1972), Petöfi (1971), Kummer (1971a, b; 1972), also for numerous further references. We cannot give a survey of textual linguistics here. Its sources are, firstly, in Harris' discourse analysis and, secondly, in European developments of structuralism, especially in Germany. The names of Hartmann, Schmidt, Harweg, Heidolph, Lang, Rieser, Drubig are associated with this direction of thought, though approached from very different angles. In eastern Europe we have especially the work of Bellert (1970), Palek, Daneš, Žolkovskij, whereas in the U.S.A. linguists treating pronominalization, especially Karttunen (1968a, b; 1969a), often make (implicit) reference to discourse structure. For a methodological foundation of textual linguistics, see Sanders (1969) and Petöfi and Rieser (1973). For general text theory, see Schmidt (1972).

grammatical and others are not, viz. that the set of well-formed texts of a language is a subset of all possible sequences of sentences. In addition to constraints upon the ordering of the sentences in the sequence, there are constraints upon the possible forms of the semantic representations of the respective sentences-in-the-sequence, so-called TRANSDERIVATIONAL CONSTRAINTS. Put more simply: the meaning (or truth) of a given sentence S_i depends on the meaning (or truth) of the ordered i-1-tuple of preceding sentences. This seems rather obvious but any adequate grammar must specify the nature of these dependency-relations between sentences in a sequence. The formal and empirical advantage of such grammars is that sentence structure is not merely described in its own right but also relative to the structure of other sentences of the text. The 'relative grammaticalness' thus defined more adequately corresponds to the actual structures of discourses (uttered texts, utterances) in verbal communication.

A sequence satisfying the necessary and sufficient conditions of dependency will be called COHERENT. Since sequences are theoretically infinite, the set of coherent n-tuples of semantic representations is also infinite. The base component of a T-grammar must recursively enumerate the members of this infinite set. It will be assumed that a coherent sequence of semantic representations determines, transformationally, the lexical, syntactic and morphophonological structures of the sequence.

2.2. The constraints upon the concatenation of sentences in a coherent sequence are of two different types. A first set determines the immediate, linear transition relations between the sentences. They are in part identical with the constraints holding between phrases and clauses in complex and compound sentences. We will call these constraints, micro-structural constraints or MICRO-CONSTRAINTS.

Our hypothesis about the form of a text-grammar, however, is much stronger. We claim that the coherence of sequences is also determined by what may be called MACRO-CONSTRAINTS. These have the whole sequence as their scope. Whereas the micro-constraints determine LOCAL well-formedness of sequences, macro-constraints operate at the GLOBAL level. The problem, of course, is how to formulate the macro-constraints and how to integrate them into the derivation of a sequence of semantic representations. Intuitively speaking, macro-constraints define the bounds within which lies the linear derivation of subsequent SR's, but how do we make explicit such a set of one-many relations between any macro-constraint and the forms of all the SR's? The way we formulate the problem suggests that we might treat the constraints as FUNCTIONS. In more grammatical terms we might say that a possible level of macro semantic structure must be mapped onto (into?)

a level of micro-semantic structure, viz. the global meaning of a text onto (into) the meaning(s) of a sentence or sequence. Such a mapping is operated by a set of transformations, of which the precise nature, however, is still obscure.

2.3. Although there are a certain number of serious linguistic and psychological arguments in favour of a postulated set of macro-constraints or global transderivational constraints, the remarks we have made above are still highly speculative, and we will not elaborate them here. In the following we will concentrate on the direct relations between subsequent semantic representations, i.e. on the local constraints upon textual coherence. It is at this 'level of feasibility' that we may formulate a first set of rules for a text logic.

3. FORMAL LOGIC AND NATURAL LOGIC

3.1. Some general remarks are in order about the relations between formal logic and natural logic. A first rather sceptical remark would be that we do know what formal logic is, but that we still largely ignore what a 'natural logic' could be.[3] That is, if the 'logic' of natural language is a logical system in the strict sense, it must satisfy at least a number of general requirements laid down in the theory of logic. If it is not a logic, but e.g. simply a part of grammar in which some logical notation is used, what then are its relations to formal deductive systems?[4] In this case we would be interested merely in

[3] The term 'natural logic', which we adopt here for reasons of simplicity – indicating 'the logic of natural language' – has found wide currency especially after Lakoff's article of the same name (Lakoff, 1970). See also McCawley's 'program' (McCawley, 1971). The status of natural logic, as discussed in Lakoff, is not wholly clear, although he treats a number of important questions which a natural logic should deal with. This is one of the reasons why we discuss at some length the general relations between logic and grammar and the status of text logic in particular.

The situation in this interdisciplinary field is somewhat confusing. Several symposia have been held on the subject now, but are attended with rather by logicians than linguists, although linguists show growing interest for the logician's approach. These reject often a Chomsky type of grammar, especially its semantic component as originally elaborated by Katz and Fodor (1964) and Katz (1967, 1971), but it is substantially different as well from the generative semantic approaches of e.g. Lakoff and McCawley. In between lies the work of Keenan (1969, 1971, 1972a, b) and Kummer (1971a, b; 1972) to which we feel attracted most at the moment. Keenan (1969:2) has explicitly compared logical proofs/systems with texts, referring to Corcoran (1969).

[4] The relations between grammar and logic have been the topic of many articles in linguistics, logic and philosophy of language, since Frege, Carnap and Quine. For a recent survey of the problems, see Fodor (1970) and the recent discussions, especially about semantics, in *Synthese* (cf. Davidson and Harman (1971)). For other work in the field, cf. the interdisciplinary reader of Steinberg and Jakobovits (1971). The Festschrift for Carnap, *Logic and Language* (1962) only contains rather brief remarks about the subject, e.g. Jørgensen's (1962) article on the differences between logical calculuses and natural language.

the non-trivial relations: since even modern logic has its remote roots in argumentative discourse (and traditional sentence structure), it will not be difficult to find many similarities. The very fact that many introductory courses in logic contain chapters and exercises in which natural language sentences (arguments) are 'translated' into logical propositions and inferences, is significant enough about these relationships.

3.2. Instead of detecting similarities between formal and natural language let us first list some important differences which seem to prohibit direct identification of any current logical system with a system of natural logic. At the same time this list may be considered as a program for what must still be done before a logic is adequate to 'represent' structures of natural language.

We begin with a set of very general, well-known characteristics setting apart a formal and a natural language:

3.2.1. FORMATION RULES in a logical language (LL) are specified merely in its syntax and do not take 'meaning' or 'interpretation' into account, of which the set of well-formed formula's (wff's) is independent. The same is true for the formation of complex structures, and, what is crucial, for derivational inference (proofs). Grammatical well-formedness in natural language (NL) is restricted also by a set of semantic rules (and the postulates of the lexicon).

3.2.2. In LL there is a direct relationship between the DERIVABILITY of wff's (from a set of axioms, definitions), their validity and their truth-value (viz. truth), whereas 'meaningfulness' in NL is never dependent on syntactic structure alone (see below Section 3.4).

3.2.3. The SEMANTICS of LL is in general based on the notion of TRUTH (in some world or model), whereas the semantics of NL – not restricted to affirmative statements as standard logic is – includes other basic concepts (e.g. applicability, happiness). Moreover, the semantics of NL essentially includes rules of meaning (intension) on which rules of reference (extension) depend (see below Section 3.4.).

3.2.4. The structure and meaning of utterances in NL crucially depends on

---

Other recent discussions are collected in the proceedings *Linguaggi nella società e nella technica* (1970), where Lewis (1970), Davidson (1970) and Scott (1970), just as on the IVth International Congress of Methodology, Logic and Philosophy of Science (Bucharest, 1971), heavily criticize present day linguistic semantics.

all sorts of formal and empirical PRAGMATIC rules and factors, whereas LL (intentionally) has no rules of 'use' or 'application' (see below Section 3.5.).

These are (some) very general divergencies. Let us now list some features of the systems (e.g. modal predicate calculi) we might consider akin to a natural logic.

3.2.5. In NL we do not have pure VARIABLES. Pronouns (pro-verbs, pro-sentences) are differentiated according to genus, case and number (pro-verbs according to state, action or possession). That is, in NL we might speak of 'semi-constants' (or, for that matter, of 'semi-variables').

3.2.6. NL has no simple distinction between ARGUMENTS AND PREDICATES. Properties and relations are expressed in all major categories (verbs, nouns, adverbs, adjectives, prepositions), which are at the same time the 'arguments' which may be quantified and predicated 'upon'.

3.2.7. The ORDERING OF ARGUMENTS in logical expressions is linear but arbitrary and does not reflect the structural (dependency) relations of NL-syntax or NL-semantics (subject, object; agent, patient, etc.). This fact makes logical expressions highly ambiguous in their interpretations.

3.2.8. QUANTIFICATION in NL is mostly restricted to selected (sub)sets of individuals with some properties or relations, and does not apply to all/some unspecified (unrestricted) sets of individuals defining a 'universe of discourse' (except of course in universal statements) (for detail, see below).

3.2.9. The STANDARD QUANTIFIERS of logical systems are not sufficient to represent all aspects of quantification in NL (*a*, *one*, *some*, *the*, *most*, *many*, *all*, *few*, *every*, *any*, *no*, etc.), although there are attempts now to provide a logic for these quantifiers.

3.2.10. TRUTH FUNCTIONAL CONNECTIVES (logical constants, logical connectives) in LL have properties which are rather different from (even the 'corresponding') intersentential connectives (conjunctions) in natural language:

– these are not (always) associative, distributive, commutative,

– disjunction is inclusive or exclusive in NL,

– material implication (conditional) is not equivalent with semantic implication; for example, in general it makes no sense in NL to say that false antecedents make an implication true. The same holds for (logical) entailment,

– the standard connectives are not inter-definable (by the De Morgan Laws)

in NL with preservation of truth/meaning (they have different presuppositions),

– logical connectives are truth-functional but are independent of the meaning of the propositions they relate (see our general point 3.2.1.),

– there are no logical analogues of the conjunctions of concession (*although*), contrast (*but*), cause (*because*, *for*, *since*), consequence (*so*, *that*), time (*then*, *when*, *since*), place (*there*, *where*, *wherefrom*, etc.), etc.,

– the logical monadic operator of negation applies in NL both to propositions and to nearly all grammatical categories of the proposition. It rather has the character of a modal operator than that of a truth functional constant.

3.2.11. The basic LAWS, PRINCIPLES and THEOREMS of standard logic do not always apply in NL:

– double negation does not mean the same as affirmation,

– the law of the excluded middle has many (stylistically relevant) exceptions in NL: contradiction is not meaningless in NL,

– as we saw above, the De Morgan Laws only hold under specific interpretations of sentential connectives in NL,

– the same is true for the associative, distributive and commutative laws,

– all valid wff's (tautologies) in LL are not necessarily tautologies (with respect to meaning) in NL, i.e. they 'convey information', in the intuitive sense of this expression,

– there seems to be no argument why such paradoxical theorems as $p \supset (p \vee q)$, $q \supset (q \vee p)$ or the like would hold in NL.

3.3. The above list is not exhaustive. It must be admitted, however, that – apart from the general principles inherent to logical systems – our remarks hold for standard systems. There have been numerous attempts to eliminate the un-intuitive aspects of the systems, or to bring the representation of logical propositions closer to those of natural language, so that inference would depend on more and 'weaker' factors. Many systems try to avoid some of the basic laws and rules of inference. Other systems introduce new quantifiers and are based on restricted quantification. Higher order calculi permit quantification of predicates, propositions, indices, etc., whereas the discussion on the status of the truth functional connectives is permanent.[5] The main set of improvements is undoubtedly due to the elaboration of all sorts of MODAL SYSTEMS and, especially, their semantics. Expressions are now available to

[5] It is impossible to list here all references to attempts to extend standard logic. For a general discussion and references we may refer especially to Rescher (1968) and Hughes and Cresswell (1969, Ch. 17).

account for necessity, possibility, time (tense), place, etc. and sentences are 'performatively' differentiated as 'statements', 'questions', 'commands', 'belief sentences', 'action sentences', etc., all with their own – though often similar – logical properties of inference.[6]

Although we take these developments to be highly interesting and as a necessary process of 'weakening' standard logic (without loss of explicitness) towards the processes underlying natural language (and argumentation), we may still note the following problems:

3.3.1. The set of well-known MODAL OPERATORS in current logical systems is still much smaller than the set of modalities in NL (where we have *likely, probably, expectably, hopefully, surely, perhaps*, etc.).

3.3.2. Modalities in logic remain (of course) LOGICAL MODALITIES, whereas modalities in NL are always contingent: logical necessity (possibility) is different from contingent (physical, psychological) necessity and possibility.

3.3.3. It is not yet clear what a serious calculus and semantics would look like having as possible operators all known modalities preceding their nuclear propositions: the problem of scope and world ordering is huge and is attacked only for some rather simple combinations of operators.

3.3.4. Some main LAWS OF MODAL LOGIC do not hold in NL. Firstly, there are those laws corresponding to their non-modal analogues – which have material implication instead of necessary (logical) implication (entailment): e.g. $q \dashv\!\exists (p \vee \sim p)$, $p \dashv\!\exists (q \vee p)$. Other laws problematic in NL are those (see 3.3.2.) relating the different modalities (dependence of necessity and possibility), the status of necessity and the relations between quantification and identity in modalized propositions (the Barcan formula).

Again it must be admitted that some logicians also reject the counter-intuitive consequences of these systems, although, in general, they are valid principles of LOGICAL inference.

[6] For *modal logic* we refer in general to Hughes and Cresswell (1968) and the work of Carnap (1957). For modal semantics, see van Fraassen (1971). For *tense logic* we may mention Prior (1957, 1968, 1971) and Rescher and Urquhart (1971).

Question (i.e. *Erotetic*) *Logic* has been studied especially by Harrah (1963, 1969) and Belnap (1969). For *Command Logic* see Rescher (1966), *Belief/Knowledge* (epistemic) *logic*, see Hintikka (1962), and for *action/event*, and in general *deontic logic*, see von Wright (1963) and Hilpinen (ed.) (1971). This list is not exhaustive, and should include especially inductive logic and the logic of preference. We mention all these directions just to emphasize the amount of work which has been done on special, though often related, fields, and the amount of work which still must be done to construct a serious synthetic system, required by a natural logic.

3.4. Some observations in the preceding paragraphs pertain to the SEMANTICS of logical systems. Although both the semantics of logical and natural languages are still under central discussion, there are some crucial divergencies in their development which merit brief attention here. Let us again focus upon (modal) predicate logic.

As was said earlier most logical work on semantics is extensional, in that individuals n_1, n_2 or n-tuples of individuals $\langle n_1, n_2 \ldots \rangle$ from a given domain D are assigned, in one or more worlds $w_1, w_2 \ldots$, to the terms of the expression; arguments being true if there are such individuals, predicates if there are such n-tuples of individuals, and propositions if both conditions hold (and the individuals for which they hold are identical); necessary propositions holding in all worlds of the set W and possible propositions in at least one w_i of W. Such an account has been of great influence in modern logic but seems to do not much as far as 'meanings' of expressions are concerned, even when we view meanings as sets of truth conditions. In the first place we have the problematic character of the notion of TRUTH itself, for which it would be more appropriate to substitute some notion like SATISFACTION[7], in order to account for non-affirmative expressions in NL (and LL). Secondly, arguments having different meanings may denote the same individuals as their extensions, whereas different predicates may have the same n-tuples as their extensions. In the third place, it is not wholly obvious that the domain of individuals should be specified independently of the worlds themselves: their 'existence' may be restricted to some worlds, so that is would be adequate to speak also of necessary and possible objects. Intuitively, then, it would be more adequate to have a semantics consisting of a model which includes a world-independent set of (basic) properties or relations, of which each member may be satisfied (or not) by the individuals or n-tuples of individuals of each world.

Even an INTENSIONAL approach does not seem to alter these facts if we take intensions as functions from expressions to extensions, or as functions from 'indices' (factors of interpretation) to extensions[8], since this would still result in the fact that all tautologies – being true in any world – or contradictions – being false in any world – would have the same value (extension) and hence have no difference of meaning. Similarly, it is problematical how to determine a function having no value (extension) at all, as is the case for all (other) intensional objects, viz. the opaque meanings of (*the*) *president*, (*the*) *neighbour*, (*the*) *girl with* (*the*) *blue eyes*, which not simply may be identified with

[7] The use of alternative notions for 'truth', e.g. satisfation, has been discussed by Harrah (1963), Hintikka (1961, 1963).

[8] This view is taken e.g. by Montague (1970a, b), and Lewis (1970).

the classes of objects satisfying these properties. We will return to these basic issues below.

3.5. Furthermore, logical systems, as we suggested, in general lack a serious PRAGMATICS. The important work which has been done in this domain is empirically much too pover to account for the numerous rules and categories determining the adequate use of expressions in NL[9]. On the other hand much of it may simply be seen as part of semantics. Not merely time, place and speaker would need explication, but also intentions, knowledge, beliefs, attitudes, and similar notions, which hitherto have been discussed mainly within philosophy and the social sciences.

3.6. The remarks of this section are not intended as a show-down of the role of modern logic in the analysis of natural language, but rather as a reminder of the difficulties and the tasks which await us in such an inquiry. In that perspective the use of current logical systems is not only fragmentary but empirically inadequate when they do not accommodate the specific properties of NL we have enumerated above. It may be rightly asked whether a natural logic which would result from the suggested adaptations is not too weak to be a logic at all. At least the principles of logical inference either would grow enormously complex or would need a complete revision, which would mean a complete redefinition of logic (and for that matter of all the formal systems based on it). These last observations seem unduly pessimistic, and the best line of research would be on the one hand to investigate which principles of current logic do in fact hold in NL or in some important fractions of NL, and on the other hand which extensions of these logics are theoretically and methodologically sound such as to account of some important structural principles of NL. Much of the preliminary research in this last part of the inquiry, however, will initially be largely informal and prepared by philosophy of language and linguistics itself. Many of our observations on text logic below regrettably belong to this stage.

3.7. A final, methodologically important, remark must be made here. Any logical system ('language') accounting for natural language is (part of) an empirical theory. Since the empirical object is a language, such a system would be a meta-language. Strictly speaking, then, logical languages are to be

[9] We think e.g. of the work of Montague (1968, 1970a, b) which bears little resemble with any form or task of (empirical) pragmatics, and we would rather range it as a specific type of syntax (and its semantic interpretation). Similar remarks hold for the, though rather different, monograph of Martin (1959). For recent discussions on the status of pragmatics, see Schmidt (1972), Stalnaker (1970), Bar-Hillel (ed.) (1971), van Dijk and Franck (1972) and van Dijk (1974).

compared with grammars not with natural languages. In this respect our list of divergencies between logic and language seems to beg the question. As part of the grammar, a natural logic would have to describe meaning (or reference) structures not 'replace' them. This is true to some extent, but the task of logic, would essentially consist in a FORMAL RECONSTRUCTION of the mechanisms of natural language, an aim which we assume to be identical with the formal derivational descriptions in generative grammars, which also generate sentences/texts together with their structural description.

4. Text logic

4.1. *Introduction*

4.1.1. The previous remarks should warn us not to assume a task like the elaboration of a 'text logic' before more is known about the logical form of sentences. Similar objections could be made against text grammars, but there is serious evidence that our understanding of sentence structure grows when we go beyond the limits of the sentence. The same, we think, may be said about a natural logic, apart from the fact that any serious logic precisely formulates the rules (LL-transformations) relating propositions in well-formed texts: proofs. Below, we will analyse in some detail this analogy between 'formal texts' and 'natural texts', and their respective 'derivations'. Furthermore, we would hardly want to construct a natural logic which does not include such fundamental concepts as presupposition and consequence, notions that can be defined only over ordered *n*-tuples of propositions/sentences, i.e. in texts. The same is true for an adequate treatment of description, quantification, identity, tense, modalities and other basic aspects of logical form, both in LL and NL.

4.1.2. In this section we want to discuss the general status, aims and tasks of a text logic and to study in some detail, though informally, some of its central problems. As such, then, our observations and suggestions are intended rather as preliminaries towards a text logic than as part of this logic itself. The problem is that it seems methodologically unadvisable to construct directly such a logic before we know what empirical facts it must account for. In order to characterize these facts we will resort to ordinary discourse supplied with some machinery from generative grammar on the one hand and modal predicate calculus on the other hand. Gradually, the discussion of some of the empirical (viz. semantic) facts will force us to extend the provisional apparatus. We do not claim that such an extended calculus (which must undergo further internal elaboration) is identical with a text logic, but it is assumed that text logic must at least contain analogous extensions with respect to standard calculi.

4.1.3. The STATUS OF A 'TEXT LOGIC' is not clear *a priori*. When conceived as a logical system in the strict sense, it cannot have empirical claims and can be tested only on the validity of its theses (theorems), i.e. on the correctness of its deduction rules, the appropriateness of its axioms, and on its consistency and completeness. At the same time it would require a formal semantics (model theory) and formal pragmatics to interpret this calculus. If it manages to take into account all relevant aspects of logical inference we have listed earlier, viz. plurality quantification, modalities (alethic, epistemic, deontic, chronological, topological), etc., it would be a sort of super-logic, which at present would be more a dream or a program than a feasible construction.

If taken as part of a generative text grammar, a text logic would have to make empirical claims as to the abstract underlying structures of sentences and texts. That is, its structures must be an appropriate input for the other grammatical rules, they must be identifiable with or relatable to meaning structures and thus make explicit such notions as ambiguity, synonymy, paraphrase, coherence, presupposition/consequence, and the like. It seems impossible to perform such a task without a corresponding lexicon. Hence the logic would contain a set of (basic) predicates, defined (derived) predicates, meaning postulates, and construction (projection) rules and constraints. This last requirement precisely would define the logic as a NATURAL logic, since its categories and rules would not only be formal but also contingent. This contingency is not the same as that characterizing natural language itself with respect to the psycho-social factors of its use in verbal communication, which an abstract but empirical grammar does not either account for, but a contingency with respect to the given empirically based structures of expressions in natural language. A natural text logic may only explicitly reconstruct not construct such structures. In this respect it is fundamentally different from a formal (text) logic, which only has internal criteria of adequacy, whatever the further analogies may be. Furthermore, these analogies are explained by the fact that modern logical systems do not develop arbitrarily, but follow roughly – in their intended interpretations and corresponding calculi – our basic intuitions about the 'logical structure' of the world, which in turn is also, though vaguely, reflected in natural language and the discourses we use to speak about that world.

Concluding these extremely general remarks we will assume, then, that a 'formal text logic' is simply identical with a very powerful (i.e. weak) modal logic, specifying all relevant rules, principles and theorems determining well-formed 'inferential texts', i.e. proofs. A 'natural text logic' is a more general and a still weaker system, part of an empirical theory (a theory of language) specifying the general rules, principles, constraints, etc. determining the abstract (meaning) structure of any text, including argumentative texts as abstractly specified by formal text logic. Formal logic, then, is the set of specific constraints defining a specific TYPE OF TEXT, *viz.* texts in which the derived statements are required to be valid (true). This does not mean that a natural text logic could not in a similar way be constructed as a deductive system, only its intended interpretation, then, must have empirical relevance, since such a system would be part of an empirical, natural grammar.

Clearly, at this point the boundaries between logic and linguistics and their respective status, aims, and tasks are blurred: both explicitly specify the abstract structure of texts and the relations between text structure (including meaning) and the world(s).

4.1.4. What, then, are the more particular AIMS AND TASKS OF A NATURAL TEXT LOGIC? Above we mentioned several times that such a logic would have to account for the 'semantic structure' of sentences and texts. Primarily, the linguist would understand, in this case, an explication of 'meaning structure', and hence the formulation of those rules of grammar determining the (grammatical) 'meaningfulness' of sentences and texts, such as any native speaker intuitively knows them, an intuition (competence) which underlies his testable judgements on his language. This knowledge of 'meaning rules', includes a purely internal knowledge of similarities and differences of meanings, both of 'words', sentences and texts: synonymy, antinomy, paraphrase, presupposition, consequence – independent of concrete use and reference. Besides a specification of the structure of propositions/sentences, a text logic more specifically determines the logical relationships between sentences in a well-formed, coherent text. These include specific constraints upon the ordering and scope of quantifiers and modal operators, relations of identity, equivalence, similarity and elementhood, inclusion and entailment between arguments, predicates and whole propositions, and the ordering of the propositions themselves. At the same time the text logic will specify the truth or satisfaction conditions for sentences-in-texts and texts, i.e. it includes a reference theory of natural language specifying the properties of the models in which they may be interpreted. Part of the textual coherence conditions enumerated above are definable only at this, extensional, level. Problematic, of course, are the precise relations between meaning structures and relations and the referential structures.

It is clear, that of all these tasks and aims we can only discuss some fragments below.

4.2. *Proofs, Systems, and Texts*

4.2.1. We suggested above that there might be some non-trivial analogy between grammatical generation of textual sequences of sentences and formal deduction in logical or mathematical PROOFS. Before we discuss some of the rules holding between sentences in coherent texts, we must make some remarks on this supposed analogy. Let us first briefly consider come characteristics of formal proofs. The crucial idea, here, is to construct a 'discourse' consisting of subsequent propositions which may follow each other under certain conditions which permit either to change a proposition (or in general a well-formed formula) into another, or to introduce a new wff. These conditions are, variably, called 'transformations', 'rules' (of deduction), 'principles', 'laws', etc. For such a discourse the following always must hold: For any formal discourse D, consisting of an ordered n-tuple $\langle S_1, S_2, ..., S_n \rangle$, of wff's: $\langle S_1, S_2, ..., S_{n-1} \rangle \dashv S_n$. That is, the last sentence logically (necessarily) FOLLOWS FROM (IS ENTAILED BY) the ordered (n–1)-tuple of preceding wff's, and is true under the following conditions

(i) that for each S_i ($S_i \neq S_n$), S_i is true,

(ii) the correct transformation rules have applied.

This entailment is false just in case $\langle S_1, S_2, ..., S_{n-1} \rangle$, the PREMISSES, are true and S_n, the CONCLUSION, false. (Whereas from false premises we may derive any proposition whatever, including S_n, which makes the entailment true).

Any wff which is part of D must belong to the following set:

(1) a wff derived from another wff by transformation rules,

(2) a definition,

(3) a previously proved theorem,

(4) an axiom.

Finally, another main characteristic of formal proof is the fact that it is based on rules pertaining to the SYNTACTIC form of wff's alone. That is, whatever may be substituted for the variables in the premisses, the conclusion will always be true if the premisses are true. Of course, in SYNTACTIC terms, the notion of truth does not enter, and we may speak only of the DERIVABILITY of a conclusion from its premisses. In SEMANTIC terms we may correctly say that a conclusion is semantically entailed by the premisses if it cannot possibly be false when the premisses are true. Any proposition which is semantically entailed by its premisses must also be formally derivable from it.

4.2.2. Let us now see in how far a derivation of a sequence of sentences, a text, can be significantly compared with such formal discourses we call proofs. A first similarity is rather superficial, viz. the fact that both appear as discourses, i.e. as ordered n-tuples of propositions. Another aspect is that in order to generate a sentence/proposition S_i after a sentence S_{i-1} a number of rules must be followed. These rules, however, are (TEXT) GRAMMATICAL RULES, whereas the rules for writing S_i after S_{i-1} in a proof are LOGICAL RULES of inference. Furthermore, it cannot simply be said that the last sentence of a natural text is either logically derivable from all its previous sentences or semantically entailed by them. The issue we started with, however, was that the basic grammatical rules relating subsequent sentences are identical with the rules relating 'logical forms' or 'semantic representation' of these sentences, and that such rules may be called to form a (natural) text logic. Such a text logic may appropriately be called a LOGIC, in the traditional sense, if its rules are 'sound principles of inference', based on the formal structure of the propositions alone.

On such an interpretation of a logic, a text logic could not possibly be a logic, because we cannot INFER sentences from (a set of) preceding ones. In more rough terms: a given sentence does not seem in any way to be 'included' in the set of preceding sentences, nor the truth of the sentence to be determined by the truth of preceding sentences.

In order to resolve such a problem of any logical approach to natural language, we may first try to weaken (or generalize) the notions of inference or logical entailment. In stead of saying that a sentence S_i necessarily/logically follows from $\langle S_1, S_2, \ldots, S_{i-1}\rangle$ we should perhaps say that S_i POSSIBLY FOLLOWS from $\langle S_i, S_2, \ldots, S_{i-1}\rangle$. That is, we should lay down the rules which formulate the conditions under which a following sentence is ADMITTED, given a set of previous sentences. In fact, this is a more general case than the logically/necessarily determined conditions of inference which of course, by $L(p) \dashv M(p)$ are always possible. Notice that in a proof we may have more than one logical consequence from a set of premisses. That is, a particular conclusion is also merely a POSSIBLE one with respect to the rules and the other POSSIBLE conclusions.

Furthermore, the notion of 'conclusion' in proofs is rather arbitrary: it may be any proposition which is the last of the derivation, and any wff derived within a proof is also a 'conclusion' with respect to the previous wff's. The difference is rather pragmatical: it is the aim of the logician to arrive by derivation (i.e. to prove) a GIVEN or ASSUMED wff.

4.2.3. Given these similarities and differences between logical (mathematical) proofs and texts of natural language, there seems to be one solution left. We must not regard any proposition/sentence/logical form of a text as a wff comparable with the wff's WITHIN a particular proof, but rather as its result, i.e. the conclusion derivable from it. That is, any sentence of a text must be seen as a THEOREM which may be derivable/proved if and only if a set of previous theorems have been derived are valid. Since this set must PRECEDE the derivation of S_i, the whole set of 'theorems' is ordered under the precedence relation. Under this interpretation we discover the analogy between a text and a THEORY, or SYSTEM, consisting of an ordered (consistent) set of theorems. Furthermore, we are close to the well-known GRAMMATICAL DERIVATION of particular sentences, starting from an initial symbol (an 'axiom') and following certain rules, although this derivation includes the FORMATION RULES, which in logic do not properly belong to proof itself, which is 'transformational' in character. Thus, a text must be formally constructed by deriving its respective sentences as theorems of our (text) logic. In these derivations, of course, the previous theorems play an important role, and precisely give the text its coherence, for if we would only apply definitions, axioms, etc. we would generate wff's, but not wff's which are well-formed with respect to the previous wff's. Hence the analogy between textual coherence and the formal consistency of logical systems. However, it remains to be seen in how far textual coherence and consistency can be compared when we realize that texts in natural language may well-contain sentences which, taken in isolation, are contradictions of each other. Clearly, notions of ordering, with respect to time or worlds, play a role here.

As for the semantical differences analogies between proofs (systems of proofs) and texts, we have already remarked that the criteria we are looking for, pertain to meaningfulness of a sentence with respect to that of preceding sentences, which in turn determines the satisfiability (truth, falsity, relevance, happiness) of the sentence in the world 'constructed' by the preceding sentences and their presuppositions and consequences. We will study the particular aspects of these general notions especially on such notions as identity, description and entailment in texts.

4.3. *The Basic Apparatus*

4.3.1. In order to be able to describe the main properties of relations between sentences in a text, we adopt the following basic apparatus, which is standard but which will gradually be modified below. The system is essentially a *Modal Predicate Calculus* (MPC) of first order.

4.3.2. *Syntax*

4.3.2.1. The syntax of the system will, initially, have the following sets of *symbols*:

(1) a set of argument (individual) variables: $x, y, z, \ldots,$

(2) a set of individual constants (arbitrary names): $a, b, c, \ldots,$

(3) a set of individual (proper) names: $n_1, n_2, n_3, \ldots,$

(4) a set of predicate variables: $f, g, h, \ldots,$

(5) a set of predicate constants (names): F, G, H,...,
(6) a set of structure markers: (,), [,], { , }, and a comma,
(7) a set of quantifiers: $\forall$, $\exists$,
(8) a set of logical connectives (dyadic operators): $\wedge$, $\vee$, $\supset$,
(9) a monadic operator: $\sim$,
(9) a set of modal operators: $\Box$; $\Diamond$.

4.3.2.2. Provisionally we take the following (standard) *formation rules* defining the well-formed formulas (wff's) of the system:

(1) A predicate variable/constant followed by an ordered set of individual variables/constants/names – which are enclosed in parentheses and separated by comma's – is a wff, called *atomic formula*, abbreviated as α.

(2) an atomic formula preceded by a set of quantifiers, binding each – non-bound – occurrence of an individual variable is a wff.

(3) Any wff as defined in (1) or (2) preceded by a set of modal operators is a wff.

(4) any wff as defined in (1), (2) or (3) preceded by the monadic (negation) operator is a wff.

(5) Any wff as defined in (1)–(4) will be called *simple*.

(6) We form well-formed *complex formulas* or *compounds* out of any simple wff's by one logical connective for each pair of simple wff's.

(7) The properties of simple wff's as specified in (2)–(4) also hold for compound wff's.

(8) No other sequence of symbols is a wff of this system.

4.3.3. *Semantics*

4.3.3.1. The (wff's of this) calculus (are) is interpreted in a Kripke-type semantics for modal predicate systems with the help of a *model* defined as a quadruple $\langle D, V, W, R\rangle$, where D is a domain of individuals ('objects') $u_1, u_2, \ldots$, where V is a value-assignment function assigning to each individual variable a member of D and to to each n-place predicate (predicate of nth degree) a member from a set of $(n+1)$-tuples of members of D and a member w_i of W, which is a set of (*possible*) *worlds* or (*alternative*) *state of affairs*, ordered by a relation R. Depending on the particuliar modal system this relation may be reflexive, transitive, symmetric, etc.

A wff has an interpretation or value in a world w_i when it is either true (satisfied) or false (non-satisfied) in that world. It is true (satisfied) just in case the $(n+1)$-tuple consisting of the values of the individual variables (i.e. members of D) and w_i is a member of the set of $(n+1)$-tuples which is the value of the n-place predicate. The values of compound formulas/logical connectives is calculated with the usual truth tables and the truth conditions for simple formulas given above. Quantified formulas are true for any or at least one value of the variable respectively (where other variables have constant value). Modalized formulas: logical necessity of a wff, if true in any member w_i of W; logical possibility, if true in at least one member w_i of W. These brief indications (which would need precision) will suffice here.

4.4. *Quantification and Identification*

4.4.1. Although we will not primarily discuss the structure of (isolated) propositions of our text logic TL, it is necessary to lay down, firstly, on which terms of the proposition the coherence relations in texts, e.g. identity, are based. That is, in order to define some relation like identity between operators, arguments, predicates or propositions, or between the individuals of the universe of discourse in which each sentence has its 'scope', we must have reliable means to IDENTIFY these individuals. This identification is traditionally defined with a set of QUANTIFIERS, $\forall$ for universal quantification, $\exists$ for existential quantification, roughly interpreted as:

$(\forall x)$: for all x: $- x -$,
$(\exists x)$: for at least one x: $- x -$,

where $(\forall x)$ may be defined as $(\sim\exists x)\sim(\alpha)$ and $(\exists x)$ as $(\sim\forall x)\sim\alpha)$, where α is any wff, containing x as a free variable, *bound* by the quantifier dominating it.

In order to represent the quantification of nouns in NL these two quantifiers are insufficient. In particular we have no means, thus, to quantify over SINGULAR INDIVIDUALS, that is, to express that our wff has a truth value in case there is just *one* individual satisfying it. Similar remarks may be made for PLURAL quantification: we may want to express that a proposition has truth value for *Many* x or *Most* x, for *Few* x, *Every* x or *Each* x, etc.

Let us concentrate on the quantification of singular individuals.

4.4.2. The extant philosophical and logical work on 'individuals', 'particulars', 'singulars' and their corresponding (in-) definite descriptions, is vast[10]. Little, however, of the main results have found their way into grammar, and only recently discussion on quantification, description and modalities also

[10] Of the numerous contributions to the study of singulars and descriptions, see Reichenbach (1947, Section 42, Section 47), Geach (1962), Linsky (1967), Strawson (1959, 1971), Rescher (1968, Ch. 9), Hintikka (1970), Donellan (1970) and Vendler (1968).

Many of the points of view, though diverging, are used in our account, although we believe that a 'textual' treatment of the issue in fact makes explicit numerous references to 'discourse' made in these approaches. In this perspective descriptions and their properties are derivable from sequences. In stead of (merely) operators we therefore introduced appropriate quantifiers, and distinguished between particular and non-particular singulars. The problem has not exhaustively been treated here and we hope to be able to treat it in more detail in future work.

becomes central in linguistic work[11]. It is impossible to review this work here and we will rather approach the problem from a systematic point of view, with special attention for the implications for text structure. Conversely, we will see that most of the unresolved problems can appropriately be restated in terms of textual relations.

Both in (text) grammar and in logic we need a general PRINCIPLE OF INTRODUCTION for referential expressions. That is, from the domain of objects – including 'abstract', 'possible', 'intensional' objects – we select a subset of objects constituting the UNIVERSE OF DISCOURSE. This well-known term significantly bears relation to the fundamental and general notion of text on which we focus. The problem is, as we will see below, that the use of unrestricted quantifiers and their (bound) variables seem to identify the universe and the universe of discourse, an identification which does not hold for any discourse.

The introduction principle we mentioned under such labels as 'ontology', 'existence', etc., is often related with a discussion on the nature of the existential quantifier (∃), which sometimes is said to have the character of a predicate and not an operator[12]. Since any object may 'exist' – according to a modal semantics – in some world, including constructed and imaginary worlds, the problem of (ontological) existence is logically irrelevant for our discussion, since existence in the actual world is merely one type of existence among, logically equivalent, others. Intuitively speaking, but theoretically crucial, is the pseudo-paradox that objects 'come to existence' by the very fact that we talk about them. This is the case for many objects discussed in ordinary, literary and scientific discourse. Now, the introduction principle simply states that reference to any individual (including classes) presupposes their explicit or implicit introduction as-individuals-for-the-discourse, viz. as DISCOURSE INDIVIDUALS, DISCOURSE REFERENTS, or the like.

The formal representations of this principle is traditionally given by existential and universal quantifiers, where the universal quantifier implies logically the existential.

Our first claim is that universal quantification in general PRESUPPOSES existential quantification, since existential quantifiers (or rather existentially quantified propositions) are implied both by the affirmation of universality and its negation.

Our introduction principle follows this line – and we will see below that it

[11] Besides the work of Lakoff (1970, 1971) mentioned above, see Bach (1968), MacCawley (1968, 1970), Karttunen (1968a, b; 1969b, 1971) and Kuroda (1971), among others. See van Dijk (1972, Ch. 2). See also Bierwisch (1971) and Bellert (1969, 1971a, b).

[12] For the use of restricted quantification, see Rescher (1968, 303, 315–318) and Keenan (1972a).

holds for all presuppositions – and requires that all introduction of discourse referents is formally accounted for by a set of INTRODUCTION OPERATORS, of which the well-known existential operator is just one. The introduction principle selects from the universal domain of objects a set of 'discourse objects', which may have a cardinality ranging from 1 (the unique set), to ∞ (the universal set). It will be assumed, however, that quantification in texts is normally of a RESTRICTED type, that is, quantification holds for subsets of individuals defined by a given property (the set of men, the set of winged horses, etc.). The denomination of the elements of these subsets is conventional, and based on a simple or complex naming procedure, i.e. either by (proper) name or by simple or complex (productive) descriptions (*Mary, girl, person next door*).

The argument variables, then, have elements of these subsets as their values (referents). Instead of *there is an x such that x is a man* (*and*...), we would directly have *there is a man* (...), written e.g. as ($\exists$ *man* x)(...x...); universal quantifiers in this restricted sub-universe may be called GENERAL QUANTIFIERS[13].

Notice that the introduction principle holds for general statements as well: *for all men*... presupposes: *there is a set of objects which are men.*

4.4.3. Taking these principles of restricted quantification – for which appropriate theorems may be specified – as our basis, we may proceed to the quantification and identification of individuals in texts. The same story is repeated here, for talking in a text of *all men,* we normally – apart from generalizations (as occur frequently in scientific texts) – refer to a subset of the set of men (which was already a subset of the universal set of 'things'). Of course, there is no limit to these restrictions, which makes quantification always RELATIVE. This relatedness in texts may be defined as a set of PRESUPPOSITIONS, or, equivalently, as a set of PRECEDING SENTENCES, IN WHICH THE SUB-SETS ARE DEFINED FOR WHICH FURTHER QUANTIFICATION IS VALID. The introduction principle regulates the definition (delimitation) of these subsets and hence the scope of further quantification. The introduction

[13] Our definition of the uniqueness quantifiers is parallel to the definition in context provided in Whitehead and Russell (1927). For a discussion, see Rescher (1968, Ch. 9) and the papers in Linsky (1971).

In van Dijk (1972, Ch. 2) we also made a distinction between particular and non-particular uniqueness, both for 'indefinites' and 'definites', but there we applied it still merely to terms, which made us distinguish between epsilon-operators and èta-operators for indefinite (non-specified) non-particular and particular terms respectively, whereas the definitivized terms would be formed with iota and lambda operators for particulars and non-particulars (abstractions) respectively. The account presented in this paper has the same purport but seems simpler to me, especially by the use of constants and (proper) names in the syntax, a procedure which we only hinted at in our book.

operators formally serve this purpose and we will now see if we need other operators besides the existential quantifier to do this job.

4.4.4. Let us take some concrete examples in order to arrive at adequate formalization.

Consider such sentences as

(1) A man is walking in the street,
(2) Mary wants to marry a Moroccan,
(3) On the corner of our street is a cinema.

The expressions *a man*, *a Moroccan*, and *a cinema* are normally interpreted as referring to ONE object, named in this case by a single lexical item. We will say that to acquire the status of discourse objects or discourse referents their corresponding expressions must be formally introduced as such, which in natural language is often manifested by the indefinite article (or another indefinite determiner). However, there is no point to use an existential quantifier in these examples since this one determines truth (satisfaction) not for JUST ONE but for AT LEAST ONE (some) individual. Of course, the truth values partially overlap but since there are different presuppositions in each case, a statement with an existential quantifier could be false and a statement including reference to JUST ONE individual true. The latter would entail that the statements when referring to more than one individual would be false.

Taking sets of men, Moroccans and cinemas as presupposed by the discourse (e.g. as implied by our knowledge of the language or the world), we want to express that these statements are valid for one individual having this property. To express this singularity we will define a UNIQUENESS OR SINGULARITY QUANTIFIER, ε, with the aid of the well-known existential and universal quantifiers:

(4) DEF 1: $(\varepsilon x)(gx)$ for $(\exists x)[gx \wedge (\forall y)(gy \equiv (x = y))]$,

or if, indeed, we want to consider $\exists$ as primitive:

(5) DEF 1′: $(\varepsilon x)(gx)$ for $(\exists x)[gx \wedge (\sim \exists y)(gy \equiv (x \neq y))]$,

which in restricted notation would be:

(6) DEF 1″: (εgx) for $(\exists gx)(\sim \exists gy)[x \neq y]$.

We use an epsilon to denote this quantifier in order to indicate that propositions closed under it are true just for one element of a set. An alternative notation would be e.g. $E_1 x$ or Ix.

Our analysis seems to follow the usual Russell-Quine line for unique descriptions. The difference, however, is that we do not introduce uniqueness in definite terms but in quantification of indefinite propositions. We thus meet the well-known objections, e.g. made by Strawson (Strawson, 1971: Chapter 1), against the russellian analysis. Indeed, definite descriptions do not assert existence or uniqueness (as in fact parts of a formal definition do not 'assert' anything at all, following Strawson's own remainder of the use-meaning distinction) but 'imply', i.e. presuppose them. On our analysis, then, these presuppositions are formally introduced, by certain operators (e.g. εx), as preceding propositions. In case there are no preceding sentences, we may consider the set of propositions which may be used to describe the pragmatical context or situation as such preceding sentences, for which the same principles are valid. In our opinion most of the interesting intuitions and proposals of Strawson, Geach, Linsky and others are thus formally accounted for. A natural link can thus be established between 'indefinite' description and definite description (see below).

Now, although the definition as proposed above seems formally in order, it remains somewhat artificial. Any calculus, and especially a number theory or a natural logic based on it, would be more elegant, it seems when providing a means to introduce direct unique quantification of singular elements of a set, e.g. by taking εx as a PRIMITIVE. This would at least avoid the rather awkward and an un-intuitive procedure for defining singulars by discarding first all other elements of a set with the identity clause.

Once introduced εx as a primitive we might speculate about a corresponding axiomatics. Its negation followed by a negation, meaning 'not for a single one not' or 'nothing(nobody) not', would then be a possible definition of the universal quantifier. We will not further discuss these possibilities here.

The uniqueness quantifier fairly well captures part of the intended meanings of (1)–(3): reference is made in each case to one single object. Notice that this quantifier makes a statement true just in case a single individual (or single class) satisfies it, but that it is not specified WHICH individual is referred to. That is, this uniqueness is INDETERMINATE and therefore may be characterized as a quantifier of CHOICE of an element from a set, just as the existential quantifier selects 'some' ('several') discourse referents.[14]

Indefinite expressions, however, may also denote one PARTICULAR element of a set, and it may be attempted to account for this fact by an appropriate quantifier. Strictly speaking, of course, quantification merely restricts the NUMBER of individuals for which a statement has truth value, and not the

[14] Notice that indeterminate (non-particular) individuals are individuals in the strict sense, not some sort of *arbitrary* individuals being 'any' member, that is *all*, members of a class, for which the appropriate symbolism is the universal or general quantifier (see below for this possible reading of our example sentence). For criticism of 'arbitrary individuals' see Rescher (1968, Ch. 8).

fact that these individuals are non-particular or particular. The notion of particularity, furthermore, seems to be based on PRAGMATIC rules, such as

(7) Speaker knows/has identified the individual a.

We will not analyze these pragmatic aspects here and merely look at the possible syntactic and semantic ways to represent particularity.[15] Since we want to include in our syntax as closely as possible the conditions which will make the propositions true or false, we will introduce a quantifier selecting a DETERMINED individual from a set, i.e. ranging over an IDENTIFIED object. We will call this quantifier a PARTICULARITY or IDENTIFICATION QUANTIFIER and will tentatively define it as follows:

(8) DEF 2 $(Ix)(gx)$ for $(\varepsilon x)(gx \wedge x = n_i)$,

or in restricted notation:

(9) DEF 2′ (Igx) for $(\varepsilon gx)(x = n_i)$.

We see that this quantifier implies (presupposes) the choice or uniqueness quantifier and imposes the further condition that the one individual of the set is identical with a 'fixed' or 'identified' individual for which we appropriately may use a *constant* as a *name*.[16]

We now seem to have the appropriate apparatus to represent the sentences (1)–(3), the ambiguity of which is now explicitly accounted for by different underlying forms, e.g. for (1):

(10) (i) $(\varepsilon x)(man(x) \wedge street(y) \wedge walking\ in\ (x, y))$,
(ii) $(Ix)(man(x) \wedge street(y) \wedge walking\ in\ (x, y))$.

(where we neglect for the moment the appropriate quantification of *street* and other aspects of meaning). The difference in meaning clearly comes out when we consider possible following sentences, on which the different readings impose restrictions. After reading (10)(i) we may have a sentence

[15] Of course, a belief logic, e.g. Hintikka (1962), may step behind this condition and make it part of the calculus. The whole problem of transparence and opacity of reference is connected with the ambiguity of 'knowing' and 'believing'. That is: I may know some individual n, without knowing him by a certain name or description, e.g. as the 'murderer of Johnson'. See Quine (1960, Ch. 4), Donellan (1971). For a linguistic account see Hall Partee (1970), especially for the related problems for pronominalization.

[16] Constants as names have been used in *Principia Mathematica* in order to refer to a particular object in the definition of definite descriptions (Whitehead and Russell, 1927, Ch. 3 and 14). Quine uses free variables to indicate existing objects in derivations (see Note 19, below). For a discussion of russellian names, see e.g. Prior (1971; Ch. 10 and Appendix). Lambert and van Fraassen (1970; Note 13) also use n to denote constants in identity relations. Cf. Lemmon (1965; Ch. 4).

like *I can hear his voice from my study*. That is, I may infer the presence of a man in the street simply from hearing his voice. There may be more men in the street and no identification of WHICH man is crying is specified. Similarly, I may say *A man cried at me from the audience* without being able to see WHO is crying, which permits a following sentence like: *But I did not see who it was*. The second reading makes such following sentences ungrammatical. Here we could have subsequent sentences such as *It is my father* or *His name is Winston Churchill*.

The same distinction holds in sentence (2), where Mary may want to marry a particular Moroccan, say Ibn Hafiz, or some, non-particular Moroccan which I have not identified, but of which I know, e.g. by hear-say that Mary wants to marry him.

In this sentence there is a third reading, based primarily on the INTENTIONAL MODALITY of the sentence as expressed by *want*. Notice that in the first reading, Mary will normally have identified WHOM she is going to marry, that is, reference to him is TRANSPARENT for her and OPAQUE for the speaker in that reading but (in some weird situation) transparent for the speaker and opaque for Mary, e.g. in case she wants to marry a particular man identified by the speaker (as being a Moroccan) but of which she does not know he is from Morocco. Now, the third reading introduces an 'intensional object', which does not refer to any particular or non-particular Moroccan at all, but to a non-particular Moroccan in the world of her intentions or dreams. In this case the statement will be made true just for ANY man if only he is from Morocco. To represent this reading we normally will use the universal (any = arbitrariness) operator and put the property in a CONDITIONAL: for all x, if x is a Moroccan, then Mary will want to marry him, or conversely: if Mary wants to marry a man, then he must be a Moroccan, which makes it a bi-conditional:

$$(11) \qquad (\forall x)\,(\text{Moroccan}\,(x) \equiv \mathsf{W}\ \text{marry}\,(\text{Mary}, x)).$$

In sentence (3), finally, we will normally have the only reading saying that I am speaking of one particular, identified cinema, which I might give a name (even a particular proper name if I remember it).

Notice that in the bi-conditional reading of sentence (2) as represented in (11) the quantifier does not imply ontological existence. In a sentence like *Mary wants to marry a millionaire from her local village* the class of objects satisfying the conditional may, in fact, be empty. Which clearly separates the world of possible or imagined creatures from the world of actual creatures and which makes the use of some modal operator for 'intentionality' necessary (e.g. 'W'). We will see below that this condition is crucial for the coherence of texts.

We do not discuss here such readings of indefinite articles which are used to express generality or definitions, e.g. in *A cinema is a house where they show movies to a public* or in *A student of literary theory should know the principles of linguistics and logic.*

4.4.5. We have discussed at some length some properties of the introduction principle for discourse referents with the aid of quantifiers, in order to have a sound basis to treat DEFINITE NOUN PHRASES and PRONOUNS in text, that is some of the surface manifestations of textual coherence. In general we may state the following intuitive PRINCIPLE OF COHERENT PROGRESSION: all discourse referents identical with those appropriately introduced by the introduction operators are to be counted as particulars in the rest of the text, if interpreted as identical in the same world(s) as those in which they were introduced. A rule of grammar, then, assigns a feature [+ DEF] to the expressions which refer to objects satisfying this principle. In English this feature selects *the* from the lexicon, whereas the introduction operators are manifested by such lexemes as *a*, *some*, *any*, etc. The principle of coherent progression also holds for cases in which a discourse referent is not – in surface structure – explicitly introduced in the text. The rule then applies to presupposed (and hence interpolatable as preceding propositions in the logical form) pragmatic propositions such as (7) above:

(12) Speaker knows/assumes that Hearer knows, that Speaker is referring to object *a* and that Hearer knows/has identified *a*.

which may be formulated in symbolic terms with the aid of the introduction operators. Such a device presupposes that a pragmatic component is associated with the logic, such as to be able to formulate underlying constraints for the logical form and its interpretation (cf. van Dijk and Franck, 1973).

Now, the problem is how we may formulate in explicit terms the different aspects of the principle of coherent progression. The terms in which it is given above are clearly extensional, and it may be asked if there are no pure meaning or intensional properties involved in coherence relations. Finally, it is necessary to have some deeper insight into the main condition of the principle: IDENTITY (IN A WORLD OR ACROSS WORLDS).

4.5. *Identity*

4.5.1. As we suggested above, coherence relations in texts often presuppose a relation of IDENTITY between (terms of) propositions or/and between the discourse referents which they denote. However, a notion like identity, as is well-known, is highly complex, both from a philosophical and a logical point of view. Again, we will omit a discussion of all relevant work in this domain and treat the issue with reference to some examples.[17]

The usual definition of the binary predicate constant IDENTICAL, which may be introduced as a primitive in the syntax, is the following:

(13) $x = y$ for $(\varphi)(\varphi x \equiv \varphi y)$,

a second order definition in which we quantify over properties.

The same definition may be reformulated in set theoretical terms. In this definition the identity relation holds, rather paradoxically, for INDISCERNABLE OBJECTS which are stated to be the same. The paradox merely lies in the fact that we use two different expressions (x and y) to refer to ONE object, just as in the basic thesis $x = x$, expressing self-identity. In this strict interpretation of identity, the identity is equivalent with self identity, which is logically necessary and hence true in each world: $(x = y) \dashv\!\!\exists \Box (x = y)$, that is, the identity of x and y entails the necessary identity of x and y, and conversely; hence $(x = y) \equiv \Box (x = y)$, (where '$\equiv$', here, means strict equivalence). In general, however, weaker notions of identity are used, also referred to as 'equivalence', 'similarity', 'analogy', etc. E.g. two symbols *a* and *a* may be said to be 'identical', but they are discernable as different occurrences (e.g. as two TOKENS of the 'same', abstract TYPE). Similarly, we may say of any two objects that they have the same properties apart from being distinct in a spatio-temporal sense. In fact this is the most strict normal interpretation for expressions like 'identity' and 'sameness'. Weaker, on this line, is identity of two distinct objects as identity from a given point of view, or IDENTITY FOR A DISCOURSE. That is, we may VIEW two written symbols, two chairs or two ideas as being identical, but closer (e.g. microscopic) analysis may reveal certain differences, which for the given occasion are neglected or ABSTRACTED from. Two uttered words may be phonologically identical but phonetically different, i.e. for the grammatical discourse they are identical (types), but they are different for a phonetic description.

[17] For a general discussion of identity, one of the main topics of logic at least since Frege, see especially Quine (1960, Section 24, 1961, Ch. 4). For identity in modal contexts see Hughes and Cresswell (1968, 192ff). One of the debatable points is the validity of $x = y \supset \Box (x = y)$. To avoid unintuitive consequences of this thesis, *contingent identity systems* have been proposed which lack it, and in which identity in a world w_i may be satisfied and non-satisfied in a different world w_j. This possibility, of course, is important above all in all *tense* contexts (cf. Prior, 1968, Ch. 7). Contingent Identity systems have been discussed by Kanger (1957). For identity in texts we may refer especially to Kummer (1971b) and – using a mathematical model – to Palek (1968).

For discussion of the implications of (modal) identity, see Hintikka (1970) and, again (the different issues treated here are closely connected and discussed often in the same papers), Linsky (1971). It has been primarily Ruth Barcan Marcus who has been dealing extensively with the problem, see Barcan Marcus (1947, 1967, 1970). Referential identity in liguistics has been treated by the authors cited in Note 11, and by Dik (1968).

On the other hand we do not merely have weaker versions of distinct-identity but also of self-identity. Physically an object is never totally identical, at different TIME POINTS t_i and t_j, which is particularly obvious for all animate objects, but nevertheless we will speak about the SAME chair, man, or university at different time points, even when all its constituting elements have been successively replaced. Many classical paradoxes have resulted from this possibility of considering a as the same object in its different physical or psychological PHASES. Also in this case the DEGREES OF IDENTITY go from strong to weak, but the important fact, again, is that the identity is assumed to be identity RELATIVE TO A GIVEN TEXT, and abstracted from the absence of 'previous' properties or the presence of 'new' properties. Clearly, the notion of TIME or STATE plays an important role here. The notion of necessary (logical) identity holding in all worlds and hence in all state descriptions or time phases, thus, cannot be compared with the notion of CONTINGENT IDENTITY we here discuss.

The fact that the 'same' object may nevertheless have different properties in different states, or be assigned different properties from different points of view, implies possible differences in referring to/naming/describing this object; e.g. as in the famous *Morning Star/Evening Star* example, where two different descriptions of two different properties denote the astronomically 'same' individual, viz. the planet Venus.

Now, the identity defining coherence in texts is based on these general principles: *a fortiori*, 'identity for a discourse' is 'identity in a text', in that extensional identity is one of the properties determining textual coherence. Let us consider some examples of identity relations in texts.

4.5.2. Consider, for example, the following texts:

(14) A girl won the beauty contest. $\left\{\begin{array}{l}\text{The girl}\\ \text{She}\end{array}\right\}$ is my sister.

(15) A girl won the beauty contest. $\left\{\begin{array}{l}\text{The girl}\\ \text{She}\end{array}\right\}$ must be very happy.

(16) A girl will win the beauty contest. $\left\{\begin{array}{l}\text{The girl}\\ \text{She}\end{array}\right\}$ will receive 5000 dollars.

The initial sentences of these examples are ambiguous along the lines sketched above. This is clear from the subsequent sentences of the text: (14) refers to a particular girl, (15) to a non-particular girl, and (16) to a non-particular girl in a future state of affairs. In all examples we may grammatically continue either with a definite noun phrase or with an appropriate pronoun, each referring to the 'same' individual as the one in the sentence preceding it. Notice, however, that the identity is not strict: in the initial sentences the only property assigned is *girl*, whereas in the second sentences we have the additional properties *sister*, *happy*, *will receive 5000 dollars.* Even if still further properties are assigned by new predicates or relations we will still consider the thus established discourse referents as identical individuals.

By embedding, transformationally, the preceding sentences into the subsequent sentences we get the following complex sentences:

(17) The girl who won the beauty contest is my sister,
(18) The girl who won the beauty contest must be very happy,
(19) The girl who will win the beauty contest will receive 5000 dollars.

The definite noun phrases 'the girl who won the beauty contest' are usually characterized as DEFINITE DESCRIPTION of a (unique) individual. But, again, these noun phrases are ambiguous: referring to a particular a non-particular and a future (possible) non-particular girl with the property of 'having won a beauty contest'.

We assume that (17)–(19) are derived from (14)–(16) because the noun phrases show the same ambiguities as the preceding sentences, and because the 'definiteness' of the noun phrase does not only obey the principle of introduction: just as in (14)–(16) we may have definite noun phrases only if indefinite noun phrases, referring to the same individual precede. If this assumption holds we would have identical deep structures both for complex sentences with embedded restricted relative clauses and for textual sequences of sentences, and the consequence that the coherence principles for (underlying) sequences also hold for complex sentences. In fact this proposal is not new and has precisely motivated the use of (generalized) transformations in early generative grammar. We will not here discuss the further grammatical aspects of these transformations but focus upon the logical structure of the deep structure sequence on which they operate.[18] Now, the classical Russellian approach to definite descriptions such as *the girl who won the beauty contest* is by introducing a *iota*-operator defining uniqueness of terms, e.g.

$$(\imath x)\,(girl(x) \wedge beauty\ contest(y_1) \wedge won(x, y_1)),$$

contextually in a similar way as we defined the uniqueness quantifier. The iota-operator merely states uniqueness (in a universe of discourse) but does not differentiate particulars and non-particulars. The interesting point is that we might probably dispense altogether with specific term-forming

[18] The grammatical aspects of (restrictive) relative clauses and descriptions have received attention in Smith (1969), Kuroda (1969) and the other papers in Reibel and Shane (1969). See also Karttunen (1971) and Kuroda (1971). Sandra Annear Thompson (1970) also derives relative clauses from sentential conjuncts in deep structure.

operators when we directly derive complex terms from preceding sentences, which directly transmits the differences between the introduced 'indefinites' to the following definites. This requires an appropriate apparatus to relate, logically, the two subsequent sentences (propositions). That is, in a rather strict sense we want that the variables of the second sentences are BOUND by the same introducing quantifiers of the preceding sentences.

The simplest way to do this would be, e.g. for (14), something like:

$$(18) \qquad (Ix)\,[(girl(x) \wedge beauty\ contest(y_1) \wedge won(x_1, y_1)) \wedge my\ sister(x)].$$

However, this formula does not seem to adequately capture the meaning of (14): we do not introduce 'a girl who won a beauty contest and who is my sister', but 'a girl who won a beauty contest' of which further information is given in the subsequent sentence. In (14) and especially in (15) and (16) this further information does not further IDENTIFY the girl, since she has been identified already, but merely further SPECIFIES her properties.

When we want to state this further predicate in a new proposition, we might either – redundantly – use a iota-description: *(and) this girl who won the beaty contest*..., or we may use a new variable bound by its own quantifier. In that case we would need of course an identity statement for the variables, e.g. as follows:

$$(19) \qquad \ldots \wedge (Iy)\,[girl(y) \wedge my\ sister(y) \wedge x = y].$$

This would also adequately account for a possible subsequent sentence like *The beauty is my sister*, where a different referring phrase is used to denote the same individual. The rule making noun phrases definite, thus, is based on referential (extensional) identity, not on syntactic (lexematic) identity. This different sentence would be written as follows:

$$(20) \qquad \ldots \wedge (Iy)\,[beauty(y) \wedge my\ sister(y) \wedge x = y],$$

or in restricted quantification, putting the identity statement in the quantifier: 'for the only y identical with x':

$$(21) \qquad \ldots (Iy = x)\,[beauty(y) \wedge my\ sister\ (y)].$$

In this case the identity predicate in the restricted quantifier precisely defines the property of definiteness [+DEF], selecting the definite article.

As a syntactic transformation rule, even of the logical system, we may normally omit identical propositions in conjunctions: $\ldots p \wedge q \ldots p \wedge r \ldots \equiv \equiv \ldots p \wedge q \ldots \wedge r \ldots$ Since $x = y$ we may consider *girl(x)* and *girl(y)* as equivalent and delete (optionally) the second occurrence where this identity is stated. We then have:

$$(22) \qquad \ldots \wedge (Iy)\,[x = y \wedge my\ sister(y)],$$

or in restricted quantification:

(23) $\ldots \wedge (Iy = x)\,[my\ sister(y)]$,

which would be the underlying structure of *(and) She is my sister*. In this approach personal pronouns and definite articles have the same source. The same holds, then, for the relative pronoun *who* in the complex definite description (17).

The method of establishing identity relations between formula followed here has the disadvantage of requiring permanent introduction of new variables and corresponding quantifiers.

Instead of repeating in each formula a new identity statement (which would probably grow more complex in each case: $x=y$, $x=y=z$, $x=y=z=u$, etc.), it is much more natural and easy to use CONSTANTS/NAMES to denote this identical individual. Actually, the very definition of the particular uniqueness quantifier (I) contains this equation of x and n_i. The coherent progression principle stated at the beginning of this section says that any individual introduced in a text acquires the status of a particular. This is not paradoxical when we recall that particularity presupposes identification. We may say that any (actual, possible, etc.) individual introduced in the text is identified for the text by the introducing statement/quantifier itself; in intuitive terms: 'precisely that individual we just have spoken about'. Since particularity may be thus established, we have the possibility of substituting n_i for x in the following sentences.

Sentence (14) would then be

(24) $\ldots \wedge ((\text{girl}(n_1) \wedge \text{my sister}(n_1))$.

or

(25) $\ldots \wedge (\text{my sister}(n_1))$,

where the constant would underly the pronoun *she*.

That the constant in the three sentences (14)–(17) still refers to particular and non-particular individuals follows from the way it is introduced: the introducing statements/quantifier DOMINATES (has as its scope) the set of sentences for which the identity condition holds, and in which, thus, n_i can be substituted for the variable of the quantifier.

The constant substituted for the x of $(\varepsilon x)(\ldots)$ is merely a DISCOURSE NAME[19] for this non-particular or arbitrary individual, optionally characterized by

[19] 'Discourse names' have been used by Keenan (1972a) who refers to Henkin's Completeness Proof for modal predicate calculi (Henkin, 1949). The principle of Existential Specification (see Suppes, 1957) also makes use of constants as 'ambiguous names' in derivations.

its main distinguishing property: e.g. *girl.* The procedure reminds of the principle of existential specification in logical inferences, which permits to use, temporarily, a constant as an 'ambiguous' name for an existentially quantified variable, under some textual restrictions. The same holds, of course for non-particular singulars and, by definition, for particular singulars.

This is a principle underlying inference in PROOFS. Similarly, the introduction of constants, or NAME INTRODUCTION, is a principle underlying any coherent text.

The use of constants, of course, is not restricted to singulars but may also be applied to name PLURALS[20], e.g. *some x, few x, many x, most x, all x.* As was remarked earlier these quantifiers do not quantify merely over general (sub)sets, e.g. as in *Some/Few/Many/Most/All boys like football,* but also over sets introduced in previous sentences of the text, as in

(26) Many girls participated in the beauty contest. Few $\left\{\begin{matrix}\text{girls}\\ \text{of them}\end{matrix}\right\}$ were pretty.

Few quantifies over the GROUP of girls introduced in the preceding sentence of the text. Assign the name n_1 to this group of participants and quantify over the constant: $(Few\ n_1, y)(...y...)$ and assign n_2 to the new subgroup. This procedure seems straightforward only if we consider groups as sets of individuals, of which EACH individual is, indirectly, 'reached' by the predicate. When the group is taken as a whole it is normally quantified as a singular individual. Notice, finally, that in example (26) the introducing *many* clearly does not quantify over the set of all girls. Like most plural quantifiers, and in general for MEASURE PREDICATES (*high, deep, expensive*), it quantifies with respect to an expected NORM or AVERAGE. This norm, of course, depends on the rest of the meaning of the sentence and hence of our knowledge of the world. In restricted quantification notation we may use the relation *For greater than/more than,* and N as a numerical variable. The definition of *many x,* would then be something like $(Many\ g, x)(...x) =_{def} (\exists g > N, x)(...x...)$. We will not further discuss the problems of plural quantification and we will retain the rule relevant for a text logic that all quantifiers in texts quantify over sets introduced in preceding sentences or presupposed by the text (as part of the lexicon or encyclopedia or as part of the pragmatical situation).

4.5.3. We have considered in some detail the relationship between quantification and identity in texts. Another important condition for this identity was, however, the identity of individuals IN THE SAME WORLD(S). That is, all

[20] For plural quantification see Rescher (1968, Ch. 10) and Altham (1971).

of our previous remarks presuppose that the MODALITIES of the subsequent sentences are kept constant. In general we cannot identify an individual introduced by a modalized sentence M_iS_i, and thus having its interpretation/extension in world(s) $w_i, w_{i+1}, \ldots$, and an individual introduced by M_jS_j, where $M_j \neq M_i$, possibly interpreted in a set of worlds $w_j, w_{j+1}, \ldots$, where possibly $w_j \neq w_i$, etc... Some concrete examples clearly show this principle:

(27) *Peter needs a secretary to type his papers. She is graduated from the University of California.

(28) *Perhaps John will visit us tonight. I am sure he will be here at eight o'clock.

(29) *Last night I dreamt that I met a very intriguing girl, named Lola. But this morning I discovered that she is systematically ignoring me.

From these examples we see that individuals of 'intended', 'possible' or 'dreamt' world (or 'state of affair') cannot simply be identified with individuals of another, e.g. actual world. In (27) we may, however, continue to qualify the needed secretary, with *She must have graduated*... Similarly, in (29) my dream may assign all sorts of fantastic qualities to Lola. In (28) the *he* may not possibly be *John* since John will be *possibly* there, and he (an other man) *surely*. This is the general rule but there is a regular possibility to establish what may be called TRANS-WORLD IDENTITY in texts. Of course, this is true, trivially, for all sentences interpretable in all or several worlds. It is also true if the domain of individuals is world-independent. Finally, regular identity of individuals is possible in different 'states' of the 'same world', i.e. all those worlds $w_{i_1}, w_{i_2}, \ldots$ 'compatible with' ('included in') a given world w_i: The John who will *necessarily* come, may *possibly* come too late. But also trans-world identity for non-compatible worlds is possible through the COUNTERPART-PRINCIPLE[21], which states that any individual u_i of a world w_i may have its 'counterpart' u_j in a world w_j. That is, there may be a real Lola of my knowledge of which I may also dream; which makes the following text coherent:

(30) Yesterday, I met a nice girl, named Lola. But tonight I dreamt that she detested me.

The pronoun *she* may refer only to Lola's dream-counterpart, which is nevertheless the 'same' Lola. Just as we may abstract – for a discourse – from certain properties of a given individual in its different phases, we may establish identity based on WORLD-ABSTRACTION, i.e. between counterparts.

[21] See Lakoff (1968a) for the linguistic implications of the counterpart principle which has been introduced by Lewis (1968).

Notice, however, that the interpretation of the whole sentence must be world consistent. It does not FOLLOW that truth for a sentence in a given world entails truth in a different world. In (29) the second sentence presupposes that I know/have met Lola, but this presupposition – against the general rule – is not identical with, or a consequence of, the preceding sentence. We will discuss the modal compatibility of predicates and propositions below.

4.6. *Partial Identity, Inclusion, and Elements of Sets*

4.6.1. Whereas the identity relations studied in the previous section may be characterized as establishing a 'static coherence', formalized as a series of constants, there is another fundamental principle of coherence, determining the 'progression' of the text. According to the introduction principle, for any individual to become a discourse referent it must be appropriately introduced by certain quantifiers. Now, this principle is not wholly FREE, that is, there are of course certain CONSTRAINTS UPON (NEW) INTRODUCTIONS. The general principle underlying these constraints is that any introduced individual must be related with earlier introduced individuals. Besides the (relative, contingent) identity relation, these relations may be of the general set-theoretic type: inclusion, element (member)-set, intersection, etc. Part of these relations have been mentioned when we discussed quantification over previously introduced subsets: one (of them), few (of them), many (of them), etc. In this case the predicates (or 'set names') remain identical, which may lead to deletion and pronominalization.

In other cases we witness part-whole relationships, where the part has a different lexical 'name' as the whole, e.g. *house-window*, *woman-eyes*, *course-student*, etc.

Now the general rule for such relations is that any individual having a specifiable relation with another already introduced individual is PARTICULARIZED by this relation and hence definite in surface structure:

(31) There were many people in the room. The women were sitting...
(32) Peter bought a new house. The front door is of massive steel.
(33) John has a new secretary. Her eyes are driving him mad.

These facts can be explained only if we keep following the introduction principle. In that case we introduce the new individuals by general rule, viz. MODUS PONENS, and a SET OF POSTULATES, lexical and encyclopedical, such that the textual existence of individual x follows contingently from the existence of individual y:

$$(\forall x)\,[\varphi x \supset \psi x], \qquad \varphi a \vdash \psi a$$

E.g. For each x, if x is a house, x has a frontdoor. Thus, when *house* (x) is stated we may infer (εy) (*frontdoor* (y)), and hence we have regularly introduced the individual. The fact that the deletion principle does not work here seems to indicate that it operates on a level where the general formula and its consequences have been deleted. That is, it only works between derived theorems/ sentences (we do not discuss the numerous grammatical problems of the ordering, forward/backward pronominalization, etc. involved here)[22].

4.6.2. At this point it becomes clear that a pure EXTENSIONAL (set theoretic) approach becomes awkward. Already in the postulates mentioned above the structure and rules for predicate logic appear: the introduction of new individuals is based on intensional relations between predicates and between propositions, and involve such relations as presuppositions and consequence. Moreover, many identity relations, normally leading to definitivization or pronominalizations, are not based on strict identity of individuals, but on inclusion, co-membership or in general identity of properties, e.g. in *I wanted to buy some apples. But they were sold out*, and in *Take care of your wallet. Peter always tries to pick it from his closest friends.* Here the individual apples I would have bought are probably not identical with those sold out, but only a subset of them, whereas in the second example we may pronominalize although there is no strict identity but merely co-membership or 'identity' of a particular wallet with any wallet. We will not pursue the details of these possible set-relations, but focus on 'intensional' coherence in texts, viz. relations between predicates and propositions.

4.7. *Intensional Coherence*

4.7.1. Texts may be coherent not only because their sentences refer to identical individuals or because they establish relations between these individuals, but also because there are relations of identity, similarity, inclusion or consequence between the properties or actions of these individuals or between propositions in general. We will call these relations INTENSIONAL[23].

When we want to maintain the description of textual relations at the pure extensional level, we may, of course, say that identity of a property of or a

[22] For discussion and reference, see van Dijk (1972, Ch. 2), Lakoff (1968a) Langacker (1969), Karttunen (1971) and Postal (1971).

[23] Although we distinguish between intension and extension, especially in the description of natural language, this distinction is not without problems, nor do we trust that intensions and meanings are similar or identical things. See Carnap (1957) for general discussion. Especially Quine (e.g. 1960, Ch. 6) and Carnap (1957) advocated the reduction of intensions to extensions. For modal intensions see Marcus (1967) and Montague (1968, 1970a, b). Lewis (1970) constructs intensions as functions from indices to extensions (following Montague). For criticism of the extensionalist stand, see e.g. Prior (1971), Ch. 4)

relation among one or more individuals can be expressed by co-membership relation of the same set of *n*-tuples, defining extensionally such a property or relation. However, such an interpretation of properties and relations both logically and linguistically leads to serious problems. The properties/relations characterizing exactly the same set of *n*-tuples would in that case be indistinct; 'thinking' and 'speaking' probably would have the same extension, although being different in meaning. The extensional definition of adjectives or adverbs would pose still greater problems. Finally, extensions for sentences are traditionally defined as truth-values (truth, falsity, applicability, or the like), but two sentences of the same extension (truth value) hardly ever have identical meanings, even when they are true in any world, as is the case for tautologies. We conclude that this sort of relationships in text are most adequately constructed as intensional, without excluding a priori the relevance of some extensional aspects of intersentential coherence, such as presupposed or entailed truth value of sentences.

4.7.2. Not only verbs, adverbs and sentences represent INTENSIONAL OBJECTS[24], but also a set of nouns and noun phrases. Thus, of the particular beauty contest in our earlier example we may say that *the girl who will win it* refers to a non-particular in a future state of affairs. But the definite expression (*the*) *girl who wins a beauty contest* does not seem to refer to any particular or non-particular at all, and rather seems to refer to a complex property, which may be assigned to a particular or non-particular individual. Intensional objects of this kind may nevertheless serve as arguments in a text, for which the usual principles hold. We may regularly continue *...normally receives a great sum of money*, and subsequent sequences may have, regularly, pronouns like *she*, which seem to require referential identity of the individuals. We may say in such cases that such expressions are interpreted as individuals of abstract or constructed worlds, established by the text itself. The 'winner of the game' for example is an entity constructed by the discourse formed of the rules defining the game. The statements of such discourse are general or universal and accompanied with necessity operators. In any world/situation in which the game is played 'the winner of the game', as an abstract expression, has an 'instantiation' in a particular or non-particular winner, which was merely a POSSIBLE winner of the game, whereas the intensional 'winner of the game', NECESSARILY wins it, by definition.

Intensional objects may be conceived of as 'names' of classes, so that their

[24] See also Note 23. 'Intensional' and in particular 'possible objects' are also topics in the general discussions in logic mentioned above. See Hughes and Cresswell (1968, p. 197). They have been treated as 'individual concepts' by Carnap (1957). For defense, see Scott (1970) Lambert and van Fraassen (1970). For attack: Quine (1960, 245ff).

interpretation in related non-abstract worlds may be the universal quantifier and a conditional: *for all girls*: *if they win a beauty contest, then they receive a great sum of money*. In the same text, as we saw earlier, this general statement may be followed by a particular statement stating that the condition is satisfied for a (non-) particular individual, from which may follow a conclusion: *Sheila won a beauty contest, therefore Sheila receives much money*. Such coherence relations are actualized primarily in generalizing, argumentative and scientific discourse, and obey the general rules for identity between arguments noun phrases or rather between individuals, of which constructed individuals, like possible, imagined individuals are just a subset, with the specific property that the worlds in which they are interpretable are also constructed by the discourse.

In a very general way this fact even seems to hold for the abstract LEXICAL MEANINGS of the words of a language. The intensional object 'girl who wins a beauty contest' does not differ in this respect from the intensional object 'girl', interpretable as name of a class, or as property, or in some vague philosophical term as 'universal particular', or something similar. This can most easily be seen from such equivalences as *sculptress–woman who makes statues* which make up the (traditional) dictionary. The restrictive relative clause defines precisely the subset of the set of 'women' or 'girls' for which the intensional object can be used as a name. We will simply consider them as properties or attributes, and not consider the philosophical and meta-logical problems related with the distinction between individuals, properties, classes, classes of classes, etc., but try to discover the characteristics of intensional relationships in texts.

4.8. *Intensional Identity. Predicates.*

4.8.1. Arguments or noun phrases in texts are submitted a general principle of introduction and progression defined on extensional identity or other set-theoretic relations. It may be asked whether such principles e.g. of introduction and progression, also determine the PREDICATE COHERENCE in texts. Apart from the predicates 'naming' the identical individuals (*a girl… the girl…*) predicates in general do not seem to be kept constant. That is, in surface structure 'new information' is usually provided by the predicate phrase of the sentence (including verbs, auxiliaries, nouns, adverbials, etc.). If this general rule is not followed, i.e. when the predicate (verb phrase) is kept constant and the subject-noun phrase differs, this is usually either assigned contrastive stress or submitted rhematization transformations (*it is… who*, etc.).

Nevertheless, there are many constraints limiting the introduction of predicates, especially the properties of combined predicates and their mutual relations (selection restrictions). Certain predicates, thus, presuppose the explicit or implicit introduction of other predicates, e.g. the predicate 'speaking' presupposes the predicate 'human' when assigned as properties to one individual. These facts are well-known from recent research in linguistics, and need no further comment here. These principles underlie not only the introduction but also the progression of predicates. Just as 'things' are related, so are their properties and the relations expressing events, actions and processes. That is, in general, certain predicates presuppose others or have others as their possible or necessary 'consequences'. These fundamental relations will be dealt with in the next section.

Predicate identity is based on the same general philosophical principles as identity of individuals: identity is 'relative identity', i.e. identity conventionally accepted for certain types of discourse. 'Water', 'communism', 'lovely', 'scientific', etc. are predicates representing intensional objects which may differ for different discourses, situations and language users. These facts are well-known and will not concern us further here. Let us consider some concrete examples in order to discover what logical principles, if any, characterize predicate identity in texts:

(34) John will go to Amsterdam this summer. So will John.
(35) Peter has forgotten his records. And so have I.
(36) Do you go to the movies tonight? No I will not go there.
(37) Jurij often plays chess. But he does not like it.
(38) Jurij often plays chess. But I do not like that.

Parts of the verb phrase are understood to be 'present' in the meaning of the subsequent sentences but transformationally deleted in surface structure, where they are represented by *so*, *it*, *that*, *there*, etc. This deletion requires some principle of deep structure identity, for which we should provide the logical form.

The (complex) predicates repeated in (34) and (35) seem to be 'go to Amsterdam this summer' and 'have forgotten (...) records', which seem to be ABSTRACTED from the preceding sentence, e.g. as follows *go* (– , *Amsterdam, this summer*), which as a complex predicate is assigned to John in a following sentence: [*go* (– , *Amsterdam, this summer*] *John.* Instead of the dash replacing the non-occupied argument place, we may use a variable and use the abstraction operator *lambda*: [(λx) (go(x, Amsterdam, this summer)] forming a predicate, with a meaning of 'the property of x such that ...x...'. The subsequent sentence takes, thus, the following form.

$$[(\lambda x)\,(go(x,\ Amsterdam,\ this\ summer)]\ John.$$

In a similar way we may make predicates of any part of a sentence.

In the last two sentences a part of the sentence and a whole sentence is repeated as a direct object *it* (*that*) in the subsequent sentence. Now, to 'what' individual does *it* refer in this case? This cannot be the sentence or part of the sentence (as indirect quotation, etc,), but must be some EVENT or ACTION, which apparently may be quantified upon. In (38) we find both readings: *that* may represent the 'activity of playing chess' (in general) or the 'event(s) of Jurij's playing chess'. Since the whole sentence expresses such an event we would need a manner to quantify over this event so that it may regularly be introduced and repeated, e.g. by EVENT SPLITTING as proposed by Reichenbach[25]: $(Ev)([\textit{Jurij plays chess}]^*\ v, \textit{often})$, where *often*, temporally qualifying the whole event may be considered as an argument of the event predicate. Another, more interesting possibility, is to consider the temporal adverbials as quantifiers or operators of the event. They strikingly parallel the pluralistic quantifiers: *no(body)-never*, *some(body)-sometimes*, *few-sometimes*, *many-often*, *all-always*. This approach is always possible of course when we use restricted quantification (over time points), e.g. $(\forall\ \textit{time}, x)$ $(\varepsilon v)\ ([\ldots]^*\ v, x)$. A similar notation may be followed to represent the topological aspect of the text.

According to the introduction quantifiers we have used earlier we may regularly introduce particular and non-particular events, both singular and plural. εv would stand for non-particular singular events, e.g. *Once John will come back*, and Iv for particular singular events: *One day John came back. It was on November 13, 1945.*

Finally, we would not merely need quantification over times, places and events but also over properties or actions expressed by the predicate, that is over a part of the sentence, not over the whole sentence. In that case we might, with Davidson[26], try something like $(\varepsilon x)\ (\textit{win}\ (\textit{girl}, \textit{beauty contest}, x)$ $\wedge\ \textit{Past}\ (x))$, or $(\textit{Many time}, x)\ (\textit{play}\ (\textit{John}, \textit{piano}, x))$, but it is not obvious what relation there might be between girl, beauty contest and the event of winning, since winning is this relation itself. It must be the event itself that has the property such that a girl wins the beauty contest. The abstraction operator suggests itself here, e.g. as follows: $[(\lambda x)\ (\textit{girl}\ (x)\ \wedge\ \textit{beauty contest}$ $(y_1)\ \wedge\ \textit{win}\ (x, y_1)]\ z$, but this would qualify a non-particular z having the same property as x. Hence we need a quantification of the predicate itself $(If)\ (\varepsilon x)$ $[(\textit{wins}\ (x, y_1))f\ \wedge\ \textit{girl}\ (x)\ \wedge\ \textit{beauty contest}\ (y_1)\ \wedge\ \textit{Past}\ (f)]$.

[25] See Reichenbach (1947, p. 247)

[26] For treatment of quantification of events or actions, including a criticism of Reichenbach's analysis of events, see Davidson (1967). See in general von Wright (1963), Binkley *et al.* (1971), Hilpinen (1971), Rescher (ed.) (1967).

Following the rules we may now introduce the predicate constant by $f=F$, such that we would have ... $\sim$*like* (I, F) in (38), where the particular activities of Jurij are disliked. In case playing chess in general is disliked we would need generalization over the previously introduced particular activities: $(\forall f)[(playing\,(x, y))f \ldots \wedge (\forall g)[(g=f) \wedge (playing\,(x, y))\, g \wedge \sim like\,(I, g)$, where the identity statement as before generates the pronoun *it* or the anaphorical demonstrative *that*.

From this brief discussion of quantification and identity of predicates in texts it has become clear that although little is known in this area, the general principles are those already discovered for first order individuals. Quantification of predicates does not seem problematic: *one, two, many, journeys* does not seem more natural than *once, twice,..., often going to Paris.*

The very fact that in natural language we may use higher predicates viz. adverbs, to assign properties to such first order properties and relations is sufficient reason to quantify over them. The same is true for whole sentences, or rather for the intensional object PROPOSITION which may be verbalized as *the fact that*... and be submitted quantification and identity. In the next section we will further analyze these textual relations between whole sentences/propositions.

4.9. *Propositions, Presuppositions, Consequences, Connectives*

4.9.1. A text logic would not be a logic if it would not specify relationships between propositions. In logic these relations are established with formation rules for complex propositions operating with dyadic connectives on the one hand, and with transformation rules defining derivability of proposition P_i from $\langle P_1, P_2, \ldots, P_{i-1}\rangle$ in a derivation (proof) on the other hand. P_i is in that case a LOGICAL CONSEQUENCE OF or ENTAILED BY $\langle P_1, P_2, \ldots, P_{i-1}\rangle$, its premisses, if it cannot possibly be false when its premisses are true. We will use the arrow ($\rightarrow$) to indicate this consequence relation: $P_{i-1} \rightarrow P_i$ having as meaning 'P_i is the 'logical consequence' of, 'logically (necessarily) follows from', or is 'entailed by' P_{i-1}'. With this relation is usually defined the (logical) PRESUPPOSITION relation between propositions or sentences, which has intuitively the following meaning: 'P_i presupposes P_{i-1}, if the truth of P_{i-1} is a necessary condition for P_i to have truth value (e.g. to be true/false, satisfied/non-satisfied, applicable/non-applicable, etc.)'. We use the double arrow '$\Rightarrow$' between two propositions (or between two sets of propositions): $P_i \Rightarrow P_{i-1}$ meaning 'P_i presupposes P_{i-1}'. The formal definition of presupposition is as follows:

(39) $\quad P_i \Rightarrow P_j \quad \text{for} \quad (P_i \rightarrow P_j) \wedge (\sim P_i \rightarrow P_j)$

that is, a sentence is presupposed by another sentence just in case it is entailed by the another sentence and entailed by the negation of the other sentence. Thus the sentence *The girl who won the beauty contest is my sister* presupposes $\left\{\begin{matrix} the \\ a \end{matrix}\right\}$ *girl won the beauty contest*, because it is a logical consequence of the first sentence and also of *The girl who won the beauty contest is not my sister*.

4.9.2. These notions, though not yet very current in standard logic, are well-known, especially in the philosophy of language and recent linguistics. They are interesting enough to attempt to construct a proper PRESUPPOSITION LOGIC[27], roughly determining the conditions under which a sentence has truth value.

Now, if we look at the example given above we see that a presupposition of a complex sentence with a definite description containing a restrictive relative clause is identical with the proposition underlying the relative clause. Earlier, we argued that this clause may be derived from a linear sequence of propositions in which the relative clause, hence the presupposed proposition, would precede the 'main clause', i.e. the presupposing proposition. If this assumption is correct a PRESUPPOSITION LOGIC IS EQUIVALENT WITH A PART OF TEXT LOGIC, since formally, the set of presuppositions of a proposition is a subset of its preceding propositions in a text. This does not mean that these must be realized in surface structure. Preceding propositions are also those which are consequences of preceding propositions. Other presuppositions of the sentence given as example would be: *there is a (one) girl, there is only one beauty contest, one girl won the beauty contest, it is possible that a girl wins a beauty contest, beauty contests have winners*, etc.... which are in part presuppositions of the presupposed propositions (the embedded relative clause). This seems to make (some) presupposition(s) TRANSITIVE:

$$((P_i \Rightarrow P_j) \wedge (P_j \Rightarrow P_k)) \rightarrow (P_i \Rightarrow P_k)$$

which follows from the transitivity of the consequence relation.

One of the disadvantages of the traditional definition of presuppositions is that it presupposes TRUTH of sentences. In the first place, it would be more adequate, in that case, to speak of 'truth in the world of knowledge of the speaker', i.e. of ASSUMED TRUTH: I may have had wrong information about

[27] A *presupposition logic* has been constructed by Keenan (1969, 1971, 1972a, 1972b). This system – though based on logical presupposition (and entailment) – features some devices and methods which we consider important also for text logic, of which presupposition logic in our view is a proper sub-system.

For presuppositions in general, see Strawson (1952) and – in linguistics – Garner (1971), Lakoff (1970, 1971a, b). See van Dijk (1972, Ch. 2) for a text grammatical treatment.

the beauty contest, which makes the presupposition factually false, though it is 'true' for the speaker.

Another problem is that there seems to be no mechanical desision procedure to define the set of presuppositions of a proposition: *John knows he is arrogant* presupposes *John is arrogant* but *John believes he is ill* does not presuppose *John is ill* or might even presuppose *John is not ill.* That is, some verbs have direct object propositions as their presuppositions others have not. In texts this problem is easier to solve since merely the propositions PRECEDING a proposition are presupposed. Others follow a proposition if they are in the scope of the verb/predicate of such a proposition (*say, believe, pretend, assume*, etc.), i.e. when they are interpretable only in a world constructed in a previous proposition.

In general we will say, then, that a sentence of a text is derivable only if its presuppositions have been previously derived, which makes presupposition a well-formedness condition for texts. Earlier, we saw that these conditions are both intensional and extensional: there must be introduced discourse referents, e.g. *girl* and *beauty contest* and an identity relation between *girl* and *girl* in the subsequent propositions underlying our example sentence. Furthermore, intensional conditions determine that *The boy who won the beauty contest is my sister* is anomalous – has 'zero' truth value – since the (lexical) presupposition of *boy* (x) is *male* (x), where *sister* (y)$\rightarrow$*female* (y), which would make $x=y$ a contradiction. Hence the further condition that the set of presuppositions of a sentence must be CONSISTENT.

4.9.3. Besides the two logical relations of logical consequence (entailment) and its specific variant, presupposition, it might be interesting to introduce some other important inter-sentential relations in texts, e.g. the 'converses' of these logical relations. The intuitive motivation for postulating a set of much weaker relations in a natural logic is the following. Relations such as logical consequence (entailment) are the principles underlying formal (deductive) derivability. This means that the conclusion derived from a set of premises is somehow 'contained' in its premises. In a natural text this may mean that a preceding sentence, e.g. as a presupposition, is, in a sense, 'contained' in some of its following sentences. Hence the divergence (if not converseness) of the notions 'logically follows from' and 'textually follows'. This is obvious when we realize that it is a principle of textual derivations that any following sentence adds new 'semantic information' to the text. As we saw above this may regularly be done by the introduction of new discourse referents or discourse predicates. We now may want to characterize formally such sentences with respect to the preceding sentences, in order to make explicit such intuive notions as 'progression', 'expansion', or the like.

Take for example logical consequence or entailment. Thus a sentence *Yesterday it rained the whole day* entails *It was raining yesterday afternoon.* Similarly, *We gave a party last night* entails *We had guests last night*, also by lexical definition. In both cases it is not possible that the antecent is true and the consequent false (when uttered the same day, by the same speaker, etc.). In a text the entailing sentence may follow, e.g. as an 'explanation' of a previous sentence: *We had guests last night, because we had a party*, or to provide more specific information: *John will arrive tomorrow. He will arrive at 5 p.m. (tomorrow).* We may say that these following sentences are COMPATIBLE WITH their preceding sentences, that is, they are not necessarily false when their preceding sentences are true. Not all sentences compatible with preceding sentences entail these, of course: *John came at 5 o'clock* is compatible with but does not entail *Peter came at 5 o'clock*, according to the definition, but incompatible with *John was sleeping at 5 o'clock*. Similarly, there are other possible following sentences entailing the same preceding sentence(s).

Now, we will use the term POSSIBLE CONSEQUENCE to denote the members of the set entailing a given sentence. We therefore provisionally define this relation as a converse of logical consequence:

(40) $p \rightsquigarrow q$ for $q \rightarrow p$,

where '$\rightsquigarrow$' means 'has as a possible consequence'. Truth in this case is disjunctive: we may have guests either because we have a party and/or because we have dinner, and/or... Whereas logical consequences are deductive, possible consequences have an INDUCTIVE character.

We here touch the general LOGIC OF CONDITIONS (cf. von Wright, 1971). Thus, the truth of *We will have a party* is a SUFFICIENT CONDITION for the truth of *We will have guests*, whereas, conversely, the latter sentence is a NECESSARY CONDITION for the first sentence. These relations are defined by von Wright (1971) with an additional CONTINGENCY CLAUSE:

(41) $$Sc(p, q) =_{\text{def}} N(p \to q) \,\&\, Mp \,\&\, M \sim q,$$
$$Nc(p, q) =_{\text{def}} N(q \to p) \,\&\, Mq \,\&\, M \sim p,$$

where N stands for 'logical necessity' and M for 'logical possibility'.

4.9.4. With the relation of possible consequence we may define the corresponding relation of POSSIBLE PRESUPPOSITION. Thus *We will have party* is a possible presupposition of *We will have many guests*, because it is a possible consequence of this sentence and of its negation. Hence the following definition:

(42) $q \not\Rightarrow p$ for $(p \rightsquigarrow q) \wedge (\sim p \rightsquigarrow q)$

where '$\not\Rightarrow$' stands for 'is a possible presupposition of'.

From the definitions we see that the converses of both the logical and the possible presuppositions are possible consequences. In other terms we may say that the possible consequences of p are the ADMISSIBLE EXPANSIONS of p, when p is given (has been derived) in a text.

4.9.5. In natural texts sentences may follow each other under still weaker conditions as those mentioned in the previous paragraphs. Take for example the perfectly coherent pair *John was walking in town. He met an old friend,* where no direct relation of entailment obtains and hence possible consequence seems undefined. Still, intuitively we know that the first sentence is a possible condition for the truth of the second sentence, but this condition is not sufficient (or necessary). Another condition would be the presence of the old friend in the same town, and the presence of both at the same place in that town. Similar remarks hold for a pair like *We had a party last night. Peter got drunk.* The only feasible way to describe such coherence relations is to account for INDIRECT POSSIBLE CONSEQUENCES, defined with a transitivity relation; DEF: q is 'indirect possible consequence' of p iff q is a possible consequence of r and r is a possible consequence of p. In many cases, in addition, entailments must be inserted, where the possible consequences hold for the logical consequences of a given sentence. Thus, in the first example given above *He met an old friend* has as a possible consequence (admissible expansion) *He met an old friend in town,* which in turn entails *He (John) is in town,* which has *John was walking in town* as a possible consequence. A similar derivation would hold for the second example.

Notice that we get INDIRECT POSSIBLE PRESUPPOSITIONS as soon as a sentence is an indirect possible consequence of p and of $\sim p$. This is actually the case in the first example given, since the first sentence is also a possible indirect consequence of *He did not meet an old friend.* It is this very weak sort of presupposition which normally defines the 'possible conditions' or 'situations' which make textual progression coherent.

An other interesting fact is that indirect possible consequences may be symmetric. John's meeting an old friend may also be a possible consequence of his walking in town (and not, say, of his sleeping at the same time). We are close, then, to the current (non-logical) notion of 'consequence' when notions of time and cause are involved (see below).

4.9.6. In fact the relation 'possible consequence' is the weakest of the contingent relations between propositions in natural texts. In the same inductive perspective we may of course introduce such important relations as PROBABLE CONSEQUENCE (CONTINGENTLY) NECESSARY CONSEQUENCE and, hence, PROBABLE PRESUPPOSITION and NECESSARY PRESUPPOSITION. In that case our definitions would contain additional contingency operators of probable and (contingently) necessary modalities. Thus the sentence *John has shot himself a bullet through the head* is an (indirect) possible consequence of its probable consequence *He was immediately dead*, whereas *Harry dropped his book* is a sufficient condition for its C-necessary consequence *The book fell down*.

4.9.7. The SEMANTICS of these relations seems rather straightforward. If p has q as its possible consequence, then in at least one world (situation) truth of p contingently entails truth of q, or, in other terms if p is true then q is not necessarily false, from the perspective of a certain world or index w_i. Similarly, we may interpret probable consequence as truth of q in most worlds (situations) where p is true (satisfied), and necessary consequence as truth of q in all worlds (situations) where p is true, again with respect to a given world w_i, e.g. in the contingent actual world with its specific psychological, biological and physical laws (of possibility, probability and necessity). Thus, in the last example of 4.9.5. the sentence *The book fell down* would be false if *Harry dropped the book* is interpreted in a different world, e.g. in the real world of outer space, or in a dream world.

4.9.8. After this very provisional discussion of some of the relevant relations between propositions (as a whole) in a text, some remarks are in order. A crucial problem, firstly, is that the set of possible consequences of a given sentence may well be infinite, which would make the logic infinitary. The only way to specify such a set would be a recursive definition based on the lexicon and the semantic rules of grammatical derivations, otherwise we would be obliged to specify a set of all inductive relations characterizing our knowledge of the world. This problem, of course, is not specific to a text logic but a major problem of linguistic semantics in general. The logic itself may only provide a set of relations (constants) and the conditions for their interpretation in some model. We thus, secondly, must realize that in a natural text logic the intersentential relations as characterized above depend on the 'meaning' of the sentences. In all our examples formal derivability hinges on different types of semantic entailment as specified in meaning postulates or lexical definitions. Thus we may infer the presence of (and hence the introduction of the discourse referent) 'guest' only if the definition of 'party' includes it; the same is true for the inductive inferences characterizing contingent consequences. This does not mean, however, that a text logic would not contain a serious syntax, otherwise it would not be a logic at all. We may of course set up a calculus where relevant theorems may independently be proved. Thus necessary consequences entail probable consequences which entail possible consequences. Further the main principles of modal calculi would hold in this system.

The main problem is whether the different modifications and extensions of the system affect these main principles of 'sound inference'. It is still not very clear, within (non-standard) logics, how 'weak' or how 'strong' relations as entailment should be in the calculus. Thus, it might well be that IN GENERAL such systems as Anderson and Belnap's (1962) pure calculus of entailment (system E), in which the well-known paradoxes of strict implication are not derivable, would turn out to provide a more appropriate basis for a text logic of natural language, but that the principles leading to these paradoxes are admitted in logics used to account for argumentation and proof in more RESTRICTED (particular) sets of texts, e.g. in mathematics and in philosophical logic. The same may hold for systems in which the axiom of necessity ($\Box p \supset p$) would not hold, or in systems (e.g. of Prior) in which $\Box p$ and $\Diamond p$ are not interdefinable. In any case the relevance of such systems, e.g. in belief or action contexts must receive detailed attention before a serious text logic can be build up. In the previous paragraphs we merely wanted to suggest that textual coherence is based on a number of relations between propositions which seem to defy even the weakest principles of such non-standard systems.

4.9.9. Finally, we may consider the problem whether the important CAUSAL relations are either identical with previously defined relations among propositions or definable in terms of them. These cause-relations are crucial in many coherent texts, e.g. in *John is ill.(So) he will not come tonight.* Without being able to resume here the vast philosophical work in the domain of 'cause'[28], we will provisionally say that *a causes b* just in case *a* is a SUFFICIENT CONDITION for *b*; in symbols: $a \dot{\underset{\cdot}{\rightarrow}} b$.

Notice furthermore, that not sentences cause each other but events, actions, state of affairs, etc. CAUSE RELATIONS, may be said to hold between propositions, i.e. between intensional objects representable by such expressions as *the fact that...*

[28] For 'cause', and in general for relations between actions and events, see the references in Note 26. For a modal treatment, see Føllesdal (1971); see the philosophical work of Chisholm (e.g. 1969). Further the early treatment of Burks (1951) and the survey of Rescher (1968, Ch. 4).

Interpreting cause as a type of possible/probable/necessary presupposition we are in line with the conditional treatment as proposed by Rescher and by von Wright (1971). Given the conditions for semantic connectedness our symbolism presupposes that when q is an effect of p, we imply that q when p (e.g. written as p/q). We will not further elaborate here the textual aspects of conditional consequence and cause.

In the example given above *John is ill* is a possible presupposition of his not coming, since he may not have come for other reasons, this possible presupposition is also a possible cause. The second sentence is a possible consequence of the first, since John's illness may have had other possible consequences. The set of (possible) causes, then, is a subset of the set of possible presuppositions, which also includes e.g. *We will have a party (tonight)*, which is not a cause of John's absence. Similarly, the set of effects is a subset of the set of possible consequences, although very often effects are probable or necessary consequences. My death is a probable consequence of the shooting of a bullet through my head, and if my brain functions cease this necessarily causes my death, i.e. my death is a necessary consequence.

Only causes which are unique with respect to a consequence may be said to be 'necessary', in the sense of physical or psychological inference.

Another basic property of cause is CHANGE, i.e. a relation relating two DIFFERENT STATES. A proposition p causes a proposition q if causation entails a difference in state description. The constraint here is chronological, a change of states entails a change of time, such that $t_1(s_1) < t_j(s_j)$. This aspect must be present in the tenses, or rather time-representations, of the related propositions. A (direct) cause is IMMEDIATELY PRESUPPOSED by a consequence-effect e_i if there is no effect e_j preceding e_i and following the cause.

This brief discussion of causation is, of course, insufficient, and it is difficult to propose some non-trivial but simple definition of the concept, and it would be wise to admit the cause relation as a primitive in the system.

4.9.10. The relations between propositions discussed in the preceding paragraphs require some remarks on the CONNECTIVES of text logic. Earlier we argued that the usual truth functional constants of standard logic are in many ways different from the connectives between sentences or clauses in natural language.

In general, natural connectives relate propositions which are each others possible presuppostion and possible consequence, that is which are 'meaning dependent' from each other. Furthermore, the general formal principles of such relations, viz. commutativity, associativity and distributivity are not always valid, although they may hold in argumentation, in which a certain degree of meaning is reduced.

We will introduce the following basic natural connectives:

(1) *conjunction*: $p \wedge q$; satisfied only if both p and q are satisfied.

(2) *disjunction*: $p \vee q$; satisfied if p is satisfied,
satisfied if q is satisfied;
non-satisfied if both p and q are satisfied,
non-satisfied if both p and q are non-satisfied.

(3) *condition*: $p \supset q$; satisfied if both p and q are satisfied,
non-satisfied if p is satisfied and q is non-satisfied,
zero (non-applicable) if p is non-satisfied.

(4) *cause/'consequence' (effect)*
$p \dot{\rightarrow} q$; satisfied if both p ad q are satisfied,
non-satisfied if p is satisfied and q non-satisfied,
non-satisfied if p is non-satisfied and q is satisfied,
zero if p is non-satisfied and q is non-satisfied.

Although there is considerable work left to be done in this domain, we will provisionally assume that all other natural connectives are definable in terms of the given primitives and negation. The provisional truth tables given here are merely intuitively based, and there are much more aspects involved, especially in 'conditions', which are not merely truth functional but also intensional.

– Consequence effect is definable as a converse of cause.

– Concession is definable in terms of negation and cause: *Although my sister is very pretty, she did not win the beauty contest*, where $p \dot{\rightarrow} q$ is a probable causation, p is satisfied but not q.

– Contrast, partly as for concession, partly negation of preceding predicates.

– Purpose is definable in terms of causation, but with the same problems of 'intention', 'want', etc.

We will not try to make these brief characterizations explicit. Let us notice merely that the conjunctions in natural language do not always cover these basic and/or derived connectives: *if... then*, not always expresses condition, *or* not always exclusive disjunction, etc. Actual use is very confusing in this domain, which seems to indicate that the rules involved are highly complex.

4.10. *A Provisional List of Derivational Principles of Text Logic*

4.10.1. Let us briefly list the main principles of inference in a text logic. These rules will be given in an informal and tentative way and the list is not intended to be complete, but has an heuristic function for the derivation provided in the next section.

4.10.2. A first set of rules contains (at least some of) those holding in standard logical systems, with the GENERAL CONDITION OF SEMANTIC CONNECTION between the formulas, laid down in the following prnciples:

(1) INTRODUCTION (INT). For any individual to become a DISCOURSE REFERENT it must be introduced with one of the introduction operators of choice for (particular or non-particular) singulars or plurals.

For any predicate to become a DISCOURSE PREDICATE it must be assigned to an n-tuple of discourse referents ($n \geqslant 1$).

(2) IDENTITY (I). Formulas are connected extensionally if their variables/constants/names refer to the same (singular or plural) discourse referent. Formulas are connected intensionally when their predicates denote identical properties or relations.

Relations of identity may be called STRONG SEMANTIC RELATIONS.

(3) RELATION (R). Identity is one (strong) type of set of (WEAKER) RELATIONS between formulas. Again, these are extensional or intensional.

Formulas are in general related (semantically) if their individual variables refer to discourse referents or classes of discourse referents d_i and d_j and if $d_i \in d_j$, $d_j \in d_i$, $d_i \subset d_j$, $d_j \subset d_i$, $d_i \cap d_j$ (where the element relation is intended also to cover part-whole relationships of any type).

Formulas are related if their predicate variables/names refer to properties or relations of/between discourse referents and if the classes they name include each other or intersect, that is, if these formulas either entail each other, logically presuppose each other or are related by possible (probable, necessary) relations of (contingent) presupposition and consequence (including cause/effect, etc.).

Any individual or predicate variable/constant referring to an individual or property (relation) related to a discourse referent or discourse predicate is counted as INTRODUCED by this relation. Individuals or properties thus introduced define RESTRICTED INTRODUCTION, whereas the introduction defined in (1) is FREE. Predicates introduced in possible (probable, necessary) consequences are called POSSIBLE (probable, necessary) PREDICATES.

(4) MODALITY. The principles as specified in (1)–(3) hold under the regular modal constraints: relations (including identity) may hold only within subsets of possible worlds (e.g. in the various states of an actual world w_0) whereas other (sets of) worlds must relate individuals through the counterpart or copying principle. This principle may introduce individuals or properties in a given world. A crucial condition for modal consistency is TENSE RELATEDNESS (and for that matter PLACE RELATEDNESS) submitted to the mentioned introduction principle and to a principle of progression for event predicates.

4.10.3. Inder these general conditions of relatedness between wff's or propositions the following general rules hold both for logical and lexical (and contingent) connectives:

(1) MODUS PONENS (MP):

$$p \cdot q, \qquad p \vdash q,$$

(where $\cdot$ is: conditional, presupposition and consequence).

(2) UNIVERSAL INSTANTIATION (UI):

$$(\forall x)\,(g\,(x)) \vdash g\,(a).$$

(3) EXISTENTIAL, PARTICULAR, NON-PARTICULAR GENERALIZATION (EG):

$$g\,(a) \vdash (\varepsilon x)\,(g(x)) \vee (\exists x)\,(g\,(x)),$$
$$g\,(n) \vdash (Ix)\,(g\,(x)).$$

(4) PARTICULAR INSTANTIATION (NAMING) (PI):

$$(Ix)\,(g\,(x)) \vdash g\,(n).$$

(5) EXISTENTIAL (NON-PARTICULAR) SPECIFICATION:

$$(\exists x)\,(gx) \vdash g\,(n),$$
$$(\varepsilon x)\,(gx) \vdash g\,(n).$$

4.10.4. As a metatheoretical principle of the system we assume a LAW OF DIFFERENCE saying that no derived theorem (sentence) may be identical with the immediately preceding theorem. $S_i \neq S_{i-1}$.

4.11. *Example of Natural Derivation*

4.11.1. Let us finally illustrate the foregoing remarks by describing a text, or rather the semantic representation of its sequence of sentences, by the principles we have so far discussed. That is, we will try to indicate for each sentence the rules which make it derivable in the text.

As an example we take a short fragment of English prose, viz. the opening lines of a well-known crime novel: James Stuart Chase's *No Orchids for Miss Blandish* (new ed. 1961).

Since the text itself is a surface manifestation of its abstract underlying structures, from which it is derived by grammatical transformations – which we will not themselves treat here –, we rewrite the fragment as an ordered set of 'basic propositions' which are more closer to the semantic propositions we want to generate.

(Let us concede, furthermore, that the fragment in question rather examplarily follows the 'normal' rules. In many other pieces of prose many specific transformations and/or literary rules apply which make the surface structure deviate from the more regular structures.) We will limit the detailed derivation to the first few propositions, and even here not all aspects of derivation can possibly be considered.

4.11.2. TEXT: *No Orchids for Miss Blandish*, Ch. 1 (ed. 1961, p. 7).

S_1: It began on a summer afternoon in July.^{S_2}

S_2: [(This) July $\begin{Bmatrix}\text{was}\\\text{is}\end{Bmatrix}$] a month of intense heat, rainless skies, and scorching, dust laden winds.

S_3: At the junction of the Ford Scott and Nevada roads^{S_4} there stands a gas station and lunchroom bar.

S_4: The Nevada road cuts Highway 54.^{S_5}

S_5: [Highway 54] is the trunk road from Pittsburg to Kansas City.

S_6: [The gas station and lunchroom bar are] a shabby wooden structure with one gas pump.

S_7: [The gas station and lunchroom bar is] run by an elderly widower and his fat blonde daughter.

S_8: A dusty Packard pulled up by the lunchroom a few minutes after one o'clock.

S_9: There were two men in the car.

S_{10}: One of them was asleep.

S_{11}: The driver$^{S_{12}}$ got out of the car.

S_{12}: [The driver was called/named] Bailey.

S_{13}: [The driver was] a short thickset man.

S_{14}: [The driver had] a fleshy brutal face and restless, uneasy black eyes and a thin white scar along the side of his jaw.

S_{15}: [The driver] His shirt was frayed at the cuffs.

S_{16}: [The driver] He felt bad.

S_{17}: He had been drinking heavily last night.

S_{18}: [And] The heat worried him.

S_{19}: He paused to look at his sleeping companion.

S_{20}: [His sleeping companion $\begin{Bmatrix}\text{is}\\\text{was}\end{Bmatrix}$] called Old Sam.

S_{21}: [The driver] shrugged.

S_{22}: [The driver] went to the lunchroom.

S_{23}: [The driver] left Old Sam.

S_{24}: [Old Sam] snored in the car.

S_{25}: The blonde was leaning over the counter.

S_{26}: [The blonde] smiled at him.

S_{27}: [The blonde] She had big white teeth.

S_{28}: [The teeth] reminded Bailey of piano keys.

S_{29}: She was too fat to interest him.

S_{30}: He didn't return her smile.

4.11.3. *Derivation*

S_1 *It began on a summer afternoon in July.*

Logical Form (LF):
$(\varepsilon y)\,[begin\,(n_1, y) \wedge summer\ afternoon\ in\ July\,(y) \wedge PAST\,(y)]$
Derivation:

(i)	$(\varepsilon x)\,(event\,(x))$	INT (in S_0; e.g.: t_0 *I tell you about*...) *INT* (*WORLD*: *Fiction*).
(ii)	$(\forall x)\,(\varepsilon y)\,(event(x) \equiv begin(x, y) \wedge TEMP(y))$	LMP (lexical meaning postulate)
(iii)	$(event(n_1))$	PI
(iv)	$(\varepsilon y)\,(begin(n_1, y) \wedge TEMP\,(y))$	MP((ii), (iii))
(v)	$TEMP\,(y)$	(iv)
(vi)	$PAST\,(y)$	INT (TENSE: $t_1 < t_0$)
(vii)	$(\exists y)\,(TEMP\,(y) \rightsquigarrow summer\ afternoon\ in\ July\,(y))$	POSS CONS
(ix)	$(\varepsilon y)\,(summer\ afternoon\ in\ July\,(y))$	MP ((v), (vii)) Int.
(x)	LF	(iii), (iv), (vi), (ix)

S_2 [*July* $\left\{\begin{matrix} is \\ was \end{matrix}\right\}$] *a month of intense heat, rainless skies, and scorching, dust laden winds.*

LF:
$[(\lambda x)\,[HAVE\,(x, y) \wedge (intense(heat))y \wedge HAVE\,(x, u)\ sky(u)$
$\wedge\ [(\lambda k)\,(\sim WITH\,(k, l) \wedge rain(l))]u \wedge HAVE\,(x, v) \wedge [(\lambda p)\,(scorch(p, q)$
$\wedge\ ANIMATE\,(q) \wedge laden\ with(p, r) \wedge dust\,(r)]v]\ month(a).$
Derivation:

(i)	$(\forall y)\,(summer\ afternoon\ in\ July(y) \rightarrow in\ July(y))$	ENTAILMENT, R
(ii)	$(\varepsilon y)\,(July(y))$	MP((i), S_1)
(iii)	$(\forall y)\,(July(y) \rightarrow month(y))$	LMP
(iv)	$(\varepsilon y)\,(month(y))$	MP((ii), (iii))
(v)	month(a)	PARTICULARIZATION I (with *month* entailed by S_1)
(vi)	$(\varepsilon z)\,(summer(z))$	S_1, R(S_1)
(vii)	$(\mathrm{M}z)\,(summer(z) \rightsquigarrow (hot\,(z))$	PROB CONS; M: for most
(viii)	$(\exists f)\,(hot\,(f) \rightsquigarrow intense(f))$	POSS CONS
(ix)	$(\mathrm{M}z)\,(\sim\exists v)\,(summer(z) \rightsquigarrow HAVE\,(z, v) \wedge rain(v)))$	PROB CONS

(x)	$(Mz)\,(\exists u)\,(summer\,(z) \rightsquigarrow \rightsquigarrow HAVE\,(z, u) \wedge wind\,(u)))$	POSS CONS
(xi)	$(\exists u)\,(wind\,(u) \rightsquigarrow hot\,(u))$	POSS CONS ((vii), (x))
(xii)	$(\exists u)\,(wind\,(u) \wedge hot\,(u) \rightsquigarrow scorch(u, p) \wedge ANIMATE\,(p))$	PROB CONS
(xiii)	$(\exists u)\,(wind\,(u) \wedge hot\,(u) \rightsquigarrow laden\ with\,(u, q) \wedge dust\,(q))$	PROB CONS
(xiv)	$(\forall\varphi)\,(\varphi\,(summer \rightarrow \varphi\,(month\ July))$	ENTAILMENT
(xv)	$[(\lambda x)\,(\varphi x)]\ month(a)$	ABSTRACTION (v)
(xvi)	LF	(xv), (vii)–(xiii)

Main rules in the derivation of S_3–S_{30} (formulas abbreviated).

S_3	(i)	INT (PLACE of event)	$(\forall x)\,(\varepsilon y)\,(event(x) \rightarrow HAPPEN\,(x, PLACE(y)))$
	(ii)	POSS CONS	$(\varepsilon y)\,(PLACE(y) \rightsquigarrow (junction\,(u, v)\,(y) \wedge$
		I (indiv.)	$road(u) \wedge road(v))$
	(iii)	POSS CONS	$PLACE \rightsquigarrow BUILDING$
		I (indiv.) NAME: n_1	$road \rightsquigarrow gas\ station\ \&\ lunchroom\ bar$
	(iv)	PROPER NAMING	*Ford Scott* (*road*) *Nevada* (*road*)
S_4	(i)	POSS CONS	$(\varepsilon x)\,(\exists y)\,(road(x) \wedge road\,(y) \rightsquigarrow cut\,(x, y)$
	(ii)	I (indiv. & pred. (name))	*Nevada road*
S_5	(i)	POSS CONS	$(\varepsilon x)\,(road(x) \rightsquigarrow trunk\ road(x))$
	(ii)	PLACE (Direction) INT	$FROM...TO\,(x, y)$
	(iii)	PROPER NAMING	*Pittsburg* (x), *Kansas City* (y)
S_6	(i)	I (PLACE)	n_1
	(ii)	POSS CONS	$(\varepsilon y)\,(gas\ station\ \&\ lunchroom\ bar(y) \rightsquigarrow (shabby...)\,(y))$
	(iii)	LMP	$(\varepsilon y)\,(gas\ station\,(y) \rightarrow HAVE\,(y, gas\ pump\,(\mathbf{z}))$
S_7	(i)	I (PLACE)	n_1
	(ii)	NEC CONS	$(\varepsilon x)\,(run(x, n_1)$
	(iii)	PRESUPPOSITION	$HUM(x)$
	(iv)	I (indiv.) NAME: $x = n_2$ $y = n_3$	$(\varepsilon x)\,(elderly\ widower(x) \wedge \wedge (\varepsilon y)\,(fat\ blonde\ girl)\,(y) \wedge \wedge daughter\,(y, x))$

S_8	(i)	PROB CONS	S_3–S_6: $(\forall x)(\exists y)(road(x) \wedge ON(x, y) \rightsquigarrow car(y))$
	(ii)	MP INT (indiv.) NAME: n_4	$(\varepsilon x)(car(x))$
	(iii)	PROPER NAMING	$Packard(n_4)$
	(iv)	PROB CONS	$dusty(n_4)\ (dust(S_2))$
	(v)	I (PLACE)	n_1
	(vi)	POSS PRED	*pull up* (n_4)
	(vii)	INT (TIME)	*a few minutes past one o'clock* (t_1) POSS CONS (*afternoons* S_1)
S_9	(i)	I	n_4
	(ii)	POSS CONS	$(\forall x)(car(x) \wedge (\exists y)(HUM(y) \rightsquigarrow IN(y, x))$
	(iii)	INT (indiv. PERSON) NAME $y = n_5$	(εy) (two men (y))
S_{10}	(i)	R (element) INT NAME: $x = n_6$	*one of* n_5: $(\mathrm{I}x)(x \varepsilon n_5)$
	(ii)	POSS CONS	$(\forall x)$ (man (x) $\rightsquigarrow$ asleep (x))
S_{11}	(i)	LMP	$(\forall x)(\varepsilon y)(car(x) \rightarrow HAVE(x, driver(y))$
	(ii)	MP, I (indiv. PERSON) NAME $y = n_7$	(εy) (driver(y))
	(iii)	I (PLACE)	n_4
	(iv)	POSS PRED	*get out of* (n_7, n_4)
S_{12}		PROPER NAMING	*Bailey* (n_7)
S_{13}	(i)	POSS CONS (pred. INT)	*short thickset man* (n_7)
	(ii)	NEC CONS	$(\forall x)(HUM(x) \rightarrow HAVE(x, (face(y) \wedge eyes(z) \wedge jaw(u))$
	(iii)	POSS CONS (I (pred.))	*fleshy brutal* (y) *restless uneasy* (z) *thin white scar along the side of* (u)
S_{15}	(i)	PROB CONS	$(\mathrm{W}x)(\varepsilon y)(\mathrm{man}(x) \rightsquigarrow \mathrm{HAVE}(x, \mathrm{shirt}(y))$
	(ii)	POSS CONS	$(\exists y)$ (shirt (y) $\rightsquigarrow$ frayed at the cuffs (y))
S_{16}	(i)	I (PERSON)	n_7
	(ii)	POSS PRED	*feel bad* (n_7)
S_{17}	(i)	I (PERSON)	n_7
	(ii)	INT (WORLD)	(MEMORY: *heavily* (*drink* (n'_7) EVENT) POSS CONS *last night* (t_j)

			INT (TIME) (PLUPERFECT) $t_j < t_i$
S_{18}	(i)	ENTAILMENT NAME $x = n_8$	$(S_1 – S_2)$ *heat* (x)
	(ii)	PROB CONS (CAUSE)	n_8 cause *worry* (n_7) PATIENT (n_7): *him*
S_{19}	(i)	I (PERSON)	n_7
	(ii)	POSS CONS	*pause* (n_7) PRESUPPOSITION: $MOVE(n_7)$ (S)
	(iii)	POSS PRED	*look* (n_7, n_6)
	(iv)	NEC CONS	*companion of* (n_6, n_7) (S_9)
	(v)	I (pred).	*sleep* (n_6)
S_{20}		PROPER NAMING	*Old Sam* (n_6)
S_{21}		POSS CONS	*shrug* (n_7)
S_{22}		POSS CONS, I (PLACE)	*go to* (n_7, n_1) n_1: *lunchroom*
S_{23}	(i)	I (indiv. pred.)	n_7: *the driver*
	(ii)	POSS CONS	*leave in* (n_7, n_6, n_4)
	(iii)	I (PLACE)	n_4: *car*
S_{24}	(i)	I (PERSON)	n_6: *Old Sam*
	(ii)	I (PLACE)	n_4: *the car*
	(iii)	POSS CONS	*sleep* $(n_6) \rightsquigarrow$ *snore* (n_6)
S_{25}	(i)	I (Indiv., pred.) (PERSON)	n_3: *the blonde (girl)*
	(ii)	POSS CONS	*leaning over* $(n_3,$ *counter* $(x))$
	(iii)	NEC CONS	$(\forall x)$ (lunchroom$(x) \rightarrow$ HAVE $(x$, counter$(x))$
S_{26}	(i)	I (PERSON)	n_3: *she*
	(ii)	POSS CONS	*smile at* (n_3, n_7)
	(iii)	I (PERSON)	n_7: *him*
S_{27}	(i)	I (PERSON)	n_3: *she*
	(ii)	NEC CONS, INT $(y = n_9)$	$(\text{W}x)$ $(HUM(x) \rightarrow HAVE(x,$ $(teeth(y))$
	(iii)	PROB CONS	$(\forall y)$ (teeth$(y) \rightsquigarrow$ white$(y))$
	(iv)	POSS PRED	$(\exists y)$ (teeth$(y) \rightsquigarrow$ big$(y))$
S_{28}	(i)	I (OBJECT)	n_9: *teeth*
	(ii)	POSS CONS	*remind* $(n_9, n_7,$ *white piano keys* $(x))$
	(iii)	I (pred.)	*white* $[(\lambda y)$ $(piano\ keys(y))]$ $(teeth)$
S_{29}	(i)	I (PERSON)	n_3: *she*
	(ii)	I (Pred.)	*fat* (S_7)
	(iii)	I (PERSON)	n_7: him

	(iv)	PROB CONS	*Fat* $\dot{\rightarrow} \sim$ *Have interest in* (n_7, n_3)
S_{30}	(i)	I (PERSON)	n_7: *he*
	(ii)	I (Pred.)	*smile* (S_{26})
	(iii)	POSS CONS	*return to* $(n_7, \textit{smile}, n_3)$

4.11.4. *Comments*

4.11.4.1. Some comment is in order after this QUASI-LOGICAL DERIVATION OF A SEQUENCE. In the first place it is very important to recognize that the transformations are necessary but not sufficient constraints to make of a coherent SEQUENCE a coherent TEXT. That is, we may derive a sequence with all the particular coherence relations without deriving structures which would be 'functional' in a more global structure. In the case of our text it seems difficult to PROVE that the fragment is a coherent part of a (crime) story. Some macro-constraints would in that case apply to the derivation as a whole. Satisfied would be the constraints of Time- and Place-introduction, Event-introduction and the introduction of 'actants' (dramatis personae) and their specific qualities, e.g. 'meanness' of the gangsters introduced here. In the non-analyzed following pages of this novel, for example, the PLAN for part of the subsequent events is manifested, viz. 'The robbery of the rich Blandish girl necklace'. It is not possible here to make explicit these (interesting) relations, between micro-structure and macro-structure.

4.11.4.2. The most frequent rules used in this fragment have been IDENTITY, POSSIBLE $\left\{\begin{matrix}\text{PREDICATE}\\ \text{CONSEQUENCE}\end{matrix}\right\}$, INDIVIDUAL INTRODUCTION, ENTAILMENT, MODUS PONENS, (PROPER) NAMING and PARTICULARIZATION.

Formally these rules seem rather satisfactory, although they are not yet fully explicit, as valid PRINCIPLES OF NATURAL INFERENCE. Problematic in this respect is the crucial notion of 'possible consequence' – and the 'possible individuals' or 'predicates' it introduces – since it seems to be based on our knowledge of the world, and hence non-formalizable. Take the lemma (iv)–(xiv) in the complex derivation of S_2: is the fact that "if 'something' is summer then 'something' is hot" a fact of the semantic structure of the language for which this statement would be valid, or merely a representation of an empirical fact? Much depends on our conception of the LEXICON, without which, apparently, no derivation can be serious. The entailments, definitions (lexical meaning postulates) must be there defined, as well as the set (if any) of basic predicates of the language and their relations with the meanings of complex lexemes. One of the ways to see possible consequences of a proposition is to say that a possible consequence is a member of the set of propositions which is CONSISTENT with a given sentence S_i, its (i-1)-tuple of preceding sentences and their consequences. Consistency in this situation is not independent of TIME/PLACE in the text. What has been presented as a true/satisfied statement may not, without specified transition marker for performatives, truths, modalities, etc. be contradictory with a preceding sentence. In our example we have only briefly accounted for TENSES in the text which is regularly the PAST TENSE (in general in narrative texts, see S_0), and the pluperfect in case events in question are represented (*he had been drinking heavily last night*). Notice, finally, that merely some basic aspects of the LOGICAL FORM have been derived. The further mapping of such structures onto syntactical and phonological structures is a next, rather obscure, chapter of text grammar. We hope to have shown that logico-semantic structures in a (textual) sequence may be accounted for by a natural logic, called TEXT LOGIC, having strong resemblances with a (mathematical or deductive) logic, with the important difference that some of its rules are inductive and based on lexico-semantic structures of natural language. At the moment we do not see a way fully different from the one attempted above for a logic of natural language.

5. SUMMARY

(1) It is assumed that the base of text grammars contains, or consists of, a type of 'natural logic', called *text logic*. This logic must specify the semantic representation or logical form of sentences and ordered n-tuples (sequences) of sentences, and the rules of natural derivation holding between sentences in a well-formed, coherent text. These rules are taken as the local transderivational constraints of T-grammaticalness. Global transderivational constraints are not discussed here.

(2) In a general discussion about the relationships between formal and natural languages and their logics a list of characteristic differences is given, which at the same time is a program for an empirically adequate natural logic, which, though based on an extended modal predicate calculus of higher order, must satisfy a number of formal and empirical requirements much too complex to be followed in the near future.

(3) A non-trivial analogy is established between (systems of) proofs and texts in natural language. Notions such as 'derivability', 'premisses', 'logical consequence', etc. may be generalized such as to hold for all types of text. In particular, sentences of a text are to be viewed as theorems derivable by a set of natural derivation rules from an ordered set of axioms, definitions (meaning postulates), derived wff's and previous theorems/sentences.

(4) In order to be able to operate these rules require appropriate propositional structures, e.g. of description, naming and quantification, representing

singular individuals and identity relations. Quantifiers ranging over particular and non-particular (arbitrary) singulars are introduced and defined in order to complete the fundamental *system of discourse referent introduction*. Referential (extensional) identity is characterized with a naming procedure, introducing constants in the derivation. These are supposed to underly the pronouns of the text. Definite descriptions and the restrictive relative clauses they may contain are derived from a linearly ordered sequence of propositions for which the mentioned rules of introduction and identity are valid. Besides these rules for extensional identity for individuals and similar rules for partial identity, membership, inclusion and part-whole relations, rules for intensional coherence between predicates, modalities and propositions are specified. Characteristic of a text logic, thus, are not only logical relations of presupposition and logical consequence but also more inductive relations such as possible, probable and contingently necessary presupposition and consequence, for which some provisional tables of satisfaction are given.

The semantics of the text logic must be adapted to be able to interpret the required specific properties of its syntax: restricted quantification, singular and plural quantification, different dyadic constants and modalities, quantification of properties and relations, etc.

(5) Finally, the initial fragment of a natural text (a crime story) is derived in some detail to illustrate the principles and the rules provisionally given earlier.

University of Amsterdam
Instituut voor Literatuurwetenschap

BIBLIOGRAPHY

Altham, J. E. J., 1971, *The Logic of Plurality*, Methuen, London.

Anderson, A. R. and Belnap, N. D., 1962, 'The Pure Calculus of Entailment', *Journal of Symbolic Logic* **27**, 19–52.

Annear Thompson, Sandra, 1971, 'The Deep Structure of Relative Clauses', in Fillmore and Langendoen (eds.), pp. 78–94.

Bach, Emmon, 1968, 'Nouns and Noun Phrases', in Bach and Harms (eds.), pp. 90–122.

Bach, Emmon and Harms, Robert T. (eds.), 1968, *Universals in Linguistic Theory*, Holt, Rinehart and Winston, New York.

Barcan (Marcus) Ruth C., 1947, 'The Identity of Individuals in a Strict Functional Calculus of First Order', *Journal of Symbolic Logic* **12**, 12–15.

Barcan (Marcus) Ruth C., 1967, 'Modalities and Intensional Languages' (1962), in Irving M. Copi and James A. Gould (eds.), *Contemporary Readings in Logical Theory*, MacMillan, New York/London, pp. 278–293.

Barcan (Marcus) Ruth C., 1971, 'Extensionality' (1960), in Linsky (ed.), pp. 44–51.

Bar Hillel, Yehoshua (ed.), 1971, *Pragmatics of Natural Languages*, Reidel, Dordrecht.

Belnap, Nuel D., Jr., 1969, 'Questions: their Presuppositions and How They Can Fail to Arise', in Lambert (ed.), pp. 23–37.

Bellert, Irena, 1969, 'Arguments and Predicates in the Logico-Semantic Structure of

Utterances', in Ferenc Kiefer (ed.), *Studies in Syntax and Semantics*, Reidel, Dordrecht, pp. 34–54.
Bellert, Irena, 1970, 'Conditions for the Coherence of Texts', *Semiotica* **2**, 335–363.
Bellert, Irena, 1971a, 'Sets of Implications as the Interpretative Component of a Grammar', in Ferenc Kiefer and Nicholas Ruwet (eds.), *Generative Grammar in Europe*, Reidel, Dordrecht pp. 48–68.
Bellert, Irena, 1971b, 'On the Use of Linguistic Quantifying Operators', *Poetics* **2**, 71–86.
Bierwisch, Manfred, 1971, 'On Classifying Semantic Features', in Steinberg and Jakobovits (eds.), pp. 410–435.
Binkley, Robert, Richard Bronaugh, and Ausonio Marras (eds.), 1971, *Agent, Action, and Reason*, Blackwell, Oxford.
Burks, A. W., 1951, 'The Logic of Causal Propositions', *Mind* **60**, 363–382.
Carnap, Rudolf, 1957, *Meaning and Necessity. A Study in Semantics and Modal Logic* (1947), Univ. of Chicago Press, Chicago, enlarged ed.
Chisholm, Roderick M., 1969, 'Some Puzzles about Agency', in Lambert (ed.), pp. 199–217.
Chomsky, Noam, 1965, *Aspects of the Theory of Syntax*, MIT Press, Cambridge, Mass.
Chomsky, Noam, 1970, 'Some Empirical Issues of the Theory of Transformational Grammar', Indiana Linguistics Club, mimeo.
Chomsky, Noam, 1971, 'Deep Structure, Surface Structure and Semantic Interpretation', in Steinberg and Jakobovits (eds.), pp. 183–216.
Corcoran, John P., 1969, 'Discourse Grammars and the Structure of Mathematical Reasoning', in J. Scandura (ed.), *Structural Learning*, Englewood Cliffs. Prentice Hall, Inc.,
Davidson, Donald, 1967, 'The Logical Form of Action Sentences', in Rescher (ed.), pp. 81–103.
Davidson, Donald, 1970, 'Semantics for Natural Languages', in *Linguaggi nella società e nella tecnica* 177–188.
Davidson, Donald and Gilbert Harman (eds.), 1971, *Semantics of Natural Language*, Reidel, Dordrecht.
van Dijk, Teun A., 1971, 'Models for Text Grammars', Paper Contributed to the IVth International Congress for Logic, Methodology and Philosophy of Science, Bucharest, August 29–September 4, 1971 (to appear in a volume published by Reidel).
van Dijk, Teun A., 1972, *Some Aspects of Text Grammars. A Study in Theoretical Linguistics and Poetics*, Mouton, The Hague (Janua Linguarum, Series Maior, No. 63).
van Dijk, Teun A., 1974, *Kontekst en Kommunikatie. Een essay in pragmatiek en sociolinguistiek*, De Bezige Bij, Amsterdam (forthcoming).
van Dijk, Teun A. and Dorothea Franck, 1973, 'Pragmatics, Presuppositions and Context Grammars', paper read at the Symposium *Zur Grundlegung einer expliziten Pragmatik*, Bielefeld, January 19–21, 1973.
Dik, Simon C., 1968, 'Referential Identity', *Lingua* **21**, 70–97.
Fillmore, Charles and Terence Langendoen, D. (eds.), 1971, *Studies in Linguistic Semantics*, Holt, Rinehart and Winston, New York.
Fodor, Janet Dean, 1970, 'Formal Linguistics and Formal Logic', in John Lyons (ed.), *New Horizons in Linguistics*, Penguin Books, Harmondsworth, pp. 198–214.
Føllesdal, Dagfinn, 1971, 'Quantification into Causal Contexts', (1965) in Linsky (ed.), pp. 52–62.
Van Fraassen, Bas C., 1971, *Formal Semantics and Logic*, McMillan, New York, London.
Garner, Richard, 1971, *'Presupposition' in Philosophy and Linguistics*, in Fillmore and Langendoen (eds.), pp. 23–42.
Geach, Peter, 1962, *Reference and Generality*, Cornell U.P., Ithaca.
Hall Partee, Barbara, 1970, 'Opacity, Coreference and Pronouns', *Synthese* **21**, 359–385.
Harrah, David, 1963, *Communication: A Logical Model*, MIT Press, Cambridge, Mass.
Harrah, David, 1969, 'Erotetic Logistics' in Lambert (ed.) pp. 3–21.
Henkin, L., 1949, 'The Completeness of the First Order Functional Calculus', *Journal of Symbolic Logic* **14**, 159–166.

Hilpinen, Risto (ed.), 1971, *Deontic Logic: Introductory and Systematic Readings*, Reidel, Dordrecht.

Hintikka, Jaakko, 1961, 'Modality and Quantification', *Theoria* **27**, 110–128.

Hintikka, Jaakko, 1962, *Knowledge and Belief*, Cornell U.P., Ithaca.

Hintikka, Jaakko, 1963, 'The Modes of Modality', *Acta Philosophica Fennica, Modal and Many Valued Logics*, 65–81.

Hintikka, Jaakko, 1967, 'Individuals, Possible worlds and Epistemic Logic', *Noûs* **1**, 33–62.

Hintikka, Jaakko, 1970, *Existential Presuppositions and Uniqueness Presuppositions*, in Lambert (ed.), pp. 20–55.

Hughes, G. E. and M. J. Cresswell 1968, *An Introduction to Modal Logic*, Methuen, London (paperback reprint with corrections, 1972).

Ihwe, Jens, 1972, *Linguistik in der Literaturwissenschaft*, Bayerischer Schulbuchverlag, Munich.

Jørgensen, Jørgen, 1962, 'Some Remarks concerning Languages, Calculuses, and Logic', in *Logic and Language*, 27–38.

Kanger, Stig, 1957, 'The Morning Star Paradox', *Theoria* **23**, 1–11.

Karttunen, Lauri, 1968a, 'What do Referential Indices Refer to?', MIT, Mimeo.

Karttunen, Lauri, 1968b, 'Co-reference and Discourse', Paper Delivered at the 43rd Annual Meeting of the LSA, New York.

Karttunen, Lauri, 1969a, 'Discourse Referents', Paper Delivered at the International Conference on Computational Linguistics, Sånga-Säby (Sweden).

Karttunen, Lauri, 1969b, 'Pronouns and Variables', in Binnick *et al.* (eds.), *Papers from the Fifth Regional Meeting of the Chicago Linguistic Society*, Chicago University, Dept. of Linguistics, pp. 103–116.

Karttunen, Lauri, 1971, 'Definite Descriptions with Crossing Reference', *Foundations of Language* **7**, 157–182.

Katz, Jerrold J., 1967, 'Recent Issues in Semantic Theory', *Foundations of Language* **3**, 124–194.

Katz, Jerrold J., 1971, 'Generative Semantics is Interpretive Semantics', *Linguistic Inquiry* **2**, 313–330.

Katz, Jerrold J. and Jerry A. Fodor, 1964, 'The Structure of a Semantic Theory' (1963) in J. A. Fodor and J. J. Katz (eds.), *The Structure of Language. Readings in the Philosophy of Language*, Prentice Hall Inc., Englewood Cliffs, pp. 479–518.

Keenan, Edward, 1969, *A Logical Base for a Transformational Grammar of English*, Ph. D. Diss., Univ. of Pennsylvania, mimeo.

Keenan, Edward, 1971, 'Quantifier Structures in English', *Foundations of Language* **7**, 255–284.

Keenan, Edward, 1972a 'Semantically Based Grammars', mimeo (to appear in *Linguistic Inquiry*).

Keenan, Edward, 1972b, 'A Presupposition Logic for Natural Language', mimeo (to appear in *The Monist*).

Kummer, Werner, 1971a, 'Referenz, Pragmatik und zwei mögliche Textmodelle,' in D. Wunderlich (ed.), *Probleme und Fortschritte der Transformationsgrammatik*, Hueber, Munich, pp. 175–188.

Kummer, Werner, 1971b, 'Quantifikation und Identität in Texten', in A. von Stechow (ed.), *Beiträge zur generativen Grammatik*, Vieweg, Braunschweig, pp. 122–141.

Kummer, Werner, 1972, 'Outlines of a Model of Discourse Grammar', *Poetics* **3**, 29–55.

Kuroda, S.Y., 1969, 'English Relativization and Certain Related Problems', in Reibel and Shane (eds.), pp. 264–287.

Kuroda, S. Y., 1971, 'Two Remarks on Pronominalization', *Foundations of Language* **7**, 183–188.

Lakoff, George, 1968a, 'Pronouns and Reference', Indiana Linguistics Club, mimeo.

Lakoff, George, 1968b, 'Counterparts or the Problem of Reference in Transformational Grammar', Paper presented to the LSA-meeting, July 27, mimeo.

Lakoff, George, 1970, 'Linguistics and Natural Logic,' *Synthese* **22**, 151–271 (also in Davidson and Harman, eds.).
Lakoff, George, 1971a, 'On Generative Semantics', in Steinberg and Jakobovits (eds.), pp. 232–296.
Lakoff, George, 1971b, 'Presupposition and Relative Well-Formedness', in Steinberg and Jakobovits (eds.), pp. 341–344.
Lambert, Karel (ed.), 1969, *The Logical Way of Doing Things*, Yale U.P., New Haven/London.
Lambert, Karel (ed.), 1970, *Philosophical Problems in Logic*, Reidel, Dordrecht.
Lambert, Karel and Bas C. van Fraassen, 1970, 'Meaning Relations, Possible Objects and Possible Worlds', in Lambert (ed.), pp. 1–19.
Langacker, Ronald W., 1969, 'On Pronominalization and the Chain of Command', in Reibel and Shane (eds.), pp. 160–186.
Lemmon, E. J., 1965, *Beginning Logic*, Nelsons, London.
Lewis, David, 1968, 'Counterpart Theory and Quantified Modal Logic', *Journal of Philosophy* **65**, 113–126.
Lewis, David, 1970, 'General Semantics', *Synthese* **22**, 18–67.
Linguaggi nella società e nella tecnica, Edizioni di Communità, Milano.
Linsky, Leonard, 1967, *Referring*, Routledge and Kegan Paul, London.
Linsky, Leonard (ed.), 1971, *Reference and Modality*, Oxford U.P., London.
Logic and Language, Studies dedicated to Prof. Rudolf Carnap on the occasion of his seventieth birthday, Reidel, Dordrecht, 1962.
Marcus, *see* Barcan Marcus.
Martin, Richard M., 1959, *Toward a Systematic Pragmatics*, North Holland Publ. Co., Amsterdam.
McCawley, James D., 1968, 'The Role of Semantics in a Grammar', in Bach and Harms (eds.), pp. 124–169.
McCawley, James D., 1970, 'Where Do Noun Phrases Come From?', in R. A. Jacobs and R. A. Rosenbaum (eds.), *Readings in English Transformational Grammar*, Waltham, Mass., Ginn.
McCawley, James D., 1971, 'A Program for Logic', in Harman and Davidson (eds.).
Montague, Richard, 1968, 'Pragmatics', in R. Klibansky (ed.), *Contemporary Philosophy*, La Nuova Italia, Firenze, pp. 102–122.
Montague, Richard, 1970a, 'Pragmatics and Intensional Logic', *Dialectica* **24**, 277–302.
Montague, Richard, 1970b, 'English as a Formal Language', in *Linguaggi*... 189–224.
Palek, Bohumil, 1968, *Cross-Reference. A Study from Hyper-Syntax*, Charles Univ., Prague.
Petöfi, János S., 1971, *Transformationsgrammatiken und eine ko-textuelle Texttheorie*, Athenäum, Frankfurt.
Petöfi, János S. and Hannes Rieser, 1973, 'Wissenschaftstheoretische Argumente für eine umfassende grammatische Theorie und eine logisch-semantische Beschreibungsprache', *Konstanzer Textlinguistikkolloquium* **1972** (= *Papiere zur Textlinguistik* **3**), Rüttenauer, M. Buske, Hamburg, (forthcoming).
Postal, Paul M., 1971, *Cross-Over Phenomena*, Holt, Rinehart, and Winston, New York.
Prior, Arthur N., 1957, *Time and Modality*, Oxford U.P., London.
Prior, Arthur N., 1968, *Papers on Time and Tense*, Oxford U.P., London.
Prior, Arthur N., 1971, *Objects of Thought.*, Oxford U.P., London.
Quine, Willard Van Orman, 1952, *Methods of Logic*, Routledge and Kegan Paul, London.
Quine, Willard Van Orman, 1960, *Word and Object*, MIT Press, Cambridge, Mass.
Quine, Willard Van Orman, 1961, *From a Logical Point of View* (1953), Harper and Row, New York.
Reibe, David A., and Sanford A. Shane (eds.), 1969, *Modern Studies in English. Readings in Transformational Grammar*, Prentice Hall. Inc., Englewood Cliffs, N.J.
Reichenbach, Hans, 1947, *Elements of Symbolic Logic*. MacMillan, London; Free Press, New York.

Rescher, Nicholas, 1966, *The Logic of Commands*, Routledge and Kegan Paul, London; Dover, New York.

Rescher, Nicholas (ed.), 1967, *The Logic of Decision and Action*, Pittsburg U.P., Pittsburg.

Rescher, Nicholas, 1968, *Topics in Philosophical Logic*, Reidel, Dordrecht.

Rescher, Nicholas and Alasdair Urquhart, 1971, *Temporal Logic*, Springer, Wien–New York–Heidelberg

Rohrer, Christian, 1971, *Funktionelle Sprachwissenschaft und Transformationelle Grammatik*, Fink, Munich.

Sanders, Gerald A., 1969, 'On the Natural Domain of Grammar', Indiana Linguistics Club, mimeo.

Schmidt, Siegfried J., 1972, *Texttheorie. Probleme einer Linguistik der sprachlichen Kommunikation*, Bayerische Schulbuch Verlag, Munich (forthcoming).

Scott, Dana, 1970, 'Advice on Modal Logic', in Lambert (ed.), pp. 143–173.

Smith, Carlota S., 1969, 'Determiners and Relative Clauses in a Generative Grammar of English', in Reibel and Shane (eds.), pp. 247–263.

Stalnaker, Robert C., 1970, 'Pragmatics', *Synthese* **22**, 272–289.

Steinberg, Danny D. and Leon A. Jakobovits (eds.), 1971, *Semantics. An Interdisciplinary Reader in Philosophy, Linguistics, and Psychology*, Cambridge U.P., Cambridge.

Strawson, P. F., 1952, *Introduction to Logic*, Methuen, London.

Strawson, P. F., 1959, *Individuals*, Methuen, London.

Strawson, P. F., 1971, *Logico-Linguistic Papers*, Methuen, London.

Suppes, Patrick, 1957, *Intoduction to Logic*, Van Nostrand Reinhold, New York.

Vendler, Zeno, 1968, *Linguistics in Philosophy*, Cornell U.P., New York.

Whitehead, A. N. and Russell, 1927, *Principia Mathematica* (2nd ed.), (to 56, paperback, Cambridge U.P., 1962).

Von Wright, Georg Henrik, 1963, *Norm and Action*, Routledge and Kegan Paul, London.

Von Wright, Georg Henrik, 1971, 'Deontic Logic and the Theory of Conditions', in Hilpinen (ed.), pp. 159–177.

IRENA BELLERT

ON VARIOUS SOLUTIONS OF THE PROBLEM OF PRESUPPOSITIONS

The problem of presuppositions has received much attention from both logicians and linguists. From the standpoint of the logician who is concerned solely with the truth value of declarative sentences, the controversy concerning presuppositions can be briefly summarized in the following way. There are declarative sentences which cause difficulties when we try to specify their truth conditions. To give a well-known example, consider the truth conditions for the sentences:

(a) The present king of France is bald,
(b) The present king of France is not bald.

According to the law of excluded middle, we can argue that if we have two statements: '*S* is *P*' and '*S* is not *P*', one of the two must be true. However, if we consider that (a) is false (for it cannot be said to be true), then it would be strange to admit that (b) is true.

Frege's solution[1] of this problem has been to differentiate between the meaning (sense) and the denotation (reference) of linguistic expressions. The expression 'the present king of France' is said to have meaning but no reference, when employed in a sentence nowadays. 'The present king of France' will thus denote a null class, and sentences (a) and (b) are neither true nor false. Although this procedure does not lead to a logical error, it is artificial and does not yield a proper linguistic analysis in other cases of presuppositions.

Another solution has been proposed by Russell[2] who treated all sentences containing expressions of the form 'The-so-and-so' as equivalent to conjunctions containing a member of the form 'there is an entity which is so-and-so'. Accordingly, the sentence (a) will be equivalent to

(a′) 'There is an entity which is now king of France and is bald'

which is obviously false, since the first member of the conjunction is false. On the other hand, the sentence (b) is treated by Russell as ambiguous, for it is equivalent either to:

(b′) 'There is entity which is now king of France and is not bald'

which is false, or to:

[1] G. Frege, 'Über Sinn und Bedeutung', *Zeitschrift für Philosophie und Philosophische Kritik*, No. 100 (1892).
[2] B. Russell, 'On Denoting', *Mind* **XIV** (1905).

J. S. Petöfi and H. Rieser (eds.), Studies in Text Grammar, 79–95.

(b″) 'It is false that there is an entity which is now king of France and is bald'

which is true (since it is a denial of (a′)).

Although Russell's proposal solves the logical puzzle concerning the truth or falsity of such statements, it cannot satisfy linguists who probably will not agree that the assertion in the form of (a) is equivalent semantically to the corresponding conjunction in the form of (a′), because the existence of an entity which is king of France cannot be said to be asserted by the use of (a), whereas it is evidently so in (a′).

We shall now recall briefly Strawson's proposal concerning the problem of presuppositions, which has been accepted by some linguists or at least has influenced the solutions proposed by others. Let us quote Strawson: "*S* presupposes *S′* is defined as: The truth of *S′* is a necessary condition of the truth or falsity of *S*".

This definition has the consequence that *S′* is *not* in any ordinary sense a component of what is asserted by *S*. The definition makes no reference at all to the belief of speakers and hearers. It does, however, have the fairly obvious consequence that where S presupposes *S′* it would be incorrect (or deceitful – the cases are different) for a speaker to assert *S* unless he believed or took for granted that *S′*. Whether or not *S* has a truth value depends on one thing, viz., whether *S′* is true. Whether or not it is correct to assert that *S* depends on quite another thing (I do not mean on this thing alone), viz., "whether or not the speaker believes that *S′*".[3]

What Strawson maintained in general was (a) that a statement containing a definite singular description was neither true nor false unless there existed something to which the speaker was referring and which answered the description, and (b) that many statements of the kind traditionally called universal and particular also lacked a truth-value unless there existed members of the subject-class. Strawson made a qualification to his own thesis:

"The main qualification that I want to make is to admit that in certain cases and circumstances it may be quite natural and correct to assign a truth-value to a statement of these kinds" (that is, those mentioned in (a) and (b) above) "even though the condition referred to is not satisfied"[4]. He gives an example:

Suppose I make a statement of the form 'The *S* is *P*' knowing that there is no *S*, with the deliberate intention to deceiving my hearer, e.g. trying to sell something and saying to

[3] The problem of presuppositions as discussed by Strawson has been summarized by him in P. F. Strawson, 'A Reply to Mr. Sellars', *The Philosophical Review* **LXIII**, (1954). This paper is a reply to W. Sellar's article, 'Presupossing', published in the same issue of the *Philosophical Revue*. All quotations from Strawson are taken from this paper.
[4] P. F. Strawson, *op. cit.*

a prospective purchaser: 'The lodger next door has offered me twice that sum' – when there is no lodger next door and I know of that.

It would be correct to reply 'that's false' and to give as a reason the fact that there was no lodger next door.[5]

Strawson draws the attention to the fact that we have a tendency to treat as logically equivalent '*S* is not *P*' and 'It is false that *S* is *P*'. We could not treat as equivalent the reply: 'The lodger next door has not offered him twice that sum' and 'The statement that the lodger next door has offered him twice that sum is not true' or 'It is false that the lodger next door has offered him twice that sum'. Strawson proposes thus to insert a proviso concerning logical equivalence: "To say that two statements are logically equivalent is to say that if both have a truth-value, then both must have the same truthvalue".[5]

The problem of presuppositions becomes more and more intricate, as appears from many discussions concerning the semantics of natural languages, for the relation of presupposition is not restricted here only to referring phrases, especially those that have no denotation. Presupposition has been shown by linguists to be a pervasive relation holding of most if not all possible utterances in natural languages. To give some well-known examples of presuppositions other than those connected with referring phrases, consider the following sentences

(1) Fred has stopped beating his wife,
(2) John woke up at five o'clock,

which would make little sense if the respective sentences

(1′) Fred has beaten his wife,
(2′) John was asleep before five o'clock,

were not true.

There are, however, many points of disagreement and confusion as to the proper description of the relation of presupposition, as to the difference between presupposition, implication and entailment in linguistic description, as to whether presupposition should belong to semantics or pragmatics, etc.

In this connection let us first consider Austin's classification of the terms 'presuppose', 'imply' and 'entail'[6].

Austin discusses three examples:

(1) Someone says 'All John's children are bald, but (or 'and') John has no children'; or perhaps he says 'All John's children are bald', when as a matter of fact, John has no children.

[5] P. F. Strawson, *op. cit.*

[6] J. L. Austin, 'Performative-Constative', in *The Philosophy of Language* (ed. by J. R. Searle), Oxford Readings in Philosophy, Oxford Univ. Press, 1971.

(2) Someone says 'The cat is on the mat, but (or 'and') I dont believe it is'; or perhaps he says 'The cat is on the mat', when as a matter of fact he does not believe it is.

(3) Someone says 'All the guests are French, and some of them aren't' or perhaps he says 'All the guests are French', and then afterwards says 'Some of the guests are not French'.[7]

Austin proposes to use the three terms 'presuppose', 'imply', and 'entail' for the three cases, respectively. Then:

(1) Not only 'John's children are bald', but equally 'John's children are not bald', presupposes that John has children. To talk about those children, or to refer to them, presupposes that they exist. By contrast, 'The cat is not on the mat' does *not*, equally with 'The cat is on the mat', imply that I believe it is; and similarly, 'None of the guests is French' entail that it is false that some of the guests are not French.

(2) We can quite well say 'It could be the case both that the cat is on the mat and that I do not believe it is'. That is to say, those two propositions are not in the least incompatible: both can be true together. What is impossible is to state both at the same time: his *stating* that the cat is on the mat is what implies that the speaker believes it is. By contrast, we couldn't say 'It could be the case both that John has no children and that his children are bald'; just as we couldn't say 'It would be the case both that all the guests are French and that some of them are not French'.

(3) If 'All the guests are French' entails 'It is not the case that some of the guests are not French', then 'Some of the guests are not French' entails 'It is not the case that all the guests are French'. It is a question here of the compatibility and incompatibility of propositions. By contrast, it isn't like this with presupposition: if 'John's children are bald' presupposes that John has children, it isn't true at all that 'John has no children' presupposes that John's children are not bald. Similarly, if 'The cat is on the mat' implies that I believe it is, it isn't true at all that to say 'I don't believe that the cat is on the mat' implies that the cat is not on the mat (not, at any rate, in the same sense of 'implies'; besides, we have already seen that 'implication', for us, is not a matter of the incompatibility of propositions)[8].

Case (1) is a clear example of what is called presupposition in the literature, both in logic and in linguistics. Case (2) and Case (3) are not at all clear examples, however. Case (2) is not really a case of implication, neither in the sense of what logicians call material implication, nor in the sense of what they call logical implication. In any case the consequent of an implication should constitute the necessary condition of the antecedent of the implication, no matter whether material or logical (the only difference being that in a logical implication the consequent follows logically from the antecedent, that is, it can be derived by the rules of logic, whereas this is not the case in a material implication). In either case an implication $p \rightarrow q$ is equivalent by definition to the incompatibility of p and $\sim q$. But Austin shows that the latter does not hold in Case (2). However, I cannot agree with Austin that the speaker's stating 'The cat is on the mat' implies that the speaker believes it is, if the term 'believe' is used in its ordinary sense. In fact, it is only *usually* the case that people believe in what they state, but then such a belief cannot be said to constitute a necessary condition of the corresponding statement, and thus

[7] J. L. Austin, *op. cit.*

[8] J. L. Austin, *op. cit.*

the term 'implication' does not seem to be appropriate for Case (2).

We may say 'The cat is on the mat' when, as a matter of fact we don't believe it is. Actually it is not so that somebody's *stating* that the cat is on the mat is what implies that the speaker believes it is, as Austin argues, but – in my opinion – somebody's stating *bona fide* that the cat is on the mat is what implies that the speaker believes it is. However, this goes far beyond semantic problems, because such an implication is dependent on the actual state of the mind of the speaker (to which we have no access, and thus we cannot decide by any formal means whether an utterance is a *bona fide* statement or not), whereas implications of interest to linguists are those which are described with reference to utterances as such, and the truth of which can be recognized by formal criteria.

Case (3) in turn is a case not only of entailment or logical implication, but of logical equivalence. And as such it constitutes a particular case of logical implication (it is a two-way implication). It corresponds to the definition of the universal quantifier in terms of the existential quantifier:

$$(\forall x)\,\varphi(x) = \sim(\exists x) \sim \varphi(x).$$

It is then obvious that in Case (3) the two statements considered by Austin are incompatible. My point, however, is that the incompatibility of statements can be shown not only in a particular case of logical equivalence, but in the case of implication. To give an example from the propositional calculus, consider the logical implication:

$$(p \wedge q) \rightarrow p,$$

and its equivalent form

$$\sim p \rightarrow \sim(p \wedge q),$$

which shows the incompatibility of the antecedent and the negated consequent. Let us now take an example from English. We may say that

(A) John sang in the opera yesterday,

implies:

(A1) John sang in the opera,
(A2) Someone sang in the opera yesterday,
(A3) John sang yesterday.

Now the negation of each of the above statements (A1), (A2) or (A3) will be incompatible with the statement (A). The relation between (A) and (A1),

(A2) or (A3) can be rightly called an implication, for (A) is a sufficient condition for (A1), (A2) and (A3); on the other hand (A1), (A2) and (A3) are each a necessary condition for (A).

Consider another example. We may say that

(B) John forced Mary to go home,

implies

(B1) Mary resisted going home,

and, by contrast, we may say that if Mary did not resist going home, it was not the case that John forced her to go. The same relation holds true of the two sentences

(C) John saw a horse,
(C1) John saw an animal.

Examples can easily be multiplied, and it is evident that implication is a most common relation concerning almost all syntactical relations and lexical items used in sentences.

As I have argued, we should not differentiate between the terms 'imply' and 'entail' along the line proposed by Austin; the difference between the terms 'imply' and 'entail' corresponds rather to the difference between material implication and logical implication, in the case of which the consequent can be derived from the antecedent by the inference rules of standard logic. I will thus return to the problem of presuppositions as discussed in linguistic literature, and then turn to the problems of implication, in order to show in conclusion that the relation of presupposition can be conveniently described as a particular case of the relation of implication, which plays an essential role in the approach that I suggest for the semantics of natural language.

Let me remind the reader of some linguistic approaches to the problem of presupposition, chosen among many others which have been proposed so far, and which can roughly be grouped along the lines described here below.

The characteristic features of the various proposals may be grouped in the following ways: (1) Presuppositions are treated as part of the semantic contents of the corresponding sentences. (2) Presuppositions of a sentence are identified as those conditions which must be satisfied before the sentence can be used in any of its semantic functions (presuppositions are treated here as conditions concerning the situational context, linguistic or not). (3) Presuppositions are considered as a subclass of logical consequences of sentences.

The approach indicated in (1) has been advocated in several papers by

Ducrot[9], who in my opinion correctly argues and presents linguistic evidence to the effect that presuppositions constitute part of the semantic contents of utterances.

The approach indicated in (2) is characteristic of Fillmore's[10] and Lakoff's[11] papers. The presuppositions of a sentence are, for instance, identified as "those conditions which must be satisfied before the sentence can be used in any of its functions". The sentence 'Please open the door' can be used as a command according to Fillmore "only if the TL" (that is, the addressee) "is in a position to know what door has been mentioned and only if that door is not at TLA" (that is, the time at which the utterance is produced) 'open'.[12] In my opinion, such an utterance should be interpreted in any case as a command, for its interpretation cannot be dependent on the fact whether the above conditions are, or are not, satisfied. If, for instance, there is a bell ringing at the door which is not in the range of vision of the speaker, he may be not aware of the fact that it is open, and may ask somebody "Please open the door". Such an utterance is intended by the speaker and interpreted by the addressee as a command in any case, independently of whether the door is closed or not. In another paper, however, Fillmore speaks of entailment rules[13], he described many other instances of presuppositions and implications, which are accounted for by what he rightly calls entailment rules.

Lakoff suggests[14] that a grammar should not generate sentences in isolation, but pairs (*P*, *S*) consisting of a sentence *S* which is well formed (grammatical) only relative to the presuppositions *P*. He raises the question whether it makes sense to speak of well-formedness in isolation, removed from all assumptions about the nature of the world. He thus assumes that the study of linguistic competence should include the relationship between a sentence and its presuppositions about the world. Among these latter are also beliefs of the speakers. For instance, Lakoff discusses the sentence

'John called Mary a Republican and *she* insulted him',

(where the italicized words are more heavily stressed), and states that the

[9] O. Ducrot, 'Les présupposés, conditions d'emploi ou éléments de contenu', paper delivered at the International Symposium on Semiotics, Warsaw, 1968, published in *Language, Sign, Culture*, Mouton, 1971.

[10] C. J. Fillmore, 'Types of Lexical Information', *Working Papers in Linguistics*, No. 2, The Ohio State Univ. November 1968; to appear in *Semantics* (ed. by Steinberg and Jakobovitz), Cambridge Univ. Press.

[11] G. Lakoff, 'Presuppositions and Relative Grammaticality', *Studies in Philosophical Linguistics* (ed. by W. Todd), Series one (1969)

[12] C. J. Fillmore, *op. cit.*

[13] C. J. Fillmore, *Entailment Rules*, mimeographed.

[14] G. Lakoff, *op. cit.*

speaker's judgements as to well-formedness will depend on his beliefs. He finds this sentence perfectly well formed, though admits that those with other beliefs may disagree.

Chomsky rightly objects to Lakoff's treatment of presuppositions saying that the relation between a sentence and its presuppositions holds independently of anyone's factual beliefs[15]. In the case of the sentence discussed above, Chomsky argues that the relation between that sentence and its presuppositions holds independently of anybody's beliefs (neither the speaker's nor John's nor Mary's beliefs).

The approach indicated in (3) is characteristic of Keenan's papers[16]. Keenan discusses various semantic relations between English sentences, and among others he defines the following relations: logical consequence, presupposition, analyticy, selectional restrictions, question-answer relation, ambiguity and paraphrases. He defines logical consequence in the following way: "A set of sentences S logically implies a given sentence S' (or S' is a logical consequence of a set of sentences S) just in case S' is true in every possible world (model) in which all the sentences of S are true"[17]. This notion is then used to define the other relations, in particular the relation of presupposition and selectional restrictions, as both appear to be a specific case of logical consequence.

The relation of presupposition is characterized by Keenan in the following way:

If a sentence S presupposes a sentence S' (or S' is a presupposition of S), then both S and its negation $\sim S$ logically imply S'.

Such a definition would be improper in a two-valued logic. A presupposition S' is a logical consequence of both S and $\sim S$, that is to say, S' is implied by S independently of the truth value of S (in all possible worlds). However, the presuppositions are not logically true sentences, which would make it possible for them to be true under all possible interpretations (in all possible worlds). In order to solve this problem, Keenan assigns a third or 'nonsense' value to sentences whose presuppositions do not hold. Thus a presupposition may be false, but then the corresponding sentence will be said to be neither true nor false.

Keenan leaves aside, however, the problem of presuppositions of questions or commands. He leaves this problem for a further study, although he

[15] N. Chomsky, 'Some Empirical Issues in the Theory of Transformational Grammar', mimeographed by Indiana Univ. Linguistic Club, 1970.

[16] E. L. Keenan, *A Logical Base for a Transformational Grammar of English*, T.D.A. Paper No. 82, Univ. of Pennsylvania, 1970.

[17] E. L. Keenan, *op. cit.*

admits that presuppositions, which constitute in his proposal logical consequences of certain sentences as well as of their negations, also can be said to follow from the corresponding questions.

Let us now consider another approach to the problem of presuppositions which has been suggested in my papers[18]. The proposal I am arguing for is in agreement with both the approach indicated in (1) and (3) discussed above. That is to say, presuppositions of a sentence are treated as part of the semantic contents of that sentence; the semantic contents of a sentence (its interpretation) is identified with a set of sentences that follow from the use of that sentence; the presuppositions will thus constitute a subset of this set.

Before I say what I mean by "a set of sentences that follow from the use of a given sentence", let me explain why instead of speaking of the consequences of sentences I speak of the consequences of sentences used. The main reason is that if we consider sentences as such, nothing can be said to follow from the majority of sentences in a natural language; not only nothing can be said to follow from sentences in the form of questions or commands, but nothing can be said to follow from sentences for which the question of their being true of false does not arise or cannot be posed, as in the case of literary texts. Keenan's proposal is evidently a very interesting one. He shows that it is possible to account for various semantic relations holding between sentences of a natural language by means of his "extended standard logical system", but what is possible to be described in this way is only a subset of English declarative sentences used in scientific prose. I do not see, however, how it will be possible to proceed further by using Keenan's basic relation of logical consequence defined in terms of truth conditions of sentences, in order to tackle the problem of the interpretation of questions, commands or sentences in literary texts. It seems to me that a possible way to cope with the problem of describing semantic relations among all sentences in a natural language is not to speak of the relation of consequence between sentences as such, but to define the relation of consequence between a sentence actually used (uttered or written) and a set of sentences following from its use and from certain pertinent implicational rules (those which constitute the description of the lexical items and relations involved). Each sentence that will be said to be a consequence of the use of another sentence will consist of a proposition together with a purported propositional attitude of the speaker or

[18] I. Bellert, 'On the Use of Linguistic Quantifying Operators in the Logico-Semantic Structure Representation of Utterances', Paper delivered at the International Conference on Computational Linguistics, Sanga Saby, 1969; to appear in *Poetics, International Review for the Theory of Literature*, Amsterdam; I. Bellert, *On the Logico-Semantic Structure of Utterances*, Osselineum, Wroclaw, Poland, 1972; I. Bellert, Sets of Implications as the Interpretative Component of a Grammar, in *Generative Grammar in Europe* (ed. by F. Kiefer and N. Ruwet), Reidel, Dordrecht-Holland, 1973.

author (belief, assertion, desire, etc.). A general implicational rule which will serve to interpret the use of all sentences of a given language with their structural descriptions may be, roughly, formulated according to the following scheme:

For all addressers (speakers or authors) A, for all receivers (hearers or readers) R, for all sentences S with their structural descriptions (D), if:

(1⁰) a sentence S is used (uttered or written) by A,
(2⁰) its structural description D satisfies condition C.

$$\text{then } A \left\{\begin{array}{l}\text{BELIEVES}\\ \text{ASSERTS}\\ \text{DENIES}\\ \text{WANTS}\\ \text{etc.}\end{array}\right\} \text{ that } S'$$

where all the terms printed in capital letters in braces[19] are abbreviations standing for the corresponding purported[20] propositional attitudes:

A BELIEVES THAT S' ≡ A purports to believe (assume) that S' (that S' is the case)[21],

A ASSERTS that S' ≡ A purports to intend to inform R that S' (that S' is the case),

A DENIES that S' ≡ A purports to intend to inform R that S' is not the case,

A WANTS that S' ≡ A purports to inform R that he wants that S' (that S' be the case).

The propositional attitude WANTS is used in some other more complex patterns, not specified in our scheme, which depending on the type of sentence (in the form of a question or command) contain the symbol R (receiver), usually identified with the subject of S'.

[19] Evidently only one of the terms in braces will be applicable in an implication in which the conditions C are specified. What I have presented here is only a scheme for the implications.

[20] A purported attitude is understood here as being independent of the actual state of mind of the speaker, who may or may not have the attitude that is implied by his linguistic behavior, by his using a given sentence.

[21] The expression 'The speaker purports to believe' should be understood as equivalent to 'The speaker behaves linguistically as if he believed', with no suggestions as to whether he actually believes or does not believe that such and such is the case. The same holds true of all the other purported attitudes. Notice that in fact we have no method for recognizing whether a speaker actually believes or wants something whether he actually intends to communicate to the receiver that such and such is the case etc. By constrast, what can in fact be recognized in all circumstances is that an utterance expresses certain beliefs or intentions purported by the speaker, for this can be inferred from the form of utterances.

Notice that in the implicational scheme, the expressions *A*, *R*, and (*S*, *D*) (addresser, receiver and sentence with its structural descriptions, respectively) are all bound by universal quantifiers, the only free variables which occur there are: (the conditions) *C*, PROPOSITIONAL ATTITUDE (that is, one of the expressions in braces) and *S'*. In order to describe a given language, we must first have a grammar generating all sentences *S* with their structural descriptions *D*, and second, we must have an interpretative component consisting of implications of the form:

$C \rightarrow A$ PROPOSITIONAL ATTITUDE that *S'*,

where *C* stands for a formula that specifies some conditions on the structural descriptions[22], PROPOSITIONAL ATTITUDE stands for one of the purported propositional attitudes listed above that applies in the case of the formulated conditions *C*, and *S'* is a sentential form of a sentence that expresses a proposition dependent on the formulated conditions *C*.

Since such implications can be considered analytical (they constitute partial definitions of the use of lexical items in specified structures and the use of syntactical rules), the consequents can be said to follow formally from the antecedents. Those implications can thus be conceived of as axioms (like Carnap's meaning postulates) which we will add to a theory of a particular natural language.

Now for every use of a sentence *S* with a structural description *D* that satisfies the conditions *C* in a certain number of axiomatic implications, we will have the same number of consequences, namely, all those sentences that satisfy the sentential form *S'* and are preceded by (embedded in) a sentence expressing the speaker's purported attitude, for they can be detached by the rule of modus ponens. The detached consequences will correspond to a part of all the conclusions that any receiver in any contextual situation can draw from the use of a sentence *S* with the structural description *D*. (Such conclusions, as a matter of fact, are drawn on the grounds of the implicit knowledge of the language, i.e. the implicit implicational rules concerning the structure of the given sentence and the lexical items which it contains.)

Returning now to the problem of presuppositions, in the proposed approach to language description, they may be said to constitute a subset of all the consequences, namely, we can say that a consequence of a sentence *S* (strictly: of the use of *S*) is a presupposition only if:

(1^0) it contains the propositional attitude BELIEVES,

[22] In general, conditions *C* may be specified in terms of a Boolean function (as a combination of conjunction, disjunction and negation) of certain conditions concerning the structural description *D*.

(2⁰) it is a consequence of an affirmative sentence *S*, as well as a consequence of the negation of *S*, of the corresponding question, order, etc.

The second condition is given here in order to define the notion of presupposition in the sense analogical to that accepted in the literature on the subject. Incidentally, I would prefer to define the term presupposition differently, so that it would cover all consequences that satisfy the first condition alone. Thus, for instance, each of the propositions (A1), (A2) and (A3) (on page 67 above), preceded by the propositional attitude 'The speaker BELIEVES that...', would be said to be a presupposition of the sentence *A* (on page 67), whenever *A* is used as an utterance. However, this is a terminological matter of no import to the present discussion.

Let us now return to the other approaches towards presuppositions as discussed in this paper, and compare them with my proposal. Consider a sentence

(a) John's children study at Harvard,

and one of its presuppositions:

(b) John has children.

If we consider just (a) and (b) (without inserting them into the respective frames as proposed by me: 'The speaker uses the sentence (a)... etc.' and 'The speaker purports to believe (b)', the only thing we can say is that the truth of (b) follows from the truth of (a) either on the grounds of our understanding these sentences, or formally on the grounds of a proper definition of the expression 'John's children'. But no conclusion can be made about John's having children unless we can verify that (a) is indeed true. However, we also can say that (b) follows from the negation of (a), that is from: 'John's children do not study at Harvard'. One therefore could argue that (b) is independent of the truth of (a) and it can be thus derived as a conclusion independently of the truth value of (a). But this is not the case, for in fact it can be derived only if either (a) is true or if its negation is true, that is when (a) is false, but not in the case if (a) is neither true nor false, that is, in the case when John has no children.

So far Keenan's proposal is perfectly adequate, because it can account for the three cases mentioned above by means of introducing a third truth value, zero or nonsense. However, this will not lead us far enough, for we know from linguistic evidence that (b) follows not only from (a) and its negation, but also from the corresponding questions, orders, doubts, wishes, etc., such as:

Do John's children study at Harvard?
Let John's children study at Harvard!
I doubt whether John's children study at Harvard.
I want John's children to study at Harvard.

And we have no way of speaking of the truth or falsity of sentences such as those. This fact is probably one of the reasons for which some linguists speak of presuppositions in terms of conditions on the world which have to be satisfied before the given sentence can be said to fulfil its semantic functions. The problem that arises here, however, is that such conditions are obviously sufficient but not necessary (they are necessary only for the truth or falsity of declarative sentences concerning matters of fact). It is not hard to show that in many cases the conditions of the factual world corresponding the presuppositions are not at all necessary conditions for interpreting a sentence; it may be very well the case that someone utters a sentence whose presuppositions expressed as conditions on the world do not hold, but the sentence is appropriately used (that is, used as an intended message according to the rules of the language) and very well understood. For instance if John is a young unmarried student of Harvard, who has no children (and who may or may not have any children in the future), we may appropriately say:

John's children will certainly study at Harvard

Or he himself may say:

My children will study at Harvard,

and the existence of John's children is not *necessarily* implied. What is necessarily implied, and what would be accounted for by the implicational rules proposed by me, is the speaker's purported belief that John will have children (In general, the tense in the consequence implied by the use of a definite description or any other argument with a linguistic quantifier[23] is dependent on the tense of the predicate used with that definite description or with that quantified argument).

To give another example which has been already discussed above, a speaker may appropriately say 'Open the door' in the case when the said

[23] For the notion of linguistic quantifier, see I. Bellert, 'Arguments and Predicates in the Logico-Semantic Structure of Utterances', in *Studies in Syntax and Semantics* (ed. by F. Kiefer), D. Reidel, Dordrecht-Holland, 1969, and my paper and book mentioned in Footnote 18 above, where I argue that if an utterance is representable by a predicate with its arguments, each argument must be somehow quantified. All linguistic quantifiers should be defined by analogy to the iota operator, that is to say, they are not sentence-forming operators (which make a sentence out of a sentential function) but they are argument-forming operators (which make an argument when prefixed to an arbitrary name, or predicate name).

door is in fact open, but is not in the range of vision of the speaker. In any case, however, one of the necessary conditions of the use of this sentence is only the purported belief of the speaker that the door is not open.

Generally speaking, we all know very well that language is not only a tool for expressing statements concerning the factual world, but also for expressing our imagination as in literary art; not only for expressing our thoughts, but also for concealing our actual thoughts, and therefore not only for saying the truth but also often for lying or saying things which are not quite compatible with the factual state of affairs, and this is done not always in an obvious way for deceiving people, but for the sake of impressing or influencing people, for the sake of propaganda. Why should we ignore all those essential functions of language? I strongly believe that on the contrary we should analyse the semantic contents of utterances and texts in a way independent of the actual conditions that hold in the world, but solely with concern to the purported meaning of utterances in terms of what is expressed by linguistic means. Only then will arise the problem of the compatibility of a given utterance or text (of its purported meaning) with the factual condition holding of the world and of the situation in which the utterance or text has been produced. But this problem does not belong any more to the field of linguistics or semantics, but rather it is a problem for a moralist or a psychologist, a political essayist or anyone who is interested whether the purported meaning of a statement, text or discourse (scientifical, sociological, political or any other) with all its implications is, or is not, compatible with the factual conditions holding of the world.

I wish to emphasize here that the point of this discussion is not to disclose any new facts about any language: I only want to discuss a method for describing semantic facts which have been shown and are known to linguists, but the proposed descriptions of which lead to controversial arguments, and no general agreement has been attained so far. Each of the proposed descriptions may be adequate either for only certain aspects of linguistic facts, or for only a subset of sentences, whereas the interpretative component of a grammar proposed here is conceived of as a convenient framework for the interpretation of all sentences used in everyday, scientific or literary discourses[24]. Thus, for instance, the sentence 'The present king of France is bald', (independently of whether used nowadays, or in a historical novel, or

[24] Since the present paper concerns the problem of presuppositions, no examples are given of other applications of implicational rules in the interpretation of utterances. In fact, as I have tried to show elsewhere (see Footnote 18), an interpretative component consisting of implicational rules is a convenient apparatus by which it is possible to account in a uniform manner for other semantic relations, such as for instance those known in linguistic literature under the term of semantic roles, selectional restrictions, semantic features (or complex structures of semantic features) contained in lexical items, etc.

as a linguistic joke[25]) would imply (would contain among its consequences) the purported belief (assumption) of the speaker (or author) that there is a king of France.

It is worth noticing that the conditions *C* specified in the antecedents of the proposed implications will usually be general enough to make a given implication applicable to an infinite set of sentences. Such will be, for instance, the conditions *C* specified for the structural description of any sentence containing a definite description (with the corresponding consequent expressing the purported belief (assumption) that there is an entity which is such-and-such); such will be the conditions *C* specified for the structural description of any sentence containing the verb 'to pretend' as its main predicate followed by an embedded *S* (with the corresponding consequent expressing the purported belief that it is not the case that *S*), etc.

I wish to add now some comments on the application of the proposed treatment of presuppositions (as a subclass of consequences) to the analysis of coherent texts or discourses. In one of my papers, the necessary condition of the coherence of texts has been shown to be definable in terms of the notion of consequence[26]. It appears that a text can be said to be coherent only if it is the case for any of its constituent sentences that its set of consequences intersects with the set of consequences of the remaining sentences. It has also been noticed that the interpretation of coherent texts involves more complex problems than the interpretation of isolated sentences, because texts or discourses cannot be interpreted only in terms of the set of consequences pertaining to the syntactical and lexical information that can be specified in conditions *C* in the antecedents of implications, but they have to be interpreted also in terms of the consequences following from additional premisses which are relevant to the given sentences, but which belong to our knowledge of the world.

Let us consider here some examples of how the consequences that correspond to presuppositions function as connectors of a coherent text. I have chosen only those examples where the consequences in question can be drawn on the basis of some additional implications pertaining to certain items in the given text, but belonging to the knowledge of the factual world rather than to the knowledge of English. The reason for my choice is that: (1) I believe that no non-arbitrary limit can be drawn between knowledge of language and knowledge of world both being used in interpreting texts or discourses, and (2) it may be interesting to realize that the semantic function of such consequences that contribute to the coherence of a text is based on the same

[25] For instance, some years ago I heard someone referring to general de Gaulle by the phrase 'the present king of France'.

[26] See. I. Bellert, 'On a Condition of the Coherence of Texts', *Semiotica*, No. 4 (1970).

principle as the semantic function of all other linguistic connectors between sentences in a text, namely, the principle of repetition. To be more precise, the necessary condition of a coherent text is that at least one consequence which we draw from each subsequent sentence of a text constitutes a repetition, that is to say, is the same as one of the former consequences. In other words, at least one consequence (presupposition) is in common with the consequences of the remaining constituent sentences of a text. Let us consider some examples:

Who is to inherit the mantle of Papa Hemingway? Who if not J. D. Salinger. Holden Gaulfield in *The Catcher in the Rye* has a brother in Hollywood who thinks *A Farewell to Arms* is terrific. Holden does not see how his brother, who is *his* favorite writer, can like a phony book like that. But the very image of the hero as pitiless phony-detector comes from Hemingway. In *Across the River and Into the Trees*, the colonel gets a message on his private radar that a pock-merked writer he darkly spies across the room at Harry's Bar in Venice has 'outlived his talents' – apparently some sort of crime. [27]

The hipster is a street-corner, bar, and partying phenomenon, a creature of mobs. One Rimbaud may be a genius, a crowd of them is a fad. An earlier fad for psychoanalysis has this in favor of it: Freud believed in the prime value of emotions, but in a necessary control by the intelligence. [28]

To the ordinary Englishman, how little the aeroplane still means! He lives as though the Wright brothers had never existed, moves and almost uninterruptedly has his being in a pre-Blériot world.[29]

For a reader who would not know that J. D. Salinger is the author of *The Catcher in the Rye*, that Hemingway is the author of *A Farewell to Arms* and *Across the River and Into the Trees*, the first text quoted above would be interpreted as a sequence of disconnected sentences. A reader who would not know anything about Rimbaud would be unable to see any possible connection between the first two sentences of the second text. The same is true *mutatis mutandis* of the interpretation of the other two sentences and the interconnection between Freud and psychoanalysis. In all these examples the factual knowledge of the world provides us with implicit implicational rules that permit us to draw consequences pertaining to a text containing such proper names.

In the third text we have a syntactical connector *he* between the two sentences. In spite of the occurrence of this connector, the text would not be interpreted as coherent if the reader did not know what the connection was between the Wright brothers, Blériot and the aeroplane. But the consequences

[27] Mary McCarthy, 'J. D. Salinger's Closed Circuit', in *Ten Masters of Modern Essay*, Harcourt, Brace and World, N.Y.

[28] Herbert Gold, 'The American Hipster', in *Ten Masters of the Modern Essay*, Harcourt, Brace and World, N.Y.

[29] Aldous Huxley, Copan, in *Ten Masters of the Modern Essay*, Harcourt, Brace and World, N.Y.

that we can draw from the use of the lexical item *aeroplane* in the first sentence will be, however, repeated in result of our knowledge of the world connected with the proper names used in the second sentence. And the text will sound thus coherent.

Finally, it is worth mentioning that although – as I have argued – the problem of the compatibility of the purported meaning and the world *is not* a linguistic problem, but the problem of the compatibility of the purported meanings of utterances used in a coherent text (that is, the consistency of a text or discourse) *is* a linguistic problem that belongs to text linguistics. And it seems to me that the proposed framework of interpretative implicational rules may be used as a convenient apparatus in the investigation of this problem.

WERNER KUMMER

PRAGMATIC IMPLICATION

1. Elements of a Pragmatic Language

In 'Pragmatics' Robert Stalnaker[1] gives a short explanation of the notion 'pragmatic presupposition' as a "propositional attitude... People, rather than sentences or propositions are said to have, or make, presuppositions in this sense... To presuppose a proposition in the pragmatic sense is to take its truth for granted, and to assume that others involved in the context do the same". In the following notes an attempt will be made to give a more elaborated account of pragmatic presupposition in terms of the notion 'pragmatic implication'.

According to Stalnaker a speaker A pragmatically presupposes a proposition p if he takes the truth of p for granted and believes that the others involved in the context, say B, take the truth of p also for granted. 'Taking the truth of p for granted' can either be glossed as 'believing' or as 'knowing', e.g.:

(1) I take it for granted that it is true that the earth is round,
(1′) I know that the earth is round,
(1″) I believe that the earth is round.

The same ambiguity holds for the second part of the definition of 'pragmatic presupposition' given by Stalnaker:

(2) I take it for granted that it is true that you take it for granted that it is true that the earth is round,
(2′) I believe that you believe that the earth is round,
(2″) I know that you believe that the earth is round,
(2‴) I believe that you know that the earth is round,
(2⁗) I know that you know that the earth is round.

It seems that the 'propositional attitudes' constituting pragmatic presuppositions can provisionally be taken as the well-known propositional attitudes of knowledge and belief. Stalnaker's definition could in this framework be spelled out as: The speaker A pragmatically presupposes that p iff he $\left\{\begin{matrix}\text{knows}\\ \text{believes}\end{matrix}\right\}$ that p and $\left\{\begin{matrix}\text{knows}\\ \text{believes}\end{matrix}\right\}$ that the audience B $\left\{\begin{matrix}\text{knows}\\ \text{believes}\end{matrix}\right\}$ that p'

[1] Robert C. Stalnaker, 1972, 'Pragmatics', in *Semantics of Natural Languages*, (ed. by Donald Davidson and Gilbert Harman), Reidel, Dordrecht-Holland.

J. S. Petöfi and H. Rieser (eds.), Studies in Text Grammar, 96–112.

or shorter in Hintikka's notation for epistemic and doxastic operators:
A pragmatically presupposes $p =_{\mathrm{Def}}$

$$\begin{Bmatrix} B_a \\ K_a \end{Bmatrix} p \cdot \begin{Bmatrix} B_a \\ K_a \end{Bmatrix} \begin{Bmatrix} B_b \\ K_b \end{Bmatrix} p.$$

(The brace notation is the notation for alternatives used in transformational grammar.)

A problem for the proposed definition of pragmatic presupposition is the exact meaning of the operators 'believe' and 'know' in this context. Irena Bellert has remarked several times[2] that the notion of belief involved in explaining language behaviour can only be that of purported belief, never that of 'real' belief, so the definiens of the definition of pragmatic presupposition should read: 'the speaker *A* purports to $\begin{Bmatrix} \text{believe} \\ \text{know} \end{Bmatrix}$ that *p* and he purports to $\begin{Bmatrix} \text{believe} \\ \text{know} \end{Bmatrix}$ that the audience *B* purports to $\begin{Bmatrix} \text{believe} \\ \text{know} \end{Bmatrix}$ that *p*'. As Bellert's claim seems basically to be correct it is either possible to treat 'purported belief' and 'purported knowledge' as undefined basic terms in a pragmatic language or to reduce them to simpler elements. The second way seems to be open, because the two terms will be shown to be reducible to the notions 'doxastic implication' and 'epistemic implication' of Hintikka's epistemic logic.

Purported belief can be characterized by an asymmetry in the defensibility of certain sets of assertions:

(3) The earth is round but John doesn't $\begin{Bmatrix} \text{believe} \\ \text{know} \end{Bmatrix}$ it.

(4) The earth is round but I don't $\begin{Bmatrix} \text{believe} \\ \text{know} \end{Bmatrix}$ it.

While the two variants of (3) are respectively doxastically and epistemically defensible, the two variants of (4) are respectively doxastically and epistemically indefensible. The definition of 'doxastically indefensible' presupposed is the one given by Hintikka:

> Let us assume that the person referred to by '*a*' makes a finite number of statements, that is, utters a finite number of declarative sentences $p_1, p_2, p_3, \ldots p_k$, on one and the same occasion. Let us assume furthermore, that every time he refers to himself in these statements he does so by using a certain term, say '*a*'. Then we shall call the set $\{p_1, p_2 \ldots, p_k\}$ doxastically indefensible for the person referred to by this term to utter if and only if the sentence: $B_a(p_1 \cdot p_2 \cdot \ldots p_k)$ is indefensible simpliciter[3].

[2] Irena Bellert, *On the Logico-Semantic Structure of Utterances*, Warsaw 1972. Irena Bellert, 1970, 'On a Condition of the Coherence of Texts', *Semiotica* **II/4**.

[3] The importance of Hintikka's epistemic logic for pragmatical languages was mentioned

Calling the proposition that the earth is round 'p' a simple proof of the doxastic indefensibility of the first variant of (4) can be given using Hintikka's definition and his method of model systems:

(1) $B_a(p \cdot \sim B_a p)\varepsilon\mu$,
(2) $p \cdot \sim B_a p \varepsilon\mu^*$,
(3) $B_a(p \cdot \sim B_a p)\varepsilon\mu^*$,
(4) $\sim B_a p \varepsilon\mu^*$,
(5) $C_a \sim p \varepsilon\mu^*$,
(6) $\sim p \varepsilon\mu^{**}$,
(7) $p \cdot \sim B_a p \varepsilon\mu^{**}$,
(8) $p \varepsilon\mu^{**}$.

From the assumption (1) an inconsistency has been deduced in lines (6) and (8), proving that the first variant of (4) is doxastically indefensible. Using doxastic and epistemic indefensibility the concepts of doxastic implication and epistemic implication can be defined:

"p implies q doxastically if and only if the set $\{p, \sim q\}$ is doxastically indefensible"[4]. Applied to (4) this definition means that (4a) doxastically implies (4b):

(4a) The earth is round,
(4b) The speaker of (4a) believes that the earth is round.

It is important not to take doxastic implication for normal, i.e. virtual implication; (4a) does not imply (4b) in a regular sense of implication. It is only doxastically indefensible for the speaker of (4a) to state on the same occasion (4a) and (4c):

(4c) I don't believe that the earth is round.

The relevant definitions were given for 'doxastic indefensibility' and 'doxastic implication', but they have strict analogues for the epistemic operator, which need not be repeated in detail. The second variant of (4) is epistemically indefensible and (4a′) epistemically implies (4b′):

(4a′) The earth is round,
(4b′) The speaker of (4a′) knows that the earth is round.

There is an interesting asymmetry between the two variants of (4), neverthe-

---

for the first time by Leo Apostel in 'Further Remarks on the Pragmatics of Natural Languages', in *Pragmatics of Natural Languages* (ed. by Yehoshua Bar-Hillel), Reidel, Dordrecht-Holland, 1971.

The quote is from Hintikka: *Knowledge and Belief*, Cornell U.P. 1962, p. 71.

4 *Ibid.*, p. 71.

less; while the first variant is not only doxastically but also epistemically indefensible, the second variant is only epistemically indefensible, which can be shown by proving that (6) is indefensible while (7) is defensible:

(6) $K_a(p \cdot \sim B_a p)$,
(7) $B_a(p \cdot \sim K_a p)$.

Using 'doxastic implication' and 'epistemic implication' not only can the concepts 'purported belief' and 'purported knowledge' be explained in a simple way, as the only test for these notions as proposed by Bellert is equivalent to Hintikka's test for doxastic and epistemic indefensibility respectively, but it is also possible to explain 'pragmatic presupposition' in these terms if it can be shown, that the definiens in the definition of this concept can be reconstructed in terms of doxastic and/or epistemic implication.

2. Truth conditions for formulas with series of epistemic operators with alternating subscripts

The second part of the proposed definiens for 'pragmatic presupposition' is a formula bound by a series of two epistemic operators with alternating subscripts. The variants are:

(a) $B_a B_b p$,
(b) $B_a K_b p$,
(c) $K_a B_b p$,
(d) $K_a K_b p$,

The only rule given by Hintikka allowing to reduce chains of epistemic operators with alternating subscripts is:

$$K_a K_b p \rightarrow K_a p.$$

As the proof for this rule is given in '*Knowledge and Belief*' it need not be repeated here[5]. Three further rules for reducing complex chains of epistemic operators with their proofs shall be given here; further rules will be derived in the next section. The names and definitions of the rules used are those of the appendix of Hintikka's *Knowledge and Belief*.

$$B_a K_b p \rightarrow B_a p.$$

Proof:

(1) $B_a K_b p \varepsilon \mu$,
(2) $\sim B_a p \varepsilon \mu$,
(3) $C_a \sim p \varepsilon \mu$, from (2) by $(C \cdot \sim B)$

[5] *Ibid.*, p. 61.

(4)	$\sim p\varepsilon\mu^*$,	from (3) by $(C\cdot C^+)$
(5)	$K_b p\varepsilon\mu^*$,	from (1) by $(C\cdot B^+)$
(6)	$p\varepsilon\mu^*$,	from (5) by $(C\cdot K)$

$$B_a K_b K_a p \rightarrow K_a p.$$

Proof:

(1)	$B_a K_b p\varepsilon\mu$,	
(2)	$\sim K_a p\varepsilon\mu$,	
(3)	$P_a \sim p\varepsilon\mu$,	from (2) by $(C\cdot \sim K)$
(4)	$\sim p\varepsilon\mu^*$,	from (3) by $(C\cdot P^+)$
(5)	$K_b K_a p\varepsilon\mu^*$,	from (1) by $(C\cdot B^+)$
(6)	$K_a p\varepsilon\mu^*$,	from (5) by $(C\cdot K)$
(7)	$p\varepsilon\mu^*$,	from (6) by $(C\cdot K)$

$$B_a K_b B_a p \rightarrow B_a p,$$

Proof:

(1)	$B_a K_b B_a p\varepsilon\mu$,	
(2)	$\sim B_a p\varepsilon\mu$,	
(3)	$C_a \sim p\varepsilon\mu$,	from (2) by $(C\cdot \sim B)$
(4)	$\sim p\varepsilon\mu^*$,	from (3) by $(C\cdot C^+)$
(5)	$K_b B_a p\varepsilon\mu^*$,	from (1) by $(C\cdot B^+)$
(6)	$B_a p\varepsilon\mu^*$,	from (5) by $(C\cdot K)$
(7)	$K_a \sim B_a p\varepsilon\mu$,	from (2) by $(C\cdot BK)$
(8)	$\sim B_a p\varepsilon\mu^*$,	from (7) by $(C\cdot K)$

As the rules given are implications and not equivalences they don't allow to reduce the number of operators in an epistemic formula; it is therefore necessary to specify the truth-conditions for formulas with more than one epistemic operator, especially for the case, in which the operators have alternating subscripts. The truth-conditions for formulas with only one epistemic operator are:

> $B_a p$ is true in μ iff p is true in every doxastic alternative of μ with respect to a,
> $K_a p$ is true in μ iff p is true in every epistemic alternative of μ with respect to a.

A simple truth-condition derivable from these conditions for a formula with two epistemic operators is e.g.:

> $B_a B_b p$ ist true in μ iff it is true for all doxastic alternatives of μ with respect to a that they have a v embedded in them, such that for all doxastic alternatives of v with respect to b it is true that p.

Analogous truth-conditions for formulas with other chains of epistemic operators can be built in the same manner as the given one.

It is obvious that the few remarks given about the problem of chains of modalities with alternating subscripts don't solve the many problems in this area, but they should provide enough background to go on in the comparison of pragmatic presupposition and doxastic or epistemic implication.

3. Pragmatic implication

Explaining the difference between definite and indefinite NP's in sentences like (8) and (9) it has often been said[6], that an utterance of (9) in some sense implies that the speaker believes the hearer knows who the girl mentioned is, while no such implication is true for an utterance of (8):

(8) I laughed at a girl,
(9) I laughed at the girl.

It is important to specify the type of implication underlying the difference between (8) and (9). If it is doxastic implication (10) should be doxastically indefensible:

(10) I laughed at the girl and I believe that you don't know who that girl is.

It is easily seen that it is not indefensible for *A* to believe that he laughed at the girl and that *B* does not know who that girl is. Therefore doxastic implication cannot be the relevant concept of implication differentiating (8) and (9).

Instead it shall be assumed that *A* believes that *B* knows that *A* laughed at the girl, and then the question is, if this belief is defensible together with *A*'s belief that *B* does not know who the girl is. To test this new kind of possible indefensibility it is necessary to give a formal version of (8) and (9) along the lines proposed by Hintikka:

(8′) (Ex) (girl$(x)\cdot$laugh at (a, x),
(9′) Girl$(b)\cdot$laugh at (a, b).

Furthermore it is necessary to specify the phrase 'to know who'; Hintikka proposes (10′) as an adequate rendering of (10):

(10) *a* knows who killed Toto,
(10′) $(Ex)K_a(x$ killed Toto$)$.

[6] E.g. P. F. Strawson, 'Singular Terms and Predication', in *Logico-Linguistic Papers*, Methuen, 1971.

The relevant portion of the proposition implied in (9) but not in (8) is:

(11) b knows, who the girl that a laughed at is,
(11′) $(Ex)K_b(\text{girl}(x) \cdot \text{laugh at }(a, x))$.

The type of indefensibility derivable from the assumption that A believes that B knows shall be called pragmatic indefensibility in distinction from simple doxastic indefensibility, which does not involve hypotheses of the speaker A about the knowledge of the audience B.

In the following it shall be proved that the set of statements consisting of (9′) and (11′) is pragmatically indefensible while the set consisting of (8′) and (11′) is not. Analogous to simple doxastic implication it will be said that (9′) pragmatically implies (11′) while (8′) does not. As the proof depends crucially on a simple rule which is not explicitly mentioned in Hintikka's work this rule shall first be derived:

$$K_a(p \cdot q) \rightarrow \begin{matrix} K_a p \\ K_a q \end{matrix} \qquad (C \cdot K \text{ and})$$

Proof:

(1) $K_a(p \cdot q)\ \varepsilon\mu$,
(2) $\sim K_a p \varepsilon\mu$,
(3) $P_a \sim p\varepsilon\mu$, from (2) by $(C \cdot \sim K)$.
(4) $\sim p\varepsilon\mu^*$, from (2) by $(C \cdot P^*)$.
(5) $p \cdot q\varepsilon\mu^*$, from (1) by $(C \cdot K^*)$.
(6) $p\varepsilon\mu^*$, from (5) by $(C \cdot \text{ and})$.

The analogous proof for the second part of the implication need not be given in detail. Using the rule $(C \cdot K$ and) the proof that (9′) pragmatically implies (11′) proceeds as follows:

(1) $B_a K_b((\text{girl}(b) \cdot \text{laugh at }(a, b)) \cdot \sim (Ex)\ K_b((\text{girl}(x) \cdot \text{laugh at }(a, x)))\ \varepsilon\mu$.
(2) $K_b((\text{girl}(b) \cdot \text{laugh at }(a, b)) \cdot \sim (Ex)\ K_b((\text{girl}(x) \cdot \text{laugh at }(a, x)))\ \varepsilon\mu^*$ from (1) by $(C \cdot B^+)$.
(3) $K_b(\text{girl}(b) \cdot \text{laugh at }(a, b))\ \varepsilon\mu^*$ from (2) by $(C \cdot K$ and).
(4) $K_b \sim (Ex)\ K_b(\text{girl}(x) \cdot \text{laugh at }(a, x))$ from (2) by $(C \cdot K$ and).
(5) $K_b(\text{girl}(b) \cdot \text{laugh at }(a, b))\ \varepsilon\nu$ (by truth-condition) from (3).
(6) $K_b \sim (Ex)\ K_b(\text{girl}(x) \cdot \text{laugh at }(a, x))\ \varepsilon\nu$ (by truth-condition) from (4).
(7) $(Ex)\ K_b(\text{girl}(x) \cdot \text{laugh at }(a, x))\ \varepsilon\nu$ from (5) by rule (108).
(8) $\sim (Ex)\ K_b(\text{girl}(x) \cdot \text{laugh at }(a, x))\ \varepsilon\nu^*$ from (6) by $(C \cdot K^+)$
(9) $(Ex)\ K_b(\text{girl}(x) \cdot \text{laugh at }(a, x))\ \varepsilon\nu^*$ from (7) by $(C \cdot KK^+)$

(8) and (9) form a contradiction, which proves that (9′) pragmatically implies (11′). An analogous attempt for (8′) and (11′) fails, because the step from (5) to (7) is not possible for (8′).

Pragmatic implication therefore seems to be an adequate explication for the difference noted between sentences like (8) and (9). A further argument for this conclusion is, that the asymmetry between (3) and (4) typical for doxastic implication also holds for (9), but doesn't hold for (8):

(9a) I laughed at the girl, and John believed you didn't know who she is.

(9b) I laughed at the girl, and I believe you don't know who she is.

While (9b) is pragmatically indefensible, (9a) isn't.

(8a) I laughed at a girl, and John believed you didn't know who she was.

(8b) I laughed at a girl, and I believe you don't know who she is.

In the case of (8) neither (8a) nor (8b) is pragmatically indefensible.

In the linguistic literature[7] it has often been claimed that sentences like (9a)–(9b) or (8a)–(8b) have the following variants:

(9a′) I laughed at the girl, and John didn't believe you know who she was.

(9b′) I laughed at the girl, and I don't believe you know who she was.

In the system of Hintikka's epistemic logic it is easy to prove that (9a) and (9b) imply (9a′) and (9b′) respectively but not vice versa:

$$B_a \sim K_b p \rightarrow \sim B_a K_b p.$$

Proof:

(1) $B_a \sim K_b p \varepsilon \mu$,

(2) $B_a K_b p \varepsilon \mu$,

(3) $\sim K_b p \varepsilon \mu^*$, from (1) by $(C \cdot B^+)$

(4) $K_b p \varepsilon \mu^*$, from (2) by $(C \cdot B^+)$

An attempt to prove the converse of the implication fails:

$$\sim B_a K_b p \rightarrow B_a \sim K_b p,$$

attempted proof:

[7] Cf. e.g. George Lakoff, 'Pronominalization, Negation and the Analysis of Adverbs', in *Readings in English Transformational Grammar* (ed. by R. Jacobs and P. Rosenbaum), Ginn and Company, 1970.

(1)	$\sim B_a K_b p \varepsilon \mu$,	
(2)	$\sim B_a \sim K_b p \varepsilon \mu$,	
(3)	$C_a \sim K_b p \varepsilon \mu$,	from (1) by $(C \cdot \sim B)$.
(4)	$C_a K_b p \varepsilon \mu$,	from (2) by $(C \cdot \sim B)$.
(5)	$\sim K_b p \varepsilon \mu^*$,	from (3) by $(C \cdot C^+)$.
(6)	$K_b p \varepsilon \mu^{**}$,	from (4) by $(C \cdot C^+)$.

Rule $(C \cdot C^+)$ does not grant that μ^* and μ^{**} are the same model set, therefore the attempted proof fails.

The concept of pragmatic implication can be used as an explicatum for Stalnaker's definition of pragmatic presupposition. In order to prove this it is necessary to prove a derived rule of $(C \cdot K$ and):

$$B_a K_b (p \cdot q) \rightarrow \begin{matrix} B_a K_b p \\ B_a K_b q \end{matrix} \qquad (C \cdot BK \text{ and}).$$

Proof:

(1)	$B_a K_b (p \cdot q)\, \varepsilon \mu$,	
(2)	$\sim B_a K_b p \varepsilon \mu$,	
(3)	$K_b (p \cdot q)\, \varepsilon \mu^*$,	from (1) by $(C \cdot B^+)$.
(4)	$K_b p \varepsilon \mu^*$,	from (3) by $(C \cdot K$ and).
(5)	$C_a \sim K_b p \varepsilon \mu$,	from (2) by $(C \cdot \sim B)$.
(6)	$\sim K_b p \varepsilon \mu^*$,	from (5) by $(C \cdot C^+)$.

It can not be proved that p pragmatically implies $B_a p$ and $B_a K_b p$. The proof proceeds in two steps, the first step proving that p pragmatically implies $B_a K_b p$, the second step proving that p pragmatically implies $B_a p$:

Proof of the first step:

(1)	$B_a K_b (p \cdot \sim B_a K_b p)\, \varepsilon \mu$,	
(2)	$B_a K_b p \varepsilon \mu$,	from (1) by $(C \cdot BK$ and).
(3)	$B_a K_b \sim B_a K_b p \varepsilon \mu$,	from (1) by $(C \cdot BK$ and).
(4)	$K_b \sim B_a K_b p \varepsilon \mu^*$,	from (3) by $(C \cdot B^+)$.
(5)	$\sim B_a K_b p \varepsilon \mu^*$,	from (4) by $(C \cdot K)$.
(6)	$B_a K_b p \varepsilon \mu^*$,	from (2) by $(C \cdot BB^+)$.

Proof of the second step:

(1)	$B_a K_b (p \cdot \sim B_a p)\, \varepsilon \mu$,	
(2)	$B_a (p \cdot \sim B_a p)\, \varepsilon \mu$,	from (1) by rule $B_a K_b p \rightarrow B_a p$.
(3)	$B_a p \varepsilon \mu$,	from (2) by $(C \cdot B$ and).
(4)	$B_a \sim B_a p \varepsilon \mu$,	from (2) by $(C \cdot B$ and).
(5)	$\sim B_a p \varepsilon \mu^*$,	from (4) by $(C \cdot B^+)$.
(6)	$C_a \sim p \varepsilon \mu^*$,	from (5) by $(C \cdot \sim B)$.

(7) $B_a p\varepsilon\mu^*$, from (3) by $(C\cdot BB^+)$.
(8) $\sim p\varepsilon\mu^{**}$, from (6) by $(C\cdot C^+)$.
(9) $p\varepsilon\mu^{**}$, from (7) by $(C\cdot B^+)$.

It shall now be tried to prove the further cases of pragmatic presupposition implied in Stalnaker's account to be cases of pragmatic implication. First it shall be shown that p pragmatically implies $K_a p$.

In order to do this the following rule has to be proved first:

$$B_a K_b p \rightarrow K_a p.$$

Proof:

(1) $B_a K_b p\varepsilon\mu$,
(2) $\sim K_a p\varepsilon\mu$,
(3) $K_b p\varepsilon\mu^*$, from (1) by $(C\cdot B^+)$.
(4) $p\varepsilon\mu^*$, from (3) by $(C\cdot K)$.
(5) $P_a{\sim}p\varepsilon\mu$, from (2) by $(C\cdot \sim K)$.
(6) $\sim p\varepsilon\mu^*$, from (5) by $(C\cdot P^+)$.

Using this rule the proof can proceed as follows:

(1) $B_a K_b(p\cdot \sim K_a p)\ \varepsilon\mu$,
(2) $K_a(p\cdot \sim K_a p)\ \varepsilon\mu$, from (1) by rule $B_a K_b p \rightarrow K_a p$.
(3) $K_a p\varepsilon\mu$, from (2) by rule $(C\cdot K$ and).
(4) $K_a{\sim}K_a p\varepsilon\mu$, from (1) by $(C\cdot K$ and).
(5) $\sim K_a p\varepsilon\mu$, from (4) by $(C\cdot K)$.

The proof that p pragmatically implies $K_a K_b p$ can only be given in outline, because it presupposes a treatment of semantic presupposition which cannot be spelled out in detail here. $K_a K_b p$ semantically presupposes $K_a p$, i.e. $K_a K_b p$ as well as its negation $\sim K_a K_b p$ necessitate $K_a p$.

Van Fraassen has proved[8] that Modus tollens does not hold in presuppositional languages. Hintikka's reductio method of model systems is crucially based on the validity of modus tollens and therefore cannot handle cases of presuppositions. The proof of necessitation for a presupposed sentence has to be given outside Hintikka's system. As it would be too complicated to establish the relevant apparatus in this paper, the result of the proof shall be assumed as given. In this case the proof of pragmatical implication for $K_a K_b p$ reduces to the proof for $K_a p$ already given.

The last proof necessary for establishing that all cases of pragmatic presupposition implied in Stalnaker's definition can be explained as cases of

[8] E.g. 'Presuppositions, Supervaluations, and Free Logic', in *The Logical Way of Doing Things* (ed. by Karel Lambert), Yale U.P., 1969.

pragmatic implication has to show that p pragmatically implies B_aB_bp. The proof runs as follows:

Proof:

(1)	$B_aK_b(p \cdot \sim B_aB_bp)\ \varepsilon\mu$,	
(2)	$B_aK_bp\varepsilon\mu$,	from (1) by $(C \cdot BK$ and).
(3)	$B_aK_b \sim B_aB_bp\varepsilon\mu$,	from (1) by $(C \cdot BK$ and).
(4)	$K_b \sim B_aB_bp\varepsilon\mu^*$,	from (3) by $(C \cdot B^+)$.
(5)	$\sim B_aB_bp\varepsilon\mu^*$,	from (4) by $(C \cdot K)$.
(6)	$C_a \sim B_bp\varepsilon\mu^*$,	from (5) by $(C \cdot \sim B)$.
(7)	$\sim B_bp\varepsilon\mu^{**}$,	from (6) by $(C \cdot C^+)$.
(8)	$B_aK_bp\varepsilon\mu^*$,	from (2) by $(C \cdot BB^+)$.
(9)	$K_bp\varepsilon\mu^{**}$,	from (8) by $(C \cdot B^+)$.
(10)	$C_b \sim p\varepsilon\mu^{**}$,	from (7) by $(C \cdot \sim B)$.
(11)	$\sim p\varepsilon\mu^{***}$,	from (10) by $(C \cdot C^+)$.
(12)	$K_bp\varepsilon\mu^{***}$,	from (9) by $(C \cdot KK^+$ dox).
(13)	$p\varepsilon\mu^{***}$,	from (12) by $(C \cdot K)$.

The pragmatic implications established by the proof given can be illustrated by comparing the pragmatic indefensibility of the (a) versions of the following sets of statements to the pragmatic defensibility of the (b) versions:

(10a) John is a fink but I don't know that he is a fink.
(10b) John is a fink but Bill doesn't know that he is a fink.
(11a) John is a fink and I don't know that you know that he is a fink.
(11b) John is a fink and Bill doesn't know that you know that he is a fink.
(12a) John is a fink and I don't believe you believe that he is a fink.
(12b) John is a fink and Bill doesn't believe you believe that he is a fink.

In the sets of statements (12a) the order of the statements is crucial. While (12a) e.g. is pragmatically indefensible (12c) is not:

(12c) I don't believe you believe that John is a fink, but John is a fink.

The same is true for (13) as compared with (13a):

(13) John is a fink but I don't think you know that he is a fink.
(13a) I don't think you know that John is a fink, but he is a fink.

Hintikka called the decisive characteristic of the pragmatically indefensible sets of statements their antiperformatory character. Uttering a statement pragmatically implies that the audience B can after the utterance be taken to believe or know what has been uttered. If the speaker explicitly denies this pragmatic implication he cancels the performatory characteristics of his utterance. Important consequences can be drawn from this fact, as it is a direct proof of the action character of statements. Certain pragmatic implications about the beliefs and knowledge of the audience are valid after a statement has been uttered, but not before it has been uttered. Some conclusions from this character of statements have been drawn elsewhere.[9]

4. Other types of pragmatic implications

The types of pragmatic implications mentioned so far don't exhaust the range of pragmatic presuppositions involved in verbal communication. As the logic of most types of pragmatic presuppositions has not been worked out so far, it will only be possible to mention some facts and to try to give some proposals for their treatment.

One important class of pragmatic presuppositions involves the concept of wanting or intending:

(14) John is a fink but I don't want you to know that he is a fink.
(14a) John is a fink but Bill doesn't want you to know that he is a fink.
(15) John is a fink but I don't want you to believe that he is a fink.
(15a) John is a fink but Bill doesn't want you to believe that he is a fink.
(16) John is a fink, but I don't want you to believe that I know that he is a fink.
(16a) John is a fink, but Bill doesn't want you to believe that I know that he is a fink.
etc.

While the non-(a) cases follow the pattern of pragmatically indefensible sets of statements, the (a) variants don't. Example (16) shows that pragmatic implications can have indefinitely many alternations of belief- or knowledge-operators with alternating subscripts. This possibility does not make necessary a major change in the proof methods outlined in 1.2. As an example for a chain of alternations the following pragmatic implication shall be proved:

$$B_aK_b(p\cdot \sim B_aK_bB_aK_bB_aK_bp)$$

Proof:

(1) $B_aK_b(p\cdot \sim B_aK_bB_aK_bB_aK_bp)\ \varepsilon\mu,$
(2) $B_aK_bp\varepsilon\mu,$ (from (1) by ($C\cdot BK$ and).

[9] W. Kummer, 'Quantifikation und Identität in Texten', in *Probleme der generativen Grammatik*, Vieweg, 1969.
W. Kummer, 'An Outline of a Model for a Grammar of Discourse', in *Poetics*, Mouton, 1971.

(3) $B_aK_b \sim B_aK_bB_aK_bB_aK_bp\varepsilon\mu$, (from (1) by ($C\cdot BK$ and).
(4) $B_aK_bC_a \sim K_bB_aK_bB_aK_bp\varepsilon\mu$, (from (3) by ($C\cdot \sim B$).
(5) $B_aK_bC_aP_b \sim B_aK_bB_aK_bp\varepsilon\mu$, (from (4) by ($C\cdot \sim K$).

....

(9) $B_aK_bC_aP_bC_aP_bC_aP_b \sim p\varepsilon\mu$, (from (8) by ($C\cdot \sim K$).
(10) $K_bC_aP_bC_aP_bC_aP_b \sim p\varepsilon\mu^*$, (from (9) by ($C\cdot B^+$).
(11) $K_bC_aP_bC_aP_bC_aP_b \sim p\varepsilon\nu$, (from (10) by truth-condition).
(12) $C_aP_bC_aP_bC_aP_b \sim p\varepsilon\nu^*$, (from (11) by ($C\cdot K^+$).
(13) $C_aP_bC_aP_bC_aP_b \sim p\varepsilon\mu^{**}$, (from (11) by truth-condition).
(14) $P_bC_aP_bC_aP_b \sim p\varepsilon\mu^{***}$, (from (13) by ($C\cdot C^+$).
(15) $P_bC_aP_bC_aP_b \sim p\varepsilon\nu^{**}$, (from (14) by truth-condition).
(16) $C_aP_bC_aP_b \sim p\varepsilon\nu^{***}$, (from (15) by ($C\cdot P^+$).
(17) $C_aP_bC_aP_b \sim p\varepsilon\mu^{****}$, (from (16) by truth-condition)
(18) $P_bC_aP_b \sim p\varepsilon\mu^{*****}$, (from (17) by ($C\cdot C^+$).
(19) $P_bC_aP_b \sim p\varepsilon\nu^{****}$, (from (18) by truth-condition).
(20) $C_aP_b \sim p\varepsilon\nu^{*****}$, (from (19) by ($C\cdot P^+$).
(21) $C_aP_b \sim p\varepsilon\mu^{******}$, (from (20) by truth-condition).
(22) $B_aK_bp\varepsilon\mu^{******}$, (from (2) by ($C\cdot BB^+$).
(23) $P_b \sim p\varepsilon\mu^{*******}$, (from (21) by ($C\cdot C^+$).
(24) $K_bp\varepsilon\mu^{*******}$, (from (22) by ($C\cdot B^+$).
(25) $P_b \sim p\varepsilon\nu^{******}$, (from (23) by truth-condition).
(26) $\sim p\varepsilon\nu^{*******}$, (from (25) by ($C\cdot P^+$).
(27) $K_bp\varepsilon\nu^{******}$, (from (24) by truth-condition).
(28) $p\varepsilon\nu^{*******}$, (from (27) by ($C\cdot K^+$).

Pragmatic presuppositions involving 'want' are not only relevant for statements, but also for questions and commands:

(17) Is Mary here? But I don't want to know whether Mary is here.
(17a) Is Mary here? But Bill doesn't want me to know whether Mary is here.
(18) Is Mary here? But I don't want you to intend for me to know whether Mary is here.
(18a) Is Mary here? But Bill doesn't want you to intend for me to know whether Mary is here.
(19) Who is here? But I don't want to know who is here.
(19a) Who is here? But Bill doesn't want me to know who is here.
(20) Who is here? But I don't want you to intend for me to know who is here.
(20a) Who is here? But Bill doesn't want you to intend for me to know who is here.
(21) Open the door! But I don't want you to open the door.

(21a) Open the door! But Bill doesn't want you to open the door.
(22) Open the door! But I don't want you to intend to open the door.
(22a) Open the door! But Bill doesn't want you to intend to open the door.

Again the (a) versions don't follow the pattern of pragmatic implication while the other variants do.

A minor problem in the treatment of the variants of (18) is the formalization of 'whether'; this concept has to be clearly distinguished from 'that' cf.:

(23) Bill knows that John has killed Mary.
(24) Bill knows whether John has killed Mary.

While the formalization proposed by Hintikka for sentences like (23) is:

(23′) $K_a p$,

the adequate formalization for sentences like (24) is:

(24′) $K_a p \vee K_a \sim p$.

An adequate logic for 'want' has not been worked out so far, but it appears that in its general outlines it might follow the pattern proposed by Hintikka for the treatment of propositional attitudes. An interesting aspect of the logic of 'want' is its close interlocking with the logic of knowledge and belief, cf:

Generally (25) does not imply (26) and vice versa:

(25) John wants to see Dr. Jekyll,
(26) John wants to see Mr. Hyde,

although it is true that Mr. Hyde is Dr. Jekyll. But in case (27) or (28) are true the implication between (25) and (26) holds both ways:

(27) John knows that Dr. Jekyll is Mr. Hyde,
(28) John believes that Dr. Jekyll is Mr. Hyde.

In this context it is important that 'want' is construed as 'intend' or 'plan' rather than as 'would like to', because it obviously can be true that John would rather like to meet Dr. Jekyll than Mr. Hyde although he knows or believes that they are identical.

Modelling for the moment the logic of 'wanting' on the logic of knowledge and belief two operators can be introduced:

I_a for '*a* intends to ...',

H_a for 'it is compatible with *a*'s intentions'.

The relation between the two operators is analogous to the one defined in the rules $(C \cdot B)$ and $(C \cdot \sim K)$:

$$(C\cdot\sim I) \text{ if } \sim I_a p\varepsilon\mu \quad \text{then} \quad H_a\sim p\varepsilon\mu.$$

In common terms the relation can be specified so, that if *A* does not intend that not *p*, then it is compatible with his intentions in the same situation that *p* and vice versa.

One of the rules for Intention has to specify that if it is true that $I_a p$ is an element of μ then in all intention-alternatives, e.g. in all states, in which *A*'s intentions are fulfilled *p* will be true. An important difference between the logic of intention and the logic of knowledge and belief is the lack of a counterpart for $(C\cdot BB^+)$ and $(C\cdot KK^+)$. It is not true that in all the states in which *A*'s intentions of a certain situation are fulfilled he has the same intentions as in the original state μ.

Another basic question for a logic of intention is as to what can be intended. One possible answer is, that only actions can be intended and this would exclude constructions like (18) or (20), in which *A* intends a certain intention of *B*: $I_a I_b p$. Generally a logic of intention will have to solve the problems of an iterated application of the operator of intention, also in cases with non-alternating subscripts like: $I_a I_a p$. For the moment iteration of intention-operators shall be allowed.

The variants of (14)–(22) following the pattern of pragmatic implication can then be formalized as follows:

(14′) $p\cdot\sim I_a K_b p.$
(15′) $p\cdot\sim I_a B_b p.$
(16′) $p\cdot\sim I_a B_b K_a p.$
(17′) $?p\cdot\sim I_a(K_a p \vee K_a\sim p).$
(18′) $?p\cdot\sim I_a I_b(K_a p \vee K_a\sim p).$
(19′) $(?x)p\cdot\sim I_a(Ex)\, K_a p.$
(20′) $(?x)p\cdot\sim I_a I_b(Ex)\, K_a p.$
(21′) $!p\cdot\sim I_a$ does bp.
(22′) $!p\cdot\sim I_a I_b$ does bp.

A precise formalization of (17′) to (20′) presupposes an explicit treatment of erotetic logic, which has been worked out by several authors and cannot be given in this paper[10]. In the same way (21′)–(22′) presuppose explicit treatment of a logic of commands and of a logic of action, which also cannot be given here[11].

[10] The model closest to Hintikka's epistemic logic is Lennart Åquist, *A New Approach to the Logical Theory of Interrogatives*, Part 1, Uppsala 1965.

[11] On the logic of commands cf. Nicholas Rescher: *The Logic of Commands*, London 1966; a review of the logic of action is given in Donald Davidson: 'The Logical Form of Action Sentences', in *The Logic of Decision and Action* (ed. by Nicholas Rescher), Pittsburgh 1968.

Using the fragments of the logic of 'want' introduced so far it can be shown that cases like (14′) and (15′) follow the model of pragmatic implication. In order to give the proofs it is necessary to specify basic truth-conditions for series of alternating intention-operators and epistemic operators with alternating subscripts. The conditions are patterned on those given for knowledge and belief and will be specified only for the interplay of K_a and I_a, as the analogues for B_a and I_a can easily be derived from them:

> K_aI_bp is true in μ iff it is true for all epistemic alternatives of μ with respect to a that they have a v embedded in them, such that for all intentional alternatives of v with respect to b it is true that p.
>
> I_aK_bp is true in μ iff it is true for all intentional alternatives of μ with respect to a that they have a v embedded in them, such that for all epistemic alternatives of v with respect to b it is true that p.

The proof that p pragmatically implies I_aK_bp can be specified as follows:

Proof:

(1)	$B_aK_b(p\cdot\sim I_aK_bp)\ \varepsilon\mu$,	
(2)	$B_aK_bp\varepsilon\mu$,	from (1) by ($C\cdot BK$ and).
(3)	$B_aK_b\sim I_aK_bp\varepsilon\mu$,	from (1) by ($C\cdot BK$ and).
(4)	$K_b\sim I_aK_bp\varepsilon\mu^*$,	from (3) by ($C\cdot B^+$).
(5)	$\sim I_aK_bp\varepsilon\mu^*$,	from (4) by ($C\cdot K$).
(6)	$H_a\sim K_bp\varepsilon\mu^*$,	from (5) by ($C\cdot\sim I$).
(7)	$H_a\sim K_bp\varepsilon v$,	from (6) by truth-condition.
(8)	$\sim K_bp\varepsilon v^*$,	from (7) by analogue to ($C\cdot P^+$)($C\cdot C$).
(9)	$\sim K_bp\varepsilon\psi$,	from (8) by truth-condition.
(10)	$P_b\sim p\varepsilon\psi$,	from (9) by ($C\cdot\sim K$).
(11)	$\sim p\varepsilon\psi^*$,	from (10) by ($C\cdot P^+$).
(12)	$K_bp\varepsilon\mu^*$,	from (2) by ($C\cdot B^+$).
(13)	$K_bp\varepsilon\psi$,	from (12) by truth-condition.
(14)	$p\varepsilon\psi^*$,	

An analogous proof can be given that p pragmatically implies I_aB_bp, as it closely follows the lines of the proof already given it will not be spelled out in detail.

Alternations of operators are also for the interplay between I_a, B_a and K_a with alternating subscripts possible to an indefinite length, cf.:

(29) I want you to believe that I believe that you want me to believe that you want me to believe that you believe that I want to go to bed with you.

(30) I want you to know that I want you to believe that I believe that you are a fink.

The proof procedures for sequences of operators as in (29) and (30) are not different from those for simpler sentences, as has been shown for the case of knowledge and belief.

5. Summary

Developing a concept of 'pragmatic implication' from Hintikka's notions of 'doxastic implications' and 'epistemic implication' it has been shown that this concept can serve as an explicatum of the notion 'pragmatic presupposition' as defined by Stalnaker. Some applications of the concept were shown and it is proposed to accept it as one of the basic terms in a pragmatic language.

Freie Universität, Berlin

WOLFRAM K. KÖCK

TIME AND TEXT: TOWARDS AN ADEQUATE HEURISTICS

> "... composition is time that is the reason that at present the time-sense is troubling that is the reason why at present the time-sense in the composition is the composition that is making what there is in composition."
>
> GERTRUDE STEIN

1. PRELIMINARIES

The title I have (finally) chosen for this paper may make some readers feel a little suspicious about its purpose and content, or may even make them wonder whether it has justifiably found its way into a collection of studies in text *linguistics*. There have been only too many assorted publications carrying titles of the general form 'Time and ...', especially in this century, after some (more or less vulgarized) knowledge about Einstein's Theory of Relativity had begun to spread among philosophers, theologians, artists, writers and, of course, their satellites, literary critics. As it is a more than trivial fact that everything is connected with, or subjected to, time in some form or other, a subject of the kind of 'Time and ...' cannot but claim to be 'interesting' wherever it is chosen to be discussed, all the more so now that, instead of the ordinary word 'time' one can use the learned expression 'the fourth dimension' (of nature, the universe, existence, or whatever). Moreover he who has dipped into the vast stock of extant writings on Time – and no human being can, in a lifetime, do more than that – will confirm the frustrating experience of bewilderment and confusion one is beset with after going through a random sample from *Sein und Zeit* to *Time and the Elementary Particle*. One is particularly disenchanted with the discussion going on at the moment in the natural sciences (– and rightly so, as one obviously has been looking in the wrong place), where one had hoped to find some guidance as to the 'reality' of 'temporal matters' that underlie – don't they? – the temporal concepts objectified in a variety of ways in the individual natural languages.[1]

[1] There is surely no need to explicitly quote the author of *Sein und Zeit* (9th ed., Tübingen 1960); it is Martin Heidegger. 'Time in Particle Physics', an essay by J. G. Taylor (*Studium Generale* **23**, 1970, pp. 1102–1107), suggested the microscopic alternative to Heidegger's global discussion. – There is also no need, I think, to record here the individual titles of

J. S. Petöfi and H. Rieser (eds.), Studies in Text Grammar, 113–124.

All this is not meant to be a statement of divine arrogance but rather a confession to error. Why then, still the title 'Time and Text'? The answer to this question will, I hope, emerge from the present article. It seems apposite, however, to try and justify briefly the course I have taken by expounding in a little more detail the reasons that are responsible for the wording 'Time and Text'.

The title is not intended to convey anything mystical or speculative in the sense I complained about above. It is nothing but a convenient formula to sum up all the problems that arise from the attempt to study the regularities in the functioning of the *linguistic* means of 'time representation' in *texts*, i.e. *not* in sentences. It is to serve as a name for the problems of textual 'time reference' or rather, textual 'temporal semantics', in a sense, however, that is *still to be characterized.* And, as the subtitle indicates, there will be much speculation too, and necessarily so, as there is very little established knowledge about the *denotata* of either 'time' or 'text' or the relationship between them, so little, in fact, that I have felt encouraged to sketch an all-embracing pre-theoretical framework within which all the intuitively relevant and essential problems can be located without neglecting or distorting any of the 'systematic' relations between them (which must obviously be part of the definitions of the respective problems). I hope that the pre-heuristic scheme outlined in the following may help to prepare the ground for an adequate heuristics for the overall problem of 'temporal semantics' in texts, and perhaps

books and articles I have read on the topic of time, though some of the titles in themselves are quite attractive, e.g. 'Creative Time' (by S. Watanabe, *Stud. Gen.* **23**, 1970, pp. 1057–1087), 'The Deification of Time' (by S. G. F. Brandon, *Stud. Gen.* **23**, 1970, pp. 485–497), 'Time as a Hierarchy of Creative Conflicts' (by J. T. Fraser, *Stud. Gen.* **23**, 1970, pp. 597–689), or 'Temporal Attitudes in Four Negro Subcultures' (by H. Bagenstose Green, *Stud. Gen.* **23**, 1970, pp. 571–586). Apart from philosophical treatments Time has been a subject of prime importance to writers and thus to literary critics, who have either concentrated on the interpretation of time by artists, or on what can be (and is) called the 'time structure' of a work of art, in particular a literary work. I shall have occasion to mention some of the works on the second-named aspect further on (e.g. those by Müller, Hamburger, Stanzel) whereas the first topic is essentially outside the domain of this paper (e.g. books like E. Staiger's *Die Zeit als Einbildungskraft des Dichters*, 1939; or the extensive work by G. Poulet, *Etudes sur le temps humain*, 1951ff. – to quote only two). So also is the bulk of scientific work on time, except for some of the biological, in particular physiological, contributions concerning the 'organic bases' of the *concept* time as it is realized by humans in various ways. This is also true of the traditional psychological work on the human time concepts as well as the corresponding psycholinguistic investigations: some of it has proved to be interesting in the present context, as far as I have been able to see. – All this, however, is not to suggest that I have read all the relevant literature in this vast domain, nor that I claim to be competent to judge its adequacy or usefulness in any more specific sense than suggested here. To pass objective judgment I would have to be in possession of a 'theory of time' which I am not, understandably enough, 'Time' takes time, too...

also for more adequate theorizing about texts in general. (The meaning of 'adequate' will be characterised presently.)

This is therefore a linguistic paper devoted to a conceptual area in language (i.e. in all natural languages, – an assumption one may make in good conscience) nameable, misleadingly again, as 'time and language', and its functioning in texts. It is not a philosophical nor psychological essay except for a certain metatheoretical bias and some scattered remarks on psycholinguistic phenomena in the context of the general scheme discussed. And the term 'linguistic' itself will be found to be different in meaning from (at least one of) its prevalent current uses, i.e. it will refer to 'theoretical linguistics' as an *empirical*, not a *formal* (or in the narrow sense 'structural') science. Fields like 'algebraic linguistics', 'computer linguistics' or the study of 'formal languages' deal, roughly, with possible, partly 'language-like' structures and have to do with natural languages only in that they are derived from intuitively evident concepts present in natural language, from which various structures are built up constructively according to specified ('exact') procedures. Such activities properly belong to mathematics, *the* formal science before all. Their *application* to problems of natural language research is strictly a matter of *empirical* adequacy and therefore depends on the (intuitively pre-classified) *data* available and the *goals* one chooses (or is allowed to choose) to associate with theoretical research in general. Such general problems are, however, outside the scope of this paper, though my attitudes and decisions in this respect are of course implicit in the views developed.[2]

[2] I definitely do *not* want to suggest here that I hold an extreme inductivist (or some such) view which would naively assume "the more data, the better the theory"; nor that I am unaware of the very complicated relationship between empirical observation and description, theory construction and theory testing, etc. But I am convinced that all formal systems derive their axiomatic bases from intuitively 'evident' concepts which are *not* above criticism; by employing certain equally basic and intuitively 'evident' – at least in Western society – means of 'inference', the principles of which may be formulated as "basic postulates" (Stachowiak [85] pp. 114ff. and pass.) or as "directives" (Reichenbach [79] p. 25 and pass.), self-contained and 'independent' structures of all sorts are built up; from among *all* possible structures the 'interesting' cases are selected (both by external and internal standards): certain 'entities' (or 'objects') are posited – usually by abstracting from some intuitive domain (as e.g. in the case of 'set' or 'space', 'number', 'line', 'body') – and their 'properties' stated; all such 'stating' technically rests on conventions established to exclude ambiguity, misunderstanding, and redundancy – the case for symbolic notation; as soon as there is agreement on these basic 'axiomatic' matters one may proceed to formulate all the 'correct' statements derivable from the initial assumptions by the accepted rules, i.e. all the statements expressing the 'behaviour' of the 'objects' *selected* for treatment for certain reasons; again the goal is to find the most 'interesting' regularities, on the one hand, and to state them as explicitly and as economically as possible, on the other, so as to achieve the supreme goal of all science: to supply instruments which are comparatively easy to handle but allow the manipulation of infinitely complex and powerful 'realities' of whatever kind. (Cf. E. Mach: "Die Wissenschaft kann ... als eine Minimumaufgabe angesehen werden, welche darin besteht,

möglichst vollständig die Tatsachen mit dem geringsten Gedankenaufwand darzustellen. *Mechanik* p. 461, quoted by Stachowiak [85] p. 211, Note 144.) – Now this is surely only a rough characterization of a 'formal system': the main point is, however, that any such formal system proceeds from the concrete to the abstract (or: general) in a *strictly controlled way*, i.e. the domain of any (abstract) concept is well-defined in relation to other concepts whose definition has been established. Thus ever-new 'interesting' objects and properties may be established on the basis of others already given, systems may be conflated, enlarged, integrated into others, etc. And all such manipulating with imaginary structures is entirely independent of empirical matters. It is a happy event then to find that regularities of an empirical nature can be symbolically expressed by some formal system already given and that therefore all the theorems of that formal system automatically hold if the 'interpretation' is *adequate*, i.e. if there *is* an exact one-one correspondence between the 'objects' in the empirical field and the imaginary 'objects' of the formal system, so that the 'empty' theorems of the imaginary system will appear as 'laws' of the empirical field. The problem then is to precisely *establish* the 'objects' and their 'properties' of an empirical domain and to examine whether their symbolic notation matches in some way that of a formal system, i.e. its axiomatically established 'objects' and 'properties'. A 'set', for instance, is "any collection of definite, distinguishable objects of our intuition or of our intellect to be conceived as a whole" (Stoll [90] quoting Cantor, p. 3). Thus there may be 'sets' in any empirical domain, but whether the set-theoretical theorems hold will depend on *what* precisely the 'elements' of the 'sets' in question are; there is no other way. It was the great illusion in the early days of machine translation to hope for the solution of all problems by blindly applying all sorts of sophisticated formal systems, e.g. topology, group theory, information theory, matrix theory, etc. The effect was devastating: there were far too many possible theorems that could be derived which were completely irrelevant and increased the 'noise' in the processing no end, on the other hand. Most of the relevant linguistic objects and their properties could not be symbolized by those formal systems! Thus it is absolutely necessary to be aware of *what a formal concept generalises over* and what must therefore be *given* (in an already 'theoretical', i.e. classified and conceptualized 'analytic' form) to fall into the domain of that concept. There must therefore always be an 'intuitive theory' first, before there can be any generalisation. It is downright wrong to expect the adequate theory of an empirical domain to 'emerge' automatically by applying a given formal system: this is no more than 'rephrasing' one's little knowledge in unnecessarily high-faluting terms, the gain may be precision, but it is empty, it has not contributed anything to knowledge. (Cf. K. R. Popper on the use of formal languages, [75] p. 21: "... the intricacy of the outfit bears no relation to its effectiveness, and practically no scientific theory of any interest can be expressed in these vast systems of minutiae".) Thus it is a fatal misunderstanding to proclaim a 'deductive' approach in the sense of an exclusively and aprioristic 'formal' approach: this is nothing but an incredible restriction of the powers of the human intellect and its range of application; it is more or less a self-condemnation to sterility *if* it is to be 'the one and only' kind of science considered permissible. As already stated there is no true 'inductive' approach in an absolute sense, but the normal way to theory building may safely bear that name: it is a continual trial-and-error process of hypothesis-making in close contact with the empirical data (which therefore can only exist relative to such hypotheses as they are conceived and tested and modified all along), striving for the most encompassing laws governing the delimited object. In such a process the primary delimitation of the 'object' will often be found inadequate in itself, new hypotheses will have to be constructed and tested until, finally, a 'primary model' may emerge picturing all the constitutive properties of the analytic elements set up previously for the empirical domain. And *only then* may one look for a formal system to express more precisely, but *without loss*, what one has established intuitively, and only then may one hope for success as regards the establishing of an *effective* instrument to manipulate the empirical data in an economical way. – The aprioristic application of a formal system without proper observation is thus bound to be misleading and wasteful: it may not only obscure

The emphasis is on *texts*. Thus the whole enterprise is oriented by a perspective that has evolved only comparatively recently: *text linguistics*. Abstractly, the ultimate aim of something like text-linguistics has to be, as I would put it, a 'linguistic theory of texts' which – *ideally*, as with every science – allows for perfect control of (all kinds of) language functioning by stating scientifically the necessary conditions for all possible (functional, i.e. usable, acceptable, not only grammatical) texts of a given language. Such a theory – obviously quite utopian, but a useful idealisation – would primarily be of use in determining the acceptable (or valid) meaning(s) of a given text, and in rejecting meaningless (parts of) texts. Assuming that 'text' means nothing but 'acceptable text' (in a purely practical everyday sense) a linguistic theory of texts would thus provide all the necessary criteria to define the set of possible texts in a given language. Such a theory would be

---

many relevant problems, but may also generate irrelevant results under the flag of 'exactness' and 'precision'. Formal systems are highly selective as to their 'content'; their application to a natural language does no more than select that aspect on which they were originally built, i.e. the intuitive aspect which originally motivated their construction: thus certain 'truth' relations between statements engendered the development of formal logic. – Thus, to sum up, it must be reflected carefully when a given formal system may be used: only in a stage where the intuitively established objects and properties can be represented adequately (congruently and economically) by it. It is therefore a waste of effort to apply certain formal systems whose foundations clearly show that they cover only a fraction of the data of a natural language, as is e.g. the case with formal logic. There is a clear distinction in interests and goals between formal disciplines and empirical ones which must not be obliterated for whatever reasons, certainly not for reasons of 'fashionableness' and 'prestige'.

These remarks are of course only fragmentary hints at a fundamental problem: the problem of the critical examination of concepts and the question of the standards employed in such examination. This problem has, upon thorough analysis, been proved unsolvable by A. I. Wittenberg [106], who has also discussed in detail the theoretical and practical consequences to be derived from a proper recognition of this problem of conceptual criticism. It is, I think, of basic importance, to be aware of what formal techniques are, how they come to be, and what they can, or cannot, do. From this follows indirectly what L. Wittgenstein has discussed repeatedly in [107], e.g. in Section 88, with respect to the *degree of exactness* required by a 'situation' according to the goal to be achieved. I think that this is important in this context too, though it must not be taken to be an excuse for slovenliness in one's work. – Formalisation is a *must* wherever it is possible, and conversely, formalisation is a must *only* where it is possible: the word 'possible' here includes concepts of 'relevance' and 'efficacity', and I shall therefore use the word 'adequate' for all these concepts. Formalisation in the wrong place is necessarily inadequate if it is not yet possible, or if it can be predicted to be impossible (as with formal logic and natural languages), if it is too selective and therefore runs idle (in Wittgenstein's sense), and if it is of no use, i.e. not fruitful and an impediment rather than a help (as generative transformational grammar, or mathematical linguistics, etc.) for the actual problems of the empirical field whose name it has assumed. The dissatisfaction with attempts of this kind in the empirical domain accounts for the present suggestions which aim at a first tentative outline of what the 'objects' of a theory of language that is to be effective and useful, seem to be. Reflections on meta-theoretical questions will therefore crop up again.

a most powerful instrument and certainly be welcome in many fields of human activity in which language and its manipulability create difficulty and trouble, for instance in law, theology, philosophy, journalism, politics, education, etc. (in fact, I am sure, there would immediately be an international war about it). It would imply nothing less than what G. Orwell, in his *1984*, pictures as the "thought police".[3]

Clearly, we are far from a theory of this degree of perfection. We are not even near a 'theory': text linguistics as a (potential) field in its own right is too young to have already developed a unified research programme and thus a generally accepted problem definition and methodology. For obvious reasons I cannot attempt to review the state of the art and all the variegated assumptions and developments that have produced it. This would involve an extensive critical discussion of all the extant writings of a text-linguistic orientation and, what is more, a very thorough discussion of the critical standards applied. The latter task is quite complex: it involves the critical analysis, interpretation, and evaluation of the various 'meta-theoretical paradigms' underlying and governing research, and this again can only be done on the basis of other, 'meta-meta-theoretical criteria' which, in turn, must be justified or, at least, be made plausible. On the other hand, this task should *not* be left to the philosophers because in the hands of these agile word-mongers it would take off the ground only too quickly and become a quixotesque battle of shadow boxers, whereas it desperately needs to be treated in close connection with concrete, object-oriented, down-to-earth research *practice*, and, in particular, the underlying 'ideologies' – I am using this word in a general, non-restricted, non-committed sense – and explicit and/or implicit political attachments of all research practice. – Some criticism of the text-linguistic scene is certainly implied by the outline of the research or problem scheme that I shall attempt to give, especially, of course, by the 'paradigm' underlying it.[4]

Despite the impossibility of a prolonged discussion I may be allowed to characterize very briefly and in a grossly simplifying way what I think the

[3] I strongly advise everybody to read Orwell's "Appendix" on "the principles of Newspeak" in his *1984* (Penguin Books, London 1971, pp. 241ff.), in which he elaborates a little on the linguistic manipulations of "The Party" to guarantee that no "heretical thought" is possible and to "make speech... especially speech on any subject not ideologically neutral, as nearly as possible independent of consciousness" by abolishing all ambiguous and polysemic words and standardizing the modes of thought and action of all citizens in such a way as to have them react without thinking, like automata. – K. Kraus's linguistic diagnoses immediately spring to mind, – but I shall resist quoting some of his work here.

[4] The expression 'meta-theoretical paradigm' is used by Th. Luckmann in his introduction to Gipper [37], p. XII, and derives from Th. S. Kuhn [63]. The problems connected with the 'values' governing the scientist's work and their influence on the quality of the 'knowl-

main orientations in text linguistics are at the moment, as this very situation has motivated the present attempt to show in a comprehensive fashion what problems are ultimately involved in the practice of something like text linguistics.

One fact about the present state of the art of text linguistics is surely indisputable: the term 'text linguistics' has no clear and unified meaning. It can be, and is, interpreted in a variety of ways, which fact may be highlighted by mere superficial comparison of the 'text-linguistic' work associated with names like Z. S. Harris, R. Harweg, P. Hartmann, W. A. Koch, W. Kummer, T. A. van Dijk, J. Ihwe, H. Rieser, J. S. Petöfi, H. Isenberg, E. Lang, S. J. Schmidt, W. Dressler, F. Daneš, T. Todorov, G. Wienold, E. Gülich/W. Raible, K. Heger, H. Weinrich, H. Brinkmann, H. Glinz, I. Bellert, M. Bense, C. Bremond, W.-D. Stempel, J. M. Lotman, L. Karttunen, R. Ingarden, – not to mention the 'text-philological' work done in the various fields of literary study, where various approaches sometimes happily co-exist side by side.[5] Excluding the purely philosophical, pseudo-philosophical, and literary approaches – which often have to be called 'pseudo-literary' as well, as they are not really investigating specifically 'literary' phenomena, but biographical, sociological, psychological, or historical 'facts', 'ideas', or as they are merely ('merely' relative to standards of scientific rigour) 'interpreting' and 'appreciating' in a 'personal' way what the text offers at a given time – it may be justified to draw a very broad distinction between two main strands of text linguistics:

(a) a broadly oriented approach, linguistic in a comprehensive and practice-determined sense, aiming at quick and as-theoretical-as-possible results to be applied wherever most urgently needed: in teaching (native and

---

edge' he provides, have been a central concern of the discussion of the bases of the social sciences and their 'logic'. Cf. for instance Acham [1], Albert [2], Topitsch [95]. It should be obvious – and Kuhn's analysis makes it clear in an illustrative way – that the natural sciences are no less bound to accepted 'values' and goals than the social sciences, though the compulsion exerted by 'the system' will be stronger there, merely because an individual who wants to survive cannot afford the experimental set-up, or will not be allowed to produce verbal monologues in his own private language.

[5] The list of names is not ordered according to rank or any other criterion and is not to suggest that I am familiar with all the different approaches implied. There is no need for a complete bibliography here, either; I shall refer only to a few works which contain most of the relevant bibliographical material; T. A. van Dijk [25], J. S. Petöfi [71], E. Gülich/W. Raible [45], K. Brinker [15], H. Weinrich [102], W.-D. Stempel [89], H. Glinz [39], [42], [43], H. Brinkmann [19], W. A. Koch [57], R. Ingarden [54], M. Bense [8], [9]. Again: this is but a selection which contains many more references to other works. – As for the traditional philological work on texts in whatever sense (textual criticism, analysis, interpretation…) there is no need to mention here all the various approaches to textual analysis. The relevant work is far too extensive and scattered to allow for condensed representation. As for linguistics and literary study in general, cf. Ihwe [53].

foreign languages and literatures), translating and interpreting, in the linguistic foundation of all areas of activity in which language is of primary importance, e.g. law, politics, journalism and the mass media, all language-dependent sciences, e.g. theology, philosophy, the philologies, psychology, sociology, as well as all fields of man-machine interaction via language (library organisation, automatic documentation, information processing, storage and retrieval, etc.), etc.; an approach that is always under pressure of time, has to be satisfied with interim solutions and ad-hoc modifications and, in the long run, with 'middle-range theories'; an approach however, that strives to be 'scientific' and 'exact' as much as any other, but is kept down constantly by the obstinacy and demands of the practical tasks that have to be accomplished and cannot therefore take the time to retire from the continual struggle into regions of (more or less) pure research and quietly reflect and experiment until an appropriate and acceptable solution would be found;

(b) the approach that is free to do precisely what has just been characterised as being denied to approach (a): it can retire into untroubled regions to quietly reflect and experiment according to strict rules, it can take time and work towards 'final' and reliable solutions, both on concrete problems as well as on all the necessary 'meta-problems'.

Both approaches – constituting the often-invoked dichotomy between 'pure' and 'applied' research – are obviously justified *and* socially 'relevant', and depend upon each other. (Establishing priorities as to given problems and ways of solving them is *quite* another matter.) – Whether a 'text' is defined (loosely) as a 'coherent sequence of sentences', as 'connected discourse', as

> eine als ein Ganzes fungierende Folge gesprochener oder geschriebener sprachlicher Elemente, das auf der Grundlage eines beliebigen (meist außerlinguistischen) Kriteriums als 'Text' ausgewiesen ist[6],

as "sprachliche Einheit mündlicher oder schriftlicher Rede, die nicht mehr Bestandteil höherer sprachlicher Einheiten ist"[7] or in an "intentionalist-sociological" way as

> von seinem Hersteller für möglichst identisches Festhalten und (Weiter-) Wirken bestimmtes sprachliches Gebilde[8]

in both these camps it has become more or less commonplace to stress that the category of 'tense' is of essential importance for the constitution of texts, i.e. that it is a necessary element determining a text as a text, or, more

[6] J. S. Petöfi [72], p. 31.
[7] H. Brinkmann [19], p. 723.
[8] H. Glinz [44], p. 123.

learnedly, the 'textuality' – as compared with the 'grammaticality' of the sentence – of the text. There is surely no need to document this fact; it is more than obvious. I may only note that the problem is not always stated in the same way. Thus, in some formal system intended to represent some kind of theoretical reconstruction of how a specific text comes about – this vague formulation is deliberate – categories like 'TEMP' or 'TEMPORAL', or something like 'temporal indices' appear, the meaning of which is intuitively fairly clear: it corresponds in some way with traditional notions like 'tense', 'time phrase', or 'time adverbial'; or one may find, in the discussion of 'intersententional relations" – in contradistinction to "sentententional description of tenses" – mention of the necessity of

> a thorough treatment of the status of temporal elements in underlying structures, e.g. in terms of a tense logic[9]

and the fact that we are

> still more ignorant ... about the temporal relations between the sentences of a coherent sequence, although we intuitively know that such temporal relations are crucial for textual well-formedness[10].

Clearly, "temporal elements in underlying structures" may refer to a variety of things, for instance, to 'tenses' only, to 'time adverbials' only, to other 'time-representational' elements, e.g. implicit in semantemes, etc., or the expression may refer exclusively to the *theoretical* constructs representing all that (and perhaps more), whereas "temporal relations" between sentences, again ambiguous, must denote something else, for instance, the purely surface relations of sentences as manifest objects, or the relations between the 'content' of the sentences, or, again, the relations between the theoretical representations of sentences... – Now, a brief and merely intuitive examination of the problems involved in the *textual* role of just *one* kind of 'temporal' linguistic element, to put it loosely, e.g. 'tense', quickly and disappointingly shows that, in order to arrive at something reasonably interesting, *all* the 'temporal' elements (whatever that be!) at work in a text must be considered and related theoretically. This fact has not always been recognised and, as a matter of fact, still seems to be little known or hardly respected, in particular by text-grammarians and text-linguists of a specifically formal or deductivist orientation. (I may note in passing that the expression 'temporal element' is intended to be understood ambiguously *venia verbo*, i.e. as meaning both 'elements' of 'time' as something *non*-verbal and prior to language, *and* 'elements' of time representation in language of the kind already hinted at, e.g. morphemes like *year/Jahr*, *are/bist-seid-sind*, *present/gegenwärtig*, *annual/yearly/jähr-*

[9] T. A. van Dijk [25], p. 9.
[10] *Ibid.*, p. 81.

lich, *last/take/dauern*, *interval/pause/Intervall/Pause*, etc.) This fact is an empirical argument for the necessity of text linguistics as well as a heuristic hint to the effect that the class of 'temporal' ingredients in a given (accepted, i.e. functional) text must be studied as an *integral component of that text's 'semantics'* (in which I should include what, *per analogiam*, has become current as 'pragmatics'; cf. infra).

To say this is clearly old hat. It has not only been stated repeatedly by traditional linguists, e.g. – to quote from the extensive relevant work of a much-maligned man – by Hans Glinz, who has maintained in innumerable statements that the problem of the tenses must be attacked through a "Feinanalyse von Texten"[11] and that "die Darstellung von Zeit" may be achieved through a great variety of means and is connected intimately with other aspects of not merely a *syntactical* and *lexical* kind (such as mood, aspect, lexical categories) but, moreover, of a strictly *textual* nature, as with the

> ...Aufbau des Textes überhaupt und ... Ort der betreffenden Aussage im Gesamttext, relativ nicht nur zu dem im gleichen Satzzusammenhang Gesagten ... sondern relativ zu vielen früheren und späteren Aussagen ... Gesamtcharakter des Textes.[12]

This is also clearly apparent in some of the most recent investigations of problems connected with 'tense', for instance, in Hauser-Suida/Hoppe-Beugel's corpus-based description of the 'Vergangenheitstempora' of German, and, in particular, D. Wunderlich's attempt to provide an explicit description of both syntax and semantics of German time reference in the wake of transformational generative grammar.

Wunderlich states explicitly,

> Mit der Aussage, ein bestimmtes Tempus ... müsse kotextrelativ interpretiert werden, ist ... impliziert, daß sich eine ausführliche Untersuchung des Tempusgebrauchs nicht mit isolierten Sätzen begnügen kann, sondern Texte zugrundelegen muß.[13]

He proceeds accordingly to give a brief sketch of problems related with the "Prozesse der Textkonstitution" and elaborates a little on the concept of "Zeitstruktur eines Textes", a notion much used in traditional philology and literary criticism, both under the label 'Zeitstruktur' and the still more popular one of 'Zeitgestaltung'[14]. Wunderlich is, *per la forza delle cose*, led to very basic modifications of the apparatus of generative transformational grammar which culminate in the introduction of pragmatic concepts meant

[11] H. Glinz [39], p. 111, Note 82.
[12] idem [40], p. 51.
[13] [108], p. 102.
[14] [108], p. 108ff. – Traditional work on text constitution and textual time structure is centred in narrative theory whose evolution has found a first definitive expression integrating earlier perspectives (in particular those of English scholars and authors) in the work of F. K. Stanzel which, apart from concentrating on the mediating process of a narration and its structure, has taken up the perspectives opened up by G. Müller. Müller

to represent certain relationships between verbal items and the situations they are uttered in. In a similar way to Wunderlich's – his most important ideas will be taken up briefly again – W. E. Bull is induced to strongly modify his original linguistic perspectives when confronted with the phenomena of time reference (by 'tense' mainly) and to argue for what he calls "systemic linguistics". Bull's concern with texts is, however, only implicit in formulations like the following:

> ...it is impossible to arrive at a satisfactory description of the function of a part without an adequate description of the nature and function of the whole.
>
> ...it may be exceedingly difficult or impossible to isolate all the parts without a thorough understanding of the function of the whole.

and especially in such 'pragmatic' statements as:

> ...the process by which a message is sent from man to man is not a system of arbitrary vocal symbols. Vocal symbols, to be sure, are used in the operation, but it has been demonstrated ... that the symbol system cannot function, cannot convey a meaningful message, without a nonsymbolic axis of orientation (the event of speaking) and without the active cooperation of the listener who derives pertinent information from a variety of nonsymbolic factors (common focus, the interaction of systems, cultural conventions, and so on). Under these conditions, the whole of which the tense system is a part is clearly something of greater magnitude than the sum of the observable vocal symbols which are said to constitute language.
>
> Precisely what constitutes this greater whole remains to be explored, but it can hardly be denied that the function of the vocal symbols in the process of sending messages cannot

---

has remained known for a couple of concepts, e.g. the distinction between 'Erzählzeit' and 'erzählte Zeit', or his notion of the 'Zeitgerüst' of a narrative. Cf. [69].

It must also be mentioned in this context that much work has been done by linguists like K. Boost, H. Brinkmann, and H. Glinz, whose views have been formed by the demands of their practical work: they have found the traditional distinction between 'normal' and 'literary' texts inadequate in teaching, for instancc, and have therefore insisted on the 'unity' of linguistic and literary textual work. In their research which represents a 'text-linguistic' tradition of at least four decades – the emphasis is on *linguistic*, not literary, or bibliographical aspects of texts only – there is special discussion of the 'relativity' of the sentence as a unit of theoretical description and the primary importance of discourse or text. In that context it has been pointed out repeatedly by Boost that a complete verbal utterance ("sprachliche Darstellung") represents a "Spannungsraum" ('space of tensions') established by the ordered arrangement and integration of the individual sentences. And here the question of the time structure is raised frequently by Boost who stresses that it is difficult to draw a straight line between grammar and stylistics. Similar views have been presented by Brinkmann and Glinz. I shall briefly mention Glinz's approach to the time structure of a text below. – Cf. Boost [12], [13], [14], Brinkmann [16], [17], [18], [19], Glinz [38], [39], [41], [42], [43], [44].

It is therefore self-evident from all this work by Boost, Brinkmann, and Glinz, that grammar is subservient to a comprehensive linguistic account of the functioning of language in discourse (as it appears in more durable form as 'text'), and that grammatical categories like 'tense' can only be profitably investigated within that unrestricted functional context. It has been H. Glinz, in particular, who has been insisting on a 'text-linguistic' approach for nearly three decades: text linguistics both as the basis *and* the goal of linguistic theorizing.

be accurately described without an analysis of the function of the nonsymbolic and nonvocal factors involved in the operation.[15]

To avoid misunderstanding, however, let me add quickly that Bull's views must not be identified with those of theoretical linguists in the narrow sense, i.e. also those underlying Wunderlich's book on time reference in German despite the latter's introduction of 'pragmatics'. Bull's critical remarks will be taken up again below as they are well in accord with the views to be outlined in the following. Though there will be little space, a few more remarks on Bull's criticism of linguistics in connection with my attempt to sketch an adequate framework for text-linguistic research will make his position clearer. Here it is enough to indicate that Bull's work, together with the work by other researchers, has not only confirmed the assumption that 'tense' is an essential element of texts but also the contention that 'tense' can only be studied sensibly in conjunction with the complete semantics (including pragmatics) of a text. He has furthermore encouraged another assumption which will be made a little more explicit presently, namely the assumption that 'text' denotes something which is *part* of a "greater whole" that "remains to be explored" and thus 'transcends' language and includes "nonsymbolic and nonvocal factors" among which "the interaction of systems" is of particular importance. This again links up with what H. Glinz said about the 'positional value' of a predication and the overall structure(s) involved in a text. Finally, mention must be made of H. Weinrich's essentially pragmatic approach to text linguistics and the problem of 'tense'. Though Weinrich's ways of arguing are neither always clear nor always acceptable he has clearly left the confines of a narrow and form-bound linguistics and thus made a step, however disputable, in the direction of an integrated study of language functioning.

These scattered remarks which will, I hope, gain a little more shape in the following systematic discussion, are of course in no way intended to give a survey report on the state of 'tense' research. This is outside the scope of this paper and also of secondary importance to the main topic to be developed. Some general remarks on the main tendencies of previous research into temporal phenomena in language will be given below, bibliographic information is given in the notes. – The main point of these introductory remarks was to motivate the title 'Time and Text' as embodying the contention that for *an adequate study of linguistic phenomena, linguistics will not be enough*, and that this is particularly true of the study of texts and the study of the temporal elements of texts (whereby 'temporal' is to be taken in both its meanings). It may also have become clear that the elaboration of the "greater whole" a

[15] Bull [21], p. 109.

text is part of, is a gigantic task and will require immense future research work. To attempt drawing a rough sketch of how this might be done adequately is the point of the present essay. Its ensuing sections will deal with the metatheoretical paradigm underlying the approach, the model of language-functioning as the overall framework for all 'punctual' work, and finally a few global hints at the problems of time and text in the sense indicated briefly above: extra-linguistic/nonsymbolic time (as constituent of text), inherent/implicit temporal elements, explicit temporal elements.

2. Note on the 'meta-theoretical paradigm'

It is standard knowledge today that there is no way of justifying any form of intellectual enterprise and its results as 'ultimate' and 'true' in an absolute sense. Thus all attempts to base human 'scientific' activity on a foundation that is unshakably and absolutely and universally, etc., true are bound to lead to an infinite regress or to become viciously circular and dogmatic. There is no difference in principle in this as far as the natural and the social, or cultural, sciences are concerned, as has become particularly clear from the research work on the foundations of either group in the last few decades. All scientific work is therefore ultimately based on, and conditioned by, a set of what may still be called 'values'. Such values will generally belong to the overall *weltanschauung* of the individual concerned and be effective on various levels of consciousness, i.e. they will be both of a global, emotional, and intuitive kind and of a more articulate, rational, and explicit kind, – all depending on the person's experience. The decision to work scientifically involves thus the acceptance of specific norms of action controlling all further experience (immediate and instrument-aided) in such a way as to make it communicable, i.e. accessible to the whole community of all those who have also chosen to work under the restrictions mentioned, but not for mutual entertainment only. Science can only progress through cooperation and economical division of labour so as to avoid all duplication of effort and to guarantee the continual elimination of error. Thus the progress of science may indeed be likened to a 'game' (with K. R. Popper) and the decision to practise science then becomes an ethical decision to accept the rules of this particular game and to play fair. The rules of this game of science are certainly not only methodological rules, nor are methodological rules the most important. Indeed, the term 'rule' does not seem to cover all the relevant determinants at work in a scientific community. A convenient term summarizing, though in rather global fashion, what *does* in effect define a scientific community or a "generation of practitioners", has been introduced by Th. S. Kuhn: it is the term 'paradigm'. It is a 'paradigm' which is acquired by the individual who wants to be initiated into the scientific community, and which directs his adjustment to a given "tradition of scientific research", i.e. defines "the legitimate problems and methods of a research field" through the complex training and conditioning the adept receives in the course of his initiation (which, as is well known, may extend over decades).[16] – This is not the place to enlarge on a discussion of these matters, however, and I shall therefore content myself with indicating a few most relevant references, and with just quoting one passage from Kuhn's book that seems particularly appropriate in the present context as it highlights the conflict between what has already been roughly epitomized as 'pure' and 'applied' science, in particular, as 'pure' or 'theoretical', and 'applied' or 'practical' linguistics:

> ...one of the things a scientific community acquires with a paradigm is a criterion for choosing problems that, while the paradigm is taken for granted, can be assumed to have solutions. To a great extent these are the only problems that the community will admit as scientific or encourage its members to undertake. Other problems, including many that had previously been standard, are rejected as metaphysical, as the concern of another discipline, or sometimes as just too problematic to be worth the time. A paradigm can, for that matter, even insulate the community from those socially important problems that are not reducible to the puzzle form i.e. a form the criterion of which is 'the assured existence of a solution' because they cannot be stated in terms of the conceptual and instrumental tools the paradigm supplies.[17]

It is no exaggeration to state that such evaluations occur daily and hourly within any scientific community. Linguistics is no exception; on the contrary, in linguistics especially, as in all other social or cultural sciences, the competition of paradigms is more than obvious and takes up a large part of the scientific activity itself. I should interpret this fact as a good sign: as scientific inquiry and its results are intimately connected with, and conditioned by, the underlying paradigm, it is part of the ethics of the researcher to be explicit and critical as to the tacit assumptions and values and motives and all other experience he introduces into the research process. It must in particular be part of his playing the game of science fair to lay his 'paradigm' open to intersubjective critical discussion and testing. Obviously there will be continual disagreement as there is no hard-and-fast method of establishing what is 'right' and 'true' and 'adequate'. The final choices are determined by more or less 'personal' values (of both a metaphysical nature and a political nature, to state the two extremes). Much may here depend on the ways and

[16] Cf. the references in Note 4. As to science as a 'game', cf. Popper [75] p. 53. Cf. also the important contributions to the discussion of the bases and determinants of scientific research *in toto* by W. Heisenberg [51], A. I. Wittenberg [106], and in particular H. Stachowiak [85] who presents an integrated discussion of all relevant aspects in precise terminology, something particularly welcome in the present situation, p. 95ff.

[17] Kuhn [63], p. 37.

means chosen for discussion, on whether the tenets of 'critical rationality' are accepted or whether other, more 'intuitive', more 'spirited', more 'original' – to voice but a few common clichés – ways of debating are cherished.

These rather scattered hints may be sufficient illustration of the integral role a chosen 'metatheoretical paradigm' will play in the practice of scientific inquiry. (For numerous illustrations cf. Kuhn's book.) Criticism of the global notion of 'paradigm' is unnecessary at this stage: as already stated I am using the term merely as a convenient abbreviation for the set of determinants (pre- or sub-rational to rational) conditioning practical research work and thus demanding explicit statement at the outset of any concrete project. I shall then proceed to state in concise form the 'meta-theoretical paradigm' of text-linguistic research as I see it at the moment. (Needless to say, in that the following is *not* 'explicit' in the specific sense of a formal system's explicitness, the reader is therefore requested to use his intuition and his intelligence to decode what is only expressed informally.)

2.1. I am not in favour of 'pure' research in the sense of a self-contained and isolated hunt for 'truth-in-itself', or as an expression of some obscure anthropological universal named 'the human striving or yearning for knowledge *per se*'. I am convinced that such metaphysical and even utopian goals can be dangerous and misleading (though they need not be inane or useless either in themselves, or by definition) and produce consequences that flatly contradict the pre-established aims and their premisses, i.e. they may inspire only too easily what P. Watzlawik has recently called the "utopia syndrome".[18]

It is important not to confuse the indicated conception of 'pure' research with the postulate of the necessary 'independence of scientific inquiry', i.e. its freedom from political or economic constraints and ties, its unlimited freedom to experiment, to cooperate and communicate over and through all political, national, and 'ideological' (in the narrow sense) boundaries.

Again, I cannot discuss the many problems involved here, in particular the questions relating to the criteria used in the decision as to the overall aim of scientific inquiry. I shall merely state that I consider scientific research as *one* mode of goal-directed activity amongst others (e.g. the artistic mode, the various 'intuitive' modes of everyday life), though as a most efficient mode as to its economy, reliability, and durability, i.e. as an activity that must yield more and more instrumental ploys to master the 'world' or, more specifically, the (both physical and cultural) ecosphere of humans, and must *help* to improve this mastery and control according to accepted 'standards of hap-

[18] Watzlawick [100]. Cf. also the references to Acham, Topitsch, and Albert, in note 4 for extensive discussion of the theoretical and practical consequences of the 'ideologization' of human work, i.e. also science.

piness' (which, in themselves, are also a legitimate subject of scientific discussion). To quote K. R. Popper's formulation:

> I ... believe that there is at least one ... problem in which all thinking men are interested. It is the problem of cosmology: *the problem of understanding the world – including ourselves, and our knowledge, as part of the world.*[19]

In the present connection I may perhaps be allowed to speak of the basic problem of 'anthropo-cosmology', i.e. of the problem of understanding this our human existence, of articulating such understanding in an explicit and controllable way so as to allow for the necessary manipulation of the 'world' with regard to specific wants, necessities, wishes, etc., in accord with a specific, socially accepted, set of values or goals which are considered to constitute a 'better' life, a 'better' world. Science thus has, in my opinion, to work towards a *continual 'optimization'* of *this* our life und world. *Not*, as pointed out above, towards some obscure 'utopia'.

This definition of the overall aim of scientific inquiry holds without any reservation or restriction for linguistics also. Thus the results of the scientific study of language functioning must allow for better manipulation of language functioning in every sense: in the public spheres of political discussion, of legal formulation, of commercial or ideological persuasion, of education and instruction of all sorts, of medical treatment, of translating and interpreting, of all critical debate, of all scientific communication, analysis and interpretation, etc.; no less, however, in the private sphere of personal communication of all sorts, e.g. in critical discussion of conflicts, in the various kinds of rhetoric used in the education of children of all ages, in the development of sound standards of critical judging of all kinds, etc. etc. There is surely no need to extensively discuss pertinent demands and goals as to an 'optimization' of language functioning. And I have used the term 'manipulation' deliberately to point to a now (and always) much-discussed case of language exploitation for certain interests, if only to show how important a channel language is for the (non-violent) mobilization of humans towards certain goals.[20]

A province of fundamental importance is education and teaching in which language quite obviously is of first-rate importance. It is especially the disappointment and frustration arising from a comparison of what goes on in scientific research and what goes on in schools which accounts for the explicit emphasis on the postulate that science should provide means for an *immediate optimization of practice*; i.e. in this case: facts and insights that

[19] Popper [75], p. 15. Popper refers to 'philosophy', but I think his formulation is applicable to scientific research in general.

[20] A discussion of concrete cases of linguistic manipulation with reference to the present German situation is given in [61].

could improve the functioning of language with children as well as adults, and thus, globally, improve their minds and actions, and as well improve *all* teaching inasmuch it is conducted via, and dependent on, language. There is a most deplorable gap between the 'splendid isolation' of universities, the no less characteristic, but less 'splendid', isolation of teachers' training colleges (now universities too), and the dreary realities of 'school linguistics' which consists in little more than the repetitive inculcation of useless pseudo-grammatical 'facts', discriminatory pseudo-stylistic 'text types' (which, in fact, are nothing but strategies for curbing and starving children's creativity, and condition their minds in a trite and completely pointless manner), extensive drill in superficials, as this is easiest to control, e.g. orthography, word collecting, etc., and perhaps some attempted work on textual analysis and interpretation, largely governed by the teacher's idiosyncrasies or hobby-horses... And, to conclude, what modern theoretical linguistics has offered so far, has, by and large, not improved the situation, but made it worse. It is precisely this demand, then, of being useful in practice, which accounts for the epithet 'adequate' in the title of this essay. A theoretical result is 'adequate' then and only then, when it allows for an 'optimization' of language functioning, when it permits effective manipulation and control of the phenomenon of language.[21]

It must be emphasized, however, that the plea for adequacy as voiced here aims primarily at the establishment of a *non-reductionist paradigm for linguistic research*, a paradigm that cannot be accused of reducing a complex phenomenon to bits and pieces which can then, 'at last', be studied 'scientifically', i.e. in accordance with certain pre-established standards of rigour and exactness making for status and political prestige rather than tangible and instrumental results. There *is* much *charlatanerie* in the attempts to force a complex phenomenon – and this intuitive postulate will surely be accepted without precise definition – "into the preformed and relatively inflexible box" (or boxes)[22] supplied by a paradigm developed in a different context for different purposes and based on a mentality – not even a philosophical and critical 'ethics' – of happy-go-lucky pragmatism and so-called down-to-earth reductivism: what you can do with a biro, i.e. take it to bits, make a million of each bit, put the bits together again, and there are a million biros, – this you can do with anything, i.e. also with language... (I must disregard all the political implications of such an attitude, e.g. the criteria of efficiency derived from it, the ideology of specialization which directly emerges from reductivism, the overall conditioning towards 'one-dimensionality' and technocracy, etc. etc.) Let me briefly illustrate this important point by a couple of

[21] I have tried to sketch what is implied in teaching a foreign language in [59].
[22] Kuhn [63], p. 24 (cf. also p. 5).

quotations from the book of a scientist, which can be applied directly to the study of language functioning:

> Science stands today on something of a divide. For two centuries it has been exploring systems that are either intrinsically simple or that are capable of being analysed into simple components. The fact that such a dogma as 'vary the factors one at a time' could be accepted for a century, shows that scientists were largely concerned in investigating such systems as *allowed* this method; for this method is often fundamentally impossible in the complex systems.
>
> ...there are complex systems that just do not allow the varying of only one factor at a time – they are so dynamic and interconnected that the alteration of one factor immediately acts as cause to evoke alterations in others, perhaps in a great many others. Until recently, science tended to evade the study of such systems, focusing its attention on those that were simple and, especially, reducible...[23]

By 'reducible' Ashby means that some 'whole' or system consists of parts or sub-systems that are "functionally independent", i.e. of parts that may indeed be studied independently of the greater whole. There is another point to be added: reductivism is bound to generate a paradigm that is endowed with the blind belief that all things can be taken to bits without loss, i.e. can be analysed so as to be re-synthesized again afterwards. This view (though certainly fruitful and effective with reducible systems and with systems that are reduced, or apparently reduced, *correctly*, i.e. without severing the functional ties between the components) implies the belief that the functioning of the whole is the sum total of the functioning of the bits. I may be allowed to illustrate this again:

> Another example showing how contradictory may be the properties in the small and the large is given by an ordinary piece of elastic. For years physical chemists searched for what made the molecule contractile.... It is now known that the rubber molecule has no inherent contractility: stretch one out and let it go, and nothing happens! Why then does rubber contract? The point is that 'stretching rubber' is not 'stretching *one*...'; the molecules, when there are more than one, jostle each other and thereby force the majority to take lengths less than their maxima....
>
> ...the point to be made is the merely negative one that in a large system there is no *a priori* necessity for the properties of the whole to be a simple copy of those of the parts.
>
> ...in such cases the scientist must be very careful about what questions he asks.[24]

I cannot say more about the problem of reducibility and reductionism here, but I shall conclude with a quotation from the book of another cybernetician on the same problem, which may be justified precisely because I shall try to outline a cybernetic scheme for the integrated study of language functioning; a scheme the status and limitations of which are most important to be recognised; a scheme the *instrumental* (= heuristic) value of which must not be transformed by a wrong process of identification into an ideological or metaphysical hypostatization! The model to be presented (presently) is

[23] Ashby [7], p. 5, p. 60.

[24] Ashby [7], pp. 112–113.

nothing but a kind of auxiliary geometric locus of all the relevant problems given by language functioning, it is in no way a mechanistic reduction of language to machines' or, worse still, the postulation of a utopian automaton reproducing the intellectual faculties of a human being, of an android that can speak:

Es wird nicht bedacht, daß *Abstraktion nicht Reduktion ist* im Sinne einer Zurückführung der verschiedenen Wirkungsgefüge etwa auf mechanische Systeme. Es wird dann nicht mehr von einer Analogie zwischen verschiedenartigen Systemen aufgrund bestimmter gemeinsamer Merkmale gesprochen, sondern es wird Identität behauptet. Man meint mit der Kenntnis der formalen Struktur der Wirkungsverknüpfung einen Sachverhalt vollständig erfaßt zu haben.... Das ist eine unzulässige und gefährliche Überbeanspruchung einer an sich fruchtbaren Methode: die Kybernetik gelangt zu bedeutungsvollen und allgemeinen Einsichten, weil sie von den Qualitäten abstrahiert. Aber gerade weil sie abstrahiert, bleiben *ihre Aussagen für jede Art qualitativer Interpretation offen.*[25]

After these scattered meta-theoretical points one brief note remains to be made: an 'adequate' heuristics can be envisaged as a paradigm reflecting that whole 'object' which, by some intuitive process, has been preconceptualized as an 'object' and thus offers itself for analysis and description as well as explanation. Needless to say that we are far from such an 'adequate' paradigm in linguistics. Only the establishment of a paradigm which is adequate in the sense characterized will allow for posing the right questions and trying to devise ways and means of answering them. Only then might one speak of having reached something like an 'adequate heuristics' guiding concrete work towards relevant goals, however difficult the work may be, however far from a (questionable) 'ideal of optimal exactness' it may lead. An 'adequate heuristics' is, however, not to be misunderstood in the sense of a set of defined discovery procedures guaranteeing success in research. Nor must there be misunderstanding as to 'inductive' and 'deductive' approaches: I do believe that the traditional, currently unpopular, way of first 'mucking about with the data' – to paraphrase Paul Ziff – and then trying to construct a hypothesis that will cover what one has found, is despite certain (questionable) arguments to the contrary, the most economical and adequate way to arrive at a substantially supported hypothesis and to avoid useless duplication of effort and multiple confusion on the way. Thus I do not agree with the current infatuation with 'deductivism' and the legalization of any private hypothesizing on the grounds that the researcher is a 'competent native speaker' himself. This is pouring the baby out with the bath-water: as there is no (absolute) inductive way, there can only be (absolute) deductive proceeding. I think that adequate heuristics has nothing to do with so narrow an approach as 'taxonomy' which seems pre-determined in every respect, but

[25] Sachsse [110], p. 7; cf. also especially pp. 231ff. ("Leistungen und Grenzen der kybernetischen Betrachtungsweise").

that it must be considered a multiple-path trial-and-error process leading from one hypothesis to another, constantly testing and modifying the intermediate 'ideas', to finally arrive at a conceptual framework which can be stated in somewhat explicit fashion so as to become available to other researchers as a well-supported framework that can be understood and tested by them. This is the only way to arrive at hypotheses, and finally theories, which are empirically relevant and may meet the demands of 'optimization of practice' that were voiced above. This also shows the place where formal instruments come in: *after* the range of phenomena one has been confronted with has been ordered into 'objects', 'properties', and their relations with each other. Every available 'formal system' has grown out of certain basic and intuitive concepts and has proceeded from there to state new concepts of all sorts and categories. To apply a formal system to a chaotic mass of 'empirical matter' thus automatically introduces the concepts underlying the formal system into that empirical domain – something which is basically inadmissible and has never been done in science, but seems to be one prevalent procedure in theoretical linguistics. I am aware of the gross generalization involved in these statements of mine, but I am sure the perceptive reader will interpret them in the right way and deduce the relevant point: only after the necessary intuitive pre-conceptualization into 'objects' and 'properties' or some such thing of a given empirical domain one wants to explain and, consequently, to control, can formalization or axiomatization be considered; to quote a mathematician:

> After an intuitive theory has been advanced to the point where its basic properties are believed known, and reliable predictions can be made with it, an axiomatization can be attempted. The first step is to list what are judged to be the basic objects discussed by the theory together with what are judged to be a set of fundamental properties which are true of these objects. Then symbols are introduced ... [26]

These remarks do not, of course, concern the status of the formal sciences in the research process: in mathematics (as now, it seems, in physics) every-

[26] Stoll [90], pp. 125–126. – I cannot resist quoting the passionate statement of J. v. Uexküll defending his 'functional' approach to the study of animal systems against the mechanistic ideas of some of his contemporaries:

> "Grundsätzlich muß ich bemerken, daß es eine Irreführung ist, wenn man (1) statt eines Kunsthistorikers einen Chemiker beauftragt, ein Bild zu beurteilen; (2) wenn man statt einem Musiker einem Physiker die Beurteilung einer Symphonie anvertraut; (3) wenn man, statt einen Biologen heranzuziehen, einem Mechaniker das Recht zugesteht, die Realität der Handlungen aller Lebewesen nur soweit anzuerkennen, als sie dem Gesetz der Erhaltung der Energie gehorchen.
> Natürlich widerspricht diese Auffassung dem 'Gesetz der Denkökonomie', mit dem sich die Mechanisten das Forschen so leicht gemacht haben. Aber Probleme beiseite schieben, heißt nicht sie lösen.

thing is possible. What is at issue here is the *use* of formal systems and an aprioristic deductivist strategy in empirical fields. This is part of a general reductivist ideology which I hold to be inadequate for the problems in hand.

2.2. Having discussed my own meta-theoretical paradigm briefly, a few words must be said about the instrumental apparatus to be used. With all the reservations made in the preceding section I should commit myself to what has come to be called 'critical rationality', i.e. to an attitude which involves the acceptance of the priority of experience, logic, and critical discussion of research practice over personal 'revelation' and metaphysical or dogmatic postulationism. This involves also the willingness to try to be as explicit as possible in the statement of the determinants, strategies, procedures, and results of one's research and thus to invite critical and rational discussion on all levels. It implies also, and this is a point rarely observed, the readiness to take into account the linguistic difficulties of explicit communication, i.e. to be willing to try to understand the *other's* points at all cost and to place the potential mistakes first within oneself, and only on careful intersubjective examination accuse the other partner.

Critical rationality has proved to be effective. Its constraints are often hard to take but have nevertheless always made for clarity and explicitness in thought and practice so as to make it possible to discover errors and correct them, to improve cooperation for mutual benefit, – in short: to acquire useful knowledge. The necessity of clarity is to be emphasized in particular and I should not hesitate to quote a much-laboured sentence of Francis Bacon's: "Truth emerges more readily from error than from confusion". The point is that 'error' is specifiable and that 'confusion' is not...

3. Brief Sketch of a Model of Language Functioning

3.1. The Anthropo-Cybernetic Model of the System 'Man-World'

...the real objects are in fact all Black Boxes ... and ... we have in fact been operating with Black Boxes all our lives. The theory of the Black Box is merely the theory of real

---

Betrachten wir die Fortschritte der Lebensforschung der letzten Jahrzehnte, soweit sie im Zeichen des 'Behaviorismus' und der 'bedingten Reflexe' gestanden haben, so kann man wohl sagen, daß das Experimentieren immer komplizierter, das Denken aber immer einfacher und billiger geworden ist.

Billiges Denken wirkt wie eine ansteckende Krankheit und erstickt alle Ansätze einer selbständigen Weltanschauung im großen Publikum..."

Uexküll/Kriszat [96] pp. 168–179.

Cf. also the remarks made above in note 2; and some further reference in [60], pp. 18ff. and note 10.

objects or systems, when close attention is given to the question, relating object and observer, about what information comes from the object, and how it is obtained.[27]

It may be useful to bear in mind that the relationship between observer and 'object' is a crucial one as regards the kind of 'knowledge' scientific research may obtain. The interdependence of observation and 'fact' has become especially clear from scientific research of this century and has thus also become part of the basic teaching of the modern philosophy of science and theory of knowledge: a 'fact' is determined by a 'theoretical' approach. – What needs mentioning in this context is the 'converse' of that statement, so to speak: there is no way of 'deriving' or 'inferring' theories from facts. As the 'world' – for *us* – is nothing but a mass of Black Boxes all we can do is to devise models and schemes that seem to 'reflect' in some way or other what 'goes on' in those Black Boxes, and thus allow us to manipulate and perhaps control them. Theories are therefore inventions of the human mind and just a special class of the set of inventions which help him to survive. This is neither new nor original. I have stated it only because the following sketch of a model is just another 'invention' that I should like to propose as a suitable framework for the study of language, a framework, however, that seems quite well-motivated and empirically plausible to me. I do certainly not maintain that this is a model *of* language functioning: it is nothing but an outline of a scheme representing the 'functional frame' within which a model of language functioning could well be developed in an empirically adequate way. The following sketch thus is a very tentative scheme meant to orientate work "towards an adequate heuristics", i.e. a paradigm which generates the 'right' = 'relevant' questions with some hope of solution.[28]

The idea of the Black Box when applied to the problem of language leads immediately to questions like "How does language behave?" or "What does

[27] Ashby [7], p. 110. As to the epistemological problems concerning 'observer' and 'reality' which have become crucial in physics and the research in the foundations of mathematics in this century, cf. Heisenberg [51], Wittenberg [106], Popper [75]. It must be noted that the consequences of these developments are of a practical nature (however ardently philosophers may speak of the 'relativity' of observation and the new 'modesty' of all science, etc.): the practical problems of devising effective means to control part of reality remain given as concrete tasks, and what has been thrown into relief is the absolute necessity of examining one's standpoint and calculating its 'creative' effect on what one does!

[28] This has been stated in a most pronounced way by Albert Einstein in a letter to K. R. Popper, from which I should like to quote the relevant bit in Popper's translation:

> "Altogether I really do not at all like the now fashionable... 'positivistic' tendency of clinging to what is observable. I regard it as trivial that one cannot, in the range of atomic magnitudes, make predictions with any desired degree of precision, and I think (like you, by the way) that theory cannot be fabricated out of the results of observation, but that it can only be invented."
>
> Popper [75], p. 458.

language do?" or "How does language function?". The history of linguistics shows that varying paradigms have provided varying answers to this kind of question. And, in fact, there have been many other disciplines which have occupied themselves with this problem in one way or another: philosophy, psychology, sociology, theology, or also mathematics. Obviously language may be studied under quite a number of perspectives and I have already hinted at the necessity to make the determinants of one's approach explicit as part of the whole scientific enterprise. Thus, as regards my own meta-theoretical paradigm and the corresponding notion of adequacy, the question of "How does language function?" cannot be answered in a down-to-earth empirical way outside an anthropological context: if, as we can observe in this age, language is discovered to be of enormous importance and influence in the working of the human mind and of human society at large, then any attempt to construct a theory that permits practical control of language functioning (for better or worse, according to interest and power) cannot but try to find out about the connections between the human mind and his natural and cultural environment. This inevitably leads into biology *via* physical anthropology, as humans share all the characteristics of living systems with the animal kingdom. Language, however, seems to be their prerogative if not a necessary instrument to assure survival and make for satisfactory existence.

Though there is no space to deal with all these questions in detail I shall make a few very brief and global remarks. – Biological research has demonstrated convincingly that every animal is part of a system 'animal-environment' the two sub-systems of which, 'animal' and 'environment', are closely interrelated and mutually dependent. J. v. Uexküll, a pioneer in what is now called 'ethology', was the first to investigate the systematic relationships between various animals and their environments. He introduced the basic notion of 'Funktionskreis' ('functional cycle') into biology and thus added to the familiar concepts of matter and energy as the only categories with which animal organisms and their relations to an ecosystem were studied, the concept of 'information' in the sense of a fixed and hereditary plan or programme of systematic behaviour. Thus a given animal is functionally related with the world it is to live in: it will perceive only signals determined as relevant by its set of instincts, it will react only to 'meaningful' stimuli in a predetermined 'meaningful' way, using what it had also developed from birth in the form of organs to make its behaviour effective (e.g. defend itself, reproduce itself, feed itself, etc.). Thus 'animal' and 'animal world' are in every single respect strictly related, they form a functional system. – This approach has now become standard in biology, and the disciplines of ecology and ethology have supplied numerous examples of such systematic connection and interaction between animal and animal environment.

What is important to note is that the animal is completely 'programmed' right from birth: it can survive more or less on its own very shortly after having been born (not so humans!) as it is fully equipped both as to the necessary 'information' (in form of instincts and reaction patterns etc.) and the necessary instruments (organs of all kinds). Thus an animal's 'language' is determined in all respects: its syntax, semantics, and pragmatics, as well as its phonology are fixed right from the start, unambiguous, and more or less 'automatic'. And indeed there is no need for the animal to be flexible: its life is perfectly regulated.

The human situation on the other hand lacks precisely this pre-determinedness: there is no fixed programme of instincts, no inventory of action-schemata, no well-developed set of organs, no clearly defined habitable and secure environment. A human is born absolutely helpless and absolutely deprived of all instrumental equipment for survival. It needs careful looking-after and intensive training for years to be able to walk and act and perform its basic life functions on its own. Every human being is thus born unprogrammed; it must be 'programmed' and trained to survive. This can only be done by social cooperation as the baby would die soon after birth. And what is more: the lack of a clearly defined world to live in securely and safely forces the human being to adapt in various ways to various environments and to be prepared to 'act' again and again, all through his life as a matter of fact, in unseen and unforeseen situations. This is only possible if the human being is able to store experience and to derive standards of evaluation of external situations from that experience so as to be able to predict and evaluate potential situations (e.g. of danger, of support, etc.). Thus a human is forced to construct a model of his world by which he can safely live, i.e. not only survive, but also exist in what he may varyingly term 'a happy way'. Such an internally stored model of the outside world enables the human being to 'think', i.e. to construct 'possible' situations, consider their value, and decide on either choosing or avoiding them. Again, however, no single human could manage to collect this kind of experience himself: he would die many times in the process. Thus again the social community takes over and provides some of the necessary 'experience' through teaching or practical instruction in such measure as to enable the individual to survive by himself. [29]

[29] By 'anthropology' I do, of course, understand *empirical* anthropology and not primarily metaphysical interpretations of the human condition, as they often appear under the heading 'philosophical anthropology'. Thus it is mainly the work of the following researchers I have relied on, though obviously the task of an 'empirical anthropology' is an enormous one and would need much more detailed research: A. Portmann [76], E. Rothacker [83], J. v. Uexküll [96], F. Thienemann [91], K. Lorenz [66] (in particular also his epistemological essays 'Induktive und teleologische Psychologie', 1942, Vol. 1, pp. 380–

Now even this extremely crude picture of the elementary functioning of the human situation will make it clear where language has to come in. Before however, I proceed to describe in a little more detail where the functional position and, consequently, the characteristic nature and performance of language for a human being must be located in this anthropological picture, it will be useful to make the picture more precise and easier to handle by means of an illustration. For this purpose the means of *cybernetics* have proved to be of great help, and not only practical in presenting the *anthropological* data in a graphic and coherent way but also as a set of valuable heuristic instruments and techniques. This can easily be seen from pertinent discussions of which I should like to mention here only one, and with special emphasis, as it has tackled the most intricate problems of both epistemology and theory of knowledge (including philosophy of science) in the most convincing manner: it is H. Stachowiak's *Denken und Erkennen im kybernetischen Modell.* The application of the basic ideas of cybernetics to a set of problems, which, so far, have been occupying different fields like psychology, philosophy, biology (in particular bio-anthropology, physiology, and neurology), and logic and mathematics, has made it possible to gain a coherent and consistent picture of the basic systems and processes underlying, and thus unifying, the diverse 'facts' discussed by the individual disciplines from their respective approaches. Thus, and this is an important fact, the cybernetic treatment – I ought to say 'anthropo-cybernetic' because it proceeds to apply the *formal* means of cybernetics to the *concepts* provided by empirical anthropology as briefly hinted at above – disregards traditional boundaries between disciplines and even renders them irrelevant (at least from a strictly theoretical point of view). On the other hand, it brings out more clearly those connections and overlaps between hitherto separated fields which call for cooperation and inter-disciplinary research. To take up a term introduced earlier one might say that cybernetics makes for a new 'paradigm' of research practice in anthropology (by which I mean *all* the fields dealing with man and his world, i.e. everything between bio-anthropology and philosophy); a paradigm rather than a theory, as it is primarily, because of its generality, a heuristic tool which provides a framework of concepts that allow the more adequate formulation of both traditional and new problems. This applies also to its use in this paper: objectifying the functional context within which

---

401; or "Gestaltwahrnehmung als Quelle wissenschaftlicher Erkenntnis", 1949, Vol. 2, pp. 255–300), A. Gehlen [32], [33], [34], and the material in [3] and [4]. – All these works contain many more references to the different approaches developed in the various traditions of empirical anthropology. They allow to draw a general scheme representing the most essential and constitutive elements of the human situation. I think that even such a global and fragmentary view will correct certain misunderstandings in the study of language.

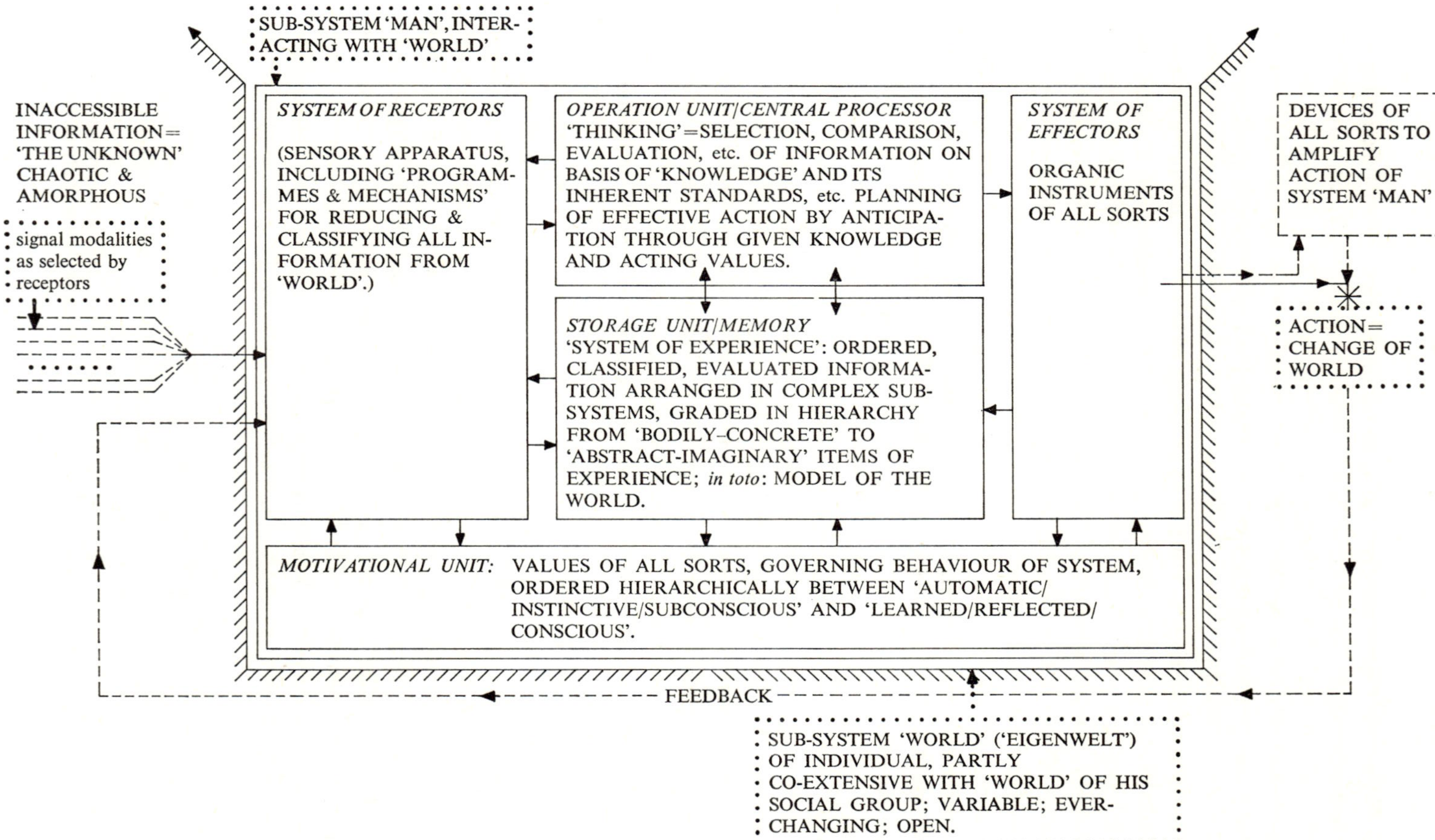

Fig. 1. The anthropo-cybernetic model of the system 'man–world'.

language can be studied adequately is only a first and very tentative step, a step, however, which pre-determines what problems can be formulated in a more or less explicit way. And my contention is that the model of the system 'man–world' as it can be drawn with the help of cybernetics on the basic of available anthropological data – a model which I shall call 'anthropo-cybernetic' – is the most promising and fruitful paradigm for adequate linguistic research, i.e. also for my specific topic 'time and text'. In the present paper I shall be unable to do much more than try and state my case as clearly as possible, and a more extensive treatment will have to be reserved to a future work. I shall therefore have to disregard most of the important details – and there are many! – relevant to an appropriate rendering of even the most basic facts, but will only try to outline those features which seem absolutely essential in the present context.[30]

Figure 1 gives a rough outline of the complex system 'man–world' (*SMW*) as sketched by the 'anthropo-cybernetic' model (*ACM*). The sub-system 'man' (*M*) has to be in constant interaction with its environment *W* to maintain its necessary stability, it is therefore in what L. v. Bertalanffy calls 'Fließgleichgewicht', i.e. its processes take place within and through relatively stable structures. Any living organism is therefore forced to maintain the necessary processes of exchanging matter and energy with its environment, thus both keeping itself running, and continually regenerating itself. In more formal terms, all organisms must counteract the increasing entropy of the universe by building up and maintaining systems and structures, i.e. redundancy, so as to avoid disintegration. This basic fact is also the origin of the anthropological notion of man as an 'active' being (in contradistinction to the 're-active' animal) though the biological aspect does not exhaust the relevance of the concept of 'action' in the human sphere. Whereas the animal's behaviour is strictly regulated by an inborn set of instincts and action-schemata that take care, and thus define, all the possible situations of an animal's life (disregarding the given learning potential of animals which is, however, negligible here), i.e. the 'world' of the animal, as v. Uexküll and many ethologists after him have convincingly shown, a human being does not possess such inborn 'programmes' except for very basic drives on the one hand guaranteeing survival of the species, and universal organic apparatuses to process 'information' from the outside world in a way complying with his needs. These universal (mainly physiological) sets of equipment and

[30] As to cybernetics I have used mainly: Stachowiak [85], Frank [29], [30], v. Cube [24], Steinbuch [88], Ashby [7], Sachsse [110], apart from a number of articles published in journals (e.g. *Grundlagenstudien aus Kybernetik und Geisteswissenschaft*, *Kybernetik*, *Studium Generale*, *Beiträge zur Sprachkunde und Informationsverarbeitung*, *Sprache im technischen Zeitalter*, etc.). – The viability of the cybernetic approach has been shown beyond doubt, I think, by Stachowiak.

their performance are of basic and distinctive importance to humans and can be said to enable them to survive. Thus, according to the extraordinary specialization as to the functions of his brain and central (and peripheral) nervous system, man has justifiably been called 'brain animal'. It is with the help of brain and central nervous system that humans are able to process 'information' from the 'world', to evaluate it, and to store it in a systematically structured and ordered way so as to retrieve it again when necessary and use it for calculating the risk involved in required or desired 'action' (=change of 'world', whereby 'world' of course comprises everything surrounding a human being, i.e. both his natural and his cultural environment, in particular his social ambience in all its aspects). To make this a little clearer let us consider the typical functional cycle interrelating the subsystem M with the subsystem W.

The external world, as a source of 'information', is constantly sending enormous and chaotic quantities of signals of various modalities to the subsystem M. The system M, by virtue of its being equipped with a set of 'receptors' (=senses, or 'sensory receptors'), selects, according to well-known laws of physiology, those signals which are potential 'adequate' stimuli for such receptors if a specific threshold is exceeded. The capacity of the individual receptor determines how much information can be received and subsequently processed. Thus the visual channel is by far the most powerful (it manages up to 10^7 bit/s), whereas, for instance, the gustatory channel has only a capacity of about 13 bit/s (disregarding all interaction between channels which may facilitate and amplify perception). But despite the enormous potential of, say, the eye, to receive millions of signals, the processing of these signals into classified and evaluated 'experience' could not be achieved if the input were not drastically cut down to the relevant minimum, especially in coordination with the information offered to all the other receptors (which are, of course, always 'open' too!). The 'relevance' of information is determined by the specific state of the system, in particular the given motivational situation (in its totality, i.e. both by its sub-conscious, automatic, and conscious sets of 'values'). What information therefore reaches the central processor, i.e. the 'mind', is determined both by automatic selection and classification processes carried out by specific physiological apparatuses (e.g. those performing 'optimalization of perception', 'lateral inhibition', etc.) *and* by what Sachsse aptly calls the "historische Reaktionsbasis"[31], i.e. the given state of the system. Thus only a fraction of the information offered gets by the in-built barriers of the mind, a fact that has been called "Enge des Bewußtseins". The space allowed for consciously received information does

[31] Sachsse [110], p. 127 and pass.

not hold more than about 10^2 bit/s, of which only about 15 bit can be effectively 'apperceived', i.e. processed in a 'moment' of consciousness. (This elementary unit of time, the 'moment', also called "subjektives Zeitquant", was first estimated by K. E. v. Baer to be about 1/18 of a second, which has, in general, been proved correct.) Thus the organic set-up of the system *M* *automatically* reduces the incoming signal quantities to manageable proportions. This is also important for our discussion of time: a system *M* cannot but, by definition as it were, process information of any kind in a linear or successive way. This is where time originates, in the before-now-after sequentiality of all conscious information processing. It must be emphasized, however, that all the sensory organs cooperate through a motivationally determined process of coordination in such a way as to yield a highly complex *and* (as to the contributing channels) composite 'picture' (or 'item' of information) which is apperceived as *one item in time*. Thus there is some meaning in saying, perception is 'synthetic', or, its output is a set of synthetic items which, though of varying sensory modality, and structured in itself, is perceived as one simultaneous whole. (The apperception of a typical autumn landscape, of a summer morning, of eating, of bodily contact, etc. consists in such complex items processed through all the senses at the same time. It is well known that, for instance, a tasty meal does not taste like anything if we have a cold, or that smoking is less enjoyable in the dark, etc.) After this first stage of quantitative reduction the actual processing of 'information' into 'experience' takes place, which is, of course, dependent on what the system 'knows' already and what it 'wants' to know, i.e. on the systems historical state. I shall here not do more than indicate very roughly what the basic process achieves: the information reaching the set of receptors is unstructured and chaotic; the receptors are connected with mechanisms of recognising recurrent patterns, of forming classes of information, i.e. of grouping the signals according to principles like 'similarity' and 'identity', in short of structuring incoming information and forming 'invariants' (or 'gestalten'). Together with this 'formal' classification (which in itself is, of course, directed by the motivational constellation in the system!) the items produced are motivationally 'evaluated' relative to their importance for the given 'values' of the system. And it is the final output in the form of classified and evaluated 'items of experience' which is passed on into the central processor where it is either used immediately, together with items from the storage unit, to form a plan for action, or passed on into the storage device to be kept as a useful 'item of experience'. Needless to say that all evaluation of incoming information is determined by what the system has 'learned' already (through 'education', 'training', or practical action). Needless to say also that these very scant remarks do less than justice to the complexity of the processes involved, and so does the illustration. But a crude outline here will be better than none, and enough for my purpose.

It remains to be added that the 'items of experience' (*IE*'s) are stored in the 'memory unit' or 'storage device' in a carefully arranged way so as to form what is called an 'internal model of the external world'. There is basically an ascending scale from the most important sensual percepts at the 'bottom' to the most abstract concepts at the 'top'.[32] Abstract items are the result of continual (and rarely regular!) analysis of original sensual items which are 'emptied' of their immediate 'synthetic' content in stages and thus may yield items which we traditionally call 'general' properties of percepts, e.g. of situations, actions, states-of-affairs, objects, events, etc., for instance: 'feature', 'set', 'responsibility', 'temperance', 'logical' etc. Clearly there are innumerable levels of abstractness, but they can only be *'above'*, or can only come *'after'*, primary perception. I shall say more about this in connection with the discussion of language in a moment. An 'internal model of the world', built up in continual interaction with the world on the basis of social existence, thus replaces the animal's set of instincts and action-schemata and enables the human being to adapt to not only varying environments but also to environments that are changing all the time. It is such an internal model and the given 'central processor' which allow humans to calculate the 'meaning' of a situation or of an action *before* actually doing something. He can relieve himself of the pressure of immediate action or re-action and 'think' first by anticipating 'possible' situations and weigh them according to his motivational state, and then choose a course of action that seems optimal. To sum up this whole characterization of the functional cycle of the system *MW* let me quote the exemplary formulation by Stachowiak:

Vermöge seiner Sinnesorgane empfängt der Mensch aus seiner Außenwelt ständig Signale, die er registriert und strukturiert sowie einem mit Wissenserwerb verbundenen Verarbeitungs- und Voraussageprozeß unterwirft. Das Ergebnis dieses Prozesses sind (oder sollen sein) Antizipationen von – im Sinne der je wirkenden Motive – optimalen Handlungen. Die als Ausgangsnachrichten der zentralen Verarbeitungsstellen den Erfolgsorganen

[32] It hardly needs pointing out that all the concepts used, e.g. 'item of experience', 'model of the world', or also the purely spatial images of 'concrete' (at the 'bottom') and 'abstract' (at the 'top'), are no more than quite abstract makeshift labels for theoretical entities whose precise properties need to be determined in concrete research. I have deliberately refrained from using more misleading notions, e.g. calling the model of the world a 'multidimensional, polyvalent, polysystematic, complex of items of experience in a plasmatic state', parts of which are 'concrete', and parts of which are 'abstract', but these concepts have no precise meaning themselves outside their systematic position of the respective item of experience: concreteness and abstractness is obviously a matter of degree: *tree* is quite abstract, though less abstract than *plant* or *shape* or *organism*. And obviously an item may assume different degrees of abstractness from position to position... There are only continual transitions between such apparently distinguished states like 'abstractness' and 'concreteness' and they can only be established within the system as a whole.

eingegebenen Meldungen lösen Aktionen des Menschen aus, durch die dieser seine Außenwelt verändert. Die veränderte Außenwelt wird zur Quelle neuer Signalkonstellationen, mittels deren er die Bewährung der vorangegangenen Handlungsantizipationen prüft. Liegt der Bewährungsgrad unterhalb einer gewissen Schwelle oder ist die Zielrichtung des Handelns infolge veränderter Motivstruktur variiert worden, so tritt der Mensch erneut in das Stadium der Verarbeitung der empfangenen Signalmannigfaltigkeiten ein, um zu verbesserten oder neuen Handlungsantizipationen zu gelangen usf.[33]

What has to be emphasized specially is the fact that all 'thinking', in the operational sense just exemplified, consists in the manipulation of items of information derived from the world and transformed by classificatory and evaluative processes into 'items of experience'. It should be noted that there has as yet been no mention of language in the restricted sense of 'vocal language'! Thus we are still concerned with thinking without or before language. And though the area of problems comprising such complex relationships as exist between language and 'reality', language and 'experience', or language and 'thought', is notoriously confused and controversial, there is good reason to assume that a clear distinction may be drawn between 'thinking' in the sense of handling 'items of experience' (or 'concepts' = 'perceptual images', to quote R. Arnheim) as the *primary* processes of human consciousness, and the *additional* and *supplementary* function of 'vocal language'. I am convinced that it is correct to speak of 'visual thinking' (or, for that matter, also of 'auditory thinking' with musicians, of 'gustatory thinking' with gourmets and cooks, of 'olfactory thinking' with cosmetic experts, etc.), though I do not think it felicitous to use the word 'language' in this connection, i.e. to speak of a 'visual language', the 'language of architecture', etc., in a technical context. In defiance of the linguistic determinists and similar language fetishists I should assert that language comes *after* primary perceptual experience, after 'perceptual thinking' *via* the individual sensual modalities with their respective (great or small) potentials, adding to 'intuitive' thinking (and cognition) another, and extremely important, 'intellectual' dimension to stabilize and preserve what is already 'there' in form of "a perceptual field of freely interacting forces".[34] By internal processing through continual analysing scrutiny of available percepts and complexes of percepts like 'tree', 'clock', 'mountain', 'road', 'flying', 'walking', etc. – the list is entirely arbitrary – new items are deduced by varying criteria (e.g. 'similarity', 'shape', 'size', etc.). Thus a tree is further analysed into items like 'trunk', 'bough', 'twig', 'branch', 'root' 'leaf' etc., but also in regard of more universal concepts like 'high', 'big', 'black', 'ugly' etc., concepts which are derived from the generalisation of invariant features observed in an infinite multitude of phenomena – a process which continues, and must con-

[33] [85], p. 5f.
[34] Arnheim [6], p. 233.

tinue, through the whole life of an individual. Everybody knows that we can distinguish innumerable patterns, forms, shapes, sizes, shades of colours etc. in a conscious way, that we do perceive complex relationships in purely formal compositions (such as those of painters and musicians or ballet dancers) without being able, or wanting or needing, to have labels for each such item of experience. We perceive and process, i.e. 'think' intuitively, in 'perceptual images', whether we be artists with a highly developed and creative sensorium whose business is experimentation, or scientists who are basically on a par with artists except for their specific norms of objectification of results, or whether we be only normal mortals with no particular verbal ability. We all get to know the world, learn how to manage it for all our life, in an 'intuitive' way, never primarily, or only, through words. And everybody also surely has had enough experience of how acute the incompatibility of *intuition* and available *verbal media* can make itself felt: in everyday life no less than in science and art. What is new is always there *before* it is labelled, and it has become actual experience only after its complete integration into the 'internal model' which, in turn, makes the vocal label naturally 'acquire' a 'new' or 'extended' meaning. All learning takes place in this intuitive way (and may of course easily be misdirected and stifled by perverting it into a memorizing of words for intuitively unassimilated 'information' – something only too common at school, something only too common with academic work). – All these only too scant remarks could be illustrated by many examples which have primarily been provided by artists and writers as well as scientists concerned with the physiology and psychology of perception and thought. They all centre in what, in many institutions, ought to become a battle-cry: "Words in their Place!" – Let me conclude with a few illustrative sentences from R. Arnheim's *Visual Thinking:*

> Language assists the mind in stabilizing and preserving intellectual entities. It does this, for example, with the perceptual concepts that emerge from direct experience. The generalities acquired in perception are embedded in the continuum of the visual world. The concept of tree rests on an endless variety of trees of different color, shape, and size; it is found inherent in each tree but is not identical with any one specimen. Furthermore, the range to which such a type concept applies is not clearly confined but slides into that of its neighbors. Trees border on shrubs, vegetables blend with fruits, violas with violins, the Romanesque with the Gothic, Miss A with Miss B. Thought needs discrete types, and perception is geared to supply it, but the structure of the raw material of experience does not furnish neat dichotomies, simple either-or's; it consists of ranges, shades, gliding scales.
>
> Here language is helpful. It supplies a clear-cut, distinct sign for each type and thereby encourages perceptual imagery to stabilize the inventory of visual concepts.[35]

I think there is need for an illustration here. The following excerpt from *Die Hornissen* by Peter Handke (1966) deals with a situation in which a com-

[35] *Ibid.*, p. 236.

plex of perceptions is realized within the 'ego' speaking. In normal life the meticulous analysis of the overall perception (as signalled by the introductory sentence) would be considered redundant and a global statement would be enough. Here, however, a sharpened sensibility takes what we might comprehend by the simple label 'Geräusche' ('noises') to pieces, labelling all the singular IE's it can separate, and thus then reports the complex and simultaneous situation (which is perceived in a fraction of the time it takes to 'tell' it) by reconstructing it bit by bit, while restricting its attention to the auditory channel only (for reasons inherent in the whole text). Here is the excerpt:

Die Geräusche

Der heiße Wind treibt den Staub durch das Fenster. Ich höre das Geräusch des Vorhangs. Ich höre das Geräusch des Sands, der gegen das Glas schlägt. Ich höre das Geräusch des offenen Schranks. Ich höre das Geräusch der nassen Blätter der Bäume. Ich höre das Geräusch des Grases unter den Bäumen. Ich höre das Geräusch von dem Kotflügel des Fahrrades. Ich höre das Geräusch des Drahtes zwischen den Pappeln. Ich höre das Geräusch des Reifens, der an der Scheune hängt. Ich höre das Geräusch der nassen Kleider über dem Draht. Ich höre das Geräusch der Schuppentür, die gegen den Holzstapel schlägt. Ich höre das Geräusch eines fahrenden Zuges. (p. 37)

There is an abstract label for the whole complex perception as it takes place (in less time, certainly, than the speaking of the text): 'Die Geräusche'. Then the perception is analysed into a series of smaller items constituting it: the 'series' is, however, entirely artificial and only a property of the *verbal* text which cannot be uttered as a whole 'simultaneously'! There is no reason at all to assume strict parallelism between the textual events and the actual perceptions: the whole complex percept will be given, then scanned and uttered. Thus the *synthetic* percept is *analyzed* into components which are 'transmitted' to the receiver of the message through artificial labels attached to them.[36] That the general direction of the acquiring of experience always takes the direction from synthesis to analysis is not only exemplified by the development of natural languages from 'holophrases' of a global kind[37] to pedantically analytical statements, but also by the language used in the text: every single noise is first of all called a 'noise' ('Geräusch') very generally, and then, by adding restrictive defining properties, specified as to the *precise percept it is* amongst all the other noises. – A still more instructive passage is to be found 10 pages on, where more specific labels for the noises are 'discussed', as it

[36] They are of course not 'transmitted' in any real sense: this is absolutely impossible. What happens is that the receiver 're-constitutes' through the signals he understands a similar (or purportedly similar) situation, in our case: 'perception'. That there can be no identity here, is obvious. The hearer concretizes what the sender tells him to concretize, on the common basis of a shared model of the world. I shall say more about this below.

[37] R. Paget's expression, quoted by Gehlen [34], p. 59.

were, thus showing in an exemplary way how different the *formal* properties of the linguistic labels used may be (determined mainly by their syntactic functions, and therefore: properties, in uttering something). For every phrase of the form "das Geräusch des/der/von dem *X*", a new label is introduced. (Not as a proper name, of course, but as the label of an open class of similar types of noise.) I shall quote only a few sentences:

Die Namen der Geräusche

Das Geräusch des Vorhangs im Wind wird selber als Wehen bezeichnet; es kann auch verglichen werden mit dem Sausen des verkohlenden Feuers in einem Ofen; ist der Vorhang aus festerem Stoff, so wird sein Geräusch im Wind als Knattern bezeichnet; dieser Ausdruck wird auch für Fahnen gebraucht. Das Geräusch des Sandes, den der Wind an das Glas schlägt, wird als Knacken bezeichnet; möglich ist auch der Vergleich mit dem feinen Prasseln eines Regens auf ein Blechdach; das festere Prasseln des Regens auf das Blechdach wird als Trommeln bezeichnet... (p. 47).

Of course this text introduces many more classificatory and evaluative features into the 'naming' of an IE than just one, i.e. 'noise', but I am sure, the reader will be able to see for himself now how precarious is the relationship between vocal signs and IE's and what basic facts it rests on: given percepts, classifying and evaluating ('analytic') procedures, a variety of types of vocal signs coordinated to IE's in an arbitrary, though systematic, fashion. – (Cf. infra, 3.1.) The case of linguistic determinism is therefore very tenuous, and probably concerns less matters of principle than matters of practice (i.e. the difficulty of changing one's habits, whether this concern the way one moves or the way one analyses the world).

After this brief exposition of a possibly plausible framework to determine the functional role of language the most important consequences for my topic (and implicitly also the study of language functioning in general, i.e. linguistics, in the comprehensive sense of an adequate theory of language functioning) may be stated. I shall of course not be able to do more than formulate some of what I think to be the most essential characteristics of the nature of the object 'language' and consequently of the theoretical representation of it for the purposes put down above. The main emphasis will naturally be on what a 'text' is and does, and what it means, therefore, to attempt constructing a 'theory of texts', and, finally, what questions might be asked as to the role of 'time' in the constitution of texts, both as 'real' time as well as the set of 'temporal-semantical elements'.

3.2. *Language*

3.2.1. *The instrument: language.* It may have become clear what humans need language for: to survive, to exist in a satisfactory way on the basis of social cooperation which, in turn, also depends on language functioning adequately; thus adequate, i.e. effective control of language is a basic desideratum for everybody; its measure will depend on his status and aspirations, it will certainly never be uniform. *Adequate* language training is therefore a most serious concern for any society; it will have to provide it in the way and measure deemed necessary. It will thus have to be aware of the natural properties and functions of the object 'language' to be able to achieve its respective aims of teaching and training. (This holds also for learning foreign languages, trivially enough, though the fact seems to find little recognition.)

3.2.2. *The virtuality and fragmentarity of language.* The ACM clearly shows that language is a *secondary* device developed to stabilize the *primary* system of perceptual experience, a system most complex and highly structured in itself; to label it so as to make it handier to manipulate (both internally, in thinking, and externally, in communicating, or thinking collectively). Language is thus a system of vocal (or: graphematic) signs representing another system of an entirely different categorial nature: experience consists in sets and complexes of *percepts* and all the ever-interacting 'field forces' (of modification and change) between them, language is a system of arbitrary and artificial, or 'virtual', *signs.* By far not everything in experience is represented in language, nor is there only one type of 'object' referred to by a linguistic sign; on the contrary, linguistic signs may denote objects of widely varying levels of abstractness, i.e. 'invariants' of all sorts. There are, for instance, the signs for bodily sensations or states like *cold, dazzle, fever, excitement, rage, passion,* all denoting sets of invariant features, structured and organized in such a way as to yield *one* consistent 'item' which is identified and recognised through all its variations. *Excitement* thus is a label for a complex item of experience, in other words, a recurring 'type' of item, or a 'class' of items; both expressions indicate that what is actually stabilized by the label *excitement* is not one, and only one, *individual* item of experience, but a set of recurring and structured features abstracted from the general flow of information, and preserved in its relevant invariant form. Thus *cold, press, hard, stink, sharp, itch* are certainly not 'spontaneous' or 'immediate' concepts in any naive sense, but results of an abstracting process picking out (according to a given, i.e. 'historical', motivational state determining 'relevancy') recurring 'items' from an ever-flowing and ever-changing process of interaction with the 'world' through the system of perceptors and their coordinated processing apparatuses. Thus obviously *excitement* may do for one situation – *the news caused great excitement* –, i.e. a particular 'historical' standard of relevancy (defining the behaviour in the corresponding situation), but may not do for another, and may have to be replaced by some more 'analytic' and more 'precise' sign, e.g. *flush, heat, tumult, fit, paroxysm, agony*, *outbreak*, *fanaticism*, *impatient*, *hysterical*, *fume*, etc. etc.[38] Here again there are various levels of abstractness to be observed, but also at least two other facts: first it must be noted that the features making up an item of experience may be of varying kinds as to the *sensory channel* concerned – *flush* may be both visual and emotional (i.e. affecting various parts of the nervous system), *hot* may concern both the sense of temperature and the gustatory sense –, and second, it may be obvious that there are various *standards of relevancy* involved which, and this is to be emphasized, also determine the *situation* in which the sign is adequate, i.e. in which it is properly functional. (In this sense it can be said that items of experience not only *classify* and *evaluate* 'information' from the world, but also – and this is obviously inherent in the 'evaluation' of information – carry '*instructions for use*'.) Thus *paroxysm* or *fit* may both be medical terms capable of still more precise interpretation and corresponding action, etc., whereas *tumult* is rather an everyday word denoting situation and behaviour of a group of people 'excited' for specific reasons (and implying, in turn, specific action according to other criteria, e.g. by the police). *Fanaticism* is quite different again as to its underlying values and corresponding instructions for action. – Finally: no such vocal label recalls an item as an isolated entity in a kind of pushdown store; on the contrary, all items of experience are systematically ordered by virtue of their being part of an 'internal model of the world'. Being quoted they immediately evoke the IE and its relevant 'model component', and all their inherent properties which govern their use, are brought into action. – To summarize: language refers to the internal model of the world in all its (varying) complexity relative to a given ('historical') motivational state. There is, therefore, no need and no reason to attribute the internal construction of

[38] NB.: The grammatical, i.e. syntactic properties of such signs as they have traditionally been recorded in form of categories of all kinds, e.g. 'noun', 'tense', 'number', etc., are basically irrelevant to the perceptual content; they may, however, – and do, in fact – assume some secondary meaning which is derived from the preferred form of 'making' statements. Thus the predominance of the subject-predicate scheme in the Indo-European languages has led to a corresponding interpretation of the respective parts of speech usually filling the principal positions of the scheme. The 'noun' has thus been associated with 'object' or 'actor', the 'verb' with 'action' or 'process', the 'adjective' with 'property' or 'quality', etc. – It would be worth examining what 'categorial' meaning can be established experimentally within a community of language users, e.g. the German native speakers, for such 'parts of speech', and on what data such 'meaning' has grown (as a set of generalised properties common to most, or all 'nouns', for instance). – In the present context it seems worth stressing that the basic distinction is to be drawn between the cognitive content of the domain of a (systematically ordered) set of vocal signs, and the signs (and their system-dependent ordering) themselves. Thus *redness, red, redden, reddish* (including *partly* related signs like *blush, flush*) represent forms with different systematic properties within the system of signs whose cognitive 'content matter' is the same: 'RED', as a percept defined by invariant characteristics, though infinitely variable as to its functioning.

that model to language and to either apotheosize or bedevil a purely instrumental entity, i.e. a system of auxiliary vocal signs, 'language'. Whatever 'concepts' there are derive from percepts organized in a "perceptual system of freely interacting forces" – to modify R. Arnheim's expression – and are definitely 'constructions' of the human mind: *apple* just as well as *topology*, and *interchangeability* no less than *toe-nail* or *vegetables*. This is not contradicted by the fact that the combination of linguistic *labels* follows certain rules: the 'semantics' of experience may be indicated in various ways through combinations of the given linguistic signals and it is only in respect of the basic law of maximum economy (or 'least effort') to organize the combination of labels into 'super-labels' of varying order (from *ouch*! to the text called *The Man without Qualities or Defects*), *not* only on the principle of strict seriality, but on many principles of systematic integration (with the help of classes, hierarchies, patterns, etc.) of labels. What a 'sentence' signals is therefore a (factual, or fictitious of any degree: potential, imaginary...) model of a 'mini-world' built out of items of experience (Wittgenstein). Whatever ways of 'predicating' one's experience are chosen, the rules of 'correctness' or 'coherence' or 'plausibility' as to the 'semantics' of the predication are to be looked for in the internal model of the world, whether they concern its 'body-near' areas or its 'imaginary worlds' of abstraction (as they are ingeniously constructed by mathematicians). And it obviously depends on what purpose the *use* of the possibility of *predicating* is to serve, i.e. again on standards of 'relevancy' (or 'adequacy'), what the conditions of the 'acceptability', i.e. of the functional effectiveness, of predications, or systems of predications, are. The fact that most of any man's experience in all its aspects is generally only made accessible through language, has led to a confused notion of language. Both the determinists and the pure formalists represent extreme approaches of which the latter seems more justified as to the nature of language as a system of 'labels for something': the only trouble is that its results must needs always be absolutely meaningless to anybody who does not know the corresponding systems of *signifiés* (including their inherent instructions for use). To attempt, on the other hand, to represent the *complete* 'model of the world' of a linguistic community, say all those speaking German as using the German *language* (as the idealised sum total of all German socio-, idio- and other -lects), means nothing less than to represent *all* the experience signalled by the German *language*. The first task is manageable, because a combinatorial formal system can be represented in some finite way: it is part of that science which studies and experiments with formal structures or systems, mathematics. The second task is impossible to complete in an ideal sense, but partly manageable in a practical sense, as is proved by the many people acquiring knowledge and experience without there being a theory of it. Thus an adequate theory of language functioning as I am envisaging it here for precisely the practical purposes of something like 'meaning control', would have to deal with the *system of signals*, i.e. language proper (in the narrow sense) on the one hand, with the *system of experience* on the other, and with the *coordination rules* between both. This view is basically in accord with both traditional and modern linguistic approaches: modern approaches have started with the combinatorial system of signals and finally got weighed down by both implicit and explicit semantic difficulties – how define those, and only those, signal combinations which actually *do* label 'meaning', i.e. (if only potential) experience (of all levels and degrees etc.)?; the determinists have realized that it is experience which determines the usability of some signal combination, but have created conflicts over certain ontological distinctions – *fruit* does not 'exist' in reality, it is a construction of the human mind like *veal* vs. *calf* or *beef* vs. *cattle*, or *chair* vs. *Sessel* and *Stuhl* – which they declared to be both the achievement and the restricting influence of language: for them it is *language* which classifies and evaluates 'information' from the world and thus constructs a 'picture' of the world preventing us from seeing it in 'another' way – the 'other' way may only be the way of another language, as W. v. Humboldt puts it in a well-known passage. I think that the hypostatization of language as something comprising both experience *and* its labels is unnecessary and highly misleading (and not only because of the extremist interpretation of such an ontological dualism (*fruit*, or *Obst*, does not 'exist' in 'reality', but neither does *tree* or *cat* or *John*: i.e. in the sense of a single 'objective' object or something like that) by the advocators of the 'linguistic relativity principle' and their political adepts, nationalist, religious, literary...: it not only seems to suggest an 'object world' which is unadulterated, as it were, by the concepts and criteria of arbitrary linguistic 'reduction', it also seems to exclude any other kind of cognition or thinking or dealing with the world except through language. This is surely inadequate; we all know that a large portion of our experience is *not* verbalised at all: the present discussion of 'time' is a case in point as will be shown later. Furthermore: to communicate 'experience', say, colour, or some shape or pattern of an object, an action, a movement etc., does not necessarily need words nor is it at all expressible in words – a well-known argument of artists, and a fully justified one! – (A trivial example is the reporter's desperate attempt to render in words to listeners what happens on the soccer pitch, though everybody in a position to watch will easily follow the game in all its intricate moves. What language *adds* to the visual picture of the soccer match is of course another matter as was briefly discussed above: the visual information which is probably – certainly to experts and fans – quite redundant, becomes re-constructed, as it were, out of available 'items of experience' and the complex flow of visual information is thus 'cut up' into quasi-defined and evaluated units: what the watcher may only dimly perceive as 'player *X* *touching* player *Y*', the commentator may render as *kicking*, *bumping*, *attacking*, *pushing*, *knocking*, *hitting*, *bashing*, *punching*... etc.). – Despite such possible criticism the basic approach 'from meaning to label' seems to me to be useful, as it has brought to light various interesting facts about how humans *may* structure their *experience*, more correctly: what cognitive categories and standards and criteria may be at work in the building up of a 'model of the world'. This surely has been a step towards an adequate theoretical account of meaning, as it allows some generalisations over the ever-changing multitude of 'models of the world'. (Much of this important research into such systematic properties of experience has been vitiated by some of the – perhaps quasi-metaphysical – underlying assumptions, and especially by a purely verbal and far too manipulable terminology.)[39] – The problem then arises: if the position and the functioning of language are established as in the ACM, what precisely *is* to be called 'language'? The system of labels, or signals? (But linguistics oriented this way ends up with studying purely formal combinations ad infinitum, if meaning is excluded completely, and these cannot be studied either without constant recourse to meaning. The system of experience, i.e. the 'model of the world'? (Then linguistics could only work if all the knowledge signalled by a given system of signals were available, and clearly this is necessary if linguistics is to provide effective means of controlling 'meaning'. But surely there is nothing 'linguistic' about distinguishing between the stinks of a laboratory and the scent on a beautiful woman: both 'items' are duly identifiable with the senses only, i.e. are classified and evaluated percepts, and have some definite effect on the experiencing person's action/re-action; both could be transmitted and even thought without words – a common thing with cooks, beauticians, chemists –, and labelling them *A* and *B* would not make any difference to either of them, it would only facilitate *talking* about them.) Thus, finally, a 'language' might be taken to consist in the peculiar *system of relationships*

[39] I am referring here to both offshoots of what was prepared by Hamann, Herder, and Humboldt in Germany: to the German form of "Inhaltbezogene Sprachforschung" around J. L. Weisgerber (cf. [103], [104]), and the American variety founded by B. L. Whorf (cf. [37], [105]). Despite the criticisms voiced only sketchily I should like to emphasize that these approaches have been valuable in many ways. Apart from extreme generalisations, they have exercised positive influence on the development of a more adequate view of the functioning and performance of language in general, on the one hand, and they have definitely supplied much interesting factual knowledge. To condemn the approach globally (as seems fashionable today) is rash and nothing but a testimony of ignorance: the work available has, of course, to be read with discrimination and a critical mind to pick out the substantial material from among the speculative and/or metaphysical framework. I am not saying that this is easy...

valid for a social group, between a given system of signals and their corresponding 'items of experience'. In this understanding 'language' would *not* exhaust *all* the experience or knowledge of the group, it would only cover *part* of it (for certain reasons). This view seems to be viable: it avoids pure formalism as well as pure ontologism, and concentrates on what is given in the well-known form of a sign: 'something', i.e. a 'signal' is related with 'something', i.e. its 'meaning' (here: an item of experience) and the relation is an arbitrary one of 'standing for', of 'representing'. Thus linguistics would have to start out from what there is in form of an inventory of signals, i.e. it would have to be structural linguistics, or – to use Bull's term – 'systemic linguistics', and would search for *what* these signals (and, of course, their possible combinations, i.e. the possible 'super-signs') 'stand for', what they 'represent'. – This is fairly traditional, but may be a little clearer in the context of the ACM. It is most important to realize that most of our experience is not labelled linguistically! In communication the appeal is *always* to the partner's 'system of experience', and it is one of the basic presuppositions of communication that both partners eke out what is *not said* by what they *know*: in communication the partners always *interpret* each other's utterances in terms of the respective 'internal models of the world'!

It might be useful to summarise very globally what the so-called 'meaning' of a linguistic 'sign' comprises:

(a) *perceptual 'matter'* (e.g. visual information, tactile information etc. as the 'concrete' matter to be processed, statable in terms of the physiology of perception: when light waves of such and such length reach... then... sensation... interpretation by brain, etc.)

(b) *classifying features* (= invariant properties defining the class of 'objects' called *cat*, the class of relationships called *series*, the class of value-bound relationships called *altruism*, etc.

Classifying features might theoretically be analysed further, e.g. into 'formal' features (e.g. *male*, *animal*, *round*, *stand*...) determining the limits of the respective 'item', i.e. delimiting it against and from among others, and into 'evaluative' features (e.g. *bad* + *male*: criminal: *bad* + *animal*: beast...), adding some 'comment' to the item defined.)

(c) *instructional features* (i.e. properties indicating the domains of adequate use of the respective label; such properties e.g. distinguish *Du-Sie*, *Tu-Vous* etc., but also *This is most interesting indeed*! from *What a load of rubbish*!, or *You are lying*! from *I am very sorry, but I cannot help thinking that there must be something to the fact that... and I cannot help to see a contradiction there, so please forgive my saying so...*, etc.)[40]

[40] This is nothing but an extremely crude hint at analytic semantics whose discussion must be left out completely here. *How* one is to proceed, i.e. from 'synthetic' IE's to more

Thus every item of experience, when evoked and realized in the mind, is not only just the recollection of some static image, but also the realization of all its defining properties which may, explicitly and implicitly, be of relevance to the action to be taken by the person involved.

The first, and most important consequence to be derived from the functional view of language in terms of the ACM can, finally, be summarized by R. Arnheim's chapter heading "Words in their place": linguistic signs are but the 'addresses' of the items of experience, as it were; as in a computer, they are helpful in identifying, moving, and manipulating items, or complete 'files' of experience, but they are *in no way* the *same* as experience. (For economy's sake the system of signals must, in order to manage an ever-changing and ever-growing stock of IE's, be structured in itself, as it would be an impossible task to have only individual-labels for the vast amount of experience to be 'addressed' and manipulated; on the contrary, every 'address' belongs to various classes and hierarchies determining its combinatorial range with other 'addresses': it is a 'noun', a 'conjunction', a 'verb', etc., it may operate in specific structures, larger (texts, or text components) or smaller (sentence patterns, word patterns). But it seems inappropriate to confuse experience and its labels and infuse certain conceptual properties into what are purely formal (or 'syntactic') entities. The difference between *His face is reddening*, *His face is growing red*, *He is becoming red in the face*,

---

'analytic' IE's, is as vaguely obvious as difficult. It is a matter of goals and interests *what* semantic units and features are posited and *how* they are systematically developed and related, i.e. it is principally a question of what a theory of 'something' is to be for and what the 'something' therefore *is*. 'Language' as a whole could ideally only be treated if there were non-linguistic means of language description, i.e. means to *describe the IE*'s which are signalled by a linguistic label (and perhaps one will come to use 'ostensive' means in linguistics, too, as in all the other disciplines dealing with 'reality'). In any event, a clear differentiation as to what part, or what kind, of 'language' is to be dealt with must be taken at the outset: *animal* in the everyday sense functions in an entirely different way from *animal* in zoology, i.e. it comprises a set of invariant properties as given in an individual SMW which will overlap with the meaning of *animal* in all the other SMW's understanding English. And so will *beast*, which may be said to embody an additional property [pejorative]. Now the global term *animal* signals *all* the distinctive properties of any single animal and may thus give rise to all sorts of deductions and inferences for whose proper analysis and notation (let alone prediction) an adequate theoretical representation of the IE *animal* would have to be presupposed for *every instance of its use*. Then a statement like *man is a tool-making animal* presupposes the IE *animal* both for the interpretation of *animal* and for *man*; thus *man* incorporates all the properties of *animal*, just as of a host of similarly abstract concepts like *matter, energy, atom, life*, etc. – It is evident therefore, that the model of the world of an individual is an intricately structured system of IE's, ordered in various ways. All the traditional thesauri of lexicographers, e.g. Roget, Hallig/Wartburg, Dornseiff, Wehrle/Eggers, are ordered in some such hierarchical way. (It may be noted that research in automatic information storage and retrieval has also developed such ideas and tried to translate them into machine-adequate form.)

Redness spreads over his face, he is blushing, etc., is primarily one of language in the sense that there are different sign sequences for what may in reality be one and the same event; the various ways of 'reconstituting' this 'event' derive from the various available IE's which are *not* language.[41] Obviously it is thus quite correct to say that there is a 'difference in seeing' the 'world', but this must be taken in the proper sense of the word: the fact of someone's blushing *is* reconstituted by using differing IE's which, in general, are to be signalled by different labels or label combinations.

3.2.3. *The fluctuating nature of meaning.* As an SMW can only survive by continual activity it is clear that there will be a constant exchange of information between the sub-systems M and W. Thus the internal model of the world will be only *relatively stable*. It is impossible that change is excluded completely. It must therefore be remembered that the IE's making up a model of the world, and characterized as complex units in a system of freely and continually interacting forces, cannot be fixed in any rigid sense. They will be variable, though maintaining a relatively invariant structure, systemic position, and function. This necessarily creates conflicts whenever the model changes, especially with people whose daily business it is (or should be) to revise and improve the society's model of the world in order to optimize the society's existence (in *all* its domains and parts). R. Arnheim has put it well:

> Philosophers and scientists constantly struggle with the verbal shells which they must use to package their thoughts for preservation and communication.... All this trouble arrives because words, as mere labels, try to keep up with the live action of thought taking place in another medium.... The struggle against the old words is only a reflection of the true drama going on in thought. To see things in a new light is a genuine cognitive challenge; to adjust the language to the new insight is nothing more than a bothersome technicality. Eric Lenneberg has stressed this point by asserting that "words tag the processes by which the species deals cognitively with its environment". Since these processes involve constant change, the referents of words cannot be said to be fixed.[42]

This is of course a most familiar theme about which much could be said. I should only like to note that there is an infinite number of variations between

[41] The term 'reconstitution' is used by Bronowski/Bellugi [20]. Their discussion of the specific performance of language for *humans* is based on a review of the report on the latest experiments with a chimpanzee taught some 'language'-similar behaviour. The article is short but important; it clearly states the difference between the *cognitive* activities and abilities of humans (and animals) and the *linguistic* apparatus used to 'reconstitute' experience for the purposes of analysis, reflection, or communication. – The controversial dichotomy 'Thinking and Language' and claims of the sort that both are the same or different, can thus be taken apart and discussed in a realistic sense. There is thinking without language. We could never do without language, however, though we may restrict its use and live primarily 'by the senses' and through action, – like artists, for instance, whose business is to experiment with their model of the world to explore possible worlds. Cf. also Slobin [84], B. L. van der Waerden [97].

[42] [6], p. 245f.

one extreme, i.e. a *minimal* use of 'words' (with artists, musicians, simple, and simply *active*, people), and the other, i.e. a *maximal* use of 'words' (writers, philosophers, academics, politicians, etc.). In all cases the relevant guiding norms and values will decide about the adequacy of language use. (Thus, for instance, the use of words in a so-called 'primitive' culture is by no means 'primitive', or in any sense less adequate than the use of so many words, spoken and written, in civilized cultures. Any judgment will have to take into account the respective underlying values. The question, of course, of whether one set of values is less 'valuable' than another, is most difficult to answer...)

3.2.4. *The schematicity of language.* A further very important point which may become clearer by being expressed in relation to the ACM is that all talk about the 'model of the world' of a society, i.e. a regularly acting group of individuals, is necessarily based on an abstraction which must be kept in mind carefully. The model of the world of a society is as idealized and abstract a notion as the (so seductive) 'spirit of the nation', the 'poverty', the 'humour' etc. of the nation. That the unheeded use of such generalisations is very dangerous and may lead to disastrous consequences does not need demonstration here. It is to be pointed out, however, that for the study of language as well, the abstract nature of the concept of 'language' of 'a society', of 'a nation' etc., must be remembered. Consequently, any linguistic sign, or combination of signs, of such a language is bound to be no less abstract, if it is to be decoded in isolation, i.e. divorced from the possibility to 'interpret' it in terms of a partially accessible system of experience. This holds for any text as well; and especially for texts which are transmitted in the impoverished form of graphematic signals! – It is to be noted therefore that *all* acquiring of experience, i.e. *all cognitive activity* of the mind is *in the individual system*, never in a 'collective' system, e.g. a team, or group, of people, however closely connected. It is only the individual system which 'experiences' and which can, therefore, *concretely* 'interpret' a linguistic label. This means saying *more* than the fact that 'not understanding' means being unable to interpret a given sign in terms of stored knowledge or experience. It means also, and this is most important for the study of texts of any sort, that all 'interpreting' of abstract linguistic signs is *conditioned* by the individual's model of the world. What the IE labelled *rose* or *bread* or *violence* or *time* is to the one, need only have minimal correspondence with what it is to the other. To quote an obvious example: D. H. Lawrence's poem *Bavarian Gentians* is naturally based on the percept of the flower called *gentian*, an IE whose invariant structure is, for instance described by botany (according to the specialised botanical system of IE's and labels, refining the everyday one). A *gentian* could *never* be defined in words if it has not been *experienced* (visually in its proper environment, or perhaps by smell, taste, and touch, or perhaps even as a medical plant). The 'meaning' of *gentian* may therefore include all sorts of aspects grouped round the 'abstract' core which is the *only* relevant part as to its *socially* valid meaning and use. Thus I think it might be useful to call the standard meaning, or the invariant of an IE which is recognized by a social group, the 'schematic' IE coordinated to a certain label, in our case the label *gentian*. It is the set of schematic IE's which is a (perhaps absolute) prerequisite of comprehensibility as to a given language. Whoever cannot differentiate for instance, between *shrub*, *bush*, and *tree*, can be said not to have mastered the respective schematic IE's as they are valid for a relevant community. – The further point to be made here, however, concerns the necessarily individual character of a person's IE's: however easily he may be able to communicate with others about plants, whether they be *geraniums*, *honeysuckle*, *roses*, or also *gentians*, he will, the closer his view and the more penetrating his reflection, always re-constitute an IE *gentian* which is *his* concrete item of experience and, in addition to the schematic and thus socially functional *gentian*, exhibits various aspects relevant to him as an individual, and thus modifying the social understanding. Thus D. H. Lawrence's IE *gentian* obviously includes Lawrencian aspects (consequences, naturally, of his motivational states) which make it a peculiar 'concretization' of the otherwise 'schematic' IE and, what is more, *condition the connectibility of the IE with other IE's.* Thus the mere uttering of a label like *gentian* may produce concretizations in a hearer or reader which, on the basis of its schematic meaning, lead to *very personal* conclusions and inferences determining the final 'interpretation' of *gentian* and, most probably, the text it is part of as a whole. It must be added that such conclusions or inferences need not be articulated explicitly, they may only be there implicit and act as hidden determinants in, say, the progression of a text. *Lawrence's* perspective may become clear from a few lines:

Bavarian Gentians

Not every man has gentians in his house
in Soft September, at slow, Sad Michaelmas.
Bavarian gentians, big and dark, only dark
darkening the day-time torch-like with the smoking blueness of Pluto's gloom,
ribbed and torch-like, with their blaze of darkness spread blue
down flattening into points, flattened under the sweep of white day
torch-flower of the blue-smoking darkness, Pluto's dark-blue daze,
black lamps from the halls of Dis, burning dark blue,
giving off darkness, blue darkness, as Demeter's pale lamps give off light,
lead me then, lead me the way.

There is no need to interpret this piece of text: it is obvious that Lawrence's deductions, as it were, from *his* IE *gentian* which he can express using the general label comprehensible to everybody knowing English, are produced by *his* concretization of *gentians* as a given IE, in the first place, and by his system of values, in the second. All the descriptive terms in the text could never have come about without there being a concrete and definite 'item of experience' labelled by *gentian*. And only on the basis of this IE the specifically Lawrencian deductions are comprehensible and plausible.

That the same (schematic) IE *gentian* may function quite differently, is shown by the familiar appearance of *gentians* in Alpine folk imagery, together with *edelweiss*, *rhododendron*, and others. In both cases – and there are many more that could be cited; that *gentian* is a 'noun', formally speaking, is irrelevant – the IE *gentian* is the very basis from which personal concretizations may be developed which, in turn, encourage further conclusions and inferences. (All the problems of literary interpretation centre in this and the establishing of the immanent 'logic' of a literary text would have to start out from the basic IE's forming an integrated whole. The difference, on the other hand, between 'personal' or 'subjective', and 'scientific' or 'objective', textual reading, can be located precisely in the difference between a (potentially) inter-subjective and 'schematic' IE and its person-, and thus always value-bound, i.e. thoroughly 'historical', 'concretization'.)

A last note may be appended: It follows from the variable nature of IE's that there are potentially innumerable combinations, i.e. possible (mini-) worlds, of IE's *via* language, only a fraction of which are actually articulated during that interval in which one might (theoretically) speak of a relatively stable model of the world among the members of a social community. This does not mean that many more such mini-worlds are not experienced or do not survive in *non-linguistic* form! It is a pecular prejudice, born from vanity, of our Western culture that there is only value in *verbal* objectifications, that *verbal* activities and relationships have inherent power to change things and that whoever is not fluent *verbally* must needs have a primitive personality. The point to be made here, apart from putting emphasis on the fact that language is far from being everything or the only essential factor in human life, concerns the fact that a theory of language functioning, i.e. a theory describing and explaining the working of the human mind as actually signalled by language, a theory thus capable of deciding about 'meaningfulness' and, consequently, capable of predicting potential 'meaningful' verbalisations, would be the only theory deserving the predicate 'adequate': only such a theory would permit effective control of meaning and therefore optimization of practical life. If the ideas presented here, are somewhere 'near the truth', such a theory would have to represent *all* potential concretizations of a social group. Is this absolutely utopian? Or might one say, it could be possible to establish the general concepts (e.g. of similarity, analogy, difference, shape, causal relations etc. etc.) guiding all processes of inference in the medium of the system of percepts. Perhaps this perspective could be taken to be a promising heuristic perspective leading the way to a comprehensive 'logic of experience' or an 'axiology of experience formation', or some such thing. Thus it would be shown again that traditional (formal) logic is a very special (and value-oriented!) case of some very complex 'logic' of experience involving 'formal' aspects of experience and especially 'valuative' processing of the 'world' of all kinds. An important step in this direction has been initiated by E. Topitsch who has discussed fundamental forms of thinking both in their genesis as well as in their influence on the development of Western thought, with especial reference to their (not always just) fossilized remains in our language.[43] But these matters cannot be followed here.

3.2.5. *The linearity of language.* A last important point is the *linear* nature of language in contradistinction to the 'synthetic simultaneity' of experience, and the consequence that what is perceived at one glance, 'synoptically' as it were, has to be rendered through a *succession* of individual language signals. This fact must obviously be of basic influence on the use of linguistic signals to evoke a synoptic complex situation or state-of-affairs in somebody's mind, to make somebody re-constitute via an extended string of language signals what *is*, in fact, a stable whole, e.g. a state of a complex system of nature, a social situation, a single vivid impression. This apparent limitation of language functioning does not only demand special ordering devices to avoid confusion (especially in long utterances) but also offers particular possibilities of exercising influence on the receiver, e.g. in an aesthetic way (suspense, tension through arousing curiosity, through sensual titillation, etc.), or also in a very practical political way (by misleading, confusing, or otherwise manipulating the receiver's mind). All such effects have been the subject of intensive study in various disciplines, e.g. rhetoric and dialectic, critical analysis of texts, stylistics, literary theory, etc. The problem has, of course, always found recognition – everybody knows about Lessing's famous *Laokoon* – but definitely needs treatment within a theory of the growth of human experience, within which both the *synthetic* and *simultaneous* sensory channels and the *linear* and *analytic* channel of language can be adequately investigated and related. – I shall have to say more about the linearity of language presently, as it is one basic factor conditioning a text's temporal semantics.

[43] Topitsch [92], [93], [94]. It is obvious that the investigation of such 'logic' of experience must take care not to become normative in a dogmatic sense, though all (ideological) criticism is bound to be directed by norms. Thus the logic of ZEN-anecdotes which completely eludes a 'civilized' Western person (like so much in the Bible, and similar writings) can *only* be called 'strange' or 'inconsistent' or 'contradictory' with reference to a presupposed standard.

3.2.6. *Communication.* It must be clear by now what is implied by 'communication': there is actually nothing 'transmitted' in the precise sense of the word except strings of vocal (or graphematic) signals; such signals can only be effective if a number of presuppositions both as to their *designata and* their proper use – which I am inclined to regard as (theoretically) inherent in the respective designatum – are valid for *all* the partners communicating. There must be, first of all, a common (portion of) 'model of the world'. Without it any kind of cooperation, i.e. also communication, is strictly impossible. What is to be emphasised particularly: language in the strict sense, i.e. as a system of signals, plays an important but *auxiliary* role, as it is but a kind of extremely sketchy shorthand for something highly complex and dynamic. It is no isomorphic mapping of the system of experience. It rather supplements the direct, or indirect, interaction of two SMW's, thus making it economical.[44] *Communication* denotes the interaction of two systems of experience using *also* linguistic means for the purposes of (value-directed) cooperation. Thus the 'pragmatics' of signs may be taken to be the instructional information inherent in IE's: knowing signals like *pot* or *shhh…! includes* knowing when to use them, and knowing the meaning of *danger* or *oil* includes knowing how to react; language signals, or combinations of them, serve to evoke and/or re-constitute experience of whatever kind, 'semantic' as well as 'pragmatic', stored to optimize future concrete interactions with the world, including communicating with a partner to mobilise exchange of experience for better (cooperative or individual) action. Language systems are therefore adapted to such situations of interaction: there are signals relating to the situation itself either explicitly (phenomena of *deixis* in the comprehensive sense: the *designatum* must be *immediate input* to the system addressed and may be referred to in various ways, e.g. by stating, exclaiming, questioning. interjecting, something – *There! Up? Go on then! Him. Silly. After, – no! Later. You see? There we are! O la la! Etc.*), or implicitly ('society-bound' signals, situation characteristic signals: e.g. Wittgenstein's example concerning the right level of abstractness of an utterance:

Denke, du sagtest jemandem statt "Bring mir den Besen!" – 'Bring mir den Besenstiel und die Bürste, die an ihm steckt!" – Ist die Antwort darauf nicht: "Willst du den Besen haben? Und warum drückst du das so sonderbar aus?"[45]

[44] The expression 'supplementation' is taken from M. Wandruszka's work which, though non-theoretical and global, does succeed to make some principally relevant points about the functioning of languages by demonstrating (with the help of 'interlinguistic' comparison), how individual languages are related with their special systems of experience. – Cf. [98], [99].

[45] [107], p. 46. Disappointing so-called 'expectation habits' is of course a principla procedure to challenge standards of experience and stimulate innovative thought processes (whatever the standards and goals involved: there is a wide variety of possibilities, including the "good soldier Schwejk" no less than "concrete poetry").

and all inherent directions for use concerning standpoint, domain of communication, e.g. factual, joking, polite, scientific, aesthetic, religious, serious, colloquial, etc.). – To sum up: human beings can only survive by cooperating; such cooperation always involves SMW's and *all* their faculties; language is *one* additional instrument to help in such cooperation by mobilising the partners' experience (for mutual benefit); thus obviously language can only operate on the basis of 'models of the world' in evidence, and in concurrence with concrete action: there is a wide variety of situations as to the 'necessary amount' of language involved, from the standardised pattern of action needing practically no supplementation by vocal signals to that standardised pattern of action involving a maximum of linguistic signals (e.g. reading a document, a novel, etc.); in all cases language functioning is dependent on a given model of the world determining concrete or inferred action.

3.3. *Text*

3.3.1. The word *text* will then best be understood as an arbitrary complex of linguistic signals of (widely) varying length, composed to supplement the interaction of SMW's (including the case of an SMW interacting with itself). A text is thus primarily a *linguistic* entity *only* (not just any complex of signs, e.g. a painting as well as a piece of music, etc.). Any set of linguistic signals functioning (in a goal-determined and *effective* way) in such interaction will be called an *acceptable*, or *functional*, text. The 'well-formedness', or the 'coherence', of texts are therefore – whatever specific aspects may be denoted by these and related expressions – determined by what the complex of signals called 'text' *stands for*: i.e. by the items of experience denoted (which include situational, or 'actional' properties). The 'acceptability' of a text is constituted by a set of 'conditions of acceptability' which must be inferred from the *denotatum* of the text in its totality. (Among such conditions one will certainly have to differentiate further: between conditions given by the set of IE's, e.g. material and formal properties identifying an item, evaluative properties, instructions for use, and conditions given by the signals and signal complexes themselves, e.g. the set of 'syntactic' conditions.)

Everything suggested so far as characteristic of language and its functioning necessarily holds for texts as well. Superficially viewed, texts are systematically combined signals, i.e. strings of signals formed according to the rules of a grammar (syntax, phonology, and graphematics). If we choose to speak of language signals as *signs* we may call any *sign combination* a *super-sign* (following information theory). Such super-signs then are emitted by a sender, a SMW, as a succession of elementary signs, built up in a systematic way. (I cannot discuss here the problem of what the elementary sign is, i.e. what the most adequate theoretical unit might be. I shall, however, continue to use *sign* and together with it *predication* to denote the most elementary unit of linguistic utterance irrespective of any theoretical approach, and use *signal* for the purely material aspect of linguistic signs, and therefore also *super-signal* for composite signals. All this is quite tentative.) – Now the material structure of such super-signs, or systems of predications, can partly be studied in its own right as a formal object to yield a formal 'grammar of signals' generating a 'language' (in the narrow sense, as suggested above). Clearly, as this *only* is of limited relevance to the study of natural language functioning and would not contribute much to an adequate theory of functional texts, it must be part of a more comprehensive undertaking aiming at a theory of the acceptability of texts.

The difficulties with such an adequate theory of text will be somewhat clear by now from the characterisation of language functioning given in terms of the ACM: texts are only shorthand for experience, more correctly: for a schematic model of the world. This is an abstraction too: it means speaking of what a text is *in general* (similar to speaking of the *langue* of a certain social community). In point of fact there is only the text coordinated to *a specific individual's* model of the world which, presupposing some minimal correspondence with another individual's model of the world, may receive an appropriate *concretization* in terms of the *other's* model of the world. Perfect interaction is therefore theoretical, in practice there will always be both loss and gain in any such interaction, a fact which offers both advantages and disadvantages. The important consequence is that the acceptability of a given text is determined by its underlying model of the world. Such a model is signalled exlicitly *and* implicitly: as stated above, language can in no way produce an isomorphic mapping of the relevant items of experience, it only crudely approximates them, suggests them; the 'rest' has to be *reconstructed* by the receiver in terms of *his* model of the world. Thus every text is naturally incomplete *and* schematic, and the conditions of its acceptability are far from being explicitly articulated: they are only partly suggested in the signal structure, most of them are to be inferred from the (mini-) world evoked.

It follows that the inherent 'logic' of a text arises from the systematic integration of the items of experience evoked, i.e. from the dynamics of its presupposed system of experience. Thus the evocation of any IE will immediately activate some mini-model in the receiver. The following IE will modify and redirect this process by cancelling out certain directions, introducing new ones, making apparent contradictions or gaps appear, thus arouse curiosity or other expectations, suggest certain implications *and* presuppositions which are (through principles of causal, or conditional, or functional, or other connection) derivable from what is being suggested, etc. In such a dynamic way a mini-model of experience (actual, or potential) is built up by the receiving system through the triggering function of linguistic signals. There may, and will, be the most intricate processes of reconstituting systems of IE's by all sorts of inferences back and forth, implications, comparisons, evaluations, etc. – This very scant description is only to suggest what has been known all the time about the functioning of texts.[46] The main point here is to emphasize that an adequate theory of texts cannot profitably limit itself to a narrow linguistic aspect (in whatever way it may be extended by ad-hoc semantics or pragmatics): it must start from the other way, i.e. the underlying model of the world, the system of IE's as a system in its own right which is only poorly labelled by a text. In other words – and quite ideally –, what is needed first is an adequate theory of experience in the comprehensive sense: a theory of the basic, and universal, ways and means to process information from 'the world'. Much is already known about this in physiology, especially in the physiology (and neurology) of perception and information processing in the central nervous system and the brain. This knowledge has gained particular interest and momentum through its being restated in cybernetic terms. Thus it seems to be possible to investigate how information is received by sensory receptors and how it is processed internally into percepts (or 'items of experience') which are, of course, not derived 'directly' from sensual experience but are creations of the human mind, conditioned by a given motivational state. – A second step would then lead to the exploration of the concrete (historical) results of such acquiring of 'ex-

[46] This is the complex problem of 'text constitution', i.e. of all the processes taking place in the progressive construction of what is here called a 'model of a mini-world': the problem has of course been the centre of all textual work in the literary disciplines (literary history, stylistics, poetics, rhetoric, etc.), to which one must add here the practical reflections and experiments of writers also. It has always been obvious with literary scholars and critics that the totality of 'meaning' and effect of any type of text is created in large measure by its structure, more appropriately, the structure of its composition. It has also always been obvious that it is the receiver (listener, reader, spectator and listener) who 'concretizes' the 'schematic' work (R. Ingarden) and that his values and standards, and in particular his knowledge and experience, are the basic ingredients in this process. These most fundamental facts are of course due to the elementary functional structure of the SMW and can be rephrased in more neutral and precise terms within the ACM. Here an adequate theory of language functioning is the prerequisite of all literary analysis and interpretation, though it does, of course, not exhaust a 'literary item' (which is part of a complex tradition of social experience and social norms as to aesthetics and morality; or, for all those who would misunderstand such a reactionary term like 'morality', I might say 'standards of relevancy' valid for the whole, or parts of the, community). – Here are the relevant problems of a theory of texts: stating all the necessary conditions of acceptable texts, explaining the 'constitution' of the 'meaning' (*and* effects) of a text and, conversely, offering precise means to 'optimize' the functioning of texts (i.e. language), wherever it occurs (= the functioning of all types of text). – The contribution of the *temporal* structure of text constitution will be discussed below.

perience', as it is carried out by a (historical) social community in a (historical) environment, driven by a (historical) set of values. Here the result must be (or should be) a theoretical account of the structure and content and working of the 'model of the world' sustaining that society. It is this model of the world as an intricately structured and dynamic 'system of experience' which is the *condicio sine qua non* of all action, i.e. all life-maintaining and life-improving active behaviour of any member of that society. It is this model of the world, too, which is the basis of all specialised experimenting, whether scientific or artistic, aiming at an optimisation of the existential situation. As no individual can survive by himself there must always be cooperation by interaction. However reduced or 'abstract' it may seem in certain situations, it is effective only because of the common model of the world. Here then language comes in to enhance the efficiency of all interacting. A third stage would investigate what portion of the internal model can be *explicitly* signalled by vocal labels, and in what way (– avoiding all hypostatization of an auxiliary instrument into a conceptual system). Thus it is in fact impossible to speak of the 'meaning' of isolated predications – as grammars do – e.g. *I am singing, you are singing, the cattle are fat*, etc. These are tremendous abstractions and can only be made use of by intelligent users who already possess the required internal model of the world within which the necessary concretization can take place. Thus the *thoroughly auxiliary and fragmentary nature of linguistic signals* cannot be over-emphasised: the only coherence they may produce is formal in the strict sense; there is *no* way to infer any criteria of coherence of meaning from the signal aspect *only*! Is there then any hope for an adequate theory of texts? There is surely no hope for an ideal theory of text in the strict sense: this is a logical impossibility; it could only be 'achieved' by 'somebody' standing outside *all* the models making up a society, and independent of the theoretical means implied by those models. (It may be added that 'theoretical' or 'scientific' activity in terms of the ACM is the attempt to stabilise parts of the ever-floating experience by objectifying them in economical form. Obviously such activity is only possible on the basis of a given model of the world which, then, is optimised again and again cooperatively and in strict obedience to accepted norms of action). There is some chance, I think, for a more practicable theory of texts if the auxiliary and fragmentary nature of language is realised and taken seriously. This means that *linguistic* semantics or pragmatics deal 'only' with special (though most important) forms to recall experience. An adequate linguistic heuristics should also incorporate a strategy involving *active use* of *experience* itself. To give a trivial example: the 'item of experience' *sparrow* must first be concretized as a visual percept before any inferences can be drawn, a cock's crow (as any 'noise' – cf. supra) must first of all be realised acoustically before it can be interpreted and made the premise of certain 'deductions', the quality *soft* can never be expressed in words if it has not been made an 'item of experience', if it has not been *felt*. And further: no linguistic signal can be sensibly *used* if it cannot be presupposed or expected that the partner is able to *infer* the corresponding situation or context of action. One cannot ask somebody, "What's the date?" and accept the answer, "Thursday". (Such overlapping or integration of systems of reference is only allowed in innovative and experimental expressions signalling potential experience. Thus a poet may speak of "a grief ago" or the "shadow of a sound" – proof of the working of the 'logic' of experience, a much more global 'logic' than the specialised kind of traditional formal logic.) Perhaps I may give a few random examples:

3.3.2. The absolute priority of the system of experience and its impoverished shorthand version by linguistic signals or signal sequences, i.e. by texts in the strict sense of the word, has always made it a particularly crucial problem to verbally 'represent' experience *adequately*, i.e. in an *effective way* (whatever the values involved!); how can one signal something complex and systematically structured, something dynamic, in a *linear* way, i.e. by signals that can only be produced and received sequentially? *I hit him* does signal some succession of *acts* (a very complex situation indeed, as everybody would agree) but there is no question at all that there was first *I*, then *hit,* and then *him.* Such a question would be adsurd though there are occasional and apparent 'symmetries', e.g. *in, out, up, back, crash*! or the famous *veni, vidi, vici* – but here we are already dealing with *texts*, i.e. predications combined into a systematic whole, into structured discourse. Such discourse can *never* 'portray' what it stands for: it does no more (and no less) than evoke the adequate model of a (mini-)world in the receiver using signals to stimulate the necessary processes of reconstituting that model out of certain essential pieces. Some of these 'pieces' – whatever labels we want to choose for them, e.g. 'actions', 'states-of-affairs', 'facts', 'events'... – are signalled *expressly* by available signals, others must be *inferred* by the receiver – in short: the 'text' offered is *always* rudimentary as to the reality 'behind' it, and it is *always* an ordered system of instructions, as it were, to *create* a model of a world (for whatever purpose: action or entertainment). Such *creation* will evidently depend upon, and be conditioned by, the *resources* available in the receiving SMW. In many cases, however, the creation of a model of a world is also guided and manipulated by the sender of the signals, and thus principally by the sequential structure he chooses for the process of reconstituting the world model he wants to be created in the receiver (i.e., *superficially* viewed by the structure of the *text*). (And again: there is only a very crude parallelism between the surface aspect of the signal sequence making up a text, spoken or written, and what *happens* as the receiver *creates* the model of a world according to the stimulation received!) There are therefore clearly many ways of rendering experience through language, though 'rendering' or 'representing' are misleading expressions as they always suggest 'direct' labelling and 'direct' retrieval of 'isolated' IE's. Thus the linearity and fragmentarity of language always stands in a specific relation of tension to what is actually signalled. This basic fact is of special significance to the problem of 'time and text': it implies the need to observe specific ordering conditions on the levels of the linguistic *signals*, and of *experience*, as well as in the relations between them. The system of experience signalled must be arranged sequentially so as to be capable of transmission and processing, and so must the 'text', and so, finally, must the process of constructing the first with respect to the latter. Thus, *one* basic and interesting task of text linguistics involves the theoretical treatment of these linguistic means which express the (semantically productive) ordering relationships between a text and the model of a world to be created by it. This relationship can, by definition, *never* be symmetrical except in a *very* superficial way.

3.3.3. The problem of the 'coherence' of texts must *appropriately* be called the problem of the 'logic' of experience 'underlying' a text. It obviously cannot be the 'text', as a structured sequence of signals, which is *coherent*: a text is *well-formed* syntactically, it is *coherent* semantically (i.e. the IE's, and the larger structures composed of IE's to form the model of a world, must be 'well-formed' as to the logic of experience in order to be *coherent* as a whole).[47] As was already shown, language can only work in conjunction with an SMW and is *one*, though important, means of action, more appropriately:

[47] R. Posner's interesting examination of phenomena of 'commenting' in texts, as one possible feature of textual coherence, thus deals with a (purposefully) restricted notion, and criterion, of coherence. Cf. the following examples:

(a) Es regnet.
(b) Daß du soeben festgestellt hast, daß es gegenwärtig der Fall ist, daß es regnet, hat kaum jemand zur Kenntnis genommen.
(a) Es regnet.
(b) Daß es gegenwärtig der Fall ist, daß es regnet, stört mich nicht.
(a) Es regnet.
(b) Daß es regnet, kommt in dieser Gegend häufig vor.

The 'comments' represent three different interpretations *less* of *It is raining* than of the situation of the interacting SMW's to which the verbal expressions are supplementary. – Comments of this kind can easily be multiplied if there is no specific indication as to the role and position of *It is raining* in a functional context. Cf. [77].

of interaction. Thus, to put it obscurely: functional language, as it appears in strongly reduced form in a 'text', is *functional* only by being *supplementary* to an SMW. It is obvious therefore, that action-relevant 'meaning' is only partially *linguistically* labelled and transmitted: it arises out of *all* the various inputs to *all* the active channels of an SMW. An *acceptable* text – and traditional 'coherence' is but an idiosyncratic aspect of such acceptability – meets conditions which are to a large extent *outside* it in a strict sense. The grammar of signals, i.e. the syntax of a text, is thus subordinated to the 'grammar' of its system of IE's and their inherent logic (which encompasses what is arbitrarily divided into semantics and pragmatics). Thus, such an extremely abstract example like *It is raining* may be an acceptable text in innumerable contexts. It may therefore be continued *logically* by a dialogue partner in a wide variety of ways, for instance:

(a) *It's raining.*
(b) Speak up!
(c) Nonsense.
(d) Nothing more relevant?
(e) Oh *men*!
(f) Beautiful rhythm!
(g) How romantic!
(h) Time for a walk.
(i) Get the dog in!
(j) At last!

An adequate theory of texts would have to explain why it is possible that a text, e.g. *It's raining. – Oh men*! is acceptable, and why *It's raining. – Time for a walk* may be just as acceptable, and so on. – I shall not hesitate to repeat: an acceptable text depends on the requirement that *all necessary conditions of acceptability* implied by what the text signals are fulfilled. The interaction of two SMW's on the basis of a common model of the world is only *supplemented* by linguistic signs whose selection and form is determined by what the partners know and want, i.e. by inferences from their own model of the world about potential action and its effects. Thus it is a simply perverted view to maintain that 'all' is in the signals and that the signals are the only 'safe' basis for 'scientific' work. This is not only dogmatic but also contradictory in itself: without all the necessary experience to be presupposed for 'understanding' any signal it would be even impossible to differentiate between signals and meaningless noises, let alone carry out any meaningful further analysis. Why then not face the real problems? Why not face a new paradigm?

3.3.4. The same point may be made in a different way: linguistic signals are but supplementary to human interaction on the basis of a common model of the world; they are fragmentary and do not state most of the relevant information which has therefore to be inferred. Thus *waiter* will never 'conjure up' in any person's mind just its 'dictionary meaning' as a well-defined "man who takes and executes orders, shifts plates, etc. at hotel or restaurant tables" (COD); instead the signal *waiter* is (and can only be) learned in the corresponding life-situation in which automatically (in most cases, or 'normally') also occur *hotel, restaurant* (and many more), *orders, plates, tables,* etc., including the still more 'abstract' IE's of *take, execute, shift*: and especially the dictionary's 'etc.'! It is a basic impossibility to define words by words (just try and look up in a unilingual dictionary the *definientia*...). Whoever has tried to learn a foreign language will know. *Waiter* then automatically makes the whole set of possible situations that it could supplement 'resurrect' in the mind and makes it therefore easy to concretize the 'meaning' of a (specifically oriented) predication:

Waiter!

as establishing a definite situation of human interaction for certain purposes (relative to the concretizing individual's model of the world). Thus *waiter!* will most probably be interpreted as the exclamation of somebody *in* a hotel or restaurant, *at* a table, etc. This situation would have to be depicted in greater detail if it could not be presupposed on the partner's part (e.g. if it was set in an exotic country, or if a particular detail was important, etc.).

In our story this is not so:

Waiter! There's a fly in my soup!

This again will not only be interpreted as an assertion of some state-of-affairs, *neutral* as to its valuative interpretation: the guest is obviously annoyed and wants the waiter to do something – everybody would take this in the same way, provided he doesn't like flies in soups, etc. Thus the waiter would be expected to apologize, 'shift' the plate, etc. – But in the story – and that is why it is a story – something surprising happens:

Waiter! There's a fly in my soup!
Don't make a fuss – they'll all want one.

There is a sharp contrast to our 'normal', action-bound, experience: we can laugh about it if it doesn't concern us, because we have understood despite the very few linguistic signals and have re-enacted, as it were, the whole situation.

And this is what we have to do all the time when confronted with linguistic signals: reconstitute the signalled piece of world in its entirety and re-enact it (whether only in the mind by simulation, or in reality). Again, the process of concretizing some 'acceptable' piece of world through its *linear* evocation by linguistic signals may be carried out through various strategies all contributing to the effect of a text on its receiver and thus constituting an important part of the text's meaning. But these problems of text composition and its effects have always been central concerns of critical discussion of texts of all kinds, based on the knowledge that language is functional only in human action which can only originate from common experience. A more detailed account of the ACM might help to make the basic problems explicit, and demonstrate with the help of some model cases what goes on when language is used. I cannot here, however, go into this discussion. The problems will be familiar to everybody who uses language and who is interested in finding out about the regularities governing such *language use*, and not only in dogmatically petrified aspects of linguistic signals and/or experience. – What was pointed out by P. and E. K. Maranda for folkloristics holds in all its astringency for any kind of normal language use, in speech or in writing:

> ...no text as such is a real folkloristic item: texts are only records of mentifacts...
> ...one should bear in mind that no recording is complete, not even a video-tape recording, since the actual situation in which folklore is presented is the only environment in which it can live. That means that the tradition-carrier and his audience, their actions and reactions, the language used and its connotations, the whole of the group's culture should be known before any accurate analysis of a given folkloristic item is made possible. That such requirements are impossible to meet does not affect their validity...[48]

[48] Cf. [67]. – I may add in passing that it is also the uncritically reductionist attitude towards language functioning which must be held responsible for all kinds of normative 'language dictatorship', e.g. in politics, social intercourse, or teaching. There are only too many examples for the utter blindness to the conditions of acceptability inherent in 'texts' belonging to so-called 'primitive' or 'sub-standard' communities. S. Pop [74] has gathered many comments, both pro and contra, on dialects and pointed out repeatedly how perverted a view it is to call such language systems 'primitive' or 'sub-standard' or 'barbaric', etc. And it is a sad fact that all too many linguists of a purportedly 'scientific' attitude are so unaware of the most elementary functional properties of language that the truth about them must be re-discovered again and again, whenever a wrongly oriented 'scientific' linguistics has run up against the natural boundaries of its approach. Today's socio-linguistics testifies to such a reaction, and it is not surprising that many of the most critical voices echo equally outspoken criticism from the past, e.g. W. Labov's discussion of the social context of language functioning, or the 'logic' of non-standard English (cf. Wunderlich/Klein eds. [56], pp. 8off., pp. 111ff.) is only different in tone from Ch. Nodier's emphatic assertion that dialects have

> "une grammaire aussi régulière, une terminologie aussi homogène, une syntaxe aussi arrêté que le pur grec d'Isocrate et le pur latin de Cicéron".
> (Cf. Pop [74], p. 28.)

3.3.5. I may conclude then by adding a few more general points. I am quite aware of the fact that an ideally adequate theory of the functioning of texts in the understanding suggested so far is absolutely impossible. It is also no *desideratum*. A feasible goal, however, is a theory developed in the awareness of *everything relevant* to the proper and individual-bound functioning of language, and therefore of texts. Such a theory would first of all have to get away from the prejudice that language exists primarily in *written* form, and that the written appearance of a text is a faithful 'reflection' of everything there is to its possible functioning. It is not necessary to stress further that this is quite misconceived. Most of what is important to the text's functioning is not articulated by it at all: without a presupposed common world of experience there is no understanding of any text in any appropriate sense. Thus it is pure fetishism to restrict a theory of texts to 'objects' given as sets of graphematic signals. And it is also dogmatic: no man can help *interpreting* the set of signals and using this interpretation as the basis of his theorising.[49] And the most basic pre-decisions in any approach to a theory of texts go far beyond the mere written appearance: judging such a theory's usefulness, for instance, or discussing a text's structure. It is also an error to assume that the application of a formal system, or a formal procedure, to a 'text' in the sense of 'structured sequence of signals' will automatically yield a linguistic theory of empirical relevance. Formal means are of invaluable assistance where the basis (of 'objects' and 'properties') for generalisation is well-established. Such a basis we have come nowhere near in the study of language functioning as understood here. And formal systems are *in no way* 'heuristic devices' or discovery procedures, as seems to be assumed by many who think the translation of some (pre-edited) 'object language' into symbolism is a 'theory'.

I am convinced that linguists are in desperate need of better acquaintance less with formal systems than with basic epistemological facts on the one hand, and much more (traditional) empirical matter on the other. It is after all a tremendous waste of energy for every 'generation' to start out from its own small basis, and to expend valuable intelligence on hypotheses which could easily have been foreseen to be inadequate. – And then: all the teachers at the schools, *what are they to do*? They *have* got to get their pupils to master the instrument of language, and they *do* need good and solid knowledge about what a text 'is' and 'does'. If they only knew the basics of language functioning, they could work out their own strategies of getting such largely intuitive knowledge 'across'. How? Through cooperative action. Never through 'words' only. Thus there would be great value in more 'negative'

[49] This is shown daily by the recurring 'misunderstanding' among humans, which is nothing but a conflict of interpretations (or concretizations) of linguistic signals.

statements about language, instead of the all-too metaphysical attitudes which seem to be current. If, as Joshua Whatmough once remarked, "meaning is goal-directed activity" – a phrase, imprecise and vague to be sure, but certainly comprehensible after what has been said – then linguistics ought to provide theoretical help to improve the teaching and training of the necessary acceptability conditions of such 'activity'. Knowing what the success of such 'activity' depends on would make every language user more critical both in his utterances and with regard to those of others.

3.4. *Time*

> Of all the important ideas those of being and of time seem to have been muddled throughout their history. And of the two, the second seems always to have won the confusion derby. Much of the time muddles come from conceiving of time as something that flows, i.e. from identifying flux and time rather than construing time as the step of becoming. That reification of time, so typical of ordinary knowledge, comes down from archaic thought...
>
> The conceptions of time as thing and as process are of course found in a number of locutions in the Indo-European languages, suggesting that time flows, flees and even fleeces us; that it can be lost and found, stolen and gained; that it is ever in a hurry to pass from past to future; that it can cause birth and death. And, at least in Spanish, time can also be killed and must even be given time (*Hay que dar tiempo al tiempo*).[50]

I have already pointed out what a harassed *concept* time is and shall therefore not spend any more time on a discussion of what 'it' possibly 'is'. There is practically no field of human activity which does not also involve some theoretical discussion of time, one more than the other, be it in the intuitive and vague terms of ordinary discourse to portray what is called the 'experience' of 'time' as (too slow or too fast) change, or in the more standardized codes of scientific discussion. Some of the latest scientific research is contained in the recent volume *The Study of Time* reporting a conference of the *International Society for the Study of Time*. This society was formed in 1966 "in response to an increased realisation among leading scientists and scholars that the interdisciplinary study of time, as a form of inquiry in its own right has come of age".[51] Most of the contributions to that conference came from physicists, biologists, psychologists, anthropologists, and philosophers. There was no word about time representation in natural languages though this problem came up in occasional remarks in various papers. It will not be necessary to give a review of what was said about 'time' in this book or of what seems currently to be held by the 'leading scientists and scholars': as said above the picture is a thoroughly confused one. Especially the physicists are throwing around concepts like 'time asymmetry', 'reversibility', 'time

[50] M. Bunge [22], p. 562.

[51] This is quoted from the circular letter of the Society, informing about aims and interests, obtainable from its secretary J. T. Fraser, P.O. Box 164, Pleasantville, N.Y. 10570, U.S.A.

invariance', 'the discrete nature of physical time', 'the time coordinate', 'cosmic time', 'time dilatation', 'astronomical times', 'atomic time', 'time reversal violations', 'Zeitmaß und Seinsschichten', 'absolute time', 'relative time', 'creative time', and many more, which clearly show that there are many theoretical approaches to the time problem within their paradigm. – The interests of biologists and psychologists are nearer those of our field, it seems, but I am not sure whether a precise description of the temporal aspects of human information processing can be of use in the theoretical representation of the 'meaning' signalled by language. There seems to be some important connection I think which might be explored: the relations between the speed of information processing (or: the relative duration of processes of the mind) and the working of language, to put it quite vaguely. This seems to be important for the concretization of texts, i.e. their 'meaning' in the sense of the 'model of the world' evoked through a complex process of re-constitution which is mediated by a linear sequence of signals. I shall come back to this very briefly a little later.

The contributions by *anthropologists* could also, I think, be of use in the sense of demonstrating differing approaches to the conceptualization of the phenomenon 'time'. This will be important both because it is surely impossible to study 'time' in the abstract in 'language' in the abstract, and because it seems a fruitful approach to concentrate on 'simple' forms and approaches on the one hand, and to insist on a basically comparative procedure on the other. An adequate theory of the functioning of language can only be constructed on such an empirical basis if it is to be more than just an exploration of ways to represent certain empirical phenomena of *one* language, i.e. if it wants to arrive at the formulation of more general hypotheses valid for all languages. Among the more *philosophical* approaches there are e.g. historical discussions of earlier conceptions of time which may be interesting for the reasons just stated, or the approaches of what has come to be called 'temporal logic', a field which wants to "systematize reasoning with propositions that have a temporalized aspect"[52] and thus is, and stays, within the confines of traditional formal logic, i.e. the field working on "an analytical theory of the art of reasoning whose goal is to systematize and codify principles of valid reasoning", having "emerged from a study of the use of language in argument and persuasion", and being "based on the identification and examination of those parts of language which are essential for these purposes".[53] I have quoted this characterization deliberately to show what logic in the traditional and specialist sense is interested in doing, and thus *can* do, and does, but also to emphasize what it leaves out as far as real languages are

[52] Rescher/Urquhart [80], p. 2.
[53] Stoll [90], p. 56.

concerned. As I have indicated earlier, 'thinking' in the sense of purposefully manipulating experience within a model of the world, is an infinitely more complex process embodying much more complex structures of 'reasoning' and a variety of principles and forms of making deductions and deriving inferences than are taken into account by formal logic in the modern sense. As languages, however poorly, also cover this global 'logic' of experience, it is obvious that logical means in the *narrow* sense cannot primarily be used for representing meaning signalled by language, let alone as heuristic devices to analyse what there is in language meaning. Thus 'temporal logic' operates with intuitive concepts of 'time', 'events', 'past', 'now', 'future', 'present', etc., introduced as 'understood', prior to various axiomatic systems precisely specifying admissible relationships between expressions containing such concepts. Temporal logic may therefore be of help to express certain features of time representation in natural languages once they have been established, it will *not*, and does not claim to, help us to *find* these.

I shall now try to point out some of the aspects of the problem of time, and, at the same time, some of the possible perspectives under which one might profitably deal with it. These remarks are, of course, of a very tentative nature but may be sufficient to illuminate potential fields of study in the interaction of time and texts.

As historical accounts of the development of time concepts, biological and psychological discussion of time concepts in the animal kingdom, and the evolution of time concepts in human development suggest, the signal *time* denotes a very abstract concept whose late ontogenetic evolution is reflected by the late phylogenetic appearance of explicit 'time' reference in language. Formulated in terms of the ACM, this means that the internal model of the world is built up in stages: after first bodily contact with the environment, mainly tactile, the processing by increased use of the visual and acoustic channels marks the evolution of more and more abstract models of the world. Thus there is first basically concrete, tactile, spatial orientation, still reflected in some of the time concepts of languages (*Zeitraum, lange Zeit, long time, short time, erfüllte Zeit, fulfilled time, time distance, Zeitabstand, Zeitspanne, time span*, etc., including, of course, temporal adverbs and prepositions etc., like *through, throughout, in, längst, round about, between*, etc.), which differentiates between situations in terms of concrete 'objects' or 'events' (*This was when the cat caught 27 mice, remember?*). As soon as a stage is reached in which the internal model of the world covers most of 'the world's' more stable and uniform aspects, information processing starts to tend to establish more abstract relations between IE's, whether these be 'objects', 'events', 'situations' or whatever. Such abstract, relations are signalled by the global concept of 'time'. 'Time' originates because of the structure of the human system, notably the narrowness of the input channel ("Enge des Bewußtseins"), which necessitates *linear* or *sequential* processing of informati on.Thus 'time' has to do mainly with the sequential *ordering* of experience in such a way as to be able to *identify* IE's for manipulation whenever needed, irrespective of their acquirement, i.e. their 'historical' position in the continuum of interaction between an individual and his environment. Thus *time* signals all sorts of orientational relations between an SMW in a given 'historical' state and some IE, be it in the process of being acquired, recalled, or otherwise 'worked on', e.g. in thinking, or communicating. One might say therefore that for the human mind as the central processor of an SMW all information processing or experience manipulating, whether on macro- or micro-levels, implies a sequential input of 'discrete' items. For two items to be discrete makes it impossible for them to be simultaneous with themselves: they must definitely be in sequence, i.e. one 'before', or 'after', the other. That in our ordinary experience lightning and thunder, or 12 a.m. and the clocks striking 12, are 'simultaneous', is another matter and shows that linguistic signals refer to very variable relationships between IE's. For the purposes of daily life, i.e. for all human interaction within an accepted model of the world, the rough-and-ready indications by linguistic signals are sufficient. This applies to all the expressions of what W. E. Bull calls 'personal time', i.e. all the ordinary distinctions between IE's as to their ordering relations relative to each other. Thus for humans there is 'simultaneity' in many ways, for other modes of processing information, differentiating more precisely, e.g. physical science, there is not.

The necessary sequentiality of all experience manipulating automatically puts every item into a specific position relative to others and, as one might say that every item requires 'space' (i.e. expenditure of matter and energy for processing), one might also speak of the 'distance' of one item from another. Thus items are not only ordered relative to each other within a 'historical' continuum of interaction (=flow of information) between a system 'man' and a system 'world' – which necessarily implies that the system 'man-world' is always the central point of reference for such ordering – it is also possible to 'measure' the distances between them, it is, in other words, possible to speak of 'intervals' between items, or, differently again: items may take up more 'space', thus make the 'distance' between an item before and after greater; items have 'duration'. – This is certainly not very clear, as it is difficult to talk about 'time' without using 'time talk'; the point is to show that 'time' originates as the name of some hypostatized 'entity' only from the fact that items of experience have to be *distinguished* from, and *related* with, each other in more or less 'precise' terms. It is from the realisation of such 'automatic' ordering in the human mind (helped of course, by the observation of natural cyclical phenomena, e.g. the seasons, weather, day and night, growth and decay, etc.) that humans generalise these specific ordering relations between IE's: i.e. they develop means to *position* every item on what becomes abstractly a 'time axis' or a 'time arrow' (from birth → death) *relative to their own position*, and they develop means to *measure* the 'distances' between IE's and themselves, or between IE and IE, etc.

An SMW will of course go through a variety of states of differing degrees of 'activity' or 'intensity' as to its information turnover. The degree of intensity of information processing will be of influence on the personal judgment of the 'distance' between two (arbitrary or conventional) items of experience: 'time' will then be 'short' or 'long'. [54] It is clear that 'time' as an abstract set of (quantifiable) relations cannot 'be' anything of that sort: 'time' *is not* without IE's ('events', 'states-of-affairs', 'situations', 'emotions', etc.), and what is 'short' is the 'distance' between two items in terms of what was 'allowed' in between, or if 'long', in terms of what was lacking or missing (in all cases relative to acting motives). Such phenomena are only too well-known, they are the essence of personal time. We all know that *in a second* may mean an *eternity* and that *in a little while* may signify *hours, days, weeks.* We also know that people have their individual internal clocks ('Zeitgefühl') relative to their cultural environment. Many examples of this have been recorded, one of the latest can be found in H. Gipper's report of his stay with the Hopi Indians and his experience of the different attitude to time among the Hopis.[55] – It is obvious that such crude personal time cannot serve as a means of orientation for the complex interaction of a social group. More precise means of both ordering and measuring are needed: clocks and calendars, i.e. 'public time'. – There is no need to discuss the working of public time, it may only be noted that there is a natural tension arising from the necessity to adapt one system of ordering to the other, i.e. in general, to have to subordinate personal to public time. That conflicts may arise if there is a break in the synchronisation of the two, e.g. by a rapid change from one time system to another, is shown by biological, medical and psychological research. Perhaps this too is an indication of the fact that *time* is the name of a very abstract hypostatization of a range of very concrete phenomena.

It seems advisable to restrict 'time' to the elementary ordering relations suggested above and to separate it from the rest of the 'semantics of experi-

[54] There is well-known psychological evidence that the information turnover is, for instance, greatly increased in certain situations (of pressure, or relief), i.e. that a person can 'experience' vast stretches of 'world' or 'life' in a split second, a fact which has been exploited by writers in many ways (including experiments with drugs).

[55] Gipper [37], pp. 205ff.

ence'. Such 'semantic' features are the results of specific classification and evaluation of IE's. A glance at the traditional listings in a thesaurus under 'time' quickly shows that explicit temporal features play a role in a large part of the vocabulary of English and German; in Roget's *Thesaurus* we find, amongst others, the following main categories under the entry 'time':

> *Course – diuturnity – transientness – perpetuity – instantaneity – chronometry – priority – posteriority – futurity – newness – oldness – morning – evening – youth – age – earliness – occasion – regularity...*

Roget does not include under TIME 'change' and 'causation', or 'motion', or 'order', etc. which certainly involve 'time', too. – Dornseiff offers a different system, his categories are, for instance:

> *Zeiträume – Zeitmessung – Nie – Immer – Dauer – Beständigkeit – Vergänglich – Vorher – Nachher – Gleichzeitig – Zwischenzeit – Gegenwart – Vergangenheit – Nahe Vergangenheit – Ferne Vergangenheit – Zukunft – Baldige Zukunft – Unregelmäßig – Regelmäßig – Kontinuität – Gelegenheit – Unzeit...*

This *ubiquity of time* in the system of experience of any culture makes it very difficult to properly circumscribe a problem like 'time and text': does 'temporal semantics' involve *all explicit* and *implicit* temporal features? It must do so, obviously, because it is the set of *all* these features – articulated or not! – which determines the behaviour of any individual predication. A heuristics of research into the *temporal constituents of texts* and their functioning in *acceptable* texts as understood here would therefore be well-advised, I think, to reflect on 'time' as well, in order to be able to differentiate 'temporal' semantics from 'other' semantic complexes, e.g. those of 'causality', or 'motion', or 'change', which all have 'time' as an important inherent feature and could therefore be of influence on the choice (in generation) or interpretation (in reception) of other temporal elements, e.g. the tenses, time adverbials, or aspectual forms. It is certainly correct to say that the tenses of verbs do not signify 'time' in the sense of 'public time', i.e. they do not explicitly refer to time as measured extensionally. They have other functions beside temporal reference, but they certainly *do* refer to 'temporal' relations between an SMW and items of experience.

It may be noted finally:

(a) the factual conditions for the emergence of the system of ordering relations called 'time' are universal to all SMW's;

(b) the ordering relations called 'time' exist *prior* to any information processing in the SMW, they are thus *prior* to language;

(c) a theoretical treatment of 'temporal semantics' might profitably start from a universal theory of time in terms of the ACM;

(d) it must be realised that, 'time' being a universal property of all information processing, there is, largely, no need to explicitly articulate temporal relations: they are either portrayed by the sequence of linguistic signals (*veni, vidi, vici*), or they are expressed implicitly (*overgrown, era, volatile*...) or explicitly (...*arrived at*... *stayed for*... *went*...);

(e) as 'time' is prior to all information processing it relates IE's of all levels: percepts just as predications, texts or parts of texts just as persons, events, situations...: it will be important to define the variables entering into temporal relations, especially those variables of differing level and magnitude, as they appear in a text.

4. Time and text

Reviewing what has been said so far about the structure of the human information processing system and its central result, the internal model of the world, further about the precarious relationship between language signs and this dynamic, though comparatively stable, model of the world (or 'system of experience'), and finally about the basic ordering relations between all 'items of experience', perceptual and linguistic, which we subsume under the label *time*, I may now briefly hint at some of the problems involved in the topic 'time and text'.

It must be evident by now that I am interested in developing an adequate theory of language functioning; more precisely, and to forestall misunderstanding: an adequate theory of the systematic foundations and the working of language within the existence of humans in general. (A description of the historical realizations of those systematic possibilities, or universal 'conditions', of language *use*, clearly has to rely on such a general theory in order to be able to make critical pronouncements on what has actually been 'done' with language; literary, or historical, or philosophical, or theological, study of 'text' as 'petrefacts' of somebody else's experience thus definitely need linguistics but cannot, of course, be supplanted by it.) In terms of the anthropo-cybernetic model (which can be stated with much more precision and detail than I have been able to do above) such a theory can be outlined in its entirety. The resulting global framework integrates what has traditionally been the subject of various disciplines, e.g. psychology, sociology, bioanthropology – a fact which will not cause delight in all those who favour working in nicely insulated boxes by artificial light and are happy with a paradigm whose guiding star is the 'eternal quest for pure knowledge'. Others will not be prepared to accept the view that psychology, sociology, linguistics, literary study, philosophy, science, etc. are 'nothing else' but specific ways of information processing, i.e. ways defined by, say the norms of critical rationality, or those of other ideologies, and that, moreover, such scholarly information processing has to do with specific portions of human information processing some of which have retained the traditional label 'psychology', others 'literature', others 'philosophy', etc. As Stachowiak's convincing demonstration shows, all the problems involved in what has traditionally been divided into disciplines like epistemology, ontology, methodology, aesthetics, theory of knowledge, philosophy of science, and other fields, can very well be integrated into a unified approach, a kind of super-theory of human information processing, within which the special problem of 'operational thinking', i.e. thinking directed at problem solving, can be discussed without quarrelling about the 'proper' domain of discussion ("This is not my field! It is psychology!" etc.), or without having to mix terminologies of different origins. The same applies to language: in the anthropo-cybernetic model of the system man-world it is primarily unnecessary to distinguish between the 'philosophy' the 'psychology', or the 'sociology' of language, all of which traditional classifications would come into a discussion of language objectifications (literary, legal, historical, political...). Instead, language can be treated as *one* specific problem: the problem of how it *functions* and what the 'meaning' of linguistic signals *is*. The distinctions between the philosophy, psychology, or sociology of language can be dispensed with at this stage: they may be relevant at a higher level, when specific interests demand the specific delimitation of factual domains – which does not concern the systematic aspects of *all* language functioning with which we are concerned here and which are of decisive influence on every kind of 'use', i.e. on all kinds of 'functionalization' of language. To state the conditions (or foundations) of all *possible* functionalizations of language would then be another characterization of the task and object of linguistic theory.

What is involved in setting up this goal may have become apparent from the previous discussion. I have stated my priorities as well as my dissatisfaction with certain tendencies in theoretical linguistics. Not, as I hope to have made clear, because I am 'ideologically' prejudiced, but because I think that formalist apriorism and deductivist reductionism operate on the basis of a very naive view of language structure and language functioning. It is precisely this dissatisfaction which accounts for the approach taken in this paper.

To summarise: the ACM allows the location of language in its functional place in the system 'man-world'. Language is a system of material signals standing for the internal model of the world (i.e. all its systematic components and properties, larger or smaller, concrete or abstract), a system which is rather static and of little mobility – relative to the 'mobility of mind' of a generation – and is to represent another system of infinite and dynamic complexity, and thus mobility and 'creativity'. It is the latter 'system of experience', or 'model of the world', which guides all information processing and thus embodies all (historical!) modes of acquiring experience of an individual. Language cooperates with this system by permitting its manipulation (in all forms of interaction) through the convenient and economical shorthand of its signals. Language thus is nothing on its own, i.e. in its purely material aspect; it works by supplementing a model of the world and, if objectified as a 'text' (of signals!), is nothing without such a presupposed model of experience.

Thus we arrive at a comprehensive characterisation of 'text': a 'text' is any linguistic signal (simple or complex) which is functional relative to a system of experience. This characterisation implies, after what was said above, that the only stable aspect of a text is its signals and all talking about 'a given text' means talking about a 'schematic', abstract, text 'underlying' – the metaphor is not to be taken literally – all possible concretizations of these signals in terms of a model of a world.

The system man-world has a very restricted input channel and is thus forced to process information item per item, i.e. sequentially. This involves explicit ordering of items within this sequence. Obviously the ordering of items, i.e. the structure of the process of reconstituting a 'piece of world', will be of influence on the result of the concretization process. The process of concretization will (or should) ultimately lead to a revision of the model of the world involved: it will, by virtue of new experience, not only restructure its 'content', i.e. the 'amount' of world covered, but also revise its inherent 'logic', i.e. add new 'axioms' or 'rules of inference' and cancel out others. A text may thus be instrumental in creating knowledge. It must be stressed, however, that 'knowledge' is to be understood in a comprehensive sense: it involves *all* types of information, and thus, the whole SMW with all its aesthetic 'memory'. (The phenomena of blushing, or trembling with rage or delight, or shivering with fear or ecstatic sensations, are definitely components of the 'knowledge' concretized through the evocation of specific IE's by verbal signals, e.g. swear words, words of despise, scorn, blame, threat, love, tenderness, etc.)

Now, the necessarily *sequential* process of reconstituting experience also creates information *qua* being sequential. What kind of information this is, will depend on the IE's involved: suspense and sensuous delight will rarely be the information of a political or legal text, of a programme or an advertisement... But to quote emotions does not exhaust the meaning created by the sequentiality of the reconstitution process: the 'temporal structure' of experience reconstitution is essential for the *meaning*, and thus the *effect*, of a text; the topic 'time and text', then, concerns this basic fact, in the first place: the *time structure of a text.* This is a genuine *text*-linguistic topic; to investigate the linguistic means of *time reference* in texts is a necessary *part* of this topic, no more and no less; no more, because it is auxiliary to the functioning of a text in the interaction of (at least) two SMW's and therefore only *one* set of acceptability conditions; no less, because it is an *essential* determinant of the time structure of a text, and thus of the text's meaning and effect.

The expression 'time structure' is, of course, very general in meaning and can therefore be applied to anything which consists of elements in a structural arrangement. As to a verbal *text* – presupposing all that has been said – the time structure can be established on various levels (or with regard to various aspects) of the text. I shall give a brief survey of some of the interesting possibilities. These possibilities may be divided into two categories:

(a) 'time structure' is understood as *that* aspect of the model of a (mini-) world (recreated through a text) which relates it with an accepted system of temporal reference, e.g. with a system of public time, of personal time, or both. Time structure in this sense means historical time structure, whereby 'historical' is to be taken in its general sense, referring to every kind of 'history', public and private, external and internal, political, philosophical, emotional, economic, etc.

(b) 'time structure' is understood as that essential *constituent of the concretization process* evoked by the *sequence* of verbal signals called 'text', as a constituent which governs and guides the construction of the model of a (mini-)world in the receiver's mind.

This basic distinction is traditional: category (a) derives from a more historicist attitude and concerns types of text, which require temporal clarity (e.g. historical, instructional, documentary texts); category (b) is a more literary category and has been treated principally in view of rhetorical and aesthetic effects (e.g. speeches, sermons, entertainment, instruction). Clearly category (b) includes category (a), and the whole distinction seems, in fact, based on rather superficial criteria, and therefore arbitrary – but practical. But this is saying no more than that a text is necessarily temporally ordered, and that the *kind* of ordering (i.e. its formal expression and its degree of explicitness) will depend on the functional status of a text, i.e. on the *type of text* involved. – I shall therefore not attempt to present a precisely differentiated system of (types of) 'time structures', but only suggest some of the interesting aspects and (also traditional) directions of research.

4.1. The time structure of the general flow of information processing by an SMW has been a concern of biology and psychology (cf. supra). We know how 'long' the human 'moment' is (in contradistinction to a snail's, or a stickleback's)[56] we know that there are rhythmic cycles of all sorts in the SMW; we know that 'time' also originates from the specific speeds of processing information, which depend on the motivational state and the amount of information to be mastered.[57] – These problems are important; they can be of significance to textual theory, especially its phonaesthetic and stylistic (i.e. rhetorical and aesthetic) aspects, if and only if all the actual information processed is adequately represented theoretically. Thus what is valued as 'fluency' of style can only be adequately determined and (experimentally) investigated with reference to a specific SMW and a precise description of every single IE to be processed. The 'fluency' of trivial, or everyday, texts is due to factors different from those determining the 'fluency' of 'great' literature, or of a political or religious speech. Thus the 'built-in' maximum or minimum speed of concretization of a text is relevant to its effect, and thus its function. It is for this reason, i.e. the dependence on the SMW involved, that 'style' has always been (and always will be) a matter of (personal) 'taste'; and that it is a doubtful enterprise to look for general laws of judgement as to linguistic performance outside a specific SMW. There must be great caution in such undertakings; the 'time structure' of information processing will definitely have to be a variable to take into account.

4.2. All classes of 'historical' texts carry some explicit reference to a system of public time: a letter bears the date as global time index (in the form of the central point of reference to which all the other implicit and explicit references in the text are meant to be related); a programme contains dates and precise time indications (both positional and durational), legal documents, contracts, certificates, laws, regulations, orders, invitations, reports, directories, speeches, lectures – all such types of text are synchronised with public time. This does not mean that the time structure of such texts is not interesting in itself for the linguist. In fact he is responsible for the precise definition of the meaning of all the *explicit* temporal elements used in texts, on the one hand, and he ought to determine the precise meaning of all *implicit* time reference. Thus no historical analysis of texts relative to their 'public-time structure' can, in principle, be carried out without linguistics. Establishing the actual duration or temporal position of events, developments, etc. in terms of public time, may, for instance, be of the greatest importance to the correct interpretation of a text, e.g. by a detective, a secret agent, a court of law, a priest... Such problems demand the use of what linguistics ought to

[56] Cf. Uexküll [96], pp. 33ff. Frank [29], Vol. II, pp. 67ff.

[57] Cf. Piaget [73], pp. 319ff. Efron [28] (with further literature). Michon [68] (with much further literature).

have determined to be the IE signalled by a given sign (word, predication, etc.); the IE'S possible implications ('back' and 'forth') derived in conjunction with the rest of the text finally yield the specific 'logic' of the text, e.g. an argument, a sequence of events, situations, processes. In the sense of 'public-time-structure' all texts could clearly be studied. It is, in fact, a distinctive feature of certain texts that they *must* be relatable to a system of public time. This often necessitates strict coordination of the actual public-time sequence of events with the sequence of predications, which is distinctive of the acceptability of such types of text. Thus it is required that a programme keeps to the strict temporal sequence of the items signalled: it is unusual to disturb the 'natural order' of items on a programme, a menu, a list of agenda, a series of instructions, a certificate, etc. This is to minimise the amount of redundancy. There are of course exceptions, both for practical reasons (strict isomorphism between predication and IE is impossible) and for reasons of priority, purpose, etc. Thus on a menu there will be strict sequence of first, second, third, and fourth courses but the beverages served off and on will usually be stated at the end, i.e. *not* where they – irregularly, though not without system – appear in the sequence of courses: aperitif, beer, wine, champagne, coffee, liqueur, etc. Apart from such references to sequence there are also indications of the duration of events; explicitly, as 'from 8 am – 10 am' or implicitly, e.g. 'after the overture to...', 'just at the opening of...'. etc.

There are of course innumerable occasions which involve explicit or implicit indication of the 'time structure' of a 'piece of world' reported by a text. There is no need here to discuss such possible time structures with reference to public time: this task is essentially the historian's, and he will have to use the information supplied by linguists to interpret his texts correctly; he, however, is *not* interested in the *linguistic means* to express temporal relations and durations as such. On the contrary, the linguist is not primarily interested in 'how much' time is used up by the 'events' reported, or narrated, by a text, or what the relationship between 'narrated' time and 'time of narration' is, or in how many 'time spheres' a novel moves, etc.[58] This may be more interesting, however, where 'personal time' is involved, because all such

[58] Cf. e.g. Glinz's analysis [39], pp. 111ff., or the recurring dichotomy 'narrated time' vs. 'time of narration' in the discussion of the so-called 'theory of the novel', inaugurated by G. Müller [69], and continued by F. K. Stanzel [86], [87].

As to the first point it is obvious that a text dealing with palaeontology or astronomy 'covers' quite different time spans from any ordinary report or the joke about the waiter above. The linguist will not be particularly interested in the 'amount' of time as such, at least not normally. Much the same holds for the ratio 'narrated' vs. 'narrating' time, which is extremely variable (as is shown by many examples from especially modern literature). The proper *evaluation* of the *function* of such 'desynchronization' is, however, once established, another matter and will indeed by a relevant concern of the text-linguist.

time reference is not precise, but derives its meaning from other interacting factors.

Texts may be constructed entirely within a system of personal time when there is no need to state precise time positions or durations, or when such precision would be irrelevant and disturbing. All human speech is usually embedded into some public-time frame, anyway. Thus purely approximative time indications are enough in many situations. In a conversation there are innumerable expressions like 'then', 'now', 'later', 'earlier', 'a while after', 'a long time', 'soon', 'recently', 'lately' etc., not to mention all sorts of indirect formulae like "waiting for hours, days, weeks, years... an eternity", "he did not run, he toddled", "she has a well-oiled mouth", "she flew up the stairs", etc. The relevant time structure of such texts, i.e. their sequence of IE's, may be inferred without any difficulty.

Finally, there are texts which seem to be 'independent' of both personal and public time except for their global attachment to an overall historical point or period. The SMW supplemented by 'theoretical' texts may be the model of an individual making 'general' statements or assertions about his world (usually without explicit reference to time, public or personal, but with implicit temporal features expressed by various operators, 'all', 'every', 'any', 'always'...), implying that these statements are valid for all other SMW's coordinated to his. Such 'timeless' assertions in the sense of statements abstracting from a given position in time to all (possible) positions and periods, are found in all kinds of discourse, from the general assertions of everyday personal life to the most highly standardised systems of statements of theories.

As already indicated, the question of the (public-, or personal-, or both) time structure in a historical sense is of less primary interest to the linguist, especially to the text-linguist. These problems may be of importance for the correct interpretation of texts, or their correct and 'logical' production, but this is mainly both a problem of semantics, i.e. the logic of experience, and of historical verification. It is the linguistic means that may be used to refer to actual time, i.e. to ordering relations between IE's, which are of interest to the linguist.

For the text-linguist, this problem is part of his investigation of textual time structure of category (b): the time structure of the reconstitution process of the model of the (mini-)world, as evoked by verbal means. Before passing on to that another point must be made.

4.3. I have, so far, been hinting at the actual time structures of human information processing and historical models of (mini-)worlds in terms of precise definition by systems of public, or personal, time, or both. In all this the direct referential connection between verbal signal and respective IE has been unproblematic. Texts may, however, not only signal some historical piece of world, verifiable according to certain standards and criteria, they may *not* be relatable to 'history' *at all* (and not claim to be), i.e. they may signal a model of a 'possible' or 'imaginary' world (which, however, must be minimally co-extensive with the 'real' world to be comprehensible). Thus the following set of predications represents a text whose modality will seem clear:

The ship Trumpeter which left London for Australia in the early eighteenth century with a hundred convicts and their families on board never reached its destination and no report of any survivor nor of any identified object connected with it ever reached the world.

There is clear reference to public time; the logic of experience seems flawless: a certain ship leaves for Australia from London, with such and such company, and disappears without trace. What inferences would we draw in real life? There could only be speculation as to possible disasters. And there would be nothing else to say about what actually *did* happen, were this in fact a 'historical' text. It would be a contradiction to say anything more about the ship's fate after the express statement that "*no* report of *any* survivor *nor* of *any* identified object connected with it *ever* reached the world". This is a general statement relative to the world of the uttering SMW. How does a reader react, however, if the uttering SMW *does* go on?

The ship's company did not entirely perish, however. The captain and the greater part of the crew ... many of the passengers ... finally over a hundred persons reached an island...[59]

There we have the contradiction mentioned above: it is a clear index that the text is *not* a 'historical' one, that it cannot be put into the 'real' order of things (though it may be in parts co-extensive with the historical world: for instance, there may indeed have been a ship Trumpeter...). And though the world depicted by the complete text is in itself completely ordered and 'logical', the ties with the historical reality of experience are cut. This is also shown by a number of other symptoms in the text indicating its special ('fictional') status, symptoms which have been discussed at length by K. Hamburger in her book *Die Logik der Dichtung*. This is the rather spectacular attempt to establish a kind of system of poetic language use by logical criteria (e.g. the criterion of 'truth', as regards the statements of novels, dramatic dialogue, and poetry – 'truth' as to reference to historical reality), an attempt which rests on specific 'logical' conventions of the interaction of SMW's which, in turn, produce the appropriate changes in the textual signal sequence, e.g. certain relaxations as to the compatibility conditions between

[59] Opening passage of Thornton Wilder's short story *The Warship*.

tense and time adverbials. (It is possible for instance, to say in a novel: "*1984 was* an interesting year...", or "*Today was* Christmas...", etc.) This kind of argument has, however, to do with only a minor aspect of the global topic 'time and text', with the problems of reference to time in the historian's sense, and certain deviations from such reference, which are discovered to be indicative of a specific use of language. There is no discussion of what temporal reference means, i.e. what the referent, 'time', is and what linguistic means there are to 'refer' to it. This is not within the confines of a poetological discussion, anyway.) On the contrary, the argument seeks to prove that the whole system of temporal reference, linguistically intact (apart from a few modifications), does not any more refer to historical time but to a *fictitious time*. This is basically correct: the whole 'model of a world' of a novel, for instance, must not be interpreted in terms of *direct* reference to some *historical* reality (biographical fallacy). It is, however, represented by the linguistic means of, and thus with recourse to, the model of the world of a specific historical period, and would otherwise be incomprehensible. The difference lies in the fact it does not claim to recapitulate what '*really*' *was* (by historical standards), but what could have been, and thus *could be*: art presents results from, and reports of, experiments with the virtual reality of the model of the world of a given period in history.[60]

4.4. The aspects of time structure with reference to texts, which I have sketchily touched so far, will also be of importance to the properly text-linguistic problem of the time structure of text constitution, i.e. of the peculiar process of reconstituting the model of a (mini-)world from a text. As I have pointed out, a 'text' in the narrow sense is a structured sequence of linguistic signals (spoken, written). As the most elementary elements of a text one may posit 'predications' (or 'propositions'); out of such propositions (whatever their form, e.g. Indo-European, or otherwise) systems of mutually dependent and mutually modificatory predications, i.e. 'texts', can be formed. A 'text' as a structured entity is definitely ordered temporally, as it can only proceed linearly, one element after another. A text, sound or letters, 'means' something. This 'something', however, has its own immanent structure which is quite distinct from the strictly linear structure of the signals: it involves the systematic arrangement and dynamic interaction of units of experience within a model of the world. As was pointed out earlier, the items of experience are complex and interact freely. And it is evidently these complex and

[60] Cf. K. Hamburger [47]. This book's first edition (1957) has largely been misunderstood and misinterpreted, to judge by the reviews and critical discussions it provoked. The present edition has taken a more or less fresh start with a 'theory of statement' ("Theorie der Aussage") which would merit serious linguistic examination.

dynamic IE's which are made to interact in a specifically directed way by being 'called up' through a sequence of linguistic signals. The basic problem of textual time structure is then *not* its reference to a system of public or personal time, but the progressive reconstitution of a multi-dimensional and dynamic system of experience through a *linear* sequence of labels. There has been much traditional research into this problem. Rhetoric, for instance, grown out of practical needs and purposes, deals with techniques of argument and persuasion, and involves, basically, the important problem of ordering the signal output for maximum efficiency relative to a given purpose; it takes into account both the elementary limitations of the input channel – '*quantum satis est*' – as well as the overall structure of the system of experience to be reconstituted in the addressee: e.g. under headings like '*dispositio*', involving '*ordo*' (which may be '*naturalis*' or '*artificialis*'), etc.[61] The working of such *principles of effective timing* can daily be observed in newspapers, political speeches, reports, as well as in all the mass media aiming at persuasion. And it is precisely the crafty exploitation of the abstract, fragmentary, and supplementary nature of linguistic signals which produces seemingly 'independent' processes of reconstitution of 'experience' in the minds of the addressees, which induce them to act in the sender's sense, though they assume that they are acting out of their own free decision. Thus the much-discussed and deplored phenomenon of 'manipulation' can, in fact, be referred back to the elementary functioning of language.[62]

I cannot, and do not want to, discuss all the various effects of the 'timing' of linguistic signal sequences, which are most readily associated, for instance with the performance of orators, actors, or comedians. Such timing works best on the actual speech level – and it may only work there – as is well known: an artist's rendering of a speech, a monologue etc., creates more, and profounder meaning in the spectator or listener. (I might note again that 'meaning' is the *total* experience of all levels or hierarchies; I do not see any necessity to divorce the 'emotional' from the 'rational' meaning: the meaning of a predication is the sum-total of the process of reaction of the addressed system.) And a joke, to quote a most obvious and trivial example, derives its effect precisely from the fact that a *first* signal sequence orients the listener and/or spectator in a certain way, 'loads' him with anticipations: i.e. makes him construct inferences or hypotheses about what is coming. A harmless question like,

"Waiter! Do you serve crabs?"

[61] Cf. H. Lausberg [65], s.v. and pass.

[62] Cf. [61] for discussion and some further references.

will immediately create the appropriate setting of a restaurant situation in the SMW addressed, but the retort of the waiter adressed explodes the first model and produces quite a different interpretation:

"Do take a seat, sir! We serve anybody."

On the level of actual linguistic speech the 'art of timing' consists precisely in sending the right amount of signals to stimulate the right amount of reconstitution processes.

To demonstrate the basic nature of the problem of effectively *reconstituting* a *system of IE's* (a 'piece' of 'world') through a *sequence of signals*, I should like to quote a passage from James Joyce's *A Portrait of the Artist as a Young Man:*

In order to see the basket ... your mind first of all separates the basket from the rest of the visible universe which is now the basket. The first phase of apprehension is a bounding line drawn about the object to be apprehended. An esthetic image is presented to us either in space or in time.... But, temporal or spatial, the esthetic image is first luminously apprehended as self-bounded and selfcontained upon the immeasurable background of space or time which is not it. You apprehended it as *one* thing. You see it as one whole.... Then ... you pass from point to point, led by its formal lines; you apprehend it as balanced part against part within its limits; you feel the rhythm of its structure. In other words, the synthesis of immediate perception is followed by the analysis of apprehension....[63]

Though this passage does not explicitly invoke language as a *secondary* means of labelling percepts of varying complexity, it beautifully captures the basic working of the human mind: from synthesis through repeated processing to an analytical model of a piece of the world, e.g. a basket, a person, an event, a situation. – The specific tension between an IE and the timed process of its analytical reconstruction via verbal signs is the writer's, or speaker's, problem. The purpose is to stimulate in the reader, or listener, a process of (creative) reconstitution yielding the similar (only ideally: the same) IE. – I shall quote a few more examples just to demonstrate what the central problem of the time structure of a text seems to be. Obviously, all *linear* linguistic rendering lags behind the synthetic apperception of IE's. An exemplary case of such linearity opposed to a simultaneous and complex 'situation' is given by Lichtenberg's report of a scene from *Hamlet*:

Garrick, upon these words, throws himself suddenly around and in the same moment falls two or three steps backward with collapsing knees. His hat drops to the floor; both arms, especially the left, are almost completely extended, the hand is at the level of the head, the right arm more bent than the left and the right hand lower; the fingers are spread out, and the mouth is open. Thus he stops, as though petrified, in a large but not excessive step, supported by his friends, who are better acquainted with the apparition and who

[63] Penguin Books 1971 (1916), p. 171.

fear he may fall. In his face horror is expressed in such a way that dread overcame me repeatedly even before he began to speak.[64]

Arnheim calls this way of describing an event which is a complex and more or less simultaneous whole, a "transcript by enumeration", and makes it clear that there is no one-one relationship between the 'objective' elements of the whole and the predications given, but that the whole description is a logically organised 'argument'. This is of course, a very highly developed form of verbalisation of an 'event', but even in more enumerative descriptions there is never just one-one scanning and labelling, there is always *interpretation*, i.e. *re*constitution. Thus a description of Degas' picture *Rehearsal on stage* most illuminatingly shows that all *direct* synoptic experience of the painting itself is different from what is created by its *verbal* representation which is evaluated and interpreted:

Degas did not represent the ballet dancers at their graceful rest, but working hard at rehearsal..., in individual postures, in side views, from the back, or standing on the sidelines awaiting their turns. One is yawning with hands clasped behind her head, another is cut off by the frame, and another stoops with her ballet skirt in back fluttering above her head. A bass viol projects into the picture, the set looks drab, but the flesh tints are warm and the stage floor a glistening green. Two men lounge in chairs...[65]

Needless to say that the description does not only not exhaust the 'information' of the picture, but *recreates* it: i.e. it *adds* information by its reconstruction, while *disregarding* other information. A *verbal* presentation of the 'content' of this painting will certainly be 'interpreted' pictorially by many different paintings! What is important is that we are clearly able to diagnose such a text as a description of *one* entity: of a picture, a scene, a situation, an event, etc., not because of its 'form' but evidently because of its content. The relationship between linear text and IE is thus tenuous, and dependent on the SMW involved. Concepts like 'events', 'situation', 'story' etc. are nothing but very global items of experience as we have *abstracted* them from our actional life. Their definition is by no means easy or plausible: it depends on the level of abstractness involved or the point of view taken, the 'depth' of analysis, etc. An 'event' in the reporter's sense, e.g. an accident, a wedding, the signing of a treaty, a battle, etc. is, or may be, infinitely complex in itself, This is shown by both scientific and artistic analyses. A medical account of so simple an event as *sneezing* could fill volumes, and a modern novelist's account of a second of a character's sensitive life *does* fill volumes. – In the following text, for instance, we always know what is going on, and what the frame of reference is, something we could never pick out from the uniform tenses and the absolute lack of express orientational signals; the specific

[64] Quoted by Arnheim [6], p. 248.

[65] From E. O. Christensen's *Pictorial History of Western Art*, New York 1964, p. 335.

meaning of the whole text (of which the excerpt is a small part) is created step by step:

> "All right", said the man, "What about it?"
> "No", said the girl. "I can't".
> "You mean you won't."
> "I can't", said the girl. "That's all I mean."
> "You mean that you won't."
> "All right", said the girl. "You have it your own way."
> "I don't have it my own way. I wish to God I did."
> "You did for a long time", the girl said.
> It was early, and there was no one in the café except the barman and these two who sat together at a table in the corner. It was the end of the summer and they were both tanned so that they looked out of place in Paris. The girl wore a tweed suit, her skin was a smooth golden brown, her blonde hair was cut short and grew beautifully away from her forehead. The man looked at her.
> "I'll kill her", he said.[66]

Just a few hints on the time structure of this fragment will be enough to show *how* the meaning of the passage is reconstructed bit by bit. A piece of dialogue between two anonymous partners recreates a very general situation: partners speak to each other, suggesting some problem, thereby characterising their relationship in a vague way. The reader has no difficulty to realise the situation, to follow the dialogue, and he will construct – according to his system of experience – all sorts of models within which this dialogue could meaningfully take place. – *Then* – and this 'then' is clear from the semantics of the text – 'the man looked at her'. But in between, arresting the dialogue, comes information modifying the reader's provisional model by sketching relevant parts of the situation: 'café', 'Paris', 'end of the summer', 'early', and depicting *one* person, 'the girl' in more detail. – It would be very difficult to distil a pattern of 'events' out of the non-dialogue passage: 'it was early' is certainly no 'event', nor 'they were both tanned', etc. – What happens is the reconstruction of a model of a situation out of *very few IE's*, from which the rest is inferred *ad libitum* (at *this stage*, of course: the text goes on!). And there are no ways of specially indicating which predications refer to *one* complex IE by way of scanning ('the girl': 'wore a tweed suit', 'skin was a smooth golden brown', 'blonde hair was cut short', 'blonde hair grew beautifully away from... forehead'), or which predications express different IE's, but IE's which are neither the same, nor simultaneous: 'It was early', 'the girl said', 'the man looked at her'. – Thus, from the text as a series of predications evoking IE's in a specific progression (i.e. according to the time structure of the text), one can infer the *actual* 'logical' sequence of the 'action' *secondarily* as one goes along, but the outcome and its effect is due to the progressive process of concretizing one IE after the other, con-

[66] E. Hemingway, *The Sea Change*, opening passage.

stantly modifying the model of the world which is being constructed since the beginning. – The sequence of predications does in no way parallel a sequence of 'events'; nor is that sequence congruent with a sequence of IE's in time: the IE's presented do not '*pass* the eye' one *after* the other, but become integrated into the model, modifying each other in various ways. – Quite apart from these meaning-creating structural properties of the reconstitution process, the normal system of temporal reference is intact: the reader has no difficulty to decode correctly the *past tenses* in the non-dialogue parts and the *present tenses* found in the dialogue, or the changing meaning of the recurring *and*, etc. – It must be clear therefore that all the complicated semantic processes going on in the reconstitution of the model of the world 'underlying' this fragment is only very crudely *articulated*: it is *inferred* in most of its components!

It is also hardly necessary to point out that the experience reconstituted is not neutrally 'descriptive' – whatever that is – but interpreted and evaluated.

Thus it may be obvious by now that the specific asymmetry between the *complex* (sequence of) IE's and the *serial* sequence of predications (as it holds on all levels, in all hierarchies of classification, evaluation, etc.) allows for the exploitation (positive and negative) of the necessary temporal ordering of the reconstitution process of experience through language: the specific temporal structure chosen creates meaning.

4.5. Finally: the temporal sequence of the reconstitution process as released by the sequence of verbal signals is not only necessarily at odds with the surface sequence of the signals, but may differ greatly from the 'logical' sequence to be inferred from the whole concretization process. What is at issue is the *actual* logical sequence of what we consider – for a given purpose – suitable units of our model of the world, e.g. 'events' or 'states', etc. – This is another aspect of the time structure of a text, an aspect which has been studied extensively (for instance, by narrative theory). We have here to do with larger units than in the foregoing: a story is said to consist of 'events' – which may take many pages each, and thus be separated into many elements – or similar 'units', whatever these are. The ordering of these units may be carried out in many ways according to the 'meaning' to be established: thus the 'events' on a menucard, or on a programme, will usually have to be kept in their 'natural' order, similarly those of 'historical' texts. No history book can speak about 1914–1918 before treating 1866. (It may do this, however, for the specific purpose of creating specific meaning: in teaching, for instance, to show the difference in warfare, politics, etc.) – This general point also implies that even historiography may rearrange the logical sequence of its events for specific purposes. This is natural with *simulated* history, e.g.

fiction which is completely at liberty to shove events and characters around to its heart's delight, though not in an *uncontrolled* way. Thus Fielding's well-known contention is true for all simulation of history through verbal composition:

> ...we intend ... rather to pursue the method of those writers, who profess to disclose the revolutions of countries, than to imitate the painful and voluminous historian, who, to preserve the regularity of his series, thinks himself obliged to fill up as much paper with the detail of months and years in which nothing remarkable happened[67]...

This has been proved adequate by various extreme experiments in our time: for instance the work by W. Faulkner, L. Durrell, G. Gaiser, M. Butor, J. Joyce, V. Woolf and many others; not to forget G. Stein, or the advocators of 'concrete poetry'; *Tristram Shandy*, the 'book of books'; or R. Musil in his conviction of the impossibility of a coherent narrative, or the representatives of the *nouveau roman*, of the drama of the Absurd, of surrealist poetry, – to name but very few in random selection.

The universal *linguistic* foundations for all such experimenting with the 'logical form' of experience have been suggested at length. It will be necessary now to show the correctness of the global hypotheses outlined by controlled and careful experiments on the reconstruction of processes of reconstitution of experience as signalled by a text.

A somewhat linguistic approach to the structural analysis of texts as to their relationship with the underlying 'logical' structure of events is demonstrated by Labov/Waletzky's 'narrative analysis'. It introduces some formal devices to represent the global time structure of 'events' as represented by verbal predications ('clauses'). The attempt is interesting in various respects and does go a little way to state more precisely what the time structure of a narrative in the sense of 'recapitulation of experience' could be. Units like 'narrative clause', or 'temporal juncture', are formally defined by their position in the ordered sequence of clauses. There is however, nothing new as to the definition of narrative and its structure (though this is not the ultimate aim of the paper, which is "correlations of the narrator's social characteristics with the structure of their narratives"). Thus the "basic narrative units" are conceived of as those units which "recapitulate experience in the same order as the original events", and the "overall structure of narratives" is analysed into such traditional units as 'orientation', 'complication', 'evaluation', 'resolution', and 'coda'. But it is certainly a merit of this investigation that it recognises the importance of differentiating between the 'primary sequence' of events as it must be inferred from a narrative by the general logic of experience, and the "linear ordering of clauses" of a narrative which is

[67] Henry Fielding, *Tom Jones* (1749), Book II, Ch. 1.

due to the "functional organisation of the narrative structure as a whole". – [68]

The "primary sequence", or logical sequence of 'events' or 'states' etc., serves thus as a *norm* by which deviations of the actual sequence of presentation may be established. It has long been recognised that the elementary 'primary sequence' works on the '*a*-then-*b*' principle, i.e. on the principle of strict congruence between the logical sequence of IE's and the series of coordinated predications.[69] This is however, talking on a very abstract level and narrowing one's perspective to the purely 'actional' *a*-then-*b* aspect of a text, an aspect which, by the way, has been effectively parodied by K. Bayer:

> ... zuerst ging goldenberg über einen acker dann über eine wiese dann durch einen wald dann trat er auf ein schneckenhaus dann stieg er auf einen berg dann fiel er über eine treppe wieder hinunter dann stand er auf dann sprang er über einen bach dann ging er im schatten dann kreuzte er einen weg dann schwamm er durch einen fluß dann stieg er über einen stein dann ging er durch ein dorf dann durch eine stadt dann lief er über ein weites feld dann stieg er auf einen baum aß einen apfel endlich fand sich goldenberg auf einer plüschbank sitzend[70]

An approach presupposing such a structure as the fundamental norm remains unaware of the complex processes of reconstituting IE's through verbal sign sequences. In fact, it soon becomes apparent, how naive the view of a basically parallel structure of experience and its linguistic representation is, a view which should have been dead and gone at least since the times of Tristram Shandy's troubles with spelling out his Life and Opinions: the reflective, language-conscious 'text producer' plagued by the impossibility of verbalising his history in all its complexity, continually running up against the fact that it just *cannot* be disentangled into nicely isolated units such as 'event', 'interpretation', 'evaluation', 'reflection', etc. Tristram Shandy does not only tell some 'story', he also demonstrates what is involved in 'ideal' story-telling, more precisely, in an ideal one-one representation of every single complex IE (consisting of 'facts', 'emotions', 'relations', 'reasons', 'values', etc. – whatever analytic concepts one likes to apply) through the serial verbalisation of the narrator. Thus narrative texts are far more interesting for the purpose of analysis, as they exhibit many more *realised* possibilities of textualising experience; – which of course, does not make it any easier. Tristram Shandy's demonstration, however virtuoso-like and scintillating, fails – as far as his proclaimed purpose is concerned –, but succeeds brilliantly as far as his capital 'philosophical' (and also linguistic, in our sense)

[68] Cf. Labov/Waletzky [64].

[69] This is also true genetically: obviously children start with thinking in events and only slowly learn to abstract from the natural 'logical' sequence of events, and thus to develop temporal concepts to become free and flexible in their manipulation of IE's. – There is much experimental research material as to these matters, cf. for instance Piaget [73], Clark [23], Bever [10], Wunderlich [108], pp. 84ff., Maranda/Maranda [67], pp. 83ff.

[70] Konrad Bayer, *Der Sechste Sinn*, Hamburg 1966, p. 258.

point is concerned. A *linear* rendering of 'life and opinions' is impossible in the sense of the historiographer walking straight ahead, recording 'event' after 'event':

For, if he is a man of the least spirit, he will have fifty deviations from a straight line to make with this or that party as he goes along, which he can no ways avoid. He will have views and prospects to himself perpetually soliciting his eye, which he can no more help standing still to look at than he can fly...

...for my own part, I declare I had been at it these six weeks, making all the speed I possibly could, – and am not yet born...[71]

Tristram makes his *whole practical* existence his theme, as far as the narration of his life and opinions is concerned, which again demonstrates the incredible variety of possible SMW's in a text; i.e. Tristram has to battle with the worlds of all his characters, as they become elements of his own, but also with the troubles of his daily existence, when actually writing his book: this whole chaotic 'world' of worlds always gets the better of his striving for '*a*-then-*b*'-logic, and he always finds himself in the constant plight to have to decide on writing about *one* at a time, as it is impossible to write about 'everything' and 'everybody' simultaneously. The following is an example (both for Tristram's unabashed mixing of worlds and his still more impudent disregard of nice logical distinctions, e.g. between 'object language' and 'meta-language'...):

...my uncle Toby ... fell asleep also.... – Dr. Slop is engaged with the midwife and my mother above stairs. – Trim is busy in turning an old pair of jackboots into a couple of mortars ... and is this instant boring the touchholes with the point of a hot poker. – All my heroes are off my hands; – 'tis the first time I have had a moment to spare – and I'll make use of it, and write my preface.[72]

Thus whereas a train conductor has no difficulty at all to coordinate his utterances with the relevant 'events' making up the train-journey – calling out the stops at the times recorded in the time-table –, the sports commentator may already get into terrible trouble synchronising his predications with what goes on in front of his eyes at a 400 yds. finish – the synoptic picture completely eludes all attempts to be rendered *serially* by verbal signs; and Tristram Shandy's philosophy of a 'history' in the form of 'Life and Opinions' is in no way synchronisable with the compulsory linearity of the utterances necessary to express them. In addition, Tristram often 'writes' in the presence of the reader – either a female, addressed 'Madam', or a male, addressed 'Sir' – addresses him directly, asks him questions, asks him for practical services (e.g. to shut the door, to hand him his cap). Thus there are many

[71] Laurence Sterne, *Tristram Shandy* (1759–67), Everyman's Library, London 1964, p. 28f. Note the various temporal references in the passage which liberally mix frames of reference, irrespective of logical levels or connections!

[72] *Ibid.*, p. 138.

different 'levels' of action, different systems of reference, all gaily mixed by Tristram to make his point: to expose the illusion of 'absolute historiography'. I should like to quote a few more examples of such mixing of reference systems, to demonstrate how intricate the mesh of IE's and utterances can be:

...It is not half an hour ago, when (in the great hurry and precipitation of a poor devil's writing for daily bread) I threw a fair sheet, which I had just finished, and carefully wrote out, slap into the fire, instead of the foul one.

Instantly I snatch'd off my wig, and threw it perpendicularly, with all imaginable violence, up to the top of the room – indeed I caught it as it fell...[73]

Here the time references are clearly to the *actual* situation of writing (which, of course, is Tristram's situation, not the author's!), and the sequence of 'events' is paralleled by the sequence of semantically coordinated predications:

(1) Mistake of throwing the wrong page into the fire: half an hour before 'saying' it;
(2) Reaction of anger upon (1) showing in throwing wig to the ceiling;
(3) Report of adequate reaction to (2): the wig is not to drop to the floor and be completely ruined, but is caught again.

In the following quotation the disentangling of various systems of reference is not so easy any more – and indeed I shall leave the gentle reader to it –:

My mother, you must know ... but I have fifty things more necessary to let you know first ... I have a hundred difficulties which I have promised to clear up, and a thousand distresses and domestic misadventures crowding in upon me, and threefold, one upon the neck of another. A cow broke in (to-morrow morning) to my uncle Toby's fortifications, and eat up two rations and a half of dried grass ... Trim insists upon being tried by a court-martial – the cow to be shot – Slop to be crucified – myself to be tristram'd and at my very baptism made a martyr of; ... poor unhappy devils that we all are! ... I want swaddling ... but there is no time to be lost in exclamations ... I have left my father lying across his bed, and my uncle Toby in his old fringed chair sitting beside him, and promised I would go back to them in half an hour; and five-and-thirthy minutes are laps'd already. ... Of all the perplexities a mortal author was ever seen in ... this certainly is the greatest, for I have Hafen Slawkenbergius's folio, Sir, to finish ... a dialogue between my father and my uncle Toby, upon the solution of Prignitz, Scroderus, Ambrose Paraeus, Ponocrates, and Grangousier to relate – a tale out of Slawkenbergius to translate, and all this in five minutes less than no time at all; ... such a head! ... would to Heaven my enemies only saw the inside of it![74]

There is no need to say that the passage is charged with meaning, not only just comprehensible, within the system of experience constituted up to its appearance in the complete text. The various elements implying temporal ordering of all sorts are therefore employed correctly and contribute through their functioning in the context of the passage to the overall message, though

[73] *Ibid.*, p. 212.
[74] *Ibid.*, p. 170: a marvellous example for logical analysis.

they would appear as completely farcical in isolation, e.g. in a grammar of the usual kind.

Such passages – and I shall quote one more further on – indicate only too clearly that all interpretation of *time reference* presupposes the establishing of the uttering SMW's coordinates of reference, as well as the definition of the (variable) 'units' entering a temporal relation.

As already said, there is a mass of pertinent material supplied by the traditional 'theory of the novel', showing a wide variety of possible 'time structures', from simple seriality, as e.g. in adventure stories, picaresque novels, and the like, to broken and rearranged seriality (novels with several plots set in different times, etc.), or special cases of the latter (e.g. novels consisting of extensive depictions of special phases of a 'hero's' life, or of a varied set of pictures representing changing aspects of one and the same complex IE) to finally novels of the 'stream-of-consciousness' type, in which the divergence between natural and logical sequence of 'events', and narrated sequence of IE's, is greatest. – This is complicated by the appearance of the author in one of various specific roles of 'narrator', and by his thus becoming part of the created world; further by the kind of experience narrated (history of generations, of one life, of a few years, a few hours, minutes, seconds, or even of utopian experience), and the kind of structure and tempo connecting the more global units of the whole (slow motion, accelerated motion, pointillist static picture, etc.) and so on. – There are infinitely many possibilities; they all need just a very small inventory of formal linguistic means to orientate the reader; and this would be impossible, were there not the common model of the world, which is systematically ordered and incorporates all the accepted modes of processing new experience: a reader *can* correctly decode such close-knit and intricate systems of temporal ordering as given, for instance, in the passage from Tristram Shandy, by reconstructing the 'natural', i.e. 'logical' model of the world of a text. –

Thus it may have become clear, at least in somewhat schematic form, what would be theoretically required for describing correctly the meaning and functioning of temporal ordering in texts, so as to allow the correct and acceptable interpretation of texts, and develop guiding rules for the production of acceptable texts.

I shall now very briefly hint at some of the most important ways of conveying temporal ordering in a text. These remarks will not be intended as a review of all the work available, but merely as hints at how 'time' is at work and understood in texts, in the form of 'temporal semantemes': non-linguistic, explicit, and implicit. And this may conclude the attempt to outline the basic requirements for devising an *adequate heuristics* for a theory of texts, in particular the function of 'time' in texts.

4.6. Most of the relevant temporal information is not explicitly verbalised at all: 'time' as a set of ordering relations is prior to language functioning as a specific determinant of the functioning of the SMW; it thus needs no specific articulation; further, language, being a system of arbitrary and virtual signs for experience, does in no way represent experience in a one-one fashion, but is abstractive, fragmentary, and tied to linear succession; furthermore, temporal meaning may be *verbalised* in a number of ways which can be classed in two sets: there is *explicit* time reference (tenses, lexical elements), or there is *implicit* time reference in the form of implications inherent in the meaning of verbal sequences. All these ways of temporal ordering (on whatever level) *cooperate* with, and *determine, each other*. It follows that the specific distribution of temporal elements (both as to selection and frequency) is basically conditioned by the type of situation of the interacting SMW, and thus the respective type of text). It is then a truism that the features of specific types of texts *cannot be exclusively verbal*: they are to be sought in the *set of acceptability conditions* determining the situation of interaction of (at least two) SMW's. Temporal elements will necessarily play important *parts* among such acceptability features. (It is premature and rash to base far-reaching, and polemical, conclusions on *verbal* temporal elements only, e.g. the tense forms.)[75]

4.6.1. There is, first, the general and little-recognised fact that temporal ordering (of experience, or predications) is expressed *without* using verbal means. Thus many kinds of texts whose functional situations are evident, do not need to label the sequence of utterances as to their order, nor do they need to introduce specific signs indicating the order of IE's. Time-tables, programmes, menu-cards, specific instruction sequences, count-downs, reports of events in progress, etc., usually dispense with explicit temporal ordering because it is quite clear that the sequence of predications 'portrays' the sequence of IE's. Time-tables, or programmes, can therefore be formulated without redundance and their temporal structure will be correctly decoded within the context of experience of the (inter-)acting SMW. It must be borne in mind that such decoding processes are complex and presuppose much information! It must also be remembered that the lack of articulated temporal meaning is on the *surface* level of linguistic *signals*, and that it is the 'semantics of experience' which allows for substantial economization of *verbal* ex-

[75] This applies both to linguistic and literary undertakings, e.g. H. Weinrich's typological dichotomy of 'Besprechen' vs. 'Erzählen' ('referential/discursive discourse' vs. 'narrative discourse') – cf. [102] –, or also H. Brinkmann's contention that tense forms express attitudes of the speaker – cf. [19], pp. 321ff. and pass. –, not to mention many similar approaches. – For an interesting document concerning non-linguists but language practitioners cf. Bloch ed. [11].

pression. It is also very important to remember that every IE, however richly supplemented by verbal utterance, has become 'past' the moment it is realised in the mind; this fact, i.e. the inherent temporality (i.e. ordering by succession) of *all* information manipulated by the mind, has profound influence on the production or the reception of a text as regards, for instance, all the possible inferences from a predicated IE in accord with the general logic of experience, or as concerns the compulsory use of linguistic devices referring back to what was *said, or* only implied, etc. Thus there is a sense in which 'pure' time (as ordering relation) is of basic relevance to the concretization and constitution of any text: a text as a structured entity is necessarily ordered in time, and this ordering may not need to be *verbalised* because it is easily deducible from the IE's *expressed, presupposed,* or *implied!* A railway timetable shows many features indicating subject and domain of the book, presupposing, however, knowledge of what a train is and what it does, etc. – Such information loses its trivial nature when it is to be manipulated by a computer which, in effect, does *not* 'know' anything of what *we* consider trivial, and will never know *most* of what we consider trivial, as it cannot 'perceive' and process in the same way as we can.) –

4.6.2. It would be a fallacy to assume, however, that such 'indexical' temporal ordering can be interpreted unambiguously in terms of its structural function. It is always the semantics of experience which determines the structural status of temporarily unspecified predication sequences. Thus the type

veni, vidi, vici: E_1–E_2–E_3

is commonly known to be congruent with what actually happened in a sequence of three distinct events. This is the easiest case; a series of IE's is synchronised with a series of labels:

...The cottage, the go-cart, the Sunday afternoon drives in the Ford – the first rheumatism – the grandchildren – the second rheumatism – the deathbed – the reading of the will – ...[76]

Here again the sequence of 'events' is paralleled by the series of signals, but this could be interpreted differently, depending on the SMW. The same 'external' kind of 'temporal' connection does *not* permit the same kind of serial interpretation in this example:

An reizvoller Lage, weltberühmt: eine einmalige Herbsterholung mit einer harmonischen Mischung von Vergnügen. Die Milde der Landschaft und des Klimas, die bezaubernde und gelöste Atmosphäre der ... Abende. Ein Sportcocktail (Golf, Tennis, Reiten, Schwimmen). Zahlreiche Unterhaltungsmöglichkeiten...

[76] Thornton Wilder, *Our Town* (1938/39), Acting Edition, New York 1938, p. 64.

Here the seriality is not in the IE's but only in the text which is to make the receiver constitute the IE 'holiday resort X' as *one* whole 'unit' by its most attractive analytic features. The surface appearance does in no way guarantee what the relationship between the individual IE's is. It is further important to emphasise that 'event' is a very abstract macro-category and that there are many texts in which it is not as easy to name what is denoted, nor make out a temporal structure; e.g. in the following well-known poem by J. Ringelnatz:

Liedchen

Die Zeit vergeht.	Die Milch verdirbt.
Das Gras verwelkt.	Die Wahrheit schweigt.
Die Milch entsteht.	Die Kuhmagd stirbt.
Die Kuhmagd melkt.	Ein Geiger geigt.

Thus it is misleading to speak of 'time structure' only in terms of events, as if every text dealt with history and facts only. Temporal ordering concerns the *complete turnover of information as well as its serial predication*, and a text can only be understood if *all* the temporal elements, explicit or implicit, are correctly concretized. As we have seen, there *may* be some rough synchronisation between IE and predication; in most texts the temporal order of IE's has to be inferred from the sequence of predications. This implies that no less than the *whole respective system of experience must be presupposed to decode a text correctly.*

4.6.3. It is of course impossible to discuss the significance of possible temporal meaning *inherent in IE's* outside the examination of whole texts. But a few hints may be given. It must be emphasised that it is obviously as impossible as unnecessary to 'say' everything, and that *linguistic* interaction merely provides labels for complex IE's which have to be reconstituted according to the progressive growth of information of the linear text. Thus, much of temporal information is naturally 'between the lines' and inferred from what is *said.* Between different entries in a diary, for instance, there may be intervals of days, weeks, months, or even years, in which 'things' happen, 'things' to be sure which can sometimes be *deduced* from later records, or 'things' which one has to posit to explain later action, etc. This is frequently the case in practice (history, criminal detection, scandal mongering, political manipulation etc.), and very often in fiction, where the interpretation of say a novel, often rests on what was *not* said but is to be inferred: thus a lapse of one year may be of extremely important consequence if it meant an interval during which, for instance, a certain project was to be carried out, a certain test was to be stood, etc. And although we are *told* nothing about what happened in that interval of silence, we may gather much information from what happens afterwards. Thus in Th. Wilder's play *Our*

Town the stage manager introduces Act Two by recalling *some* of the (necessary) events that have taken place since the close of the action of Act One:

> Three years have gone by. The sun's come up over a thousand times. Summers and winters have cracked the mountains a little bit more and the rains have brought down some of the dirt. Some babies that weren't even born before, have begun talkin' regular sentences already...[77]

Of course there are many ways of reporting *implicitly* what has happened during a certain time interval. All I want to point out here is that it depends on the IE's presented what deductions the reader will make or will be both enabled, and led, to make. Thus the predication *They spent three happy years after getting married* implies something different from a phrase containing instead of *happy* the word *changeful* or *hard* or *calm*, or if *getting married* is replaced by *moving to Constance* or *finishing with the project*, etc. Thus the complete reconstitution of the meaning of a text ultimately always depends on the SMW at work and its potential of hypotheses and logic of experience. In this way *any* predication may be important to the temporal ordering of the experience expressed, and thus also *any* type of linguistic sign may be cooperative in establishing IE's by being positioned in a textual sequence in a specific way: *ouhh!* no less than the longest period by Thomas Mann. Of course there is a scale of explicitness of temporal reference, from the most explicit expressions using systems of public time (or the still more refined systems of physics) to more general temporal elements (implying regularity, change, causality, motion, order, succession, simultaneity, development, etc. etc.). The troubling truth is that 'time' is implied by practically any item of the dictionary, as its specific position within the system of a text will determine the set of presuppositions as well as implications that *can* be inferred at that juncture. – It is of course important to be aware of 'more explicit' inherent lexical properties – especially with nouns, adjectives, and verbs, but also with adverbs, prepositions, conjunctions –, as their functioning within a text will partly determine the functioning of the rest of temporal elements. Categories like 'inchoative', 'durative', 'ingressive', 'iterative', 'perfective', 'imperfective', etc. have always claimed attention, but, in concluding I can only repeat again that temporal implications and presuppositions are equally well connected with nouns or adjectives – but this is an incorrect way of speaking: temporal meaning may be generated by predications independent of *explicit* temporal features in the elements making up the predications; the position of the predication within its context and the kind of situation supplemented by the text are much more important and constitute the greater whole which must be realised *first* before the contribution of any

[77] *Ibid.*, p. 37.

single item can be established *a posteriori.* Thus it is for example impossible to decode the following passage correctly if one does not know the situation supplemented by it – something any listener can easily supply from his processing of the concrete situation:

First automobile's goin' to come along in about five years – belonged to Banker Cartwright, our town's richest citizen. Lives up in the big white house up there on the hill.

There is a flat contradiction in an 'automobile's *going to come along in five years*' and the *same* 'automobile's belonging' to *X* in the *past*, with *X* obviously living '*now*', i.e. at the point of speaking. This is an unfair example as it is a text spoken by a character of a play on stage demonstrating a town at a certain point in time ('now') which constitutes his 'axis of orientation', a point which is in the past from the respective evening the play is performed. Thus the confusing system of reference is created by rapidly changing the perspective: from the perspective of 'now' – therefore future: *is going to come along* – to the narrator's perspective looking back – *belonged* – then returning to 'now' (different from actual *now* of performance) *–lives* –.

A similar situation is Tristram Shandy's: he also moves around 'in time' as he likes, mixing both his actual situation and the individual situations of his characters – creating a still more complex picture than the stage-manager in *Our Town.* The receiver who is adequately trained can, however, easily adapt himself and correctly constitute the world he gets transmitted via signals, signals which in no way parallel what 'actually' happens.

4.6.4. Of all seemingly 'explicit' linguistic means of time reference, the so-called 'tenses' have received most attention. I shall not review the situation here: it is enough to say that the tense forms of verbs may be *one* among many factors cooperating in ordering both the experience signalled as well as the series of signals itself. There is no question that tenses do not *exclusively* refer to 'time', whether public or personal. Their various functions can therefore, in fact, only be established from actual language functioning, i.e. from texts – though in the sense proposed here. – Present research shows how profoundly semantic and pragmatic elements determine the working of tense forms[78], even where the central point of interest is explicitly 'time reference', as with the three standard works by Koschmieder, Bull, and Wunderlich. Their approaches must rank among the most serious and clear-headed: they all concentrate on the category 'tense' (though Wunderlich and Bull examine also what Bull calls 'non-systemic' functions of tenses, i.e. their specific functions in specific contexts, e.g. in the neighbourhood of time adverbials,

[78] Cf. in particular Hauser/Hoppe [49] (which is somewhat text-oriented) and especially the substantial discussions by Koschmieder [62], Bull [21], and Wunderlich [108], not to forget the extensive work by Glinz, Brinkmann, and others.

or temporal expressions, and though Koschmieder, too, deals with the problems of lexical categories as to time, and particularly with 'aspect'). There is a wealth of material to be taken into account, both theoretical, and factual. – I do not think it necessary to quote such material here: this would require the critical analysis of the paradigms underlying the different approaches, and also the alternative of a properly text-linguistic theory of language functioning, which we have not yet established. How important this theory is, is demonstrated by a collection of interviews of writers as to their criteria for choosing preterite, or perfect, tenses in German.[79] This book shows that the rules underlying the distribution of these tenses in German texts (together with the other tenses) are of a varying kind: they are due to semantic and pragmatic factors governing the obligatory and/or optional use of either preterite or perfect, as usual: they are, however, far less precise than, for instance, in English, where it is impossible to say *I have seen him yesterday*, because there are *regional* norms of all types and kinds favouring either preterite (North, and Standard, German) or perfect (South, and colloquial, German) – for historical reasons –; and there is constant interference between the two, which in turn is not regularized on any level but tends to vary strongly with the type of text involved. This most fascinating (and amusing as well as annoying) document may be taken to confirm the demand put forward here that there is no sense in investigating *one* aspect of language functioning *in isolation* but that the only profitable way of going about the construction of viable theoretical models requires (*at least*) the awareness of *all* the *relevant* conditions of acceptability at work in a given text. This implies automatically that it is never just a tense morpheme which has temporal, or modal, or aspectual, or some pragmatic, '*meaning*'.

5. Concluding remarks

I have tried to demonstrate what is involved in a heuristics aiming at regularities in the temporal aspects of texts as linguistic objects, *if* a certain metatheoretical paradigm is adopted. The attempt to motivate a paradigm which conceives of all scientific work as basically goal-oriented in the concrete sense of 'optimizing' actual language use, is based on considerations deriving from the history of the sciences as socially embedded activities, on the one hand (for which one does not need especial ideological bias of a narrow-minded sort), and from the precarious and in many ways conflicting relationships between theory and practice in present linguistic research. Though I have not been able to critically review the 'state of the art', and though

[79] Bloch ed. [11].

many of my characterizations may, if only for their brevity, sound too clear-cut and global, the essential points may have become clear to all those who have cared enough to try to understand. This is, however, in no way intended to insinuate a concealed shifting of responsibility for what has been said: I have tried to express my views as clearly as possible, wherever I was able to, even at the risk of repetitiveness, and I am very much aware of the fact that all such textual transmitting of heuristic thinking is bound to gather noise on the way, to become confused and misleading. Apart from such obvious matters I may stress again that the present paper was meant to sketch all those *relevant* aspects of language functioning which must, according to the paradigm, be taken into account for a properly devised heuristics of research into the temporal semantics of texts (on all structural levels). Thus the *towards* in the paper's title is important. All those who miss the material on temporal semantics available at present, should therefore not be disappointed: it would have made the article far too long and unbalanced to critically discuss such data, i.e. *re*-examine them in the context of the framework presented. This will be the object of future studies. Let me emphasize that I have not at all passed over all that vast material lightly, it had no place within a very general discussion on the one hand, and a *text*-linguistic perspective on the other. The research to be undertaken now can therefore concentrate on sample analyses and more exact and formal theoretical modelling of results. It will be conducted strictly in the awareness of the fundamental difficulties outlined: it will therefore concern itself with well-delimited 'types' of text, especially 'simple' forms, and it will *not* shirk the arduous task of establishing *all* the *relevant* conditions of acceptability determining the 'meaning' of a text, – though they could all too easily be pushed aside by declaring them to be 'non-linguistic', 'outside scientific possibility', etc.

University of Constance
DFG-Projekt 'Textlinguistik'

BIBLIOGRAPHY

[1] Acham, Karl, *Vernunft und Engagement*, Sozialphilosophische Untersuchungen, Wien 1972.
[2] Albert, Hans, *Plädoyer für kritischen Rationalismus*, München 1971.
[3] *Anthropologie – Fischer Lexikon* (ed. by G. Heberer, G. Kurth, and I. Schwidetzky-Roesing), Frankfurt/M. 1961.
[4] *Anthropologie, Neue* (ed. by H.-G. Gadamer and P. Vogler), ca. 6 Vols.; publ. Vols. 1–3 (bio-anthropology and social anthropology), dtv, München 1972.
[5] Arnheim, Rudolf, *Art and Visual Perception.* A Psychology of the Creative Eye, London 1956.
[6] Arnheim, Rudolf, *Visual Thinking*, Berkeley/Los Angeles 1969.
[7] Ashby, W. Ross, *An Introduction to Cybernetics*, London 1964.

[8] Bense, Max, *Theorie der Texte*, Köln 1962.
[9] Bense, Max, *Aesthetica*, Baden-Baden 1965.
[10] Bever, Thomas G., 'The Comprehension and Memory of Sentences with Temporal Relations', in: *Advances in Psycholinguistics* [78] pp. 285–29.
[11] Bloch, Peter André (ed.), *Der Schriftsteller und sein Verhältnis zur Sprache, dargestellt am Problem der Tempuswahl*, Bern/München 1971.
[12] Boost, Karl, *Arteigene Sprachlehre*, Breslau 1938.
[13] Boost, Karl, 'Der deutsche Satz. Die Satzverflechtung', *Deutschunterricht*, Berlin/ Leipzig, Jahrg. 1949, Heft 3, pp. 7–15.
[14] Boost, Karl, *Neue Untersuchungen zum Wesen und zur Struktur des deutschen Satzes*. Der Satz als Spannungsfeld, Berlin 1956.
[15] Brinker, Klaus, 'Aufgaben und Methoden der Textlinguistik', *Wirkendes Wort* **XXI** (1971), 217–237.
[16] Brinkmann, Hennig, 'Die Konstituierung der Rede', *Wirkendes Wort* **XV** (1965), 157–172.
[17] Brinkmann, Hennig, 'Der Satz und die Rede', *Wirkendes Wort* **XVI** (1966), 376–390.
[18] Brinkmann, Hennig, 'Die Syntax der Rede', *Sprache der Gegenwart* (ed. Inst. f. dt. Sprache/Mannheim) Vol. 1 (1967), Düsseldorf 1967, pp. 79–88.
[19] Brinkmann, Hennig, *Die deutsche Sprache*. Gestalt und Leistung, 2. neubearbeitete und erweiterte Auflage, Düsseldorf 1971.
[20] Bronowski, J. and Bellugi, U., 'Language, Name and Concept', *Science* **168** (1970), 669–673.
[21] Bull, William E., *Time, Tense, and the Verb*, Berkeley/Los Angeles 1968.
[22] Bunge, Mario, 'Time Asymmetry, Time Reversal, and Irreversibility', *Studium Generale* **23** (1970), 562–570.
[23] Clark, Eve V., 'How Young Children Describe Events in Time', in: *Advances in Psycholinguistics* [78] pp. 275–284.
[24] von Cube, Felix, *Kybernetische Grundlagen des Lehrens und Lernens*, Stuttgart 1965.
[25] van Dijk, Teun A., *Some Aspects of Text Grammars*, The Hague 1972.
[26] van Dijk, Teun A., Ihwe, J., Petöfi, J. S. and Rieser, H., *Zur Bestimmung narrativer Strukturen auf der Grundlage von Textgrammatiken*, Hamburg 1971.
[27] Dornseiff, Franz, *Der deutsche Wortschatz nach Sachgruppen*, Berlin 1954.
[28] Efron, Robert, 'The Measurement of Perceptual Durations', *Studium Generale* **23** (1970), 550–561.
[29] Frank, Helmar G., *Kybernetische Grundlagen der Pädagogik*, 2. völlig neubearbeitete und wesentlich erweiterte Auflage, 2 vols. Baden-Baden 1969.
[30] Frank, Helmar G. (ed.), *Kybernetische Maschinen*. Prinzip und Anwendung der automatischen Nachrichtenverarbeitung, Frankfurt/M. 1964.
[31] Fraser, J. T. (ed.), *The Study of Time*, New York/Heidelberg 1971.
[32] Gehlen, Arnold, *Der Mensch*. Seine Natur und seine Stellung in der Welt, 8. Aufl. Frankfurt/M. 1966.
[33] Gehlen, Arnold, *Anthropologische Forschung* (Aufsätze), Hamburg 1961.
[34] Gehlen, Arnold, *Urmensch und Spätkultur*, Frankfurt/M. 1964.
[35] Gehlen, Arnold, *Zeitbilder* Zur Soziologie und Ästhetik der modernen Malerei, Frankfurt/M. 1966.
[36] Gelhaus, H. *et al.*, *Der Begriff Tempus – eine Ansichtssache?*, Beiheft 20 zur Zs. Wirkendes Wort, Düsseldorf 1969.
[37] Gipper, Helmut, *Gibt es ein sprachliches Relativitätsprinzip?*. Untersuchungen zur Sapir-Whorf-Hypothese, Frankfurt/M. 1972.
[38] Glinz, Hans, *Die innere Form des Deutschen*, 5. Aufl. Bern 1968.
[39] Glinz, Hans, *Grundbegriffe und Methoden inhaltbezogener Text- und Sprachanalyse*, Düsseldorf 1965.
[40] Glinz, Hans, 'Zum Tempus- und Modussystem des Deutschen. Einige grundsätzlice Bemerkungen', in Gelhaus *et al.*, pp. 50–58.
[41] Glinz, Hans, *Der deutsche Satz*, 6. Aufl. Düsseldorf 1970.

[42] Glinz, Hans, 'Methoden zur Objektivierung des Verstehens von Texten, gezeigt an Kafka "Kinder auf der Landstraße"', *Jahrbuch für Internationale Germanistik* **1** (1969), 75–106.
[43] Glinz, Hans, *Sprachwissenschaft heute*. Aufgaben und Möglichkeiten, Stuttgart 1970.
[44] Glinz, Hans, *Linguistische Grundbegriffe und Methodenüberblick*, *Deutsche Grammatik I; Deutsche Grammatik II*, Frankfurt/M. 1971.
[45] Gülich, E. and Raible, W. (eds.), *Textsorten*. Differenzierungskriterien aus linguistischer Sicht, Frankfurt 1972.
[46] Hallig, R. and Wartburg, W. v., *Begriffssystem als Grundlage für die Lexikographie*. Versuch eines Ordnungsschemas., 2. Aufl. Berlin 1962.
[47] Hamburger, Käte, *Die Logik der Dichtung*, 2. stark veränderte Auflage, Stuttgart 1968.
[48] Hartmann, Peter, 'Zur Berücksichtigung der Zeit in der Sprache', *Der Deutschunterricht* **4** (1958), 47–75.
[49] Hauser-Suida, U. and Hoppe-Beugel, G., *Die Vergangenheitstempora in der deutschen geschriebenen Sprache der Gegenwart*. Untersuchungen an ausgewählten Texten, München/Düsseldorf 1972.
[50] Heger, Klaus, *Monem, Wort und Satz*, Tübingen 1971.
[51] Heisenberg, Werner, *Physik und Philosophie*, Frankfurt 1959.
[52] Hockett, Charles F., *The State of the Art*, The Hague 1968.
[53] Ihwe, Jens (ed.), *Literaturwissenschaft und Linguistik*. Ergebnisse und Perspektiven, 4 vols., Frankfurt 1972.
[54] Ingarden, Roman, *Das literarische Kunstwerk*, Tübingen 1965.
[55] Ingarden, Roman, *Vom Erkennen des literarischen Kunstwerkes*, Darmstadt 1968.
[56] Klein, W. and Wunderlich, D. (eds.), *Aspekte der Soziolinguistik*, Frankfurt 1971.
[57] Koch, Walter, A., *Vom Morphem zum Textem*, Hildesheim 1969.
[58] Koch, Walter A., *Varia Semiotica*, Hildesheim 1971.
[59] Köck, Wolfram K., 'Acceptability and the Teacher of English. Some Theoretical and Practical Remarks', *The English Language Journal*, Buenos Aires **1** (1970), 227–238, 341–355; and **2** (1971), 15–30, 117–128, 217–231.
[60] Köck, Wolfram K., 'Grundproblematiken der Theorie einer Literaturwissenschaft', in *Zur Grundlegung der Literaturwissenschaft* (ed. by S. J. Schmidt), München 1972, pp. 14–40.
[61] Köck, Wolfram K., 'Manipulation durch Trivialisierung. Elementare Möglichkeiten der Konsumprogrammierung', in *Sprache und Gesellschaft* (ed. by A. Rucktäschel), München 1972.
[62] Koschmieder, Erwin, *Zeitbezug und Sprache*, Leipzig 1929; Neudruck Darmstadt 1971.
[63] Kuhn, Thomas S., *The Structure of Scientific Revolutions*, 2nd ed., Chicago 1970.
[64] Labov, W. and Waletzky, J., 'Narrative Analysis: Oral Versions of Personal Experience', in *Essays on the Verbal and Visual Arts* (ed. by J. Helm), Seattle and London 1967, pp. 12–44.
[65] Lausberg, Heinrich, *Handbuch der literarischen Rhetorik*, 2 vols., München 1960.
[66] Lorenz, Konrad, *Über tierisches und menschliches Verhalten*, Gesammelte Abhandlungen, 2 vols., München 1965.
[67] Maranda, P. and Maranda, E. K., *Structural Models in Folklore and Transformational Essays*, The Hague 1971.
[68] Michon, John A., 'Processing of Temporal Information and the Cognitive Theory of Time Experience', *Studium Generale* **23** (1970), 149–265.
[69] Müller, Günther, *Morphologische Poetik*, Gesammelte Aufsätze, Darmstadt 1968.
[70] Palmer, Frank R., *Grammar*, Penguin Books 1971.
[71] Petöfi, János S., *Transformationsgrammatiken und eine kotextuelle Texttheorie*, Frankfurt/M. 1971.
[72] Petöfi, János S., 'Zu einer grammatischen Theorie sprachlicher Texte', *Zeitschrift für Literaturwissenschaft und Linguistik* **3** (1972), 31–58.

[73] Piaget, Jean, *Die Bildung des Zeitbegriffs beim Kinde*, Zürich 1955.
[74] Pop, Sever, *La dialectologie*, 2 Vols., Louvain 1958.
[75] Popper, Karl R., *The Logic of Scientific Discovery*, London 1968.
[76] Portmann, Adolf, *Zoologie und das neue Bild des Menschen*, Hamburg 1956.
[77] Posner, Roland, 'Die Kommentierung – oder: Ein Weg von der Satzgrammatik zur Textlinguistik', *Zeitschrift für Literaturwissenschaft und Linguistik* **5** (1972), 9–30.
[78] *Advances in Psycholinguistics*, (ed. by G. B. Flores d'Arcais and W. J. M. Levelt), Amsterdam/London 1970.
[79] Reichenbach, Hans, *Elements of Symbolic Logic*, New York 1947.
[80] Rescher, N. and Urquhart,., *Temporal Logic*, Wien/New York 1971.
[81] Roget, Peter Mark, *Thesaurus of English Words and Phrases* 1852), abridged version, Penguin Books 1960.
[82] Rothacker, Erich, *Logik und Systematik der Geisteswissenschaften*, Bonn, 1948.
[83] Rothacker, Erich, *Probleme der Kulturantropologie*, Bonn 1948.
[84] Slobin, Dan I., 'Universals of Grammatical Development in Children', in *Advances in Psycholinguistics* [78], pp. 174–184.
[85] Stachowiak, Herbert, *Denken und Erkennen im kybernetischen Modell*, 2. Auflage Wien/New York 1969.
[86] Stanzel, Franz K., 'Die Zeitgestaltung in W. Faulkners *The Bear*', *Die Neueren Sprachen* (1953), pp. 114–121.
[87] Stanzel, Franz K., *Typische Formen des Romans*, Göttingen 1964.
[88] Steinbuch, Karl, *Automat und Mensch*. Kybernetische Tatsachen und Hypothesen, Berlin/Göttingen/Heidelberg 1965.
[89] Stempel, Wolf.-D. (ed.): *Beiträge zur Textlinguistik*, München 1971.
[90] Stoll, Robert R., *Sets, Logic, and Axiomatic Theories*, San Francisco & London 1961.
[91] Thienemann, August F., *Leben und Umwelt*. Vom Gesamthaushalt der Natur, Hamburg 1956.
[92] Topitsch, Ernst, 'Vom Mythos zur Philosophie. Vorphilosophische Grundlagen philosophischer Probleme', *Studium Generale* **11** (1958), 12–29.
[93] Topitsch, Ernst, *Vom Ursprung und Ende der Metaphysik*, Wien 1958 (dtv., München 1972).
[94] Topitsch, Ernst, 'Sprachlogische Probleme der sozialwissenschaftlichen Theoriebildung', in *Logik der Sozialwissenschaften* [95], pp. 17–36.
[95] Topitsch, Ernst, (ed): *Logik der Sozialwissenschaften*, 6. Aufl. Köln 1970.
[96] Uexküll, J. v. and Kriszat, G., *Streifzüge durch die Umwelten von Tieren und Menschen/Bedeutungslehre*, Frankfurt 1970 (urspr. 1934, 1940).
[97] van der Waerden, B. L., 'Denken ohne Sprache', *Acta Psychologica* **10** (1954), 165–174.
[98] Wandruszka, Mario, *Sprachen. Vergleichbar and Unvergleichlich*, München 1969.
[99] Wandruszka, Mario, *Interlinguistik*, München 1971.
[100] Watzlawick, Paul, 'Das Utopie-Syndrom', *Neue Zürcher Zeitung* 8.10.1972.
[101] Wehrle, H. and Eggers, H., *Deutscher Wortschatz*, Stuttgart 1961.
[102] Weinrich, Harald, *Tempus*. Besprochene und erzählte Welt, 2. völlig neubearbeitete Auflage, Stuttgart 1971.
[103] Weisgerber, Leo, *Die vier Stufen in der Erforschung der Sprachen*, Düsseldorf 1963.
[104] Weisgerber, Leo, *Zur Grundlegung der ganzheitlichen Sprachauffassung*, Aufsätze 1925–1933, Düsseldorf 1964.
[105] Whorf, Benjamin Lee, *Language, Thought, and Reality*, London 1956.
[106] Wittenberg, A. I., *Vom Denken in Begriffen*. Mathematik als Experiment des reinen Denkens, 2. Aufl. Basel 1968.
[107] Wittgenstein, Ludwig, *Philosophische Untersuchungen*, Frankfurt 1971.
[108) Wunderlich, Dieter, *Tempus und Zeitreferenz im Deutschen*, München 1970.
[109] McCawley, J. D., 'Tense and Time Reference in English', in *Studies in Linguistic Semantics* (ed. by Ch. J. Fillmore and T. Langendoen), New York 1971, pp. 97–113.
[110] Sachsse, H. *Einführung in die Kybernetik*, Braunschweig 1971.

JÁNOS S. PETÖFI

TOWARDS AN EMPIRICALLY MOTIVATED GRAMMATICAL THEORY OF VERBAL TEXTS*

I. SENTENCE GRAMMARS AND TEXT GRAMMARS

0. *Introduction*

The ever increasing intensity of (linguistic and non-linguistic) text theoretical research makes it possible and, at the same time, also necessary to take some of the basic points of the theory of grammar under closer examination.

Although I only intend to deal with the basic questions of the theory of grammar of verbal texts, it seems to be necessary to give an outline of the broader context of this topic, too.

The term *verbal* is used for the precise specification of the text-domain under investigation, i.e. for separating it from the *non-verbal* (musical-, motional/dance-, pictorial-, scenic-, etc.) text-domains, with which, though through appropriate transfer, the term 'grammar' can also be brought into connection.

The term *text* will refer in this context to a sequence of spoken or written verbal elements functioning as a single whole, which is qualified according to some (mostly extralinguistic) criterion as being a 'text'.

The term *grammar* indicates the complex of a system of syntactic, semantic and phonological rules and of a lexicon (a specially built up dictionary of a language).

1. *State of the Grammatical Theory of Verbal Texts*[1]

1.1. First of all I consider it necessary to make clear that the grammatical

* This study is built up of two main chapters. The first chapter ('Sentence Grammars and Text Grammars') is a partly revised version of the first part of (1971e) while the second chapter ('A Not Fixed Linearity Text Grammar. The Present Stage of Its Development') is a new and the most detailed summary of the grammatical conception referred to in the title until now. The present form of this conception is not at last a result of discussions within the frame of the Project 'Textlinguistics' at the University of Constance and I owe, first of all, very much to the common work (still being) done together with H. Rieser. [Cf. Petöfi-Rieser (1972a), (1972b).] My works contained in the bibliography inform both about the phases of the development of the text-theoretical conception serving as a broader framework and of the 'not fixed linearity text grammar'. The notes given here refer to this bibliography.

[1] As regards the general text-theoretical framework cf. (1967a), (1967b), (1971a), (1971b), (1971i), (1972d).

J. S. Petöfi and H. Rieser (eds.), Studies in Text Grammar, 205–275.

theory of verbal texts (in the following: GThVeT) has a *direct* (i.e. from the application independent) aim and task.

Its *direct aim* is to describe the knowledge of the 'ideal native speaker/listener' concerning the grammatical structuredness of verbal texts (i.e. his *verbal grammatical competence*).

Its *direct task* is to carry out this description such as to comply with those requirements of the theory of science which can be met within the frames of linguistics.

1.2. Besides the direct aim and task, the GThVeT also has an *indirect* aim and task.

The *indirect aim* of the GThVeT has different aspects. These aspects are hierarchically ordered in the following way:

– first of all, the GThVeT has to become part of the description of the knowledge of the 'ideal native speaker/listener' concerning the full verbal structuredness of verbal texts (i.e. his *full verbal competence*);

– the GThVeT has to provide the basis for the description of the ordinary verbal activity (i.e. of the verbal activity without artistic intention) of the 'ideal native speaker/listener' (more precisely, of his creating and receiving non-artistic texts, i.e. of his *full verbal performance*);

– the GThVeT has to become part of the description of the knowledge of the 'ideal homo poeticus' concerning the structuredness of verbal works of art, or, in a broader sense, of works of art which also have a verbal component (i.e. of his *poetic competence*);

– finally, the GThVeT has to become part of the science which makes possible the description of the poetic activity of the 'ideal homo poeticus' (more precisely, of his creating and receiving verbal works of art – in a broader sense: of works of art having a verbal component – i.e. of his *poetic performance*).

Besides the direct task these indirect aims entail different *accessory (indirect) tasks*. Namely, the GThVeT has to be built up such that

– the description of the sound-textural (euphonetic and rhythmic) structure of verbal texts can be made compatible with the description of their grammatical structure. (This guarantees the possibility of describing the full verbal competence and performance within the frame of a homogeneous theory);

– it allows for the optimal analyzability of the non-verbal structures (of the 'world' sui generis of the particular texts, their sociological, ideological, poetic and aesthetic structure) implied by the verbal structure, and accounts for the possibility of relating the interpretation of the non-verbal structures with the interpretation of the verbal structure. (This guarantees the possibility of describing the poetic competence and performance within the frame of a homogeneous theory.)

The complexity of these tasks determines the chance of establishing a GThVeT to a great extent. In my opinion in the present stage of research nothing more can be expected than to raise the relevant questions. Maybe, the answer to them will be more simple than their actual formulating.

In the following, I want to deal with the probelms related to the *direct* aim of the GThVeT, thus as to make allowance for the requirements called for by the accessory tasks, too.

As a matter of fact, the above formulation of the direct aim and task is a generalisation of the aim and task resulting from the sentence grammatical research of recent years. As a starting point, I will discuss briefly the basic traits of the types of grammar developed in the course of this sentence grammatical research, together with some questions concerning the possibility of establishing an *integrated sentence grammar*.

2. *Some General Questions Concerning the Set-Up of Sentence Grammars*[2]

2.1. Within the domain of the sentence grammar the following three main problems can be distinguished:

(1) the problem concerning the *universal sentence grammar*, that is, the investigation of how the syntactic, semantic and phonological components, and the lexicon should be built up in general;

(2) the problem concerning the *sentence-grammar of a given language*, that is the investigation of how the grammar of a given language can be built up according to the principles formulated in the universal sentence grammar;

(3) the problem concerning the *grammatical description of a given sentence* (more precisely, of a given linear sentence-manifestation), that is the investigation of how a given linear sentence-manifestation a structural description can be assigned.

2.1.1. The above mentioned problems (1) were (and still are) investigated, above all within the framework of the so-called generative transformational research.

Almost all of the 'schools' working within this frame base their investigations on the hypothesis that the description of the 'competence' is independent of the aspects of communication (i.e. of the different verbal activities of the speaker and the listener).

[2] When dealing with the building up of sentence grammars I have considered almost exclusively the generative grammatical conceptions. As regards the analysis of these sentence grammatical conceptions cf. also (1971b), (1971c), (1972a).

Since several theoretical questions remained unsolved so far, it is only quite natural that no generative transformational sentence grammar has been elaborated for any of the languages.

'Grammatical description of a given sentence' within the frame of this conception means to show that the grammar in question is able to generate even this given sentence as well.

The most important trait of the generative transformational research, which, in my opinion, makes it more powerful than other types of research, is that it distinguishes between *deep*-structure and *surface*-structure.

2.1.2. The above mentioned problems (2) and (3) were (and are still) dealt with – though not always under the aspect of a universal grammar – mainly in the research done in machine translation, in certain contrastive linguistic researches and in the theory of documentation.

Among the problems arising from these branches of research stress can be laid on the investigation of the question, what kind of an automatizable procedure can be elaborated in order to analyze the sentence structures out of the surface (linear) sentence manifestations.

2.2. The main conceptions, with respect to the questions of the universal sentence grammar, can be summed up as follows.

The following four levels of the sentence structure will be referred to:

(1) *linear (sentence-) manifestation:* a segment of a spoken or written 'text' which is classified – generally on the basis of some extra-linguistic criterion – as a 'sentence'; it will be denoted by *LiM*;

(2) *surface (sentence) structure:* a structure – given in the form of a diagram or labelled brackets – which is only the subject of the linearization-operation in order to become a linear manifestation; it is denoted by *SuSt*;

(3) *deep (sentence) structure:* a structure – given in the form of a diagram or labelled brackets – which contains all informations necessary for the semantic interpretation and for getting at the surface structure by means of transformations; it is denoted by *DSt*;

(4) *semantic (sentence) representation:* a 'sentence-meaning representation' by means of abstract semantic units; it is denoted by *SeR*. (As for the formal structure of the semantic representation, there are several conceptions known. The two main types are the following: (a) a diagram or a labelled-bracketed-construction, the terminal elements of which are abstract semantic units; (b) an expression built up of abstract semantic units by means of a predicate-logic. – The status of the 'abstract semantic units' is not yet clear.)

These structure levels can be arranged graphically as shown in Figure 1.

----- LiM -----
----- SuSt -----
----- DSt -----
----- SeR -----

Fig. 1.

2.2.1. The model developed out of the *conception of Chomsky* (the 'CKP – *Chomsky-Katz-Postal* – model', as it is called by Katz, or the 'classical transformational theory', as it is called by Postal) generates DSt-s to which the SeR-s are assigned by a transformation-like semantic interpretative rule-system, and which are transduced into SuSt-s by the aid of syntactic transformation rules and phonological interpretative rules. – The questions of how to get the LiM are considered to be phenomena belonging to the sphere of 'performance'.

2.2.1.1. The main characteristics of the *generating rule system* of Chomsky consists in the context-sensitive way of determining the syntactic features of the verbs and adjectives in 'predicate position'. In other words, this means that in the generation nouns will be categorized first – in a context-free way – and the verb and the adjective functioning as 'the predicate of the sentence' will be categorized according to the features of these nouns.

The choosing of the concrete lexical units is governed by the categories obtained in this way. The *lexicon* of the model contains lexical units furnished with the appropriate 'lexicon-accessories', i.e. with the sets of the appropriate phonological, syntactic and semantic features.

The grammatical functions 'subject', 'predicate', 'object' etc. can be stated on the basis of the 'dominance-relations' of the diagram (or the labelled-bracketed-expression).

An attempt to correct the generating rule system as conceived by Chomsky is the *Operators and Nucleus model* by P. Seuren which, as far as its basic conception is concerned, belongs to the same type of model as that of Chomsky.

One of the characteristics of this model is that it draws a distinction between 'sentence', 'proposition' and 'nucleus' in the sentence-structure.

Another characteristic of this model is that it is the verb or the adjective functioning as the 'predicate of the sentence' which are chosen first. The selection of the nouns is governed by the lexical representation of the verb or the adjective in the lexicon. On the one hand this means that the separation of the nominal part, functioning as the subject, from the verbal part, functioning as the predicate (as it is the case in Chomsky's grammar) is abandoned. On the other hand, it is necessary that the lexical representations of the verbs and adjectives receive a special structure, a structure distinct from that in the Chomskyan grammar.

Seuren does not apply diagrams for the representation of the sentence structures; he represents the structure-informations which he considers to be relevant in a way analogous to the way of writing expressions in a predicate-logic.

The functions 'subject', 'predicate', 'object' etc. are indicated by 'function-categories' written into the lexical entries.

Another attempt to correct the model of Chomsky is the *Case Grammar* as conceived by C. Fillmore. Even this model can still be considered as belonging to this model-type, although it differs much more from the model of Chomsky than Seuren's model.

The model of Fillmore suggests to choose a 'predicate-frame' as first step in the generation. The way in which the lexical units capable of functioning as 'predicates' are represented in the lexicon, is analogous to the representation given in the model of Seuren. However, while Seuren uses 'surface case categories' ('subject', 'object', 'indirect object', etc.) in these representations, Fillmore thinks it necessary to apply 'deep case categories'. The 'deep case categories' suggested by Fillmore are: Agent, Experiencer, Instrument, Object, Source, Goal, Place and Time.

2.2.1.2. The *semantic interpretation* component fitting the syntactic conception of Chomsky has been elaborated by Katz and Fodor, and Katz and Postal, respectively.

Katz and Fodor (KF) specified the task of semantics as follows: determination of the number and the meaning of the possible readings of the particular sentences, disclosure of the occasional semantic anomalies, disclosure of the paraphrase-relations among sentences – and the taking into consideration of all semantic properties and relations playing a role in these operations. However, the interpretative rule system outlined in KF can only solve the first and the second task immediately, and even this can only be done within the boundaries determined by the syntactic component. More precisely, it can assign the possible readings only to the 'deep-structures'.

The syntactic and semantic rule system cannot handle the question of syntactic ambiguities (i.e. the determination of how many different deep-structures can belong to a linear manifestation like e.g. *the shooting of the hunters was terrible*); and the question of the paraphrases (i.e. the determination, in which syntactically and/or lexically different surface structures the particular sentence-readings can be manifested).

This would only be possible within the frame of this model, if we assumed that we have the deep-structure, the semantic representation, the surface-structure and the linear manifestation of *each* sentence at our disposal together with an 'ordering apparatus' which is able to choose, on the one hand, those 'structure descriptions' which lead to the same linear manifestation and, on the other hand, those 'structure descriptions' which lead to the same semantic representation. (In the latter case it has to be assumed, that the paraphrases have an identical semantic representation.) This assumption, however, is inconsistent with the aim of the KF-conception, namely, according to this assumption, instead of a potentially infinite set of structures an actually infinite set of structures ought to have been taken into consideration.[3]

A semantic interpreting component can in principle be attached both to the modified generating rule system suggested by Seuren, and to that suggested by Fillmore.

2.2.1.3. In connection with the *syntactic transformational component* I only wish to make the following remarks: (1) in this conception the DSt does not determine unambiguously the LiM-s which can be derived from it and, as a consequence, it does not determine the transformations to be carried out either; (2) the transformational component of none of the versions of this conception is elaborated to such an extent as to permit to judge whether it has taken into account all transformational possibilities leading to well-formed LiM-s, and only those, or not.

I do not want to deal with the questions of the phonological interpretative component here.

2.2.2. The type of conception which has been outlined so far (let us call it conception-type *A*) has been subject to criticism because of the role semantics plays in it. On the basis of this criticism a new type of conception (let us call it conception-type *B*) arose.

2.2.2.1. The kernel of this new type of conception can already be found in the theory of U. Weinreich.

Weinreich took the position, contrary to the KF-theory, that

> ...the preoccupation of KF with disambiguation appears to be an entirely unjustified diversion of effort. Semantic theories can and should be so formulated as to guarantee that deep structures (including their lexical components) are specified as unambiguous in the first place and proceed from there to account for the interpretation of a complex

[3] This criticism refers only indirectly to the KF-model, namely it concerns the objective and not the set-up of the model. What I think necessary is to give a broader interpretation of the notion of competence; this means that I also interpret the task of the grammar in a broader sense.

expression from the known meanings of its components. (Weinreich, 1966; p. 339.)

2.2.2.2. The new type of conception which has actually been based upon the criticism of Weinreich, is generally called *generative semantics*. (See the works of Bach, McCawley, Lakoff, and Postal in the bibliography.)

The essentials of generative semantics have been summed up by McCawley as follows:

> in each language there is simply a single system of processes which convert the semantic representation of each sentence into its surface syntactic representation and that none of the intermediate stages in the conversion of semantic representation into surface syntactic representation is entitled to any special status such as that which Chomsky ascribes to 'deep structure'. (McCawley, 1967; p. 18.)

This means, in other words, that the base-component of the grammar has to generate immediately semantic representations; since, as a consequence of this, there does not exist a semantic interpretation as such within the frame of generative semantics, semantic interpretative rules will not be needed either.

The generative semanticians are not concerned with the question of 'generation'. In the notation of the semantic representations they apply a predicate-calculus which seems to be near to the object-language. They attempt to establish such a form of representation which unambiguously determines the LiM.[4]

The lexicon applied in generative semantics should be built up in such a way that it is the semantic representations the lexical units (or phrases) manifesting them are assigned to – i.e. the set-up of the lexicon is quite the opposite of that of the conception-type *A*.

2.2.2.3. A. K. Žolkovskij and I. A. Mel'čuk, by investigating the problems of machine translation, arrived at a conception similar to that of generative semantics – independently from the development of the latter, in fact, even preceding it in time.

They think that the problems of semantics reflect, as a matter of fact, the difference of the roles the speaker and the listener play in communication:

> ...the grasping of a 'meaning 'manifests itself on the side of the speaker in the capability of expressing the same idea in different ways, while on the side of the listener in that he is capable of recognizing identity or relatedness of meaning of verbal utterances which, on the strength of their form, seen to be different.

In this respect, the decisive trait of this model is, to use the terminology of

[4] The further development of the conception of Chomsky has been disregarded here – it does not concern the basic questions significantly. [For this question cf. Maclay (1971).

the authors, the 'mass character' of the semantic synthesis, i.e. the goal, that the system of the synthesis

> ...has to guarantee that every given meaning can be expressed through a maximal variety of lexically and/or syntactically different sentences. (Žolkovskij and Mel'čuk, 1967; pp. 177, 178)

The *semantic synthesis* of Žolkovskij and Mel'čuk is built up as follows:
– the 'sentence-meanings' (SeR-s) are written in a so-called 'basic-language'; (The authors did not deal in an explicit way with the question whether the meanings themselves can be generated or not. The basic-language contains elements – 'basic lexical-units' and 'parameters' – which are formally analogous to the elements of a predicate-logic.)
– from these 'sentence-meanings' written in the basic-language the '(lexico-) syntactic structure' of all possible (synonymous) representations belonging to the particular meanings will be derived by means of a rule system containing lexico-syntactic transformations;
– out of these '(lexico-) syntactic structures' (the formation of which is called 'semantic synthesis' by the authors) the so-called syntactic and morphological synthesis forms the LiM-s.

The semantic synthesis works with a special dictionary in which the 'units of the basic language' are assigned the appropriate lexical units. (Cf. Apresjan *et al.*, 1969.)

2.2.3. In addition to the above mentioned conceptions belonging to these two conception-types, there could certainly other conceptions be enumerated as well. However, my aim was only to take into account the *relevant problems*, not the particular conceptions. Before I proceed further, I want to sum up briefly these relevant problems.

The 'direction' of the succession of the operations required by the different conception-types and the differences between them, mapped in Figure 1, can be demonstrated in the way shown in Figure 2.

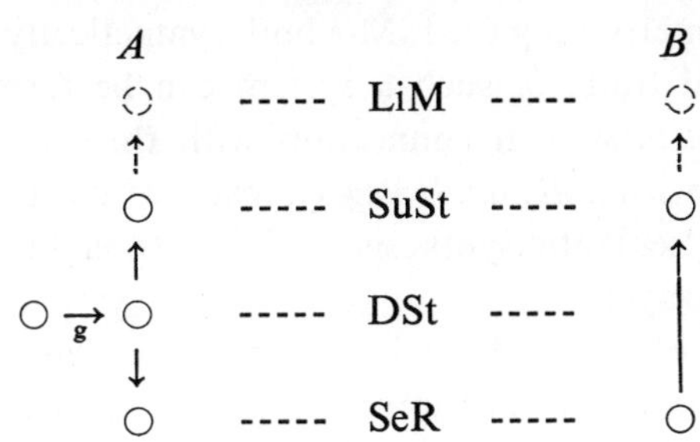

Fig. 2. ○→g indicates the generation of DSt-s.

The succession of the operations in conception-type *B* is *uni-directional*: it leads from the SeR to the SuSt. The model is able to generate the paraphrases, however, it cannot give an account of whether the LiM-s obtained manifest only the intended meanings or other meanings as well. That is, it cannot account for either the syntactic ambiguity or the possible readings of the LiM-s.

The succession of the operations in conception-type *A* is *not uni-directional*; it leads from the DSt-s to the SeR-s and to the SuSt-s, respectively. The model can account for the possible readings of the DSt-s, but not for the syntactic ambiguity of the LiM-s, nor for the paraphrases of the SeR-s. The modified version of the conception of Chomsky as given by Seuren and Fillmore, respectively, reduces the differences between the two conception-types in a certain 'formal' respect; namely, the second conception-type (the conception-type *B*) operates generally with verbal units which are analogous to the expressions of a predicate-logic, and both Seuren and Fillmore apply units of this kind.

For the time being it remains unmotivated whether it is necessary to apply abstract case-categories as suggested by Fillmore. The question of the relation of the two conception-types to the grammatical competence also remains undecided. I shall come back to these points later.

2.2.4. When analyzing Figure 2, the possibility of a third conception-type, namely the *full inverse of conception-type B* – let us call it conception-type B^{-1} – arises. (The theoretically not so interesting question of how the sequence of operations of conception-type *B* can be completed until the LiM is reached will not be dealt with here; however, when referring to the inverse conception, I think of a complete sequence of operations.)

It is not likely that a model which could immediately generate LiM-s can be set up. More precisely, it is not likely that such a model can be set up economically for *any* of the languages and can be adequately motivated in a grammatical respect. Thus, one possibility remains: to elaborate a system capable of interpreting the LiM-s both syntactically and semantically. Only a few general traits of such a system can be formulated, however, since the problems arising in connection with this are language-specific.

Such a *syntactico-semantic analyzing system* – to use this inverse term as opposing the term 'semantic synthesis' – can be thought of as realizable in the following two ways:

(1) as a system of rules (B_1^{-1}) by means of which the LiM-s will be assigned all possible DSt-s thus joining a grammar of conception-type *A*;

(2) as a system of rules (B_2^{-1}) by means of which the LiM-s will be assigned all possible (syntactico-) semantic representations (i.e. SeR-s), the

set-up of which is independent from that of a grammar of conception-type *A*.

Taking this conception-type into consideration, too, these three conception-types can be summed up as follows (see Figure 3).

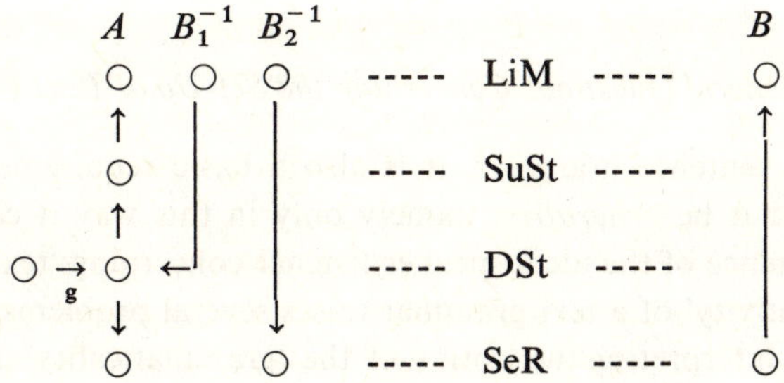

Fig. 3.

Although none of the grammars of conception-type *B* raised the question of 'generativity', it can be assumed that even a grammar of this type can be built up in a generative way; that is, also SeR-s can be generated. Now the question of how the generativity can be guaranteed in an inverse model (i.e. in a grammar of conception-type B^{-1}) arises, namely, it is not likely that LiM-s can be generated. – To maintain generativity is by all means desirable, since only in this way the modelling of the knowledge concerning the structure of the *infinite* number of sentences can be guaranteed.

In my opinion, generativity is only feasible on the basis of a combination of the conception-types $(A+B_1^{-1})$. A combined model of this type would function as follows: the model of type *A* generates DSt-s and transduces those into SuSt-s (and into LiM-s belonging to the particular DSt-s). Then, the model of type B_1^{-1} analyses these LiM-s and shows whether they manifest only the generated DSt-s or whether other DSt-s can also be assigned to them. If the latter proves to be the case, the model determines these DSt-s. After this the semantic interpretation component of the model of type *A* interprets all possible DSt-s belonging to the particular LiM-s. In other words, it determines all possible SeR-s belonging to the particular LiM-s. Thus, a combined model like this would be able to account for both the syntactic and the semantic ambiguity (if the LiM-s contain such ambiguities).

Furthermore, if it were possible to build up the models of the types $(A+B_1^{-1})$ and *B* in such a way as to make them correspond to each other, i.e. so that the model of type B_1^{-1} and the semantic interpreting rule-system of the model of type *A* can be the inverse of the rule-system of the model of type *B*, then the model of type $((A+B_1^{-1})+B)$ would be able to account not only for the syntactic and the semantic ambiguity but also for the paraphrases in an economic way. The model of type B could assign all possible paraphrases to the SeR-s generated by the model of type $(A+B_1^{-1})$. Thus a model of type $((A+B_1^{-1})+B)$ could reflect the full sentence-grammatical competence of the ideal speaker/listener in an operative way.

3. *Some General Questions Concerning the Set-Up of Text Grammars*[5]

3.1. As for a sentence grammar, it is also a basic requirement for a text grammar, that it be *generative*, namely only in this way it can reflect the verbal competence of the ideal speaker/listener concerning 'texts'.

The 'generativity' of a text grammar raises several problems, the first one being that of interpreting the notion of the 'grammaticality' of texts. Since we consider the grammar to be the complex of a syntactic, a phonological and a semantic component, the notion of 'grammaticality' has to be interpreted from the point of view of each of these components. With respect to semantics this was already found to be complicated enough in the case of the sentence grammar, because an unambiguous line of demarcation between 'linguistic semantics', 'ontological semantics' and 'pragmatical semantics' cannot be drawn; the necessary and sufficient scope of semantics which should be taken into consideration within the frame of a generative sentence grammar cannot be determined in some a priori way.

The determination of the grammaticality of a linguistic structure is carried out on the basis of those relations which exist among the elements of the structure.

Within the frame of an expounded simple sentence the 'constituent-structures' are organized to an 'organic whole' on the basis of relatively unambiguously definable grammatical relations. However, if we try to order the types of the complex sentences according to the 'organicality', we find that their organicality will gradually become looser and looser such that it comes to sentences which manifest a connection of structures which cannot be motivated any longer because of linguistic aspects alone.

In order to be able to establish grammaticality or, to use a somewhat more general term, 'textuality', we also have to find an analogon for 'organicality' –

[5] The thematic restriction concerning the discussion of the sentence grammars (see Note 2) is, of course, followed by consequences with respect to the discussion of the text grammars, too. The analysis of other than generative-type sentence grammars from the point of view of text grammar will be the topic of a forthcoming study.

Here I also want to observe that, as a natural consequence of the development of grammatical research, I was originally considering the completion of a Chomsky-type grammar to a text grammar and it was only later that I attempted to outline a more powerful conception. Concerning the first endeavour (building upon Chomsky's conception) see (1967a), (1967b), (1968), (1969a), (1969c), (1969d), (1969e), (1971a); (1969b) and (1970) already show the amplification of the conceptional framework.

the relations guaranteeing organicality – with respect to text structures.

First of all it seems to be advisable to distinguish between *grammatically continuous* and *grammatically discontinuous* sequences of sentences.

A sequence of sentences can be considered as *grammatically continuous*

(a) if a constituent-structure (i.e. NP- or VP-subtree) in the consecutive sentence-structures of the sequence is recurrent. (This recurrence can be manifested in the form of a 'pro-form', a 'synonym' or on the basis of some other relation fixed in the grammar qualifying as a recurrence);

(b) if the sequence of sentences is well-formed with respect to the 'topic-comment' order;

(c) if the sequence of sentences is well-formed with respect to the order of logical and/or temporal 'antecedent(s)-consequence' (in a given case 'cause and effect') relation.

With regard to grammatical continuity there can be a difference between a sequence resulting from the succession of 'sentence-bases' and a sequence resulting from the succession of the 'linear manifestations of the sentence bases'. This question will not be considered here, however.

To guarantee the fulfilment and to meet the requirement noted in point (a) seems to be more or less easy. It certainly needs the application of well-defined 'inter-sentential' operations.

To guarantee the fulfilment and to meet the requirement noted in point (b) presupposes that more specific 'inter-sentential' operations be stated. In this case, the problem of the 'sentence-stress' also has to be taken into consideration.

The fulfilment of the requirement noted in point (c), though it is not impossible theoretically, calls for the elaboration of a very complicated apparatus. In this apparatus the semantic characterization of the lexical units and, above all, the presuppositional entries assigned to the particular lexical units – together with a rule-system capable of operating with these presuppositions – have to play the basic role. The 'normal arrangement' of a sentence-sequence can possibly be established with the aid of all these means.[6]

If a sequence of sentences does not fulfil the above requirements, it will be called *grammatically discontinuous.*

However, if we only apply this distinction to the succession of sentences, it is not even sufficient for the characterization of the 'organicality' ('cohesion', 'coherence') of texts as far as grammatical aspects are concerned. Namely, there exist certain types of texts in which the sentences of two grammatically continuous sentence-sequences intersect in such a way that

[6] Cf. Petöfi-Rieser (1972b).

the text ought to be classified as grammatically discontinuous, although this classification conflicts with both our grammatical intuition and the actually provable grammatical relationships ranging over the elements which are responsible for the discontinuity. In my opinion, this problem can only be solved, if we define the text-basis as being a different, a 'deeper' structure than the succession of the sentence-bases constituting the text, and if we define a continuity-relation concerning the 'text-basis', too.

After this short introductory analysis, I shall treat the problems of text grammar on the basis of distinguishing two main classes of text grammar types:

(1) the class of the so called '*fixed linearity text grammars*', i.e. text grammars, in which the text basis essentially corresponds to the linear succession of the bases of the sentences constituting the text;

(2) the class of the so called '*not fixed linearity text grammars*' i.e. text grammars, in which the text-basis is a 'deeper' structure than the linear succession of the sentence-bases constituting the text and in which a constituent of the basis can be separated from the informations determining the linear manifestation.

These two types can also be observed in connection with the sentence grammars: most of the sentence grammars conceived mainly for the purpose of machine-analysis belong to the former type, while those operating in one or another form with a 'deep structure' belong to the latter type.

In the following I want to deal with the possibilities of the realization of the particular text grammar types belonging to these two classes.

3.2. The sentence grammars, on the one hand, serve (or can serve) as *models* for setting up text grammars, on the other hand, they also must be an *organic part* of them.

3.2.1. The types of the *fixed linearity text grammars* are developed from the types of sentence-grammatical conceptions discussed in the preceding chapter, by means of the *linear expansion* of the sentence-grammatical operations. (That is why text grammars will be referred to as being of conception-type LiA, LiB, LiB^{-1}, etc.)

Thus, the problems of the types of text-grammatical conceptions interpreted in this way reflect, in addition to the problems which concern the maintaining of the textuality, also the basic problems of the type of sentence grammar chosen as their model.

The problems of *textuality* can be taken as being identical both in conception-type LiA and LiB. (Within a fixed linearity text grammar I do not see any sufficiently motivatable way of accounting for the generation of 'coherent' texts consisting of a grammatically (linearly) not continuous sentence-sequence. For this reason I shall treat here only the problems of the grammatically (linearly) continuous sentence-sequences.)

From the criteria for grammatically continuous sentence-sequences I shall not consider requirement (c) for the time being, because the problems of its application are not yet clear. As for the requirements (a) and (b), one part of requirement (a) belongs to the problems of the *generation*, while its other part together with requirement (b) belong to the problems of the *transformation*.

The formation of the 'identical constituent structures', which guarantee the grammatical continuity of a sequence of sentences, has to be provided by the *generation*. With respect to the 'NP-constituents', this makes the application of 'reference-indices' necessary. (The term 'reference-index' will be used here in the sense of 'co-textual identifier', that is, the only task to be fulfilled by the reference-indices is to reveal whether the elements occurring in the text (no matter whether they are identical or different in their 'outward form') refer to the same 'referent' or not. (The 'reference-semantic' aspects of the 'references' themselves are not concerned.)

If the depth of the semantic characterization of the lexical units ranges as far as to contain certain markers of 'ontological' character (even if it does not go deeper than the Chomskyan or Seurenian theory), the lexicon component has to contain in conception-type Li*A* as well as in Li*B* such additional special arrangements which guarantee the fulfilment of a Chomsky-type as well as a Seuren-type insertion possible with respect to these semantic markers, too. Namely, in the generation it may become necessary to insert both verbs depending on nouns and nouns depending on verbs already chosen. It is, of course, important, in which way the generation is carried out: from sentence to sentence, or simultaneously ranging over the whole sequence of sentences.

In conception-type Li*A* the task of the *transformational* component is to carry out the pronominalizations. Conception-type Li*B*, in addition to this, has to establish the surface-manifestation of the recurring identical elements. In carrying out either these transformations or those determining the order of the constituents of the sentences, we cannot dispense with the structure-analyses of the surface-and deep-structures of the sentences preceding the sentence in question in the given sequence of sentences. Thus, the carrying out of the transformations is based on making allowances partly for information inside the sentence-structure, partly for information outside the sentence-structure.

Presumably, in conception-type Li*B* the structure-analysis of the preceding sentences is also necessary for carrying out the synonym-structure-forming (in the model of Žolkovskij and Mel'čuk: lexico-syntactic) transformations.

In conception-type LiA the semantic interpreting rule-system has to be built up in such a way that it is able to interpret a grammatically continuous sequence of sentences as one single whole.

As far as the *individual traits* of the particular conception-types are concerned, it is true of these text-grammatical conception-types, too, that (*within the frame of the linearly fixed sentence-sequences*)

(1) conception-type LiB is able to generate paraphrases, although it cannot account for the possible syntactico-semantic ambiguity of the generated sentence-sequences;

(2) the generative inverse of conception-type LiB the conception-type Li$(A+B_1^{-1})$ can be, which is complementary to conception-type LiB also in so far as it accounts for the syntactico-semantic ambiguity;

(3) the conception-type LiB_1^{-1} (and LiB_2^{-1} which is also conceivable here) requires a special 'text-analysing method' capable of disclosing the syntactico-semantic structure of the particular sentences of a grammatically continuous sequence of sentences. In addition to this, it must also be capable of determining the reference-indices which can be (must be) assigned to the particular NP-constituents;

(4) the description of the full grammatical competence concerning the grammatically continuous sequences of sentences is only conceivable within the frame of a conception-type Li$((A+B_1^{-1})+B)$ which has to be built up according to the requirement of 'economy', so that the model-parts Li$(A+$ $+B_1^{-1})$ and LiB be maximally coordinated.

3.2.2. In summing up the sentence-grammatical conceptions I have only mentioned that there are also models which argue for immediately generating surface structures, that is, – in terms of the present terminology – for 'fixed linearity' already within the sentence frame. Since the class of the text grammars just discussed can actually be considered as an *analogous extension* of such a conception, one can also think of a text grammar which contains, as its sentence grammar, a 'fixed linearity sentence grammar'.

In this case a conception-type LiB' can be conceived which can be assigned an inverse generative conception-type Li$(B_2^{-1})'$; consequently, a conception-type Li$(B'+(B_2^{-1})')$ may be conceived, too.

Concerning only the fixed linearity text grammars, no objection can be raised against such conception-types from the point of view of the operations guaranteeing 'textuality'. Namely, these operations can be reinterpreted thus as to apply to such types as well, and not even these types can be considered as being less effective, if in their set-up allowance is made for the relevant characteristics of the competence similarly to other fixed linearity text-grammatical conceptions.

Objections can be raised, however, against the principle of the 'fixed linearity' applied within the frame of the sentence, namely, in the case of more complicated sentence-structures rules have to be applied which cannot be grammatically motivated. However, if we consider that the use of computers is indispensable for the analysis and synthesis of text-structures, and, if it can be proved that there exists a language (or that there exist languages) the machine analysis and synthesis of which can be carried out by the application of such grammars considerably simpler than by the application of other grammars, then even the dropping of this objection can be justifiable.

3.2.3. A fixed linearity text grammar – as we have seen – can generate *only* grammatically (*linearly*) continuous sequences of sentences.

In connection with the class of this type of grammars an additional difficult problem arises, namely the problem of defining a 'normal form' of sentence sequences and its reconstruction from actual sentence-sequences. This 'normal form' is indispensable for revealing the semantic relations of the sentence-sequences.[7]

Because of these problems I think fixed linearity text grammars to be uncapable to function as optimal empirically motivated text grammars; however, the experiences accumulating in the course of the investigation of this class of grammars contribute in some form or other to the development of a method for the characterization of the linear manifestation.

3.3. The above enumerated structural features (empirical shortcomings) of the fixed linearity text grammars make it practically impossible to carry out such basically important text-grammatical tasks as the formation of paraphrases which disorganize the succession of the text-sentences, and the disclosing of all possible syntactico-semantic relations (co-hyponymy, etc.) between texts.

As we have seen it, the shortcomings of these text grammars are due to the fact, that no matter, which type of sentence grammar they derive from, all of them are generalizations of the *conception* of a fixed linearity sentence grammar (i.e. a phrase-structure-grammar). This generalization allows only

[7] Though the problem of the 'normal form' also exists with respect to the revealing of the semantic relations among sentences, it only becomes a difficult problem in the case of the description of languages with free word-order. In the text grammar, however, this problem equally affects all languages. – The root of the problem is roughly as follows: how can the semantic representations of texts differing from one another only in the succession of their constituents be noted in an *identical* form. (This form permits to reveal also other types of syntactico-semantic differences.)

such an application of the operations of the sentence grammar chosen, by which the single sentences of a sentence-sequence can be generated only according to a determined succession and can be analyzed under similar restrictions, respectively. This basic structural property will not be altered in the least by the necessity that the sentence-grammatical operations must be complemented by inter-sentential operations.

Thus, it is a characteristic of the grammars of this text grammar class that the order of the sentences building up the text is already fixed in the text-basis. The difference of the single text grammars is due to the fact that the operations within the sentence-frame are carried out by means of different types of sentence grammars. (The most consistent among these text grammars is the LiB', which requires fixed linearity in the sentence-frame, too. This LiB' has at the same time the most restricted possibilities.)

In order to be able to develop more effective text grammars, it is necessary, in my opinion, to generalize the *conception* of a not fixed linearity sentence grammars (i.e. the conception of those sentence grammars which also operate with a semantic representation that is separatable – linearly independent – from the manifestation). Through this generalization those text grammar types come into being which I call the types of the *not fixed linearity text grammar*. The main characteristic of a grammar of this type is, as I have already mentioned, that it interprets the text-basis as being of a 'deeper' structure than the linear succession of the bases of the sentences constituting the text.

It is obvious that all of the sentence grammars analysed can be developed not only into fixed linearity text grammars (Li-grammars) but also into not fixed linearity text grammars (NLi-grammars).

Since in the sentence frame the complex sentence grammar type $((A+$ $+B_1^{-1})+B)$ alone proved to be suitable for describing the whole verbal competence, I only want to deal with the generalization of the conception of this type, i.e. with the not fixed linearity text grammar of type NLi $((A+B_1^{-1})+B)$. For symplicity's sake I shall omit the indication of the type further on.

II. A 'NOT FIXED LINEARITY TEXT GRAMMAR'. THE PRESENT STAGE OF ITS DEVELOPMENT[8]

0. *Introduction*

By way of introduction I want to express my conviction that it is necessary

[8] As regards the integration of the different kinds of sentence grammatical conceptions into one single text-grammatical framework cf. (1971b), (1971c), (1971d). For the text-grammatical problems of 'generativity' as well as for some basic questions concerning (text) semantics and text-typology cf. (1971f). – The most detailed presentation of this text grammar preceding the present study is (1972b).

to build up a *text theory* which is able to serve as a framework for treating *any* problems related to texts.

Within an all-embracing text theory I propose to distinguish two components which can be separated by definition. According to this distinction I speak of a *co*-textual and a *con*-textual text-theoretical component.

The domain of investigation of the former is concerned with the *internal properties* of text-structure which can be revealed by means of an explicit text grammar and an explicit theory of (non grammatical) form. The domain of the latter is concerned with all so-called *text-external relations* (relations concerning the production and reception of texts; language-historical, form-historical, socio-historical relations; criticisms, interpretations with given purposes, etc.).

In order that a text grammar:

(1) be capable of describing the verbal competence taken in its widest sense,

(2) may become an integral part of an interdisciplinary branch of science serving for the description of verbal performance taken in its widest sense, and finally

(3) be also empirically motivated, too, i.e. capable of meeting all requirements which may be raised by the different fields of application,

not only the co-textual, but also the con-textual aspects have to be taken in consideration in its set-up.

0.2. With this object in view I have attempted to show in my text-grammatical studies up to now the necessity of a special 'not fixed linearity text grammar', which first of all specifies the 'deep structure' of a text. Within this deep structure ('Text Basis'/TextB/) a component (the 'Text Semantic Representation'/TextSeR/) is separated from the information-block (/TextΩ/) determining the linear arrangement of the given text. The independence of the TextSeR from the linear arrangement means that the TextSeR contains all semantic 'basic units', out of which one particular text is (or will be) built up, without, however, determining the final succession of the sentences of the text and the syntactico-semantic construction of the single sentences.

This 'not fixed linearity text grammar' should be able

(Aa) to assign to any given text (TextLiM) all of its possible syntactico-semantic representations (TextB-s), i.e. to *analyse* texts,

(Ab) to generate all types of TextB-s, i.e. to *synthesize* texts,

(B) to establish the syntactico-semantic relation between any two given texts unambiguously, i.e. to *compare* texts.

Generation – more precisely, the generation of TextB-s – means, according to this conception, the generation of complexes of 'elementary structures' ('basic units') from which a 'not linear TextB' can be developed.

Of course, no 'perfect' carrying out of these tasks can be expected thus far. At the moment I rather think of an 'optimal approximation'.

This text grammar contains the following components:

(1) a formation rule system /FR/
(2) a transformation rule system /TrR/
(the rules of both rule systems should be applicable in both directions i.e. both in the direction of analysis and that of synthesis)
(3) a lexicon /$\mathscr{L}$/
(4) an algorithm for the analysis of texts /A_A/
(5) an algorithm for the synthesis of texts /A_S/
(6) an algorithm for the comparison of texts /A_C/
(these algorithms should be as exhaustive as possible).

0.3. Though in this paper I only intend to describe the single components of the grammar outlined above, I think it necessary to point out some relations this grammar to a con-textual text-theoretical component.

As we have already seen, one part of the con-textual aspects concerns the text-production and the text-reception, while another part of it concerns the further interpretation (from one or another aspect) of a text which has already been described grammatically.

0.3.1. Assuming, that the basic components of a communication-theoretical model and the relations between them are generally known, let us now turn to the analysis of the process of text-production and text-reception, and the relations between these processes and their grammatical aspects. (See Figure 4.)

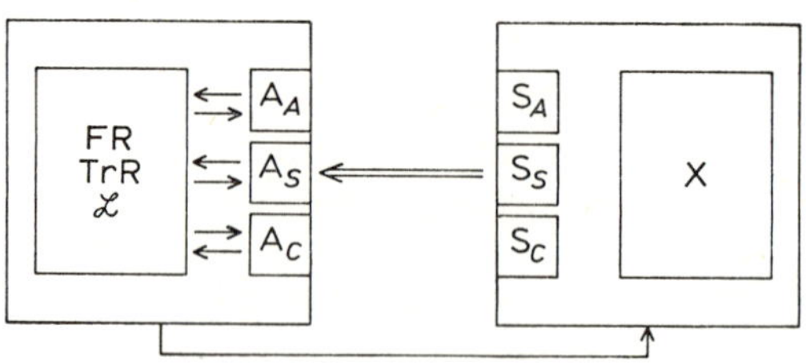

Fig. 4.

The symbols in the right-hand-side block of this figure will be interpreted as follows: 'X' refers to those (most possibly hierarchically superposed) theoretical components, which describe human (verbal and non-verbal) communication. S_A is a strategy for text-analysis, S_S is a strategy for text-synthesis and S_C is a strategy for the comparison of texts.

The difference between the 'strategies' and the 'algorithms' is that while the algorithms have to account for all theoretical possibilities, the strategies only have to direct the selection from among these possibilities according to the actual communicational situation.

These considerations are, at present, of course, only of hypothetical character since only some initial attempts have been made at setting up a 'communicational grammar' until now. The main intention was to point out that a text grammar should also be manipulatable by 'informations coming from outside', if the claim is raised that it be emprically founded with respect to communication processes, too. (As regards the problems of verbal communication cf. Bar-Hillel (ed.), 1971; Harrah, 1963; and Schmidt, 1972.)

0.3.2. As far as the aspects of the further-interpretation of a grammatically described text are concerned, it must be said that they obviously depend on the 'type' of the given text. Thus, we can speak of the con-textual interpretation of 'literary texts', 'juridical texts', 'theological texts', etc.

In connection with this the following question has to be briefly touched upon: the question of whether the single text-types (and so the single con-textual text-theoretical components) require specific grammars (i.e. grammars differing from each other) or whether the claims of all con-textual aspects can be met by one single grammar.

I am convinced, that all text types and aspects can be treated by *one and the same* text grammar, since the different con-textual aspects are determined by the difference of the goals and ways of the further-interpretation. However, this text grammar has to meet the *basic claim* of all con-textual interpretations.

This basic claim can be formulated as follows: the object of the con-textual interpretation of texts is not only (we could say not in the first line) the *verbal structure* of the text, it is rather the relation between the world manifested by the verbal structure and the actual world. Thus, a text grammar has to provide the description of this world, too. This statement, naturally, does not amount to the denial of the fact that from certain synchronic and/or diachronic points of view the verbal structure is primary. However, the theory of literature is concerned with the relation existing between the 'world manifested by the text' and the 'actual world' (which exists at the same time with the production or reception of the text). Similarly, the theory of jurisdiction is concerned with the problem of how the 'world of a juridical fact' is made up by different elements (e.g. evidences, statements, records, etc.) and with the relation existing between this world and the 'world manifesting itself in juridical norms or an admissible interpretation of them'. Theology is concerned, among other things, with the problem of how certain types of sacral texts 'constitute' the 'world which has been fixed in the dogmas' and which relation this world has to the 'actual world' of the simultaneously existing epoch and of the different single epochs, respectively.

Thus the con-textual interpretations are always concerned with the comparison of two worlds: the world manifesting itself in the text under investigation and the world manifested in doctrines, juridical norms, ideologies, sciences, etc. The result of this comparison can be tested in an intersubjective way, provided that the structure of both worlds compared are given in an explicit form. This, however, can only be guaranteed by using *one* text grammar, since the form of manifestation of all 'world-representations' is (or must be) a text.

I want to emphasize that, in my opinion, the only task to be fulfilled by a text theory is to carry out the operation of comparison (i.e. the text comparison). The checking of whether the world descriptions provided by the special branches of science for carrying out the comparison correspond to the 'reality' or not, is no task of a text theory.[9]

1. *The Formation Rule System*[10]

1.1. The *general characteristics* of the formation rule system of this text grammar are:

(1) the rule system generates complexes of elementary structures; the elementary structures will be called *predicates* (the term 'predicate' is used to mean a "'functor' + 'its arguments'");

(2) the rule system is based on a lexicon in which

(a) the lexical units and their semantic representations are given in the form of '*predicate-functions*' (therefore it is more appropriate to speak of 'lexical representations' instead of 'lexical units');

[9] Some aspects of the application (more precisely the possibilities of the application) of this text grammar are discussed in (1972d), (1972e), (1972g).

[10] The formation rule-system was formulated first in (1971f). This rule-system has been taken over with a minimal alteration in (1972b) (and consequently also in (1971g)). – The representation of the arguments (see R9) has undergone the greatest changes. [This question is discussed in details in (1972h).] The main cause of these changes is that the 'homogeneity' of this grammar (i.e. the basic identity of the semantic representation of a lexicon item, a 'sentence' and a text) became only gradually clear. [For this question cf. (1972c), (1972f).] The present form of the rule-system is more detailed than it was in the earlier studies, because several rules represented in a contracted form until now were separated in this version.

(b) all predicate-functions are assigned '*selectional characteristics*' relating them to all other predicate-functions (or predicate-function classes, i.e. sets of predicate-functions which have the same characteristics), with respect to all possibilities of a 'structural expansion';

(c) the predicate-functions are also classed according to the different combinations of the selectional characteristics;

(3) the rule system allows for a '*bi-directionality*' of double character:

(a) on the one hand, its 'lexicon rule' inserts either *lexical representations* (here the grammar functions as 'interpretive grammar' or the grammar of the 'decompositional' part, i.e. as the grammar for analysis) or *semantic representations* (here the grammar functions as the grammar of the 'compositional' part, i.e. as the grammar for synthesis);

(b) on the other hand, the rules are *not ordered*; this guarantees that the generation of a complex can begin with choosing any of its elementary structures. (This fact is of basic importance, since in the generation of the complexes building the elements of a text-basis the generation of each new complex can be manipulated by the structures of the complexes generated already and/or other informations, according to different points of view; thus, a maximal flexibility of the grammar has to be guaranteed.)

1.2. A formation rule system having the traits enumerated above is represented by the rule system given in **(1)**

(1)

R1 $\quad \mathrm{KB} :=: \mathrm{K}\Omega \,\S\, \Sigma^{\square} \; [\equiv \mathrm{KSeR}]$

R2 $\quad \Sigma^{\square} :=: \left| \begin{array}{l} \Sigma \\ [\varphi^{\mathrm{C}}]\,\{\Sigma^{\square}, \Sigma^{\square}, \ldots \Sigma^{\square}\} \end{array} \right|$

R3 $\quad \Sigma \;:=: [\varphi^{\mathrm{P}}]\,\{\mathrm{a}\!: \mathrm{Pers.1} \quad \mathrm{e}\!: \mathrm{Pers.2} \quad \mathrm{o}\!: \Pi^{\square}\}$

R4 $\quad \Pi^{\square} :=: \left| \begin{array}{l} \Pi \\ [\varphi^{\mathrm{C}}]\,\{\Pi^{\square}, \Pi^{\square}, \ldots \Pi^{\square}\} \end{array} \right|$

R5 $\quad \Pi \;:=: [\varphi^{\mathrm{T}}]\,\{\kappa\}$

R6 $\quad \kappa \;:=: [(^{*}\varphi^{\mathrm{t}}) \wedge (^{*}\varphi^{\mathrm{l}})] \left\{ \left| \begin{array}{l} [(([([\varphi'']) \; \varphi']) \; \varphi] \\ [(([([\varphi'']) \; \varphi']) \; \varphi]) \; \delta_{//\varphi^{0}{}_{\mathrm{C}} = \Delta \ni \ulcorner\delta\urcorner}] \end{array} \right| \{A\} \right\}$

R7 $\quad A \;:=: \alpha_{\mu_1} \!:\! \xi_1 \ldots \alpha_{\mu_n} \!:\! \xi_n$

R8 $\quad \varphi^{''/'} :=: \left| \begin{array}{l} \mathrm{F}^{''/'}_{\sigma_k} \\ \alpha_{\mu_i} \!:\! \xi_i \end{array} \right|$

R9(a) $\quad \xi_i \;:=: \left| \begin{array}{l} \delta//\varphi^{0}{}_{\mathrm{C}} = \Delta \ni \ulcorner\delta\urcorner \\ \Pi^{\wedge}_{\mathrm{LeR/SeR}} \\ \Sigma^{\wedge}_{\mathrm{LeR/SeR}} \end{array} \right|$

(ba) $\delta//\varphi^{0}{}_{C} = \Delta \ni \ulcorner \delta \urcorner :=:$

$$\left\langle \begin{array}{l} \left| \begin{array}{l} \rho^{v} \equiv \varphi^{v}//\varphi^{0}{}_{C} = \Delta \ni \ulcorner \varphi^{v} \urcorner \\ \rho \equiv [U//\varphi^{\omega} \in Q] \; \{\varphi^{\omega}(.\varphi^{\omega\omega}) \left\{ \left| \begin{array}{l} xN//\varphi^{0}{}_{C} = \Delta \ni \ulcorner xN \urcorner \\ zN//\varphi^{0}{}_{C} = \Delta \ni \ulcorner zN \urcorner \\ yN//\varphi^{0}{}_{C} = \Delta \ni \ulcorner yN \urcorner \end{array} \right| \right\} \} \end{array} \right| \\ \left(\llcorner\Sigma//\sqsupset\rho^{v}/\rho/ \left| \begin{array}{c} N \\ C/A \end{array} \right| \; \left| \begin{array}{c} xN \\ zN \\ yN \end{array} \right| \right) \end{array} \right\rangle$$

(bb) $\Pi^{\wedge}_{LeR/SeR} :=: {}^{\llcorner}\Pi_{LeR/SeR}$

(bc) $\Sigma^{\wedge}_{LeR/SeR} :=: {}^{\llcorner}\Sigma_{LeR/SeR}$

R10 $\varphi^{\triangle} :=: F^{\triangle}_{\sigma_k}$ where ${}^{\triangle} = o\;|\omega|\;\omega\omega\;|c|\;\bar{s} \quad \varphi\bar{s} \equiv \varphi$

R11 $\alpha_{\mu_i} :=: a_k$

R12 $U :=: R/H/M/V$

R13(a) $\rho^{v} :=: RN$

(b) $\rho :=: UN$

R14(a) $xN//F^{0}_{\sigma_k} = \Delta \ni \ulcorner xN \urcorner :=: \left| \begin{array}{c} LeR_i \\ ESeR_i \end{array} \right| \in \mathbf{p}^{0}_{\sigma_k}$ where $LeR_i =_D ESeR_i$

(b) $zN//F^{0}_{\sigma_k} = \Delta \ni \ulcorner zN \urcorner :=: \left| \begin{array}{c} LeR_i \\ SeR_i \end{array} \right| \in \mathbf{p}^{0}_{\sigma_k}$ where $LeR_i =_D SeR_i$

(c) $yN//F^{0}_{\sigma_k} = \Delta \ni \ulcorner yN \urcorner :=: \left| \begin{array}{c} \Sigma^{\wedge}_{LeR} \\ \Sigma^{\wedge}_{LeR} \end{array} \right| {}_{Des} = \Delta \ni \ulcorner yN \urcorner$ where $\Sigma^{\wedge}_{LeR} =_D \Sigma^{\wedge}_{SeR}$

R15(a) $F^{\diamond}_{\sigma_k} :=: \left| \begin{array}{c} f^{\diamond}_{LeR_i} \\ f^{\diamond}_{ESeR_i} \end{array} \right| \in \mathbf{p}^{\diamond}_{\sigma_k}$ where $\diamond \equiv "/'/o/\omega/\omega\omega/c/\bar{s}$

$LeR_i =_D ESeR_i$

(b) $F^{\diamond}_{\sigma_k} :=: \left| \begin{array}{c} f^{\diamond}_{LeR_i} \\ SeR_i \end{array} \right| \in \mathbf{p}^{\diamond}_{\sigma_k}$ $\quad LeR_i =_D SeR_i$

(c) $F^{v}_{\sigma_k} :=: Name_i \in \mathbf{f}^{v}_{\sigma_k}$

(d) $\varphi^{T} :=: f^{T}_{i}$

(e) $\varphi^{P} :=: f^{P}_{i}$

R16(a) ${}^{\llcorner}\Pi_{LeR/SeR} :: \{\Pi^{\square} \wedge \ldots \wedge \Pi^{\square}\}$

(b) ${}^{\llcorner}\Sigma_{LeR/SeR} :: \{\Sigma^{\square} \wedge \ldots \wedge \Sigma^{\square}\}$

The symbols used in my convention of writing rules are interpreted as follows:

KB the basis (B) of a first order composition uni (K) (K: 'text-sentence');

KΩ the set of the K-internal and K-external informations governing the transformations which determine the linear manifestations;

$\Sigma^{\square}$ a S-constituent-complex variable
(a complete S-constituent – i.e. a S-constituent-complex, to which R2 will not be applied again, or a simple S-constituent – will be called the semantic- or lexical-representation of K (KSeR or KLeR));

Σ a (simple) S-constituent variable;
$\Pi^{\square}$ a proposition-complex variable;
Π a (simple) proposition variable;
κ a kernel (a predicate-complex) variable;
δ a variable standing for a description functioning as an argument-description or a 'grammatical predicate';

The functor-variable types are the following (the particular types perform different grammatical functions; thus, the distinction of the different types amounts to the explicit indication of their grammatical function):

φ^{T} a functor determining 'tempus'; there are three 'general tempora': one which is indicating 'simultaneousness' (SIM), one which is indicating 'past' (PAST) and one which is indicating 'future' (FUT), as compared to the time of the act of 'performance' (which is always 'present'); the actual tense-relations will be determined by transformation-rules;
φ^{C} a functor representing a 'connection' (which can also be manifested in the form of a not-sentence-closing punctuation mark);
φ^{P} a functor determining the 'assertive' (ASS), 'interrogative' (QUE), 'imperative' (IMP), 'exclamative' (EXC) ... character of a proposition; these 'topmost performative predicates' are manifested in speech by intonation, while in writing by sentence-closing punctuation marks – or even by special morphemes;
φ^{t} a temporal adverbial complement;
φ^{l} a local adverbial complement;
φ' an adverbial complement of manner;
φ'' an adverbial complement of degree;
φ a verb, adjective or 'relation-of'-noun functioning as a 'grammatical predicate';
φ^{0} a noun functioning as an argument-description or a 'grammatical predicate';
φ^{ω} a quantifier (including the cardinal numbers and the fractions; – as for the quantifiers see the remark concerning R9;
$\varphi^{\omega\omega}$ a 'complement' of a quantifier (e.g.: the names of the different measures and weights, and such 'quantifying words' as for example '*piece*', '*head*', '*bunch*', etc.);

The corresponding predicate-variables are:
$\pi^{T}, \pi^{C}, \pi^{P}, \pi^{t}, \pi^{l}, \pi', \pi'', \pi, \pi^{0}, \pi^{\omega}, \pi^{\omega\omega}$

The constants belonging to the variables enumerated up to now are indicated by the respective latin letters to which a number-index is attached as a right-hand-side subscript:
$f_i^{T}, f_i^{C}, f_i^{P}, f_i^{t}, f_i^{l}, f_i', f_i'', f_i, f_i^{0}, f_i^{\omega}, f_i^{\omega\omega}$,
$p_i^{T}, p_i^{C}, p_i^{P}, p_i^{t}, p_i^{l}, p_i', p_i'', p_i, p_i^{0}, p_i^{\omega}, p_i^{\omega\omega}$,

A the n-tuple of the arguments belonging to a functor φ or a δ functioning as a 'grammatical predicate' at one and the same time;

ξ_i a metavariable standing for an argument;

α_{μ_i} an argument-label variable;

a_k a concrete argument label;

The system of the argument-types still has to be elaborated; for the present a slightly modified version of the Fillmorian system is applied. It contains the following labels:

a: *a*gent,
e: *e*xperiencer (in my earlier works e2),
h: '*h*abens' (in my earlier works e1),
i: *i*nstrumental,
o: *o*bject,
s: *s*ource,
g: *g*oal,
r: '*r*ole-indicator',
c: '*c*ounter-part',
l: place (*l*ocus),
t: *t*ime,

and different kinds of double-labels:

ca: *c*ounter *a*gent, lg: place-*g*oal,
... ts: *t*ime-*s*ource,
ls: place-*s*ource, tg: *t*ime-*g*oal;

φ^v a variable standing for a 'proper name';

Δ a variable standing for a set of 'objects';

$\Pi^\wedge$ a variable standing for an unordered set of propositions and/or proposition-complexes;

$\Sigma^\wedge$ a variable standing for an unordered set of S-constituents and/or S-constituent-complexes;

(A latin-letter-symbol printed in heavy-faced types indicates a class of the respective elements.)

ρ a variable standing for a 'reference-index' indicating an argument-description;

ρ^v a variable standing for a 'reference-index' indicating a 'proper name';

UN an actual reference-index;

RN a constant standing for an actual 'proper name';

U a variable standing for a reference-index specificator (an 'identificator'); the 'values' of U are:

R (*r*eferencializable) M (*m*ediately referencializable)
H (*h*alf referencializable) V (*v*ariable);

xN a variable standing for the definiendum or the definiens of a definition in the lexicon, where the definiens is an elementary semantic representation (ESeR);

z*N* a variable standing for the definiendum or the definiens of a definition in the lexicon, where the definiens is not an elementary semantic representation (SeR);

y*N* a variable standing for the definiendum or the definiens of a definition which is not contained in the lexicon (i.e. the definiens cannot be expressed by one single word in the given language);

⌜X⌝ a symbol standing for the 'denotatum of X', where X is a metavariable (it occurs as ⌜x*N*⌝, ⌜z*N*⌝, ⌜y*N*⌝, ⌜δ⌝, ⌜φ^{v}⌝);

F_{σ_k} a symbol indicating a set of functors; it refers to a class the element of which have the properties referred to by F_{σ_k}; the symbol indicating this class has the same super- and subscripts as F;

X $_{D}$= Y, X $_{C}$= Y, X $_{Des}$= Y means: 'X defines Y', 'X characterizes Y' and 'X describes Y', respectively;

: = : the sign for 'bidirectional rewritability';

§ the sign linking two 'elements' having different functions in a mutually interdependent way (in R1: if KΩ is determined first, the structure of the KSeR/KLeR must be developed so as to make the application of the transformations included in KΩ possible; if the KSeR/KLeR is developed first, it is the structure of the KSeR/KLeR which determines the transformational possibilities);

: the sign linking two elements having different functions in a non-mutually determining way;

. the sign linking together a quantifier and its 'complement';

: : the sign for embedding;

≡ the sign indicating identical substitution;

( ) the sign for 'optionality': the element contained in it can either be chosen or disregarded in the generation;

| | the sign for 'quasi optionality': one of the elements contained in it must be chosen in the generation;

/ means: exclusive 'or' (*a*/*b*/*c* is read: either *a* or *b* or *c*);

// means: 'under the condition that' (//*A* is read: under the condition that *A*);

⊐ means: 'being a constituent of a structure' (*B*⊐*A* is read: *A* is a constituent of *B*);

∈ or ∋ means: 'being an element of a set/list/class';

[ ] { } the sign for a "'functor'+'argument(s)'"-relation which yields a 'grammatical predicate';

[[]] the sign for a "'functor'+'argument(s)'"-relation which yields a 'complex functor';

The relation of the functors and their admissible argument '*n*-tuples' (or, the other way round: the relation of the argument '*n*-tuples' and their admissible functors) has to be determined by the lexicon. Thus, the relation "'functor'+'argument(s)'" means in any case a mutual interdependence.

$^{\llcorner}\Sigma$ a dummy-symbol standing for S-constituents;

$^{\llcorner}\Pi$ a dummy-symbol standing for propositions;

$\langle\ \rangle$ the sign for an ordered set;

$\{\ \}$ the sign for an unordered set;

$\wedge$ the sign linking elements which are K-externally dependent from each other

$\{\Sigma^{\square} \wedge \ldots \wedge \Sigma^{\square}\}$ and $\{\Pi^{\square} \wedge \ldots \wedge \Pi^{\square}\}$, which make it possible to generate any number of $\Sigma^{\square}$-s or $\Pi^{\square}$-s of any complexity, reflect the recursivity of the rule-system by means of which also 'texts within texts' can be developed in a *recursive* way. Namely $\{\Sigma^{\square} \wedge \ldots \wedge \Sigma^{\square}\}$ form a 'TextB within a TextB'.

1.3. As a general remark to the formation rule-system I want to note that it provides only an attempt at setting up a bidirectional rule-system; some details of it will necessarily have to be modified in the course of further research. My aim concerning the construction of an all-embracing text grammar is to develop a theoretical framework, which enables to investigate the details so that the general theoretical framework can be maintained without

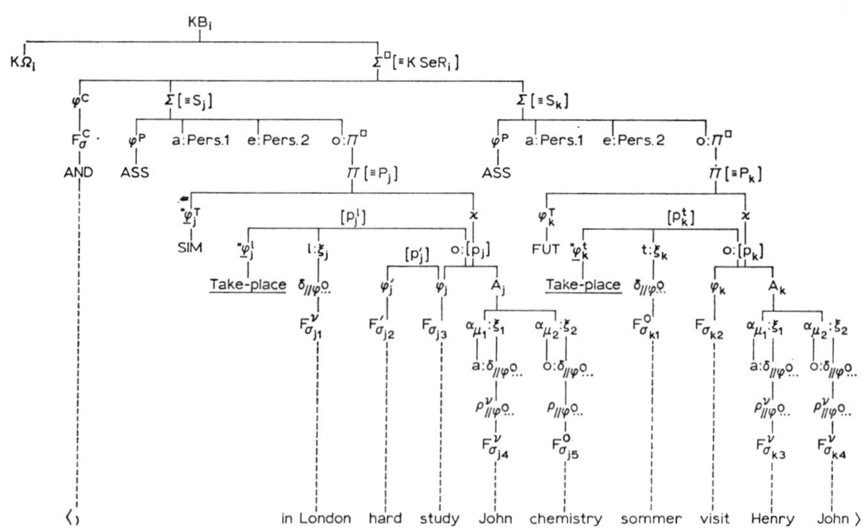

Fig. 5.

greater change. The integrability of the results of the widely ramified researches may be guaranteed only in this way.

Now I shall turn to some of the rules of the rule-system.

In order to make the interpretation of rules R1–R7 easier, let us see a (more or less simple) diagram which can be constructed by applying these rules. (See Figure 5.)

R1. Rule 1 can be regarded as the definition of a KB. According to it a KB is composed of a semantic representation-part (a KSeR, i.e. a complete S-constituent-complex) and an information-block (KΩ). Here, the basic question concerns the relation of these two parts to one another. This relation leads to some problems which are also connected with the question of bi-directionality already touched upon.

Chomsky was forced to change the 'standard theory' because it has become obvious that also the 'surface structure' plays a role in the 'semantic interpretation'.

By the definition of the KB suggested here this problem seems to be eliminated, namely, according to this definition the KB does not consist only of a semantic representation which is 'neutral' from the point of view of the surface structure, but it also consists of an information-block which fully and entirely determines the linear manifestation. However, this determination does not claim to be clear-cut in the sense as it is required by 'generative semantics'. The component called SeR here is a so-called 'standard (or canonical) form' which should enable us to derive all linear manifestations that can be built from this standard form. The specific linear manifestation will be determined by the information-block assigned to the semantic representation.

Further research must decide, how all posssible information-blocks (i.e. the informations which determine all possible linear manifestations that are derivable from the given representation) can be assigned to a given 'standard form' (semantic representation) and which of these informations should be regarded as K-internal and which of them as K-external (but co-text-sensitive) ones.

In the generation of a KB, the 'content' of the KΩ can be determined only if we have the above mentioned informations at our disposal.

R2, R4: In these rules the so-called 'connective functors' play the basic role.

Until now linguistico-logic investigations based on the propositional calculus are mostly concerned with the structure of the so-called 'assertive sentences' in order to guarantee the application of the logical apparatus, and only those logical (modal logical) operators are considered, the theory of which can be regarded as more or less elaborated.

The linguistic description of the connective functors (the investigation of the pre-conditions of their 'possible arguments') should be concerned with the description of all 'connections'. The investigation of the linguistic/logic functioning of the elements which do not belong to the propositional calculus has not yet been attempted.

R3: The term 'assertive sentence' used above is identical with the logical term 'proposition'.

The notion of 'proposition' defined in the grammar outlined here is not identical with the notion of 'proposition' as used in logic. This 'proposition' will be a 'proposition in the logical sense' only if its functor determining 'tempus' meets certain requirements (for example if it is 'present') and if it will be – to use my terminology – an 'o'-argument of a performative predicate function, which expresses 'assertion'. This means that the same proposition (a proposition taken in my sense) can build not only the 'kernel' of any assertion but also that of questions, commands and even exclamations.

R6: This rule allows to generate a complex composed of predicate-functions of different degrees and/or different states. Such a complex will be called here an S-constituent-kernel (abbreviated simply as 'kernel'.)

The line containing 'δ' is the representation of the so-called 'nominal predication'.

$^*\varphi^{l}$ and $^*\varphi^{t}$ are 'special functors', they can be interpreted in two ways. Concerning $^*\varphi^{l}$ thi simplies that it can be either interpreted as "*Lokal* l:δ h:p" (read: the place of the realization of the 'action/event-relation' expressed by the predicate p is $\ulcorner\delta\urcorner$), or as "*Take-place* o:p l:δ" (read: the realization of the 'action/event-relation' expressed by the predicate p takes place in $\ulcorner\delta\urcorner$). By way of analogy $^*\varphi^{t}$ canal so be interpreted in two ways. – In my studies up to now I applied a representation matching the first interpretation (applying 'el' instead of 'h', as mentioned above).

R5: φ^{T} can be interpreted analogously to $^*\varphi^{l}$ and $^*\varphi^{t}$.

R8: This rule serves to specify the functors which are not first grade in R6 further. As a matter of fact, the first line on the right hand side of the rule has a 'subcategorization-rule'-character, similarly to *R10*. Both of them assign the label of a functor-class to a functor-variable. The second line guarantees the possibility of generating 'complex adverbial constructions' such that it provides the basis for the applicability of R9.

The rules R9 and R12–14 need special analysis. (These rules have undergone the most changes until now.)

R9: Rule R9a serves first of all for the specification of the argument-metavariable ξ_i.

An argument can be selected from three main types. It can be

(a) a 'namable object' (in the terminology of Bellert), this is indicated by δ,

(b) a proposition, a proposition-complex or an unordered set of proposition, this is indicated by $\Pi^\wedge$,

(c) a S-constituent, a S-constituent-complex or an unordered set of S-constituents, this is indicated by $\Sigma^\wedge$.

The variables $\Pi^\wedge$ and $\Sigma^\wedge$ can be specified further by the rules R9bb, R9bc, R16b, R2, R4... As examples for type (b) the arguments of the 'verba sentiendi' can serve, for type (c) the arguments of the 'verba dicendi'.

Type (a) itself can be subclassified (see R9ba): a 'namable object' can be denoted by a 'proper name' (ρ^{v}) or by a 'description' ρ (in the narrower sense of the word) and both of them can optionally be attached a S-constituent, a S-constituent complex or an S-constituent-set.

The structure of the 'description' (in the narrower sense of the word) has, globally seen, a three-fold arrangement:

'Identifier' + *'Quantifier'* + *'Variable'*.

The problems of the 'definition' of the *variables* are deeply connected with the problems of the lexicon. R14 represents, how the different kinds of variables can be assigned a 'defining expression' consisting of a LeR or a SeR out of the lexicon (see R14a, R14b) or how such an expression can be generated (see R14c, R9bc, R16b, R2...).

The constituents of the *quantifier* φ^ω indicate the following quantifiers:

(2) (a) N: NONE (of)

(b) *Q*: 'quantity' with the following specifications:

- Qr: r, where 'r' is a real number,
- Q<r: LESS-THAN-r,
- Q>r: MORE-THAN-r,
- Qu: NOT-SPECIFIED-QUANTITY,
- Qg: SOME,
- Qc: FEW,
- Qm: MORE,
- Qj: MUCH/MANY,
- Qa: ALL (=RESTRICTED ALL),
- Q_in: EVERY-n, where 'n' is a rational number,

(c) G: IN-GENERAL,

A: ALL (=NOT-RESTRICTED-ALL),

A_in: EVERY-n, where 'n' is a rational number.

The difference between the 'RESTRICTED-ALL/EVERY (Qa/Q_in)' and the 'NOT-RESTRICTED-ALL/EVERY (A/A_in)' can also be formulated in this way: while A/A_in is always valid for the whole of the 'world' in question, Qa/Q_in is only valid for a defined part of this 'world'.

The *identifiers* (*U*) can be defined as follows:

R: the 'namable object' can be referentialized for both the speaker and the listener,
H: the 'namable object' can be referentialized for only one of them,
M: the 'namable object' can be referentialized only mediately for both of them,
V: the 'namable object' can be referentialized for none of them.
(It is always the performative predicate which serves as a frame for determining the referencializability; in the case of a given text the referencializability can be decided on the basis of the determiners applied and the co-text, while in the process of generation, it can be decided freely, and in this case the decision determines the selection of the determiners and the generation of the co-text.)

An 'identifier' can only be applied, if the quantifier is of type Q. It would be nonsense to speak of the identification of an expression quantified by a quantifier of type (a) or (c).

The identification-types enumerated above can be illustrated for example by the following utterances:

(1) *I saw the great film,*
(2) *I saw a great film,*
(3) *I heard, that he saw a great film,*
(4) *I would like to see a great film once.*

In consequence of *R9(*b*a)* the variable-part of the argument-description can be indicated by a symbol complemented by an adjacent number. Let us indicate the definition 'great film' by, say, *y21*. The expression '1 great film' can, then, be indicated by Q1*y21*.

The type of identification can be expressed

in (1) by RQ1*y21*,
in (2) by HQ1*y21*,
in (3) by MQ1*y21*
and in (4) by VQ1*y21*.

However, following *R13* only the symbols 'R', 'H', 'M' and 'V' complemented by an adjacent number will stand in an argument-place, e.g. 'H27' instead of 'HQ1*y21*', where the numbers from 1 to *n* (independent of the type of identifier) enumerate those 'objects', which are referred to in the given text.

I call these identifiers complemented by an adjacent number 'reference-indices'. (Taken in a wider sense, the expressions having a quantifier 'N'/ 'G'/'A'/'A_in' can also be ranked among the reference-indices.)

The reference-indices can be further-specified by means of different kinds of symbols, in order that these indices express as many informations as possible. One possible way of further-specifying a reference-index is the following:

$$^{m}UN_{d}^{w}$$

where in the place of 'd' the symbol of the variable-type can be inserted, in the place of 'w' a symbol expressing the 'world-reference' (fictitious, real, belonging to a world W_i, etc.) and in the place of 'm' a symbol indicating that a 'person' is referred to.

(In connection with the identifiers and their specifications lots of further questions have to be settled.)

The rules of the rule-system can be classified as follows:

R1–R7, the second line of R8, R9 and R11 are 'generative rules',
the first line of R8 and R10 are 'subcategorization rules',
R11 and R13–R15 are 'insertion rules',
R16 is a 'special composition rule'.

2. *The Transformation Rule System*[11]

2.0. Before characterizing the transformation rule system I think it necessary to outline the structure of the Text B.

Figure 5 illustrates the set-up of a KB. As a matter of fact a KB can also be represented as a *set* consisting of a KΩ-block and different kinds of predicates. (See Figure 6 which is a transcribed form of Figure 5.)

$$\begin{array}{lll} KB_i \equiv \, < K\Omega_i & & \\ & KSeR_i \equiv \, < & p_j^P,\ p_k^P \\ & & p_j^T,\ p_k^T \\ & & p_j,\ p_k \\ & & p_j^I \\ & & p_k^t \\ & & p_j' \\ & & p_i^C \qquad >> \end{array}$$

Fig. 6.

[11] As far as the transformation rule-system is concerned, only the general framework has been developed up to now. The original plan was that J. Ihwe would undertake the elaboration of this rule-system in the frame of the Project 'Textlinguistics' at the University of Constance [cf. (1971g), (1972b)]; however, because of his changed affiliation this plan is unlikely to be realized.

(The predicates p^l, p^t, p', p^C are 'optional' i.e. they do not occur as basic units in all KB-s.)

From this set the diagram can be reestablished unambiguously, this is due to the fact that the indices of the predicates unambiguously indicate the dependency-relations.

It is also obvious, that this KB-structure is a 'contingent' structure, that is the 'content' expressed by the KB could also be expressed by a KB having a different structure or even by two or more KB-s. We obtain a KB having a different structure, for example, if we turn the information of the KΩ-block concerning the order of the constituents S_j and S_k in the linear manifestation into the opposite. We obtain two KB-s, for example, if we delete p_i^C, and if the elements with the index 'j' and 'k', respectively, will be put into different KB-sets. From the elements with the index 'j' two separate KB-s could be built up by separating the (optional) predicate p_j^l from the set of the remaining predicates with the index 'j' and constructing a distinct KB from it. In such a case the building of KB-s is carried out by the application of the principle that the optional predicate belonging to the expansion of the kernel predicate will be assigned the hierarchy-higher predicates of the kernel predicate as proposition- and S-constituent-building predicates. If we build several KB-s from one KB, this implies, of course, that the original KΩ-block will be divided into several KΩ-blocks, too.

These alternatives can be illustrated by restructuring the KB_i in Figure 5. (For simplicity's sake I only enumerate the different linear manifestations.)

(1) *Henry will visit John in summer, John studies chemistry hard in London.*

(2) *John studies chemistry hard in London. Henry will visit JOHN in summer.*

(3) *John studies chemistry hard. JOHN STUDIES CHEMISTRY HARD in London. Henry will visit JOHN in summer.*

(The capitals indicate 'pronominalizability', more precisely 'pro-form-building'.)

The set-representation of the KB-structure (and the fact that a considerable part of the KB-structures is 'contingent') allows (and suggests, respectively) the extension of this way of representation to the text-basis, too. Per analogiam a TextB can be represented in the following way: (see Figure 7)

$$
\begin{array}{l}
\mathrm{TextB_i} \equiv \langle \mathrm{Text}\Omega_\mathrm{i} \\
\qquad \mathrm{TextSeR_i} \equiv \langle\!\langle \mathrm{p}_1^\mathrm{P}, \ldots, \mathrm{p}_\mathrm{j}^\mathrm{P}, \ldots, \mathrm{p}_\mathrm{n}^\mathrm{P} \rangle \\
\qquad\qquad \langle \mathrm{p}_1^\mathrm{T}, \ldots, \mathrm{p}_\mathrm{j}^\mathrm{T}, \ldots, \mathrm{p}_n^\mathrm{T} \rangle \\
\qquad\qquad \langle \mathrm{p}_1, \ldots, \mathrm{p}_\mathrm{j}, \ldots, \mathrm{p}_\mathrm{n} \rangle \\
\qquad\qquad \langle \mathrm{p}_\mathrm{k1}', \ldots, \mathrm{p}_\mathrm{kn}' \rangle \\
\qquad\qquad \langle \mathrm{p}_\mathrm{k1}'', \ldots, \mathrm{p}_\mathrm{kn}'' \rangle \\
\qquad\qquad \langle \mathrm{p}_\mathrm{k1}^\mathrm{l}, \ldots, \mathrm{p}_\mathrm{kn}^\mathrm{l} \rangle \\
\qquad\qquad \langle \mathrm{p}_\mathrm{k1}^\mathrm{t}, \ldots, \mathrm{p}_\mathrm{kn}^\mathrm{t} \rangle \\
\qquad\qquad \langle \mathrm{p}_\mathrm{k1}^\mathrm{C}, \ldots, \mathrm{p}_\mathrm{kn}^\mathrm{C} \rangle \qquad \rangle\!\rangle \rangle
\end{array}
$$

Fig. 7.

(The values of the indices 'k1',..., 'kn' are different in the different predicate-classes.)

It is, however, necessary to introduce some supplementary arrangements into the representation of a TextB. This supplementation aims, first of all, at making explicit the structure of the 'world' manifesting itself in the text and it only concerns the set of the kernel predicates.

The structure of the 'world' manifesting itself in a text can be made explicit by the representation of the set of the reference-indices and the representation of the relation among them. If a kernel predicate contains several arguments, the set of the reference-indices functioning as arguments and the relation among them are represented by the predicate itself. However, it is necessary to find some means for representing them with respect to the whole of the text, too. Such means can be

(a) a reference-index list,
(b) the so-called thematic nets,
(c) the so-called reference-relational diagram

and

(d) the so-called communicative nets.

The *list of the reference-indices* enumerates on the one hand the reference-indices together with those 'identifier + quantifier + variable' structures which are represented in an abbreviated form by them, on the other hand the 'definitions' belonging to the different variable-types.

The simplest way of developing *thematic nets* is to construct a net with respect to each reference-index in which we gather all the predicates containing the given reference-index as one of their arguments. – The natural consequence of this procedure will be that certain predicates will have to be arranged into more than one net. Though the repeated occurrence of the single predicates can be avoided by applying certain redundancy-principles (this was the solution I have chosen in my studies thus far), the question of which solution is more useful cannot be considered as already settled.

The single thematic nets can be considered as being analoga of the single reference-indices. As an analogon of a predicate relating reference-indices to one another the so-called *reference-relational diagram* can be constructed, which has the form of a matrix. The reference-indices (taken the term 'reference-index' in the wider sense) build the columns of this matrix, while the single thematic nets and the sets built up from the predicates belonging to the expansion of the kernel predicates represent the lines of it. The elements of the matrix are '+'-signs indicating which reference indices belong to which nets. This matrix shows which reference-indices are mediately or immediately related by the predicates of the thematic nets and which are not.

${}_0p$	*Communicate*	a:A e:X o:T_i,
${}_0p^t$	*Temporal*	o:${}_0p$ t:TEM,
${}_0p^l$	*Local*	o:${}_0p$ l:LOC,
${}_1p$	*Entitle*	a:A o:T_i r:'TIT',

A ≡ the author of T_i,
X ≡ variable standing for a receiver of T_i,
T_i ≡ a text defined by the $TextB_i$,
LOC ≡ the place of the production of T_i,
TEM ≡ the time of the production of T_i,
TIT ≡ the title of T_i,

$TextB_i \equiv \langle Text\Omega_i$
$TextSeR_i$ ⟪the set of the $p^C_{k_i}$-s⟩
⟨the set of the p^P_j-s⟩
⟨the set of the p^T_j-s⟩
⟨the set of the p^t_j-s⟩
⟨the set of the p^l_j-s⟩
⟨the set of the p″-s⟩
⟨the set of the p′-s⟩
⟨the set of the communicative nets (CN_k)
the reference-relation diagram
⟨the set of the thematic nets (TN_j)⟩
the list of the reference-indices
the list of the argument-variables and the defining expressions belonging to them ⟫⟩

Fig. 8.

The *communicative nets* represent another type of supplementary structure These can be developed such that each so-called communicative predicate ('A *Communicates* to B that ...', 'A *Communicates* to C that ...', 'B *Communicates* to A that ...', etc.) will be assigned a net which gathers the kernel predicates of the communicated sentences and sequences of sentences belonging to the given communicative predicate. The presence of explicit communicative predicates is not necessary. However, each text (TextB) must be assigned a 'topmost communicative predicate' which can be expanded in the same way as the kernel predicates. The predicates belonging to the expansion express the place, time etc. of the production of the work. (Even if the topmost communicative predicate can be considered as the super-structure of the 'performave predicates' of the single sentences of the text, it is advisable to treat it separately.)

The entire representation of the TextB of a 'descriptive' text which has a title can be given as in Figure 8.

2.1. Examining in this connexion the structure of the TextΩ-block and that of the KΩ-blocks, I can say the following about them:
A TextΩ-block belonging to a TextB must contain:

(1) the information concerning the order of the KB-s constituting the text and

(2) information determining which predicates belong to the particular KB-s.

A KΩ-block belonging to a KB must contain the following informations:

(1) determination of the order of the S-constituents (if the KSeR contains a connective predicate, too),

(2) specification of the internal structure of the single S-constituents, that is

(a) the determination of the succession of the 'sentence-parts' ('subject', 'object', 'predicate', 'adverbial-complements', etc.),

(b) the determination of which kind of basic units constitute these 'sentence-parts' and how they should be developed (without 'pro-form'-building and deletion),

(c) the specification of the insertions.

In short: a KΩ must contain all informations necessary for the unambiguous determination of the LiM to be developed out of the given KB, except those concerning the 'pro-form'-building and the deletion.

A *basis* (both a KB and a TextB) contains, as I have already emphasized several times, all informations which are necessary to develop a LiM assignable to the given SeR, i.e. *the* SeR and *one single* Ω-block. This means with respect to the Ω-blocks of a TextB to provide *one* succession of the

KB-s constituting the text and *one* Ω-block for each KB. Let us call this case a '*one-one* possibility'.

However, in connection with the TextLiM-s which are assignable to a TextSeR we can speak of a '*many-many* possibility'.

The determination of the '*many-many* possibility' (more precisely the '*every-every* possibility'), i.e. the assigning of all possible Ω-s to a *given* TextSeR is the task of the synthesis-algorithm. (All algorithms have their specific formational-, transformational- and lexicon instructions. The statement above can thus be formulated more precisely as follows: the determination of the TextΩ-s is the task of the transformational instructions of the synthesis-algorithm.)

2.2. Before the transformation rule-system starts to work it is necessary to reduce the '*every-every* possibility' to '*one-every* possibility'. This means, that *one* possible KB-order must be selected, however, *every* possible KΩ-block for the single KSeR-s must be preserved.

Thus the transformation-rules begin to operate on the following ordered string of sets [see (**3**)]:

$$
(\mathbf{3}) \qquad \begin{array}{llll}
\mathrm{KSeR}_1, & \mathrm{KSeR}_2, \ldots, & \mathrm{KSeR}_i, \ldots, & \mathrm{KSeR}_n \\
\mathrm{K}\Omega_{11} & \mathrm{K}\Omega_{21} & \mathrm{K}\Omega_{i1} & \mathrm{K}\Omega_{n1} \\
\mathrm{K}\Omega_{12} & \mathrm{K}\Omega_{22} & \mathrm{K}\Omega_{i2} & \mathrm{K}\Omega_{n2} \\
\vdots & \vdots & \vdots & \vdots \\
\mathrm{K}\Omega_{1p} & \mathrm{K}\Omega_{2q} & \mathrm{K}\Omega_{ir} & \mathrm{K}\Omega_{ns}
\end{array}
$$

The following types of transformation rules must be contained in the set of transformation rules:

(1) rules, by means of which 'first sentences' (KLiM_1-s) can be built (if it is possible at all to formulate explicit conditions concerning 'first sentences'),

(2) rules, which select the appropriate $\mathrm{K}\Omega_{i+1}$ on the analysis of the following ordered string (see (**4**)) – where the value of 'i' can be 1, too – and complete it by the possible and/or necessary 'pro-form'-building and/or deletion instructions, i.e. rules, which produce the appropriate completed KB_{i+1},

$$
(\mathbf{4}) \qquad \begin{array}{llll}
\mathrm{KSeR}_1, & \mathrm{KSeR}_2, \ldots, & \mathrm{KSeR}_i, & \mathrm{KSeR}_{i+1} \\
\mathrm{KLiM}_1, & \mathrm{KLiM}_2, \ldots, & \mathrm{KLiM}_i, & \mathrm{K}\Omega_{i+1\ 1} \\
 & & & \mathrm{K}\Omega_{i+1\ 2} \\
 & & & \vdots \\
 & & & \mathrm{K}\Omega_{i+1\ r}
\end{array}
$$

(3) rules, by means of which a syntactico-semantic structure can be converted into a paraphrastic structure (a subset of these rules are most probably lexicon-rules),

(4) rules, by means of which all KB-internal transformations can be carried out.

2.3. The transformation component sketched above still has to be elaborated; I only wanted to outline its set-up and its tasks here. However, on the basis of the characterization of these rule-types one can perhaps get an idea of how this component is supposed to work.

3. *On the Structure of the Lexicon*[12]

3.0. Within this text-grammatical conception the lexicon plays a basic role. The formation-rule system is, as a matter of fact, a combinatorical system operating on the definitions in the lexicon.

The lexicon will contain the following sectors:

(1) the sector of the definitions,

(2) the sector of the convertibility-relations,

(3) the sector of the thesauristic arrangements.

3.1. The *sector of the definitions* is based on the hypothesis that within the set of lexical units (more precisely, the set of 'lexemes', i.e. the different readings of the lexical units) of any natural language it is possible to separate a proper subset which can be declared to be the set of *elementary semantic units.* In other words, this means, that a proper subset can be found, the elements of which function as undefined basic units in the grammar of the given language, and by means of these each unit belonging to the complementary set can be defined. (A universal theory of grammar must, of course, examine the question, whether it is possible to define a set of universal elementary semantic units. However, I do not want to treat this question here.)

The expressions 'lexeme', 'readings of a lexical unit' need some further interpretation. Namely, the lexicon does not contain 'words' but special 'frames' as its 'units'; thus, the lexicon does not contain for example *tell* but *somebody tells something, somebody tells somebody something, somebody tells somebody something about something*, etc.

The representations of these frames are called 'predicate functions' (for

[12] As regards the structure of the lexicon see the following: A summary of the general ideas concerning the set-up of the lexicon in (1971b). General characterization of the lexicon component of this text grammar in (1971d), (1972b) (in the latter the relation between the lexicon items and a (modal) predicate logic has been analysed, too). Outline of a project preparing the setting up of a lexicon is represented by (1971h). As for the first partial results of this project cf. 'In prep.' ('In prep.' will contain a potential set of ESeR-s and the convertibility relations existing among the ESeR-s.) Concerning the relation of the lexicon items and the TextSeR cf. (1972c), (1972f) and Petöfi-Rieser (1972b).

example: 'tell$_i$ a: somebody o: something') and the lexicon indicates in each case, which predicate-function-class the predicate-function in question belongs to (with respect to the example mentioned above it is the class 'p'). I will therefore avoid the expressions 'word', 'lexical unit' and 'frame' in the lexicon and call the representations of the units of the object-language *lexical representations* (LeR), the grammatical constructs *semantic representations* (SeR). Both representations are, as far as their form is concerned, 'predicate functions'. The functors have an index indicating the 'reading' in question. In the above example only an index-dummy is written instead of an index. For simplicity's sake index-dummies will be left out further on, however, they are automatically implied by each functor.

Thus a *definition* in a lexicon is a LeR and a SeR connected by the definition sign ($=_D$). Within the definition the LeR is the definiendum, while the SeR is the definiens; th symbol 'D' is always on that side of the equality sign where the definiens stands. (Thus a definition is indicated either by LeR$=_D$SeR or by SeR$_D$=LeR.)

The definiendum is always one single LeR, while the definiens is either one elementary SeR (ESeR) or an ordered set of ESeR-s.

A considerable part of those definitions, the definiens of which is one single ESeR, are so called 'degenerate definitions'. A degenerate definition is for example

$$\text{p wish e:}_1\text{x1 go:}_1\text{x2e} =_d {}_1\text{p WISH e:}_1\text{x1 go:}_1\text{x2e}$$

if we consider 'WISH e:$_1$x1 go:$_1$x2e' to be an ESeR. (Functors representing objects referring to the units of the object language are written in small letters, functors indicating linguistic constructs are capitalized. The 'degenerate' nature of a definition will be indicated by using the symbol '$=_d$' instead of '$=_D$'.)

However, the definition

$$\text{p want e:}_1\text{x1 go:}_1\text{x2e} =_D {}_1\text{p WISH e:}_1\text{x1 go:}_1\text{x2e}$$

will not be regarded as a degenerate definition. These two definitions together illustrate, that the ESeR 'WISH e:$_1$x1 go:$_1$x2e' can be manifested either by a LeR 'wish e:$_1$x1 go:$_1$x2e' or by a LeR 'want e:$_1$x1 go:$_1$x2e' (i.e. by a specific *wish*- and by a specific *want*- reading in the object language).

The term 'definition' will be used further on only to indicate 'not-degenerate definitions'. The degenerate definitions will always be referred to as 'degenerate definitions'.

Those definitions, the definiens of which consists of more than one ESeR can be classified roughly into the following two subclasses: the subclass of the so-called *ESeR-homogeneous* definitions and that of the *not ESeR-homo-*

geneous definitions. The indications 'ESeR-homogeneous' and 'not ESeR-homogeneous' are only technical expressions. With respect to the representation the former is intended to indicate that all predicate-functions of the definiens are ESeR-s, while the latter indicates that among the elements of the definiens there are also predicate-functions of not-ESeR-character i.e. LeR-s. (The definiens of a LeR will be indicated by $\langle \text{LeR} \rangle_{\text{Ds}}$, however, for simplicity's sake, in the case of a $\langle \text{LeR} \rangle_{\text{Ds}}$ occurring in a definiens, I shall indicate by an asterisk put before the functor that actually a $\langle \text{LeR} \rangle_{\text{Ds}}$ is concerned.)

The not ESeR-homogeneous definitions will be reducible to ESeR-homogeneous definitions in a finite number of steps. In connection with this the very interesting problem of the 'depth' of the definitions arises, i.e. the analysis of the distribution of the definitions within the set of the definitions which can be made ESeR-homogeneous in 0, 1, 2,..., *n* steps and the question of what the maximal *n* within the given lexicon is.

In the argument-places of the definitions stand 'variables'. In the argument-places of the argument of type *A* 'x1', 'x2' and 'x3' are applied as 'individual variables'. These distinctions indicate already a global information concerning the insertion in that *x1* stands for 'somebody', *x2* for 'something' and *x3* for 'somebody or something, where it is not decided, which one is concerned'.

In order that the insertion be better determined, the class of the 'individuals' must be subdivided. This is the aim, for example, of the categorization-system of the Chomskyan grammatical conception, too. It is obvious, that this categorization-system needs to be specified further (and most probably it must be supplemented by another (or other) categorization-system(s)); however, for simplicity's sake and just for illustrating the working of the categorization I shall apply part of the categorization-system of Chomsky here (see Figure 9). The elements OBJECT 21, OBJECT 22,... standing at

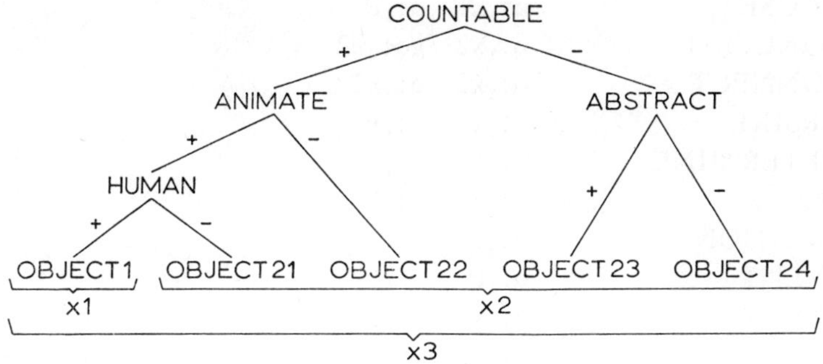

Fig. 9.

the terminal nodes will be used as 'categorizing predicates' for the further categorization of the arguments of type 'x2'. OBJECT 1 is unambiguously defined by the application of 'x1'. It is obvious, that this categorization-system contains the variables 'event' and 'fact', which can be gained from propositions, too, because they can be regarded as 'special x2'-s. Since, however, the variables 'event' and 'fact' play a distinguished role (first of all concerning the transformations), they will be indicated by the symbols 'x2e' and 'x2f', respectively.

If we have to use more than one of a certain variable-type within a predicate-function and these do not refer to the same 'some...' they will be distinguished by a subscript put before them (for example $_1$x2, $_2$x2,...).

We must, of course, subcategorize the arguments of all types of predicates, thus, among others, the arguments of the predicates of type $[[\varphi'] \varphi]$, too. Here the *f*-functors function as arguments which can be classified into different subclasses. For example, with respect to the *f*-functors the categories 'Quality', 'Relation', 'Action', 'Emotion',... can function as categorizing elements. Of course, further subclasses must be specified here, too.

If we assume that the elements enumerated under (**5**) are ESeR-s, the lexicon can contain, for example, the following degenerate definitions (see **6**) and (not degenerate) definitions (see **7**). I want to emphasize once more that this is only a 'formal' illustration; the final determination of the set of the ESeR-s and the final set-up of the single definitions can only be given together with the actual set-up of a lexicon.

(**5**)

p	ABLE	e:$_1$x1	o:$_1$P
p	ABSTRACT	o:$_1$x2	
p	ACTION	o:$_1$P	
p^0	AIM	o:$_1$x2	
p	ANIMATE	o:$_1$x2	
p^0	ARRANGEMENT	o:$_1$x2	
p	CAUSE	a:$_1$x1	o:$_1$P
p	CONCERN	o:$_1$x2	go:$_2$x2
p	CONNECT	o:$_1$x2	g:$_2$x2
p	DESIRE	e:$_1$x1	o:$_1$P
p	DETERMINE	a:$_1$x2	o:$_1$P
p	DO	a:$_1$x1	o:$_1$P
p^0	EMOTION	o:$_1$P	
p^0	EVENT	o:$_1$P	
p	EXPECT	e:$_1$x1	o:$_1$P
p	FEMALE	o:$_1$x1	
p	FIRST	o:$_1$x3	

p GOOD $o:{}_1x2$
p HAVE $h:{}_1x1 \quad o:{}_1x2$
p HUMAN $o:{}_1x1$
p^0 INFORMATION $o:{}_1x2$
p IDENTICAL $o: \ \mathrm{AND} \ {}_1x2 \ {}_2x2$
p KNOW $e:{}_1x1 \quad o:{}_1x3$
p KNOW $e:{}_1x1 \quad o:{}_1x2 \quad so:{}_2x2$
p LOOK $e:{}_1x1 \quad o:{}_1x2$
p MAKE $a:{}_1x1 \quad go:{}_1x2$
p^0 NAME $o:{}_1x2$
p^0 OBJECT $o:{}_1x2$
p^0 PLAN $o:{}_1x2$
p^0 PRESENT $o:{}_1x2$
p^0 PURPOSE $o:{}_1P$
p^0 QUALITY $o:f$
p^0 RELATION $o:f$
p SAY $a:{}_1x1 \quad o:{}_1x2 \quad e:{}_2x1$
p SETTLE $a:{}_1x1 \quad go:{}_1P$
p TELL $a:{}_1x1 \quad o:{}_1x2 \quad e:{}_2x1 \quad so:{}_2x2$
p WISH $e:{}_1x1 \quad go:{}_1P$

(6)

p good $o:{}_1x2 =_d \langle$ QUALITY $o:f$
p GOOD $o:{}_1x2\rangle$
p^0 plan $o:{}_1x2 =_d \langle$ OBJECT 22 $o:{}_1x2$
p^0 PLAN $o:{}_1x2\rangle$
p^0 present $o:{}_1x2 =_d \langle$ OBJECT 22 $o:{}_1x2$
p^0 PRESENT $o:{}_1x2\rangle$
p say $a:{}_1x1 \quad o:{}_1x2 \quad e:{}_2x1$
$=_d \langle$ ACTION $o:f$
p SAY $a:{}_1x1 \quad o:{}_1x2 \quad e:{}_2x1\rangle$
p tell $a:{}_1x1 \quad o:{}_1x2 \quad e:{}_2x1$
$=_d \langle$ ACTION $o:f$
p TELL $a:{}_1x1 \quad o:{}_1x2 \quad e:{}_2x1\rangle$
p present $a:{}_1x1 \quad o:{}_1x2 \quad g:{}_2x1$
$=_d \langle$ ACTION $o:f$
p PRESENT $a:{}_1x1 \quad o:{}_1x2 \quad g:{}_2x1\rangle$

(7)

p^0 book $o:{}_1x2 =_D \langle$ OBJECT 22 $o:{}_1x2$
${}_1p^0$ *collection $o:{}_1x2$
${}_1p$ *collection-of $o:{}_1x2 \quad s:qu_2x2$
${}_2p$ PURPOSE-OF $h:{}_1x2 \quad o:{}_1P \sqsupset {}_3p$

	$_3p$	*read	$a{:}_1x1$ $o{:}_1x2$	
	$_2x2$			
	$_2p^0$	*sheet	$o{:}_2x2$	
	$_4p^T$	PAST	$o{:}_4p$	
	$_4p$	*print	$lg{:}_2x2$ $a{:}_2x1$ $o{:}_3x2$	
	$_3x2$			
	$_3p^0$	*text	$o{:}_3x2$	$\rangle$
p	buy $a{:}_1x1$ $o{:}_1x2$ $s{:}_2x1$ $co{:}_2x2$			
	$=_D\langle$	ACTION	o:f	
	$_1p$	CAUSE	$a{:}_1x1$ $o{:}_1P\sqsupset_2p$	
	$_2p$	HAVE	$h{:}_1x1$ $o{:}_1x2$	
	$_3p$	*give	$a{:}_1x1$ $o{:}_2x2$ $g{:}_2x1$	
	$_2x2$			
	$_1p^0$	*money	$o{:}_2x2$	$\rangle$
p	call $a{:}_1x1$ $e{:}_1x2$ $ro{:}`_2x2'$			
	$=_D\langle$	ACTION	o:f	
	$_1p$	*give	$a{:}_1x1$ $g{:}_1x2$ $o{:}`_2x2'$ $ro{:}_3x2$	
	$_3x2$			
	$_1p^0$	NAME	$o{:}_3x2$	$\rangle$
p	dislike $e{:}_1x1$ $o{:}_1x3$			
	$=_D\langle$	EMOTION	o:f	
	$_1p$	NEG* like	$e{:}_1x1$ $o{:}_1x3$	$\rangle$
p	decide $a{:}_1x1$ $go{:}_1P$			
	$=_D\langle$	ACTION	o:f	
	$_1p$	SETTLE	$a{:}_1x1$ $go{:}_1P$	$\rangle$
p	discover $a{:}_1x1$ $o{:}_1x2$			
	$=_D\langle$	ACTION	o:f	
	$_1p$	*find	$a{:}_1x1$ $o{:}_1x2$	
	$_1x1$			
	$_2p$	FIRST	$o{:}_1x1$	$\rangle$
p^0	discovery $o{:}_1x2$			
	$=_D\langle$	OBJECT 24	$o{:}_1x2$	
	$_1p^0$	EVENT	$o{:}_1x2$	
	$_1p$	IDENTICAL	o: AND $_1x2$ $_1P\sqsupset_2p$	
	$_2p$	*discover	$a{:}_1x1$ $o{:}_2x2$	$\rangle$
p	famous $o{:}_1x3$			
	$=_D\langle$	QUALITY	o:f	
	$_1p$	KNOWN	$e{:}qj_1x1$ $o{:}_1x3$	$\rangle$
p^0	gift $o{:}_1x2$ $=_D\langle$	OBJECT 22		

$_1p^0$ PRESENT $o{:}\,_1x2$ $\rangle$

p give $a{:}\,_1x1$ $o{:}\,_1x2$ $g{:}\,_2x1$
$=_D \langle$ ACTION $o{:}f$
$_1p$ CAUSE $a{:}\,_1x1$ $o{:}\,_1P \sqsupset {}_2p$
$\underline{_2p}$ HAVE $h{:}\,_2x1$ $o{:}\,_1x2$ $\rangle$

p hope $e{:}\,_1x1$ $o{:}\,_1P$
$=_D \langle$ EMOTION $o{:}f$
$_1p$ DESIRE $e{:}\,_1x1$ $o{:}\,_1P$
$_2p$ EXPECT $e{:}\,_1x1$ $o{:}\,_1P$ $\rangle$

p^0 interest $o{:}\,_1x2$
$=_D \langle$ OBJECT 23 $o{:}\,_1x2$
$_1p^0$ CONDITION $o{:}\,_1x2$
$_1p$ IDENTICAL $o{:}$ AND $_1x2$ $_1P \sqsupset {}_2p$
$\underline{_2p}$ *want $e{:}\,_1x1$ $go{:}\,_2P \sqsupset {}_3p$
$\underline{_3p}$ KNOWN $e{:}\,_1x1$ $o{:}\,_2x2$ $\rangle$

p interested $a{:}\,_1x1$ $o{:}\,in\ _1x2$
$=_D \langle$ ACTION $o{:}f$
$_1p$ *want $e{:}\,_1x1$ $go{:}\,_1P \sqsupset {}_2p$
$\underline{_2p}$ KNOWN $e{:}\,_1x1$ $o{:}\,_1x2$ $\rangle$

p interesting $o{:}\,_1x2$
$=_D \langle$ QUALITY $o{:}f$
$_1p$ *arouse $a{:}\,_1x2$ $o{:}\,_2x2$
$\underline{_2x2}$
$_1p^0$ *interest $o{:}\,_2x2$ $\rangle$

p^0 novel $o{:}\,_1x2 =_D \langle$ OBJECT 22 $o{:}\,_1x2$
$_1p^0$ *story $o{:}\,_1x2$
$_1p$ *long $o{:}\,_1f^0$
$_2p$ *imaginary $o{:}\,_1f^0$ $\rangle$

p plan $a{:}\,_1x1$ $go{:}\,_1P$
$=_D \langle$ ACTION $o{:}f$
$_1p$ MAKE $a{:}\,_1x1$ $go{:}\,_1x2$
$\underline{_1x2}$
$_1p^0$ PLAN $o{:}\,_1x2$
$_2p$ CONCERN $o{:}\,_1x2$ $go{:}\,_1P$ $\rangle$

p read $a{:}\,_1x1$ $o{:}\,_1x2$
$=_D \langle$ ACTION $o{:}f$
$_1p$ LOOK $a{:}\,_1x1$ $o{:}\,_1x2$
$\underline{_1x1}$
$_2p$ ABLE $e{:}\,_1x1$ $o{:}\,_1P \sqsupset {}_3p$
$_3p$ *understand $e{:}\,_1x1$ $o{:}\,_1x2$

$\frac{{}_1x2}{{}_4p}$ *write a:$_2$x1 o:$_1$x2 ⟩
p scientific o:$_1$x2
=$_D$⟨ QUALITY o:f
$_1$p CONNECT o:$_1$x2 g:$_2$x2
$\frac{{}_2x2}{{}_1p^0}$ *science o:$_2$x2 ⟩
p science-fiction o:$_1$x2
=$_D$⟨ QUALITY o:f
$_1$p CONNECT o:$_1$x2 g:$_2$x2
$\frac{{}_1x2}{{}_2p}$ NEG*real o:$_1$x2
$\frac{{}_2x2}{{}_1p^0}$ *science o:$_2$x2 ⟩
p sister-of o:$_1$x1 h:$_2$x1
=$_D$⟨ RELATION o:f
$_1$p FEMALE o:$_1$x1
$_2$p IDENTICAL o: AND $_3$x1 $_4$x1
$\frac{{}_3x1}{{}_3p}$ *parents-of o:$_3$x1 h:$_1$x1
$\frac{{}_4x1}{{}_4p}$ *parents-of o:$_4$x1 h:$_2$x1 ⟩
p successful o:$_1$x3
=$_D$⟨ QUALITY o:f
$_1$p *reach o:$_1$x3 g:$_1$x2
$\frac{{}_1x2}{{}_1p^0}$ AIM o:$_1$x2
$_2$p AIM-OF o:$_1$x2 h:$_1$x3 ⟩
p want e:$_1$x1 go:$_1$P
=$_D$⟨ EMOTION o:f
$_1$p WISH e:$_1$x1 go:$_1$P ⟩

Let us now examine the internal structure of a 'definiens', taking the definition 'p^0 book o:$_1$x2=$_D$ ⟨...⟩' as an example.

Since a definition must express a 'mutual and unambiguous connection' between the definiendum and the definiens, the definition can be read in two ways. Concerning the definition of *book* it can be read, on the one hand as

'something [$\equiv {}_1x2$] is a *book*, if ...',

on the other hand as

'if something [$\equiv {}_1x2$] is a *book*, then ...'

The dots indicate the definiens. Simplifying a bit this definiens can be read as follows:

> "this something [$\equiv_1$x2] is a countable non-animate object; – more closely: this something [$\equiv_1$x2] is a collection; this something [$\equiv_1$x2] is a collection of a certain number [$\equiv$qu] of sheets [$\equiv_2$x2], on which somebody [$\equiv_1$x1] printed [PAST] a text [$\equiv_3$x2]; this something [$\equiv_1$x2] has the purpose of being read by somebody [$\equiv_2$x1]".

Since it is a not ESeR-homogeneous definition, its reading must be continued by a suplementation

> "where 'collection', 'collection-of', 'read', 'sheet', 'print' and 'text' can be definied in the following way:...

In place of the dots the definitions of the elements enumerated must be inserted. (A better solution is to make the definition ESeR-homogeneous first and to read the definiens afterwards.)

On the basis of the above example we can say that the definientes can be manifested by a 'text'. If this is true, it means that a definiens must be a 'TextB'. However, the definientes of the definitions presented up to now are no TextB-s – at least not explicitly –, namely, none of the definientes are assigned a TextΩ-block. They cannot be regarded as full TextSeR-s either, because they neither contain performative predicates nor tempus-determining predicates and, in addition, the arguments of their predicates are incomplete. However, these insufficiencies are only *virtual* ones.

The definientes in the lexicon function as TextB-s, both as their form and their content is concerned, even if they are special TextB-s. Their special nature results

(1) concerning their content from the fact that the arguments of their predicates are so-called 'defined variables' (that means, 'reference indices' of the types *R*, R, H and M do not occur at all or, cautiously formulated, only very seldom as arguments in a definiens);

(2) concerning their form from the realization of the hypothesis, according to which in the representation of the definientes a number of redundancy-rules can be applied:

(a) it is not necessary to give a TextΩ, because with respect to the LiM-s of the definientes a so-called 'normalized form' can be interpreted (for example: from each kernel predicate a KLiM must be built up – by means of applying K-internal transformations which can be specified so that they are valid with respect to the whole lexicon –; the order of the KLiM-s within the manifestation is equal to the order of the kernel predicates in the definiens; no K-internal transformations must be applied);

(b) the 'performative predicate' expresses in each case an 'ASSERTION', thus it can be omitted from the single definientes;

(c) the 'tempus-determining predicate' is mostly SIM (or a special present-manifestation of SIM), this can also be omitted; however, those tempus-determining predicates which are not of SIM-character, must be indicated;

(d) it is not necessary to interpret 'supplementary structures' on the set of the kernel predicates, because only one 'communicative net' occurs generally in the definientes and the function of the 'thematic nets' concerning the definientes is irrelevant (each definiens is ab ovo grammatically continuous);

(e) as we have seen the arguments in the TextB have a three-fold structure:

$$\left|\begin{array}{c} R/\mathrm{R} \\ \mathrm{H} \\ \mathrm{M} \\ \mathrm{V} \end{array}\right| \quad \left|\begin{array}{c} \mathrm{N} \\ \mathrm{G/A} \\ \\ \\ \mathrm{Q} \end{array}\right| \quad \left|\begin{array}{c} \mathrm{x}N \\ \mathrm{z}N \\ \mathrm{y}N \end{array}\right|$$

As far as the 'variable'-part is concerned, within a definiens in a lexicon all three types can occur (in the definition of *book* ${}_2x2$ is a 'variable' of type 'y', ${}_3x2$ is a 'variable' of type 'x'); an extra indication of the type is superfluous, the representation unambiguously indicates the type;

A definiens in a lexicon generally contains 'G'-s as 'quantifiers', thus they can be omitted; it is, however, necessary to indicate the possible occurrence of other identifiers. (The symbols are written in small letters in the lexicon, see for example 'qu' – not 'Qu'.)

I want to emphasize again, that all representational instructions enumerated in point (2) are based on the hypothesis that with respect to the whole lexicon it is possible to specify redundancy-conventions which allow the representation of the definientes as 'reduced TextB'-s. (Namely, the redundancy-conventions permit to complete them to 'well-formed TextB'-s.) Neither the validity of this hypothesis nor the determination of the single redundancy-conventions can be regarded as definitely settled.

However, the basic hypothesis, that the definientes in the lexicon are TextB-s, can in my opinion, be regarded as sound. This fact considerably simplifies the set up of the text grammar (and, at the same time, it serves as an evidence for both the necessity and the indispensability of a text grammar).

As far as the lexicon is concerned I have only dealt with the sector of the definitions up to now. As regards the two other sectors, I only want to make some remarks.

3.2. The *sector of the convertibility relations* must fulfil a double function. The first function concerns the ESeR-s, the second one concerns the LeR-s.

3.2.1. Though the ESeR-s have the character of 'basic notions', the possibility of paraphrasing holds for them as well. This is due to the nature of living languages. These possibilities can be formulated similar as regards the definitions – using the sign of the convertibility relation (=C=) instead of that of the definition. The sector of the convertibility relations concerning the ESeR-s represents these paraphrasing possibilities. The 'convertendum' is always an ESeR, the 'convertens' is either an ESeR-homogeneous or a not-ESeR-homogeneous ordered set (see (**8**) and (**9**) respectively).

(**8**)

p^0 PLAN $o{:}_1x2$ =C= <		OBJECT22	$o{:}_1x2$	
	$_1p^0$	ARRANGEMENT	$o{:}_1x2$	
	$_1p$	DETERMINE	$a{:}_1x2$ $o{:}_1x2e$	
	$_1x2e$			
	——			
	$_2p$	DO	$a{:}_1x1$ $o{:}_1x2e$	
	$_2p^T$	FUT	$o{:}_2p$	>
p^0 PRESENT $o{:}_1x2$				
=C= <		OBJECT22	$o{:}_1x2$	
	$_1p^0$	GIFT	$o{:}_1x2$	>

(**9**)

p TELL $a{:}_1x1$ $o{:}_1x2$ $e{:}_2x1$ $so{:}_2x2$				
=C= <		ACTION	$o{:}f$	
	$_1p$	*give	$a{:}_1x1$ $o{:}_3x2$ $g{:}_2x1$	
	$_3x2$			
	——			
	$_1p^0$	INFORMATION	$o{:}_3x2$	
	$_2p$	CONCERN	$o{:}_3x2$ $go{:}_2x2$	>

The not-ESeR-homogeneous sets can obviously be traced back to ESeR-homogeneous sets by applying appropriate definitions.

It is, however, also possible to convert those ESeR-homogeneous sets which function as 'convertentes'. The principle of conversion is here that any of the ESeR-elements of a 'convertens' can be conceived as a 'convertendum' and can be replaced by the appropriate convertens, if this does not contain the original convertendum as one of its elements.

By means of (many-step) convertibility relations it is, further, possible to convert all definientes, too. Through these conversions a maximal paraphrasing possibility is guaranteed, with respect to all linguistic units.

3.2.2. In the convertibility relations concerning the LeR-s the convertendum is a LeR, the convertens is either an ESeR-homogeneous or a not-ESeR-homogeneous ordered set. In these relations any LeR (i.e. either the convertendum or any LeR in the convertens) can be replaced by its definiens, as a result of which we obtain such quasi-definitory identities that cannot be found in the sector of the definitions. Since we can apply the convertibility relations to these definientes, too, this allows for new ways of paraphrasing.

The actual performance of the paraphrasings, as I have already hinted at when dealing with the transformation rule-system, requires appropriate rules. The convertibility relations have the purpose of guaranteeing the applicability of these rules.

3.3. The *sector of the thesauristic relations* contains the LeR-s and the ESeR-s in different kinds of arrangements. The identical syntactico-semantic behaviour, the different semantic relations (co-hyponymy, hyperonymy) etc. serve as basis of these arrangements.

These arrangements are of basic importance both in the generation and in the application of the transformations.

3.4. Concerning the lexicon a very important question to be dealt with is *the relation of colloquial and technical language*. Namely, it is obvious that the colloquial use of language presupposes the knowledge of much less detailed and much less precise definitions than the use of particular technical languages does. The problem arising here is, that while the requirements concerning the 'precision' of the definitions in the technical languages are given within the particular 'theories', no such requirements can be formulated with respect to the use of colloquial language. These requirements can only be motivated by the help of such 'aspects' as the guaranteeing of the maximal paraphrasing of the expressions of the colloquial language (by means of expressions of the colloquial language) where it can only be decided on the basis of some concensus, whether the single expressions of a language are 'expressions of the colloquial language' or not.

In order that a text grammar be capable of generating and analysing any kind of texts, it is necessary for this grammar to contain a complex of 'lexica' not only one lexicon. The kernel of this complex should be provided by the lexicon of the 'colloquial language' and a series of lexica of the different technical languages should be attached to it. Each lexicon should, of course, be set up according to the same principles.

4. *The Algorithm for the Analysis of Texts*[13]

The task of the analysis is to assign the admissible text-bases to the linear manifestation of a given text (Analysis I) and to reveal the 'macro-structures' manifesting themselves in the text (Analysis II).

4.1. *Analysis I* starts from the TextLiM (=KLiM-string) and reaches the TextB through the KB-string.

The *direct task* of Analysis I can be formulated as follows: it must assign to all sentences of the text that basis (or those admissible bases), of which the analysed text-sentence can be considered as its (their) linear manifestation. In this assigning process such basic problems have to be solved as the disclosure of the possibilities of completing 'defective' sentences, the disclosure of syntactico-semantic structural homonymy, the elimination of all PRO-type reference-elements (PRO -noun, -adjective, -adverb, -verb) by substituting the 'original' elements for them, the determination of the definit-, indefinit- and general- character of the arguments, etc.

The *indirect task* of Analysis I is the disclosure of the objects (sets of objects) of the 'world' manifesting itself in the text and the relations existing between them. – In order that Analysis I also fulfil its indirect task, we have to reconstruct the TextB after the reconstruction of the KB-string(s).

4.2. Let us now briefly consider the scope of task of *Analysis II.*

Recent text linguistic research often refers to so-called 'macro-' or 'global-' structures. [Cf., for example, van Dijk (1972) and Ihwe (1972).] These structures refer to structures concerning the whole of the text, as opposed to the structure of the single sentences of the text.

I do not intend to deal with the problems of the structures belonging to this category that have been exposed in the literature thus far; I only want to outline those 'macro-structures' which can be interpreted within the framework of the text grammar presented here. The task of Analysis II is to disclose these macro-structures.

Among the three structure-levels (TextSeR, KB-string, KLiM-string/= =TextLiM/) interpreted with respect to the text, the two latter ones can, under a common name, be called 'text-surface-representation (TextSuR)'.

[13] I have dealt with the 'simulation' of the analysis first in (1969b) and (1969c). A special question, namely that of the problems of the grammatical analysis of poetic images was discussed in (1969a). (The text-grammatical framework was then still an amplified Chomsky-type sentence grammar.) As regards the aspect of the analysis of the text-grammatical conception presented in this study cf. (1972d). – Since a complete text is the demonstration material in each study, each study touches mediately the aspect of the analysis, too.

The TextSeR and the TextSuR, of which the former one is indifferent towards the linear arrangement while the latter one is already linearly arranged, are opposed to one another. Since these structure-levels show an essential difference, we must interpret a 'macro-structure' with respect to *both* of these levels separately.

4.2.1. The macro-structure interpreted with respect to the TextSeR is the *reference-relation-diagram*.

4.2.2. The macro-structure interpreted with respect to the TextSuR is the so-called *compositional TextSuR*.

The compositional TextSuR must express through what kind of higher order composition units the structure of the whole text can be reached starting from the consecutive KLiM-s.

4.3. The *algorithm for the analysis* must treat the possibilities of the performability of the operations of Analysis I and Analysis II.

The disclosure of the KB-s on the basis of the KLiM-s is considered the basic operation among these. In order to carry it out, it is necessary to elaborate a special parsing system, i.e. one operating with the rules of the given text grammar. After having already constructed the set of admissible KB-structures, the performance of the remaining tasks can be said to be more or less easy. The elaboration of the algorithm for the analysis requires that the rule-systems be elaborated and a lexicon be set up.

In the course of my investigations concerning these problems, I have only presented some empirical studies dealing with the 'simulation' of the analysis of given texts.

In this study I want to show, how the text grammar works in the direction of the synthesis (composition). Since the analysis is, as a matter of fact, the reversal of the synthesis (decomposition), under the condition that the problems concerning the synthesis are clear it is possible to reconstruct the outlines of the process of the analysis, too.

5. *The Algorithm for the Synthesis of Texts*[14]

In Figure 8 the entire 'communicative basis' of a so-called descriptive text

[14] I dealt with the aspect of the synthesis first in (1971b). (1971f) contains the first presentation of the formation rule-system together with the analysis of some problems of the synthesis. For the discussion of the presuppositions and consequences in connection with the synthesis cf. Petöfi-Rieser (1972b). (The last remark made in Note 13 also holds with respect to the synthesis).

A supplementary remark to the handling of the demonstration texts: the general frame-

having a title has been shown. The first main sector of this basis contains the general communicative informations concerning the text as one single element, while its second main sector contains the grammatical (co-textual) informations concerning the internal structure of the text.

In this second main sector a further internal arrangement can be observed. This internal arrangement can also be interpreted as an operational arrangement.

5.1. My remarks concerning the *synthesis* (text-generation) will be made with reference to this Figure, i.e. according to the succession of the elements enumerated in it.

Let us start with the elements contained in the lowermost block of these hierarchically ordered blocks. (The question, in which succession the generation should proceed, is most probably a misformulated question. The succession, or at least the starting informations, must be provided by the 'strategy for the synthesis' depending on the text-type to be generated. However, I do not want to deal with this problem here.) My aim is only to present those elements, out of which a TextB can be constructed and to point out some aspects which must be taken into consideration when generating a TextB.

5.1.1. The entirety of the elements enumerated in the lowermost block of Figure 8

communicative nets
....
reference-relations-diagram
thematic nets
list of the reference-indices
list of the argument-variables and of the defining expressions belonging to them

can be called a *potential TextB-kernel.*

When developing a potential TextB-kernel, the first question to be decided is, whether the TextB should be built up of LeR-s or SeR-s (that is, whether we intend the text grammar to function as an interpretive grammar or as a synthesis grammar starting with 'semantic representations').

---

work of the working-process, i.e. of the text-grammatical description is always the same. Only the representation of the arguments and the principle of constructing thematic nets show certain deviations. As far as the former is concerned, the cause for the deviations is, that the threefold arrangement of the representation of the arguments (identifier + quantifier + variable) was only developed gradually, while the cause concerning the latter is the testing of the different possibilities of eliminating redundancies.

To make his distinction clearer, let us consider the following example.

The problem 'LeR or SeR' concerns on the one hand the selection of the 'defining expressions' which will be assigned to the argument-variables, on the other hand the construction of the thematic nets.

Depending on how this problem was decided, we can choose the 'defining expressions' given in (**8**) or in (**9**) from the lexicon (see (**6**) and (**7**)) by applying rule R14b and assign them to a variable of type 'zN'.

(**8**)	z01	$:=:$	p_1^0	book	o:z01		
(**9**)	z01	$:=:$	$<$	OBJECT22	o:z01		
			p_1^0	*collection	o:z01		
			p_1	*collection-of	o:z01	s:qu_1x2	
			p_2	PURPOSE-OF	h:z01	o:$P_3 \sqsupset p_3$	
			$\underline{p_3}$	*read	o:z01	a:$_1$x1	
			$\underline{_1x2}$				
			p_2^0	*sheet	o:$_1$x2		
			p_4^T	PAST	o:p_4		
			p_4	*print	lg:$_1$x2	a:$_2$x1	o:$_2$x2
			$\underline{_2x2}$				
			p_3^0	*text	o:$_2$x2	$>$	

(The principle applied in the transcription of the symbols of the lexicon is, that the reference indicated by the symbols within the *whole* TextB must be unambiguous.)

Let us build now reference-indices from these 'z01'-s: (let us select (according to R9ba), for example, a 'Qu' indicating 'NOT-SPECIFIED-QUANTITY' as 'φ^{ω}', and 'V' indicating 'variable' as 'U'.

(**10**) V01 ≡ VQuz01; where z01 is defined in (**8**)
(**11**) V01 ≡ VQuz01; where z01 is defined in (**9**)

Let us add, as a new reference-index, the proper name 'John' indicating a definite (male) person:

(**12**) *R*02 ≡ John

Let us now build argument-pairs from (**10**)+(**12**) and from (**11**)+(**12**), respectively applying the Rules R7, R11, R9a and R9b in such a way that (**10**) and (**11**) will be assigned to the argument-label 'o', (**12**) will be assigned to the argument-label 'a'. Thus we obtain (**13**) and (**14**), respectively.

(**13**) A_1 $:=:$ {a:*R*02 o:V01/$_{\mathbf{LeR}}$}
(**14**) A_1 $:=:$ {a:*R*02 o:V01/$_{\mathbf{SeR}}$}

(For simplicity's sake I refer to V01 defined in (**10**) with the symbol $V01/_{LeR}$, and to V01 defined in (**11**) with the symbol $V01/_{SeR}$.)

Let us now look for a predicate-function assigning a functor to these argument-pairs (according to the upper line of Rule R6). (**15**) will serve as a set of subclassificational characteristics (F_{σ_k}), which results from the classificational predicates of the 'proper name' and the 'defining expression' assigned to the variable z01 functioning as arguments.

$$\textbf{(15)} \qquad F_{\sigma_k} \equiv \begin{bmatrix} \text{a:HUMAN} & \text{o:OBJECT22} \\ \text{MALE} & \end{bmatrix}$$

Since the 'characteristics' belonging to the 'a' is indicated by 'x1', the 'characteristics' belonging to the 'o' is indicated by 'x2' in the lexicon, we must look for a predicate-function with the argument-pair 'a:$_1$x1 o:$_1$x2'.

If we apply for example rule R15b (that is if we look for a definition in the definition-sector of the lexicon the definiens of which is not an ESeR) we can select the functor '*interested*' and the SeR belonging to the LeR having the functor 'interested'. In the former case we obtain (**16**), in the latter case (**17**). When building (**16**) we simply must write the functor selected before the argument-pair while when building (**17**) the elements of the argument-pair must be inserted in place of the corresponding argument-variables of the SeR.

(**16**) p_1 interested a:*R*02 o:*in* $V01/_{LeR}$
(**17**) <p_5 *want e:*R*02 go:$P_6 \sqsupset p_6$
p_6 KNOWN e:*R*02 o:$V01/_{SeR}$>

Besides demonstrating the LeR/SeR problem, this example could perhaps also give an idea of how the rule-system functions. (Those predicates not provided with a predicate-symbol play a decisive role in the application of both the formation and the transformation rules as F_{σ_k} elements.) With respect to the predicate obtained the generation can be continued as follows:

As already emphasized earlier, a predicate expresses only a 'relation'. (**16**) can, for example, be read in the following way:

> "a relation between the elements 'John', 'books' and '(be) interested in'".

If we do not want to complement this predicate by utilizing the possibilities supplied by rule R6 to a 'kernel' having the functors f′, f″, f^t and f^l, too, it can be immediately complemented by the application of rule R5 to a proposition and then, by the application of R3, to a S-constituent; thus it can already function as a KLeR.

Let us turn back to the components of the potential TextB-kernel after this digression.

For simplicity's sake I want to demonstrate a more or less simple TextB ($TextB_1$) which is suitable for giving an idea about the most important aspects. The elements of this TextB are LeR-s. Consequently I shall use the symbols KLeR and TextLeR instead of the symbols KSeR and TextSeR.

(a) List (**18**) contains the argument-variables belonging to the potential $TextB_1$ together with the respective 'defining expressions'.

(b) List (**19**) enumerates the reference-indices (the reference-indices stand on the left hand side of the equivalence-sign, the reference-descriptions stand on the right hand side).

(c) List (**20**) enumerates the thematic nets. No redundancy principle will be applied in the construction of the single nets, therefore some predicates occur in more than one net. (For simplicity's sake in list (**20**) only the symbols indicating the predicates have been enumerated after the symbols standing for the single thematic nets. The predicates themselves are contained in an extra list.) Within the single nets also the embedding-relations are represented in parentheses. The symbol '∅' represents an empty net; the 'emptiness' is the consequence of the fact that the reference-index in question takes only part in the construction of another reference-index. NEG1 is the representation of 'simple negation' (*not*) while NEG2 represents a sort of 'emphasized negation' (*not at all*).

The reference-relation-diagram and the set of the communicative nets is, as a matter of fact, a superstructure built upon the lists enumerated in (a), (b) and (c).

(d) The reference-relation-diagram is shown in Figure 10.

(e) The communicative nets are enumerated in list (**21**). According to the reference-relation-diagram all reference-indices are immediately or mediately connected. A Text B which has this property is called a grammatically continuous TextB. (With respect to $TextB_1$ the $TextB_1$-kernel already has this property.)

$TextB_1$ contains three communicative nets, each of them consists of one element only i.e. to each of them belongs one proposition to be communicated. The communicative nets are closely connected with each other, since their arguments 'a' and 'e' together contain in each case the same reference-indices (*R*02, *R*03 and *R*04).

(18)	z01	:=:	<	OBJECT22	o:z01
			p_1^0	book	o:z01>
	y02	:=:	<	OBJECT22	o:y02
			p_2^0	book	o:y02
			p_1	good	o:f_2^0>
	y03	:=:	<	OBJECT22	o:y03

p_3^0 book o:y03
p_2 interesting o:y03>
y04 :=: < OBJECT o:y04
p_4^0 novel o:y04
p_3 famous o:f_4^0
p_4^T PAST o:p_4
p_4 write a:*R*05 o:y04
p_5^T PAST o:p_5
p_5 call a:*R*05 o:y04 ro:'*R*06'
*R*05 ≡ Dickens
*R*06 ≡ Oliver Twist>
y05 :=: < OBJECT o:y05
p_5^0 novel o:y05
p_6 science-fiction o:f_5^0>
y06 :=: < OBJECT22 o:y06
p_6^0 book o:y06
p_7 f_7 o:y08
f_7 H14≡HQ1y07
y07 :=: < OBJECT22 o:y07
p_7^0 discovery o:y07
p_8 scientific o:f_7^0>
y08 :=: < OBJECT22 o:y08
p_8^0 topic o:y08
p_9 have o:y08 h:y06>>
y09 :=: < OBJECT1 o:y09
p_9^0 sister o:y09
p_{10} sister-of o:y09 h:*R*03>

(19) *R*01 ≡ John
*R*02 ≡ George
*R*03 ≡ Henry
*R*04 ≡ Steven
*R*05 ≡ Dickens
*R*06 ≡ Oliver Twist
V07 ≡ VQuz01 *(books)*
V08 ≡ VQuy02 *(good books)*
V09 ≡ VQ1y03 *(≈ an interesting book)*
R10 ≡ RQ1y04 *(≈ the famous novel written by Dickens called 'Oliver Twist')*
H11 ≡ HQ1y05 *(≈ a science-fiction novel)*
H12 ≡ HQ1y06 *(≈ a book the topic of which is a*

scientific discovery)
R13 ≡ RQ1y09 *(Henry's sister)*
H14 ≡ HQ1y07 *(≈ a scientific discovery)*
(The descriptions in brackets do not belong to the actual list, they only have a function of supplementary explanation.)

(20)

TN01 $\ni$ $\{p_{11}, p_{12}, (p_{13}::p_{11}, p_{12}), p_{21}, p_{22}, p_{23}, (p_{20}::p_{21}, p_{22}, p_{23}),$
$p_{24}, p_{27}, (p_{26}::p_{27}), p_{30}, (p_{29}::p_{30}), p_{32}, (p_{31}::p_{32}), p_{37};\}$
TN02 $\ni$ $\{p_{13}, (p_{13}::p_{11}, p_{12}), p_{16}, (p_{16}::p_{17}, p_{18}, p_{19}), p_{17}, p_{20},$
$(p_{20}::p_{21}, p_{22}, p_{23}, p_{24}), p_{21}, p_{24}, p_{25}, (p_{25}::p_{26}, p_{27}), p_{29},$
$(p_{29}::p_{30}), p_{31}, (p_{31}::p_{32}), p_{32}, p_{34}, (p_{34}::p_{37});\}$
TN03 $\ni$ $\{p_{14}, (p_{14}::p_{11}, p_{12}), p_{16}, (p_{16}::p_{17}, p_{18}, p_{19}), p_{18}, p_{20},$
$(p_{20}::p_{21}, p_{22}, p_{23}, p_{24}), p_{22}, p_{24}, p_{25}, (p_{25}::p_{26}, p_{27}),$
$p_{26}, p_{27}, p_{29}, (p_{29}::p_{30}), p_{31}, (p_{31}::p_{32}), p_{35}, (p_{35}::p_{37});\}$
TN04 $\ni$ $\{p_{15}, (p_{15}::p_{11}, p_{12}), p_{16}, (p_{16}::p_{17}, p_{18}, p_{19}), p_{19}, p_{20},$
$(p_{20}::p_{21}, p_{22}, p_{23}, p_{24}), p_{23}, p_{24}, p_{25}, (p_{25}::p_{26}), p_{28}, p_{29},$
$(p_{29}::p_{30}), p_{30}, p_{31}, (p_{31}::p_{32}), p_{36}, (p_{36}::p_{37});\}$
TN05 $\ni$ $\{\emptyset\}$ [*R*05∈R10]
TN06 $\ni$ $\{\emptyset\}$ [*R*06∈R10]
TN07 $\ni$ $\{p_{11}, p_{12};\}$
TN08 $\ni$ $\{p_{21}, p_{22}, p_{23}, (p_{20}::p_{21}, p_{22}, p_{23}), (p_{37}::p_{21}, p_{22}, p_{23}, p_{24});\}$
TN09 $\ni$ $\{p_{24}, p_{33}, (p_{37}::p_{21}, p_{22}, p_{23}, p_{24});\}$
TN10 $\ni$ $\{p_{32}, (p_{31}::p_{32});\}$
TN11 $\ni$ $\{p_{28}, p_{30}, (p_{29}::p_{30});\}$
TN12 $\ni$ $\{p_{27}, (p_{25}::p_{26}::p_{27});\}$
TN13 $\ni$ $\{p_{33};\}$
TN14 $\ni$ $\{\emptyset\}$ [H14∈H12]

(When setting up the list of the predicates I have omitted for simplicity's sake the classificatory predicates (ACTION,...).)

p_{11} NEG1 interested a:*R*01 o:V07
p_{12} NEG2 read a:*R*01 o:V07
p_{13} dislike e:*R*02 o: AND P_{11} P_{12}
p_{14} dislike e:*R*03 o:AND P_{11} P_{12}
p_{15} dislike e:*R*04 o:AND P_{11} P_{12}
p_{16} decide a:AND *R*04 *R*02 *R*03 go:AND P_{17} P_{18} P_{19}
$\underline{p_{17}}$ do a:*R*02 o:$_1$x2
$\underline{p_{18}}$ do a:*R*03 o:$_2$x2
$\underline{p_{19}}$ do a:*R*04 o:$_3$x2

p_{20}	plan	a:AND *R*02 *R*03 *R*04 go:AND P_{21} P_{22} P_{23}
$\underline{p_{21}}$	tell	a:*R*02 e:*R*01 so:V08
$\underline{p_{22}}$	tell	a:*R*03 e:*R*01 so:V08
$\underline{p_{23}}$	tell	a:*R*04 e:*R*01 so:V08
$\underline{p_{24}}$	present	a:AND *R*02 *R*03 *R*04 o:V09 e:*R*01
p_{25}	say	a:*R*03 e:AND *R*02 *R*04 o:P_{26}
$\underline{p_{26}}$	want	e:*R*03 go:P_{27}
$\underline{p_{27}}$	tell	a:*R*03 e:*R*01 so:H12
p_{28}	read	a:*R*04 o:H11
p_{29}	say	a:*R*04 e:AND *R*02 *R*03 o:P_{30}
$\underline{p_{30}}$	tell	a:*R*04 e:*R*01 so:H11
p_{31}	say	a:*R*02 e:AND *R*03 *R*04 o:P_{32}
$\underline{p_{32}}$	tell	a:*R*02 e:*R*01 so:R10
p_{33}	buy	a:R13 o:V09
p_{34}	hope	e:*R*02 o:P_{37}
p_{35}	hope	e:*R*03 o:P_{37}
p_{36}	hope	e:*R*04 o:P_{37}
p_{37}	successful	o:AND P_{21} P_{22} P_{23} P_{24}
p_{38}	plan	a:AND *R*02 *R*03 *R*04 go:P_{24}

The predicate-symbols underlined refer to predicates which are the kernel predicates of a proposition standing in an argument-place of some other predicate. (P_i indicates a proposition developed out of a p_i.) The TN-s are given as unordered sets in (**20**), however, these sets can be ordered (in fact, in certain cases they must be ordered – Cf. Chapter 6).

	R 01	*R* 02	*R* 03	*R* 04	*R* 05	*R* 06	V 07	V 08	V 09	R 10	H 11	H 12	R 13	H 14
TN01	+	+	+	+			+	+		+	+	+		
TN02	+	+	+	+			+	+	+	+	+	+		
TN03	+	+	+	+			+	+	+	+	+	+		
TN04	+	+	+	+			+	+	+	+	+	+		
TN05										[+]				
TN06										[+]				
TN07	+						+							
TN08	+	+	+	+				+						
TN09	+	+	+	+				+	+					
TN10	+	+	+	+						+				
TN11	+	+	+	+							+			
TN12	+	+	+	+								+		
TN13									+				+	
TN14												[+]		

Fig. 10.

(**21**)	KN01	p_{25}	say	a:*R*03	o:AND *R*02 *R*04	o:P_{26}
	KN02	p_{29}	say	a:*R*04	o:AND *R*02 *R*03	o:P_{30}
	KN03	p_{31}	say	a:*R*02	o:AND *R*03 *R*04	o:P_{32}

5.1.2. The block

the set of the $p' - s$
the set of the $p'' - s$
....
the set of the $p_j^l - s$
the set of the $p_j^t - s$

contains the predicates belonging to the expansion of the kernel predicates.

For simplicity's sake no predicate of type p′ is assigned to the kernel predicates. Thus the set of the predicates of type p″ remains empty.

No predicates of type p^l (i.e. predicates expressing *local* circumstances) will be assigned to them either.

Even if no predicate of type p^t is present in an explicit form (that is, even if no such predicates expressing *temporal* circumstances as e.g. *yesterday, tomorrow, in two weeks* occur) an implicite 'time-determination' belongs to each predicate. These time-determinations will be indicated by the symbol 'τ_i' furnished with the subscript of the respective kernel predicate. (τ_i is a relational time-variable.) In setting up the Text Ω – in the determination of the succession of the KSeR-s/KLeR-s these $\tau_i - s$ play an important role.

5.1.3. The block

the set of the $p_j^T - s$
the set of the $p_j^P - s$

contains the predicates building propositions and S-constituents.

The predicates building propositions (the 'tempus determining predicates' (p^T)) indicate the 'global tempus-determinedness' of the relation expressed by the expanded kernel. They are related to the implicit temporal elements of the performative predicates (performative propositions) which function as a constant with respect to all text-sentences. In relation to this constant the 'global tempus-determinedness' of the single propositions will be SIMultaneous, PAST or FUTure.

The p^T predicates are contained in list (**22**). For simplicity's sake I only enumerated the symbols of the kernel predicates after the labels PAST, SIM and FUT instead of the p^T predicates themselves.

(**22**) PAST: p_{28};
SIM $p_{11}, p_{12}, p_{13}, p_{14}, p_{15}, p_{16}, p_{20}, p_{25}, p_{26}, p_{27}, p_{29}, p_{31}, p_{34}, p_{35}, p_{38}$;
FUT: $p_{17}, p_{18}, p_{19}, p_{21}, p_{22}, p_{23}, p_{24}, p_{30}, p_{32}, p_{33}, p_{37}$.

A performative predicate 'p^P ASS a:Pers.1 e:Pers.2 o:' belongs as an *S-constituent*-building predicate to each proposition. The propositions (more precisely their kernel predicates) are enumerated in list (**23**).

(**23**) ASS a:Pers.1 e:Pers.2 o:$p_{11}, p_{12}, p_{13}, p_{14}, p_{15}, p_{16}, p_{20}, p_{25}, p_{28}, p_{29}, p_{31}, p_{33}, p_{34}, p_{35}, p_{36}, p_{38}$;

5.1.4. The last block of elements belonging to the TextSeR_i

the set of the $p^C_{k_i}$ *– s*

contains the so-called 'connective predicates'.

These *connective* predicates could as well be called S-connective predicates, since they indicate the building of complex S-constituents. (The predicates indicating the building of complex propositions are given within the respective kernel predicates.)

When enumerating the predicates p', p'', p^l, p^t, p^T and p^P it was possible to give the different kinds of lists in a simplified form because these predicates are furnished with the same subscripts as the kernel predicates they belong to. This is not possible, however, in the case of p^C-type predicates therefore these predicates must be presented in their full form. This presentation is contained in list (**24**).

(**24**)
p^C_1 AND o:S_{13} S_{14} S_{15}
p^C_2 AND o:S_{20} S_{38}
p^C_3 AND o:S_{34} S_{35} S_{36}
p^C_4 AND o:S_1 S_2
p^C_5 BECAUSE s:p^C_4 g:S_{16}

The arguments of the connective predicates can be given in different ways. On the one hand they can be given without argument-labels; in this case, if the arguments fulfil different 'functions' the succession of the arguments enumerated is relevant. (This way of representation has been applied in my works until now and also in this study where the connective predicates contain proposition arguments.) On the other hand the arguments can also be represented by labels – as it is the case here, where 's' indicates 'cause'/'antecedent', 'g' 'effect'/'consequence'.

By having developed the list of p^C – s the generation of the TextLeR_1

more precisely that of the potential TextLeR_1 is completed. The next task is to start with the determination of the $\text{Text}\Omega_1$ – block.

5.1.5. By having set up list (**24**) the condition for constructing the pre-transformational $\text{Text}\Omega_1$-block is already given. As we have already seen, the pre-transformational TextΩ-block must contain on the one hand the structural (not transformational) informations belonging to the single KSeR-s/ /KLeR-s; on the other hand, it must contain the information determining the succession of an admissible KB-sequence.

The structural informations of the KLeR-s indicate, which predicates the single KLeR-s are derived from. These informations are contained in list (**25**).

(**25**)	KLeR01	:=:	S_1	KLeR07	:=:	S_{25}
	KLeR02	:=:	S_2	KLeR08	:=:	S_{28}
	KLeR03	:=:	S_3	KLeR09	:=:	S_{29}
	KLeR04	:=:	S_5	KLeR10	:=:	S_{31}
	KLeR05	:=:	S_{11}	KLeR11	:=:	S_{33}
	KLeR06	:=:	S_{12}			

An *admissible KB-succession* is represented by (**26**). The succession is indicated by the subscripts attached to the symbols enumerated in (**25**).

(**26**) KLeR05_1, KLeR06_2, KLeR01_3, KLeR04_4, KLeR02_5, KLeR10_6, KLeR08_7, KLeR09_8, KLeR07_9, KLeR11_{10}, KLeR03_{11}.

5.1.6. The determination of the pre-transformational Text Ω_1-block has to be followed by the determination of the admissible KΩ-blocks belonging to the single KLeR-s; then all those rules of the transformation component are applied which reduce all sets of $\text{K}\Omega_i$-blocks to one single $\text{K}\Omega_i$-block. As a matter of fact this is the last step in developing the Text B. (I want to add some remarks to these operations under point 5.2.)

5.1.7. In Figure 8 the TextB_i is still assigned different kinds of predicates. The functors of these predicates are constants. With respect to a given text this means that it is only necessary to determine the value of their argument-variables. For example, concerning the TextB_1 generated above, the following values of variables can be given:

A: *N.N.* pupil
LOC: in the *n*-th class of the elementary school of the village *V*,
TEM: on the *D*-th day of the month *M* in year *Y*,
TIT: *'John and the books'*.

5.1.8. In order to develop the $TextLiM_1$ (which is the last step of the text-derivation) it is necessary to carry out the K-internal transformations and to linearize the terminal elements obtained, including the placing of the elements enumerated under 5.17. The result of an admissible text-derivation is shown in (**27**).

(**27**) On the *D*-th day of the month *M* in year *Y*

John and the books

John is not interested in books. He does not read books at all.

George, Henry and Steven dislike this. Therefore they decide to do something.

They plan to tell him about good books and to present him with an interesting book. George says, that he wants to tell him about the famous novel of Dickens, called 'Oliver Twist'. Steven has read a science-fiction novel. He says, that he will tell John about it. Henry says, that he wants to tell John about a book on a scientific discovery. The interesting book they want to present him with will be bought by Henry's sister.

They hope, that their plan will be successful.

N.N.pupil,
in the *n*-th class of the elementary school of the village *V*

5.2. The task of the *algorithm for synthesis* is to give an algorithm comprising all admissible possibilities concerning the generation of TextB-s and the application of the formation and transformation rule-system, respectively.

5.2.1. With respect to the formation rule-system this means that an algorithm is needed in order to realize all combinatorial possibilities of the predicate-functions (and their arguments). Namely, the formation rules are unordered and it is (and must be) possible to reach a whole KSeR/KLeR starting with any of the rules. In generating the KSeR-s/KLeR-s one of the most difficult tasks is the application of p^C predicates and the characterization of their arguments such as to direct their application. Most probably the characteristics determining the insertion of the arguments cannot be fixed in the lexicon; the application of a p^C must in each case be preceded by the syntactico-semantic analysis of the respective propositions and S-constituents, respectively.

5.2.2. The development of the Ω-blocks and the set-up of working transformation rules is a more complicated task.

In developing the TextΩ-block the most difficult task is to establish the admissible KB-successions. This requires a thorough semantic analysis of the single KSeR-s. (From this also follows, of course, that if we make the text grammar work as an interpretive grammar, the single KLeR-s must be semantically interpreted before establishing the KB-successions.)

In the course of the semantic analysis, it is first of all necessary to derive all presuppositions and consequences belonging to the given KSeR from the SeR-s building the KSeR and from the entire KSeR itself, respectively. Then it must be possible to establish the admissible anteriority-posteriority and/or simultaneity relations on the basis of the KSeR-set declared to be the potential TextSeR and of the set of presuppositions and consequences which can be assigned to them. Taking these relations into consideration the 'detailed temporal superstructures' built upon the elements τ_i can be developed within the global PAST SIM FUT structure. (To use the terminology of Reichenbach, the set-up of the admissible 'point of speech' – 'point of reference' – 'point of event' relations is concerned here.)

As far as the development of the KΩ-blocks is concerned, the algorithm must allow for the possibility of assigning all admissible KΩ-blocks to all KSeR-s. The problems arising here concern the argument-labels, the informations assigned to the definientes of the single LeR-s and also the syntactic structure of the KSeR-s.

The functioning of the (different types of) transformation rules was outlined in Chapter 2. The synthesis algorithm must, of course, also be capable of commanding the admissible ways of performing these operations.

6. *The Algorithm for the Comparison of Texts*[15]

The disclosure of a possibly existing syntactico-semantic relation between two texts is a basic operation to be carried out, if several theoretical (and applied) linguistic tasks are to be solved. This operation will be called the 'comparison of texts'.

6.1. Concerning the *comparison of texts* I only want to point out one problem here.

The text-grammatical conception presented here must guarantee the 'homogeneity' of the grammar as regards two aspects. One aspect concerns the identical way of handling the linguistic structures of different orders. The point is here the following: since both the definitions in the lexicon and the argument structures themselves are 'text-structures' (they can be conveyed

[15] As regards the problems of the comparison of texts cf. (1971f), (1972e).

into a manifestation consisting of several text-sentences) both must be handled in the same way as the whole of the text is handled. This aspect has been hinted at several times until now.

While the above aspect of homogenetity is first of all of a 'formal' nature, the other aspect concerns the 'content' in so far as it concerns the comparability of texts. Namely the syntactico-semantic comparability of two texts does not only require that the structure of both texts be described globally in the same form but also that the TextB of both texts be built up identically even in their smallest details. In other words this means that the single thematic and communicative nets, the sets of the different kinds of complementing predicates and the internal structure of the single Ω-blocks be normalizable in such a way as to allow for the fact that different analysers of a given text assign TextB-s to the given text which are identical with respect to the whole internal structure, too.

If it is possible to define such a 'normalized internal structure', concerning this structure different kinds of 'reduction'-operations can be given, by means of which it is also possible to establish the hyponymy and hyperonymy relation of texts.

6.2. Concerning this latter aspect of homogeneity *the algorithm for comparison* must contain rules to check whether the TextB-s are normalized or not, rules for normalizing the not normalized TextB-s and rules concerning the performance of the admissible basis-reductions.

7. *Concluding Remarks*

First of all I want to emphasize two points again. The first one concerns the character of the text-grammatical conception outlined here in general, the second one concerns the present stage of elaboration of this conception.

7.1. Concerning the *character* of this conception I want to point out the double aspect of the universality, which is the aim of this conception.

7.1.1. First this conception aims at being universal in that it is intended to serve as a general framework for solving *all* grammatical problems which arise in connection with the constitution of texts of a *given language.* This means, in other words, that it is intended to handle all text-grammatical and sentence-grammatical problems within one homogeneous framework. (The 'discussion of grammatical problems' should, of course, – as it has been exposed in the introduction of this study in detail –, be understood such that all extra-grammatical communicational aspects, which can be considered within a grammar at all, must be taken into consideration, too.)

7.1.2. Furthermore this conception aims at being universal as regards the description of the *universal properties of natural languages.*

Both, the different kinds of predicate functions and the dependency-relations existing among them are, in all probability, of universal character; therefore, the formation rule-system presented here can be conceived as a universal formation rule-system. (When presenting this rule-system the use of such language-specific categories as 'verb', 'noun', etc. was only made to make the interpretation easier. The predicate-functions themselves are always interpreted by the lexicon, where no such categories are needed.) As opposed to the universality of the rule-system, the lexica of the single given languages represent the individual characteristics of the given languages. This means, that this grammar is aimed at being applicable to the description of all languages, the lexica of which are built up according to the requirements of the grammar. (The formation rule-system is, as already referred to, a combinatoric system built upon the elements of the lexicon.)

As far as the transformation rule-system is concerned the aspect of universality and that of individuality can also be shown. (The aspect of individuality appears here, first of all, in the lexicon-informations.)

7.1.3. Since this conception is a *text-grammatical* conception, in the set-up of which the aspect of *universality* plays the basic role, a grammar developed along the lines of this conception will perhaps be more suitable for describing the grammatical system of the single languages than the grammars developed until now. This will also be true for handling such problems, as for example

– the description of the grammatical aspect of the acquisition of the mother-tongue,

– the description of the problems of translation and the carrying out of the translation itself,

– the description of the grammatical aspect of sub-languages (e.g. child-language, dialects, technical sub-languages, etc.) of a given language,

– the description of the language-historical changes of the grammar of languages,

– the description of the grammatical aspect of language-disturbances,

– the carrying out of investigations in the domain of contrastive grammar, etc.

I want to point out finally, that although the grammar developed along the lines of this conception is a formal mechanism, since (almost) all of its categories can also be interpreted empirically and the rule-systems operate on the lexicon items (definitions) of the single languages, it is suitable for being applied in the language teaching of *any* levels. – This fact entails further (interdisciplinary) consequences, too.

7.2. Concerning the *present stage of elaboration* of this conception the following can be said.

The elaboration of this text grammar does not go beyond a detailed theory-outline at present. However, it has already been examined as to its capability of solving different kinds of individual grammatical problems and also as to its applicability from different points of view.

The immediate tasks to be solved are the following:

(a) To set up a system of argument-labels which, on the one hand, functions as the full system of the 'deep-semantic case categories', on the other hand, which allows for the mapping of these 'deep-semantic case categories' onto different kinds of 'surface forms' specific for given languages.

(b) Having the system of argument-labels already at one's disposal to set up a 'defining vocabulary' and a so-called 'minimal lexicon' (1–2000 lexicon items).

(c) Having established such a lexicon, it will be possible, on the one hand, to test and improve the formation rule-system as a synthesizing rule-system and, on the other hand, to elaborate the system of the necessary transformational informations and to develop the transformation rule-system in order to permit the testing of the whole grammar from the aspect of the synthesis and to permit the elaboration of an analysing algorithm.

The elaboration of the system of the transformational informations presupposes the investigation of such important questions as the examination of the aspects of the presuppositions and consequences concerning the lexicon items and the different structures built up from these, and the examination of the internal structural regularities of the admissible $_i$-complexes.

7.3 The tasks and problems enumerated above are in the first line of *grammatical* character, they concern the rule-systems and the algorithms. However, when outlining the broader context of a text grammar it has also been mentioned, that the text grammar is only one (co-textual) component of a text theory, and that it should be set up so as to allow various kinds of con-textual components to be attached to it.

A pair of a co-textual and a con-textual text-theoretical component builds a *partial text theory*. As an example for those tasks which can only be carried out with the aid of a partial text theory consisting of a text grammar and one of the con-textual text-theoretical components, I mentioned the 'further interpretation' of the grammatically analysed text from some aspect, as well as the analysis of the 'text production' and of the 'text reception'. To conclude, I want to make some remarks in connection with these points.

7.3.1. A text grammar, as we have seen it, should make it possible to reveal the 'world' manifesting itself in a text. 'Further interpretation' means in the first line the interpretation of this world, that is the assigning of an '*extensional interpretation*' to it (and its possible comparison with' (an) other world(s).

Extensional interpretation means on the one hand the combinatorial assigning of the predicates 'exists in w_i', 'does not exist in w_i' to the 'objects' of the world-manifestation of the text, on the other hand the combinatorial assigning of the predicates 'true in w_i' 'false in w_i' to the 'facts', 'events', etc. of the world-manifestation of the text. This latter is directed by the text-coherence.

A partial text theory capable of carrying out this task – let us call it a 'text structure world structure theory (TeSWoST)' – is analogous to the theory which e.g. Montague refers to as *universal grammar*. Among the different partial text theories the elaboration of a TeSWoST is of primary importance.

7.3.2. The next step can be – as far as possible already with a theory-outline concerning a TeSWoST at one's disposal – to make attempts at the elaboration of that particular partial text theory, the task of which is the *theoretical description (reconstruction) of the verbal communicative activity*. Let us call this partial text theory 'text structure communication structure theory (TeSCoST)'.

In order to be able to develop a TeSCoST, by means of which the relations of the algorithms and the strategies can be disclosed, it is necessary to start as soon as possible with the empirical investigation of – more or less simple – 'communicative situations' (as for example 'question and answer', 'dialogues', etc.) from both communicative and grammatical points of view.

The 'effectiveness' of a text grammar developed on the basis of the gra m-matical conception outlined here can only be evaluated definitely after having these tasks already solved (and partly possibly in the course of the solution, respectively). However, the solution of these tasks requires common efforts of several researchers (and research-groups).

University of Bielefeld,
Fakultät für Linguistik und
Literaturwisserschaft

BIBLIOGRAPHY

Apresjan, Ju. D., Mel'čuk, I. A., and Zolkovskij, A. K.: 1969, 'Semantics and Lexicography: Towards a New Type of Unilingual Dictionary', in F. Kiefer (ed.), 1969 (see below).

Bach, E. and Harms, R. (eds.): 1968, *Universals in Linguistic Theory*, New York.

Bar Hillel, Y. (ed.): 1971, *Pragmatics of Natural Languages*, Dordrecht.

Chomsky, N.: 1965, *Aspects of the Theory of Syntax*, Cambridge Mass.

Chomsky, N.: 1967, The Formal Nature of Language in E. H. Lenneberg (ed.), 1967.

van Dijk, T. A.: 1972, *Some Aspects of Text Grammars*, The Hague.

van Dijk, T. A., Ihwe, J., Petöfi, J. S., and Rieser, H.: 1971, 'Textgrammatische Grundlagen für eine Theorie narrativer Strukturen', *Linguistische Berichte* **16**, 1–38.

van Dijk, T. A., Ihwe, J., Petöfi, J. S., and Rieser, H.: 1972a, *Zur Bestimmung narrativer Strukturen auf der Grundlage von Textgrammatiken* (= *Papiere zur Text-linguistik/Papers in Textlinguistics*, Band 1).

van Dijk, T. A., Ihwe, J., Petöfi, J. S., and Rieser, H.: 1972b, 'Two Text Grammatical Models; A Contribution to Formal Linguistics and the Theory of Narrative', *Foundations of Language* **8**, 499–545.

Fillmore, C. J.: 1968, 'The Case for Case', in E. Bach and R. Harms (eds.), 1968.

Fillmore, C. J.: 1971, 'Some Problems for Case Grammar', in C. J. Fillmore (ed.), 1971.

Fillmore, C. J. (ed.): 1971, *Working Papers in Linguistics No. 10*, The Ohio State University.

Harrah, D.: 1963, *Communication: A Logical Model*, Cambridge, Mass.

Hartmann, P. and Rieser, H. (eds.): 1973, *Angewandte Textlinguistik I* (= *Papiere zur Textlinguistik/Papers in Textlinguistics*, Band 2), Hamburg.

Ihwe, J.: 1972, *Linguistik in der Literaturwissenschaft. Zur Entwicklung einer modernen Theorie der Literaturwissenschaft* (= *Grundfragen der Literaturwissenschaft* **4**), München. (An English version is to appear in the series 'De proprietatibus litterarum', The Hague.)

Ihwe, J. (ed.): 1972, *Literaturwissenschaft und Linguistik. Ergebnisse und Perspektiven*, I-III., Frankfurt.

Katz, J. J. and Fodor, J. A.: 1963, 'The Structure of a Semantic Theory, *Language* **39**, 170–211.

Katz. J.J. and Fodor, J. A.: 1970, 'Interpretive Semantics vs. Generative Semantics', *Foundations of Language* **6**, 220–259.

Kiefer, F. (ed.): 1969, *Studies in Syntax and Semantics*, Dordrecht.

Koch, W. A. (ed.): 1972, *Structurelle Textanalyse – Analyse du récit – Discourse Analysis*, Hildesheim.

Lakoff, G.: 1971, 'Linguistics and Natural Logic', *Synthese* **22**, 151–271.

Lakoff, G.: 1971, 'On Generative Semantics', in D. D. Steinberg and L. A. Jakobovits (eds.), 1971.

Lenneberg, E. H. (ed.): 1967, *Biological Foundation of Language*, New York.

Maclay, H.: 1971, 'Linguistics', Overview, in D. D. Steinberg and Jakobovits L. A. (eds.), 1971.

McCawley, J.: 1967, 'Meaning and the Description of Languages', *Kotoba No Uchu 2*.

McCawley, J.: 1968, 'Concerning the Base Component of a Transformational Grammar, *Foundations of Language* **4**, 243–269.

Petöfi, J. S.: 1967a, 'Some Problems of the Linguistic Analysis of Poetic Works of Art', *Actes du Xe Congrès International des Linguistes Bucarest 1967* III, Bucarest, 1970.

Petöfi, J. S.: 1967*b*, 'On the Structural Linguistic Analysis of Poetic Works of Art', *Computational Linguistics VI*, Budapest; also in W. A. Koch (ed.), 1972.

Petöfi, J. S.: 1968, 'Notes on the Semantic Interpretation of Verbal Works of Art', *Computational Linguistics VII*, Budapest; in German translation in J. Ihwe (ed.), 1972.

Petöfi, J. S.: 1969a, 'On the Structural Analysis and Typology of Poetic Images', in F. Kiefer (ed.), 1969.

Petöfi, J. S.: 1969b, 'On the Problems of Co-textual Analysis of Texts', COLING (International Conference on Computational Linguistics in Stockholm), Preprint No. 50; in German translation in J. Ihwe (ed.), 1972.

Petöfi, J. S.: 1969c, 'On the Linear Patterning of Verbal Works of Art', *Computational Linguistics VIII*, Budapest.

Petöfi, J. S.: 1969d, 'On the Complex Analysis of Languages as Synchronic Systems', *Revue (Liège)* **1**, 1–18.

Petöfi, J. S.: 1969e, cf. 1971i.

Petöfi, J. S.: 1970, 'Von der Explikation des Begriffes 'Satz' zu der 'Explikation der Texte'' (Zur Frage einer generellen Text-theorie), Preprint, University of Gothenburg, Research Group for Modern Swedish.

Petöfi, J. S.: 1971a, 'Zur strukturellen Analyse sprachlicher Kunstwerke', in J. Ihwe (ed.), 1972.

Petöfi, J. S.: 1971b, *Transformationsgrammatiken und eine ko-textuelle Texttheorie. Grundfragen und Konzeptionen*, Frankfurt.

Petöfi, J. S.: 1971c, 'Transformationsgrammatiken und die grammatische Beschreibung der Texte', *Linguistische Berichte* **14**, 17–33.

Petöfi, J. S.: 1971d, cf. 1972a.

Petöfi, J. S.: 1971e, 'Towards a Grammatical Theory of Verbal Texts', *Working Paper*, University of Gothenburg, Research Group for Modern Swedish; in German translation *LiLi, Zeitschrift für Literaturwissenschaft und Linguistik* **2** (1972), 31–58.

Petöfi, J. S.: 1971f, ''Generativity' and Textgrammar', *Gothenburg Papers in Theoretical Linguistics* **9**, also *Folia Linguistica* **V** (1972), 277–309.

Petöfi, J. S.: 1971g, 'Modell (2)' (in Zusammenarbeit mit J. Ihwe), in T. A. van Dijk, J. Ihwe, J. S. Petöfi, H. Rieser, 1971; in English translation in T. A. van Dijk, J. Ihwe, J. S. Petöfi and H. Rieser, 1972b.

Petöfi, J. S.: 1971h, 'Problems of the Syntactico-Semantic Aspects of the 'Lexicon-structure'' (Motives and outline of a lexicological project), *Working Paper*, University of Gothenburg, Research Group for Modern Swedish.

Petöfi, J. S. 1971i, 'On the Comparative Structural Analysis of Different Types of 'Works of Art'', *Semiotica* **III**, 355–378.

Petöfi, J. S.: 1972a, 'On the Syntactico-Semantic Organization of Text-Structures', *Poetics* **3**, 56–99.

Petöfi, J. S.: 1972b, 'Modell (2)' (In Zusammenarbeit mit J. Ihwe), in T. A. van Dijk, J. Ihwe, J. S. Petöfi, and H. Rieser.: 1972a.

Petöfi, J. S.: 1972c, 'Textlinguistic aspects in the Grammatical Theory of Sentence', *Actes du XI*[e] *Congrès International des Linguistes Bologna 1972.*

Petöfi, J. S.: 1972d, 'Text Grammars, Text Theory and the Theory of Literature', To appear *Poetics* **7**, 36–76.

Petöfi, J. S. 1972e, 'Juristische Texte und eine Textgrammatik mit nicht-linear festgelegten Basis', in D. Rave *et al.* (eds.), 1972; also in P. Hartmann and H. Rieser (eds.), 1972.

Petöfi, J. S.: 1972f, 'Zum Aufbau eines 'Lexikons'', in D. Rave *et al.* (eds.), 1972; also in P. Hartmann and H. Rieser (eds.), 1972.

Petöfi, J. S.: 1972g, 'Sprachunterricht und eine Textgrammatik mit nicht-linear festgelegten Basis', in P. Hartmann and H. Rieser (eds.), 1972.

Petöfi, J. S.: 1972h, 'Einige Probleme der Repräsentation der 'Argumente' im Rahmen einer Textgrammatik', in M. Rüttenauer (ed.), 1973.

Petöfi, J. S.: *Towards a Well-Defined 'Defining Vocabulary'*, in prep.

Petöfi, J. S. and Franck, D. (eds.): 1973, *Präsuppositionen in Philosophie und Linguistik/ Presuppositions in Philosophy and Linguistics*, Frankfurt.

Petöfi, J. S. and Rieser, H.: 1972a, 'Wissenschaftstheoretische Argumente für eine umfassende grammatische Theorie und eine logisch-semantische Beschreibungssprache', in M. Rüttenauer (ed.), 1973; also in *Folia Linguistica* **VI** (1973).

Petöfi, J. S. and Rieser, H.: 1972b, 'Präsuppositionen und Folgerungen in der Textgrammatik', in J. S. Petöfi and D. Franck (eds.), 1972.

Postal, P. M.: 1970, 'On the Surface Verb 'remind'', *Linguistic Inquiry* **1**, 37–120.

Rave, D., Brinckmann, H., and Grimmer, K. (eds.): 1972, *Syntax und Semantik juristischer Texte.* Referate und Protokolle der Arbeitstagung im Deutsches Rechenzentrum Darmstadt, 11. bis 13. Mai 1972.

Rüttenauer, M. (ed.): 1973, *Konstanzer Textlinguistikkolloquium 1972* (= *Papiere zur Textlinguistik/Papers in Textlinguistics*, Band 3), Hamburg.
Schmidt, S. J.: 1973, *Texttheorie. Probleme einer Linguistik der sprachlichen Kommunikation*, München.
Sebeok, T. A. (ed.): 1966, *Current Trends in Linguistics* **III**, The Hague.
Seuren, P.: 1969, *Operators and Nucleus. A Contribution to the Theory of Grammar*, Cambridge.
Steinberg, D. D. and Jakobovits, L. A. (eds.): 1971, *Semantics. An Interdisciplinary Reader in Philosophy Linguistics and Psychology*, Cambridge.
Weinreich, U.: 1966, 'Explorations in Semantic Theory', in T. A. Sebeok (ed.), 1966.
Žolkovskij, A. K. and Mel'čuk, I. A.: 1967, 'O semantičeskom sintéze', *Problemy Kibernetiki* **19**, 177–238.

** Since the completion of this study first steps have been made in the analysis of the problems of the 'partial text theory' mentioned in point 7.3.1. Studies dealing with this topic are contained in Petöfi, J. S. and Rieser, H.: 1973, *Probleme der modelltheoretischen Interpretation von Texten* (= *Papiere zur Textlinguistik/Papers in Textlinguistics* **7**), Hamburg: Buske.

HANNES RIESER

SENTENCE GRAMMAR, TEXT GRAMMAR, AND THE EVALUATION PROBLEM

Some Remarks Concerning the Theoretical Foundation and the Possible Application of Text Grammars

0. The text grammars set up so far generalize the formal properties of specific types of sentence grammar.[1] This procedure, widely accepted among text linguists, led us to the assumption that text grammars developed from a specific type of sentence grammar will have the formal and empirical properties of this model sentence grammar. This assumption will be dealt with in this paper.[2] Another feature of the text grammars set up so far is closely connected with the theoretical and practical aims such text grammars try to meet: We think that not only the sentence grammar chosen as a model for the construction of a text grammar and the practical interests which led to its construction determine its theoretical power but also its supposed domain of application. Thus the meta-theoretical part of a text grammar may include the postulate that the grammar must reconstruct the semantic relations between two arbitrary texts belonging to a certain extensionally delimitable subset of the set of all texts of a natural language. This subset might e.g. consist of the legal texts valid during some time interval. The domain of application of the text grammar in question would then be this subset of the set of all texts of a given natural language.[3] If two text grammars are said to obey the same theoretical postulates and to cover the same domain of application it may be inferred that the text grammars in question are equivalent relative to the underlying theoretical postulates and the chosen domain of application. Supposing now that one grammar out of the two proves to be more successful in meeting the theoretical postulates and in covering the pre-set domain of application, then this success would naturally count strongly against the other type of text grammar. The test as to whether two text grammars are equivalent relative to a given domain of application may thus serve as an evaluation procedure and, as far as we can judge, this kind of evaluation, informal and intuitive as it may be, is at least one possible way to get better and more powerful text grammars. It must be added that the

[1] Cf. e.g. J. S. Petöfi's goal to set up a text grammar according to the principles of generative semantics in [19], pp. 248–273, [21], pp. 33–47 and [24]; van Dijk treats somewhat analogous problems in [7], pp. 12–23 and 34–159; the question of the generalizability of PSGs is discussed in [30], [31], [32], and [33].

[2] This hypothesis was discussed first in [3], [32], and [33].

[3] This specific domain of application was chosen for practical reasons, cf. [3], [27], and [28] for further information. Other interesting domains of application are discussed by T. A. van Dijk, J. Ihwe and J. S. Petöfi in their contributions to this volume.

J. S. Petöfi and H. Rieser (eds.), Studies in Text Grammar, 276–299.

kind of evaluation proposed is not only of considerable theoretical interest but also of practical importance to those linguists, who want to apply the findings of text linguistics to the solution of practical problems, e.g. the reconstruction of the semantics of subsumption and argumentation in jurisdiction.

Naturally this test or other tests could provide reasonable answers to the question whether some field of text linguistic research proves to be empirically relevant, i.e. useful for meeting some stateable practical interests. We think that this notion of empirical relevance should guide the theoreticians work. Let us consider the first hypothesis concerning a sentence grammar, serving as the model for a text grammar:

(a1) Let G_i be a sentence grammar defined by a set of formal properties $F(G_i)$.

(a2) G_i generates a set of sentences (a language) L_d^1.

(a3) L_d^1 can be mapped into L_d^0, the corresponding set of utterances of the object language in question.

(a4) L_d^1 proves to be incomplete if it is compared with L_d^1, i.e. $[L_d^1]^0 \subset \subset L_d^0$ may be asserted. $[L_d^1]^0$ is the image of L_d^1 in L_d^0.

(a5) $[L_d^1]^0 \subset L_d^0$ serves as a sufficient criterion for the empirical inadequacy of G_i.

(a6) The empirical inadequacy of G_i is considered to be the result of a set of formal properties $R(G_i)$, where $R(G_i) \subset F(G_i)$.

(a1′) Let TEG_i be a text grammar with $F(TEG_i)$ such that there is a partial syntactic isomorphism between G_i and TEG_i, or such that G_i is a proper sub-grammar of TEG_i, then the following hypotheses may be valid:

(a2′) TEG_i generates a set of texts (a language) $\mathscr{L}_d^1$.

(a3′) $\mathscr{L}_d^1$ can be mapped into $\mathscr{L}_d^0$, the corresponding set of texts of the object language in question.

(a4′) $\mathscr{L}_d^1$ proves to be incomplete if it is compared with $\mathscr{L}_d^0$, i.e. $[\mathscr{L}_d^1]^0 \subset \mathscr{L}_d^0$. $[\mathscr{L}_d^1]^0$ is the image of $\mathscr{L}_d^1$ in $\mathscr{L}_d^0$.

(a5′) $[\mathscr{L}_d^1]^0 \subset \mathscr{L}_d^0$ serves as a sufficient criterion for the empirical inadequacy of TEG_i.

(a6′) The empirical inadequacy of TEG_i is considered to be the result of a set of formal properties $R(TEG_i)$, where $R(TEG_i) \subset \subset F(TEG_i)$.

If TEG_i does not contain any rules which modify the sub-grammar G_i then it is resaonable to assume that the proof of empirical inadequacy may be given for G_i first and may then be generalized with respect to TEG_i.

In the following we try to provide such a proof with respect to a certain type of sentence grammar, namely a context-free phrase structure grammar (PSG)[4] specifying a set of sentences the elements of which are considered to be theoretical equivalents of norms or directives of the German language of jurisdiction. The German language is the object language, the German language of jurisdiction is regarded as a proper subset of this object language.

1. Some remarks on the meta-theoretical postulates and conventions to be used

1.1. Let L_d^0 be the set of all utterances $\{SAT_1^0, \ldots, SAT_n^0\}$ spoken or written at a given time interval T, i.e. the object language. The subscript 'd' indicates that the object language in question is German; the superscript 'o' indicates that the theoretical level of L_d^0 is 0 (= zero), which means that *neither its syntax nor its semantics have been explicitely stated.*

1.2. A sentence grammar $G_{d_i}(L_d^0)$ is defined as a quadruple of sets: $G_{d_i} = \langle VNT, VT, R_{sy}, R_{se} \rangle$.

1.2.1. VNT is a set of nonterminals, i.e. a finite set of syntactic categories whose elements are set up by *operational definition.*

We call a parsing procedure, leading to a denumerable set of well-defined syntactic categories *taxonomical classification.* This taxonomical classification provides the syntactical elements for a descriptional language (a meta-language defined on L_d^0).

In VNT a set VNT_{se} of syntactic-semantic categories is included (cf. 2.2.1. and 2.2.2.).

1.2.2. VT is a set of semantically interpreted terminals, i.e. a set of objects that correspond to the words of L_d^0, where $VNT \cap VT = \emptyset$.

1.2.3. $VNT \cup VT$ constitute V, the vocabulary or alphabet of $G_{d_i}(L_d^0)$.

1.2.4. R_{sy} is a finite set of syntactic rules defined on VNT.

1.2.5. R_{se} is a finite set of semantic rules defined on VNT and VT, such that $R_{se_i}(A_i, a_i)$, where $A_i \in VNT$ and $a_i \in VT$.

1.3. L_d^0 provides the empirical basis for the construction of G_{d_i}.

1.4. All and only the sentences generated by G_{d_i} are elements of the set of sentences (of the language) L_d^1.

G_{d_i} enumerates all and only the sentences $\{SAT_1^1, \ldots, SAT_n^1\}$ of the language L_d^1. There exists an isomorphism between L_d^1 and a (proper) subset of L_d^0.

[4] For a discussion of the properties of PSG's cf. [11], pp. 81–118, pp. 183–186, pp. 217–229; for a practical application of PSG's cf. [4] and [5].

$SAT_i^1 \in L_d^1$ is said to be confirmed, if at least one speaker of L_d^0 asserts the isomorphism $IS(SAT_i^1, SAT_i^0)$ as valid and if this assertion can be repeated within a stated time interval C.

1.5. G_{d_i} permits the recursive definition of $\{SAT_1^1, \ldots, SAT_n^1\}$, $SAT_i^1 \in L_d^1$. G_{d_i} serves as an enumerating algorithm as well as an algorithm to be used for recognition tests. This is equivalent to saying that G_{d_i} enumerates $\{SAT_1^1, \ldots, SAT_n^1\}$ on the one hand and that on the other hand it is possible to submit $SAT_i^1 \in L_d^0$ to G_{d_i} and to decide after a finite number of operations whether the corresponding SAT_i^1 belongs to L_d^1.

If this recognition test proves to be successful for a set $\{SAT_i^0, \ldots, SAT_r^0\}$, $SAT_i^0 \in L_d^0$, we say that G_{d_i} generates a decidable sub-language of L_d^0.

1.6. $R_{sy_{n+1}}$ may be added to R_{sy}, if $R_{sy_{n+i}}$ is used in the derivation of SAT_i^1 and if $IS(SAT_i^1, SAT_i^0)$ is valid.

Analogous conditions hold for $VNT \cup \{A_{n+i}\}$, $VT \cup \{a_{n+i}\}$, and $R_{se} \cup \cup \{R_{se_{n+i}}\}$. Clearly the reverse operation of reduction is also possible; this operation leads to the contraction of G_{d_i}.

2. SOME INFORMAL REMARKS ON THE STRUCTURE OF G_{d_i}, I.E. THE PHRASE STRUCTURE GRAMMAR (PSG) TO BE USED[5]

2.1. The syntactic component of G_{d_i} consists of a set of binary (cf. e.g. rules 9, 10, 11 on pp. 282–83) and monary context-free phrase structure rules. The complex syntactic categories constituting *VNT* consist of main categories and sub-categories. These complex categories are considered as variables. Since at least one rule of R_{sy} is recursive, G_{d_i} generates an infinite language. When a proof within G_{d_i} is given, i.e. when SAT_i^1 is derived, it has to be decided, how often a recursive rule must apply and which categorial constants must be chosen. The first decision determines the length of the resulting (non-) terminal string, the second decision determines agreement as to gender, number, case, tense, and mood (cf. p. 282).

2.2. The assignment of syntactic categories to the corresponding semantic categories as proposed here provides a necessary but certainly not a sufficient stage in the development of an interpretative semantic component. In the present stage of elaboration this semantic component is restricted to the descriptively adequate definition of sense relations between the lexical units constituting *VT*, between sub-trees within a theorem SAT_i^1 and between distinct theorems SAT_i^1, SAT_k^1. This semantic component does not

[5] This grammar was developed in [8], [9], [10], [30], [31], and [33].

attempt to treat contextual, i.e. referential and world-(or model-)related 'well-formedness'.

In this stage of development, the semantic component of G_{d_1} consists of:

2.2.1. an ordered string of pre-preterminal complex syntactic categories $\langle X_1,\ldots, X_n\rangle$, to which definite semantic interpretations are assigned by rewrite rules (productions) of the form: $X_i : X_i(d_j)$,

2.2.2. lexical entries (nonterminals), defined as the ordered pairs $x_i(d_j)$ consisting of the graphematic sequence x_i and a set of semantic features d_j,
2.2.3. the condition that a rewrite-rule $X_i(d_j) : x_i(d_j)$ applies iff $d_{jX_i} = d_{jx_i}$ (cf. p. 283).

2.3. The complex category d_j consists of:

2.3.1. a basic semanteme that is either axiomatically set up or derived as a theorem from a given set of axioms; such basic semantemes receive arbitrary names (cf. p. 284, BEIM, EINBIEG, DER, ANDER etc.),

2.3.2. secondary semantemes which are assigned to their corresponding syntactic main categories and sub-categories necessary for the syntactic description of L_d^0 (cf. p. 284, cas (1)*, num (1)*, gen (1)*, ADJ (0.1)* etc.; secondary semantemes are considered as functions of basic semantemes or as functions of incomplete semantic categories of the nth degree.

2.4. The semantically interpreted ordered sequences of graphemes $\langle x_1(d_j), \ldots, x_n(d_r)\rangle$ are assigned to their directly dominating semantically interpreted syntactic categories $\langle X_1(d_i), \ldots, X_n(d_r)\rangle$.

This assignment procedure is repeated continually until the higher syntactically labelled nodes are reached. The position of the lexical entries in the higher nodes thus corresponds from left to right to their position in the terminal string, i.e. the semantic ordering relation is determined by syntactic ordering relations.

In the actual stage of development of this model the double information caused by the synthetically determined substitution rules is of no importance. This redundancy is motivated, however, by the provision of further extension. That is, if additional necessary semantic parameters (e.g. selection restrictions for NOP and HAV representing ontological 'well-formedness'; co-textual and world -(model-) related referential indices; truth functions of the sentences in texts; presuppositions, etc.) are known so as to allow of formulation in the form of general rules, the proposed substitution rules will be justified.

3. Specification of the Categories Used

3.1. *Main Categories of VNT*

ADJ(0.1)	adjective in the positive degree
ADV	adverb
ART(2)	indefinite article
HAV	verbal constituent directly dominating VEF(typ) and INF(typ)
INF(3)	prefix+'zu'+infinitive, e.g. *auszuführen, auszulöschen,* etc.
NOM(0)	substantive which selects PRA(typ) but not ART(typ)
NOM(2)	substantive which selects ART(2)
NOP	nominal phrase, e.g. ART(2)+ADJ(0.1)+NOM(2) etc.
NPP	prepositional phrase, e.g. PRE(1)+ART(2)+NOM(2); PRA(2)+NOM(0) etc.
PRA(2)	complex preposition; preposition in the dative case+ dative morpheme of the definite article, e.g. *beim, zum* etc.
PRE(1)	simple preposition in the accusative case
SAT[IMP](1)	imperative sentence with inversion of NOP gen num cas(0) and VEF(typ) per num tem mod(3) for pos(1)
VEF(3)	finite verb, directly dominating VEF(3) per num tem mod for pos and NOP gen num cas(0).

3.2. *Sub-Categories*

gen(∅, 1, 2, 3)	indices for genus
num(∅, 1, 2)	indices for number
cas(∅, 0, 3, 2, 1)	indices for case
per(∅, 1, 2, 3)	indices for person
tem(∅, 0, 1, 2, 3, 4, 5)	indices for tense
mod(∅, 1, 2, 3)	indices for mood, e.g. (0) = indicative, (1) = subjunctive 1, (2) = subjunctive 2, (3) = imperative
for(1, 2)	indices for active and passive
pos(0, 1, 2)	indices for the position of HAV and VEF(typ), e.g. (0) = normal position, (1) = inversion, (2) = = final position of HAV or VEF(typ)

3.3. *Numerical and Other Indices*

(typ)	variable, index for types of ADJ, ART, INF, VEF
[1]	index indicating position or distinction of complex categories which consist of main and sub-categories
NOM(0)*	asterisk indicating the semantic category corresponding to the syntactic category NOM(0)

*i.	asterisk assigned to the number of a rule, indicating that some specific applicability-conditions are required for its operation
:	symbol equivalent to the rewrite symbol

3.4. *Semantic Relations*

ANTO(ENG, WEIT)	symmetrical relation of antonymy between e.g. the basic semantemes 'ENG' and 'WEIT'
HYPO(BLU, ROS)	non-symmetrical relation of hyperonymy between e.g. the basic semantemes 'BLU' and 'ROS'
SYNO(ARE, REE)	symmetrical relation of synonymy between e.g. the basic semantemes 'ARE' and 'REE'

4. A SENTENCE GRAMMAR G_{d_1} GENERATING A SET OF SENTENCES (A LANGUAGE L_d^0) OF WHICH THE SENTENCE SAT[IMP]$(1)_1^1$ IS AN ELEMENT

4.1. *Syntactic Rules*

(1)	SAT [IMP](1)	:	NPPgen(3) num(1) cas(2) HAVper(3) num(1) pos(1)
(2)	NPPgen(3) num(1) cas(2)	:	NPPgen(3) num(1) cas(2) NPPgen(2) num(1) cas(1)
(3)	NPPgen(3) num(1) cas(2)	:	PRA(2) NOM(0) gen(3) num(1) cas(2)
(4)	NPPgen(2) num(1) cas(1)	:	PRE(1) NOPgen(2) num(1) cas(1)
(5)	NOPgen(2) num(1) cas(1)	:	ART(2)gen(2) num(1) cas(1) NOM(2)gen(2) num(1) cas(1)
(6)	NOM(2)gen(2) num(1) cas(1)	:	ADJ(0.1)gen(2) num(2) cas(1) NOM(2)gen(2) num(1) cas(1)
(7)	HAVper(3) num(1) pos(1)	:	VEF(3)per(3) num(1) tem(0) mod(3) for(2) pos(1) INF(3)
(8)	VEF(3)per(3) num(1) tem(0) mod(3) for(2) pos(1)	:	VEF(3)per(3) num(1) tem(0) mod(3) for(2) pos(1) NOP[1]gen(1) num(1) cas(0)
(9)	NOP[1]gen(1) num(1) cas(0).	:	ART(2)[1]gen(1) num(1) cas(0) NOM(2)[1]gen(1) num(1) cas(0)
(10)	NOM(2)[1]gen(1) num(1) cas(0)	:	ADJ(0.1)[1]gen(1) num(1) cas(0) NOM(2)[1]gen(1) num(1) cas(0)

(11)	VEF(3)per(3) num(1) tem(0) mod(3) for(2) pos(1)	:	VEF(3)per(3) num(1) tem(0) mod(3) for(2) pos(1) ADV[1]
(12)	ADV[1]	:	PRE(2)[1] ADV[1]
(13)	VEF(3)per(3) num(1) tem(0) mod(3) for(2) pos(1)	:	VEF(3)per(3) num(1) tem(0) mod(3) for(2) pos(1) NOP[2]gen(1) num(1) cas(0)
(*14)	NOP[2]gen(1) num(1) cas(0):	:	ART(2)[2]gen(1) num(1) cas(0) ADJ(0.1)[2]gen(1) num(1) cas(0)
(15)	VEF(3)per(3) num(1) tem(0) mod(3) for(2) pos(1)	:	VEF(3)per(3) num(1) tem(0) mod(3) for(2) pos(1) ADV[2]
(16)	ADV[2]	:	PRE(2)[2] ADV[2]

4.2. *Semantic Rules*

(17)	PRA(2)	:	PRA(2) (PRA(2)*(BEIM))
(18)	NOM(0)gen(3) num(1) cas(2)	:	NOM(0)gen(3) num(1) cas(2) (cas(2)*(num(1)*(gen(3)* (NOM(0)*(EINBIEG)))))
(19)	PRE(1)	:	PRE(1)(PRE(1)*(IN))
(20)	ART(2)gen(2) num(1) cas(1)	:	ART(2)gen(2) num(1) cas(1) (cas(1)*(num(1)*(gen(2)* ART(2)*(DER)))))
(21)	ADJ(0.1)gen(2) num(1) cas(1)	:	ADJ(0.1)gen(2) num(1) cas(1) (cas(1)*(num(1)*(gen(2)* (ADJ(0.1)*(ANDER)))))
(22)	NOM(2)gen(2) num(1) cas(1)	:	NOM(2)gen(2) num(1) cas(1) (cas(1)*(num(1)*(gen(2)* (NOM(2)*(STRASS)))))
(23)	INF(3)	:	INF(3)(INF(3)*(AUSFÜHR))
(24)	ART(2)[1, 2]gen(1) num(1) cas(0)	:	ART(2)(1, 2)gen(1) num(1) cas(0)(cas(0)*(num(1)*(gen(1)* ART(2)*(DER)))))

(25) ADJ(0.1)[1]gen(1) num(1) cas(0) : ADJ(0.1)(1)gen(1) num(1) cas(0)(cas(0)*(num(1)*(gen(1)*(ADJ(0.1)*(ANTO(WEIT, ENG))))))

(26) NOM(2)[1]gen(1) num(1) cas(0) : NOM(2)[1]gen(1) num(1) cas(0) (cas(0)*(num(1)*(gen(1)*(NOM(2)*(BOG)))))

(27) PRE(2)[1, 2] : PRE(2)[1, 2](PRE(2)*(NACH))

(28) ADV[1] : ADV[1](ADV*(ANTO (LINKS, RECHTS)))

(29) ADJ(0.1)[2]gen(1) num(1) cas(0) : ADJ(0.1)[2]gen(1) num(1) cas(0)(cas(0)*(num(1)*(gen(1)*(ADJ(0.1)*(HYPO(ANTO (ENG, WEIT), BOG)))))))

(30) VEF(3)per(3) num(1) tem(0) mod(3) for(2) pos(1) : VEF(3)per(3) num(1) tem(0) mod(3) for(2) pos(1)(pos(1)*(for(2)*(mod(3)*(tem(0)*(num(1)*(per(3)*(VEF(3)*(sein))))))))

(31) ADV[2] : ADV[2](ADV*(ANTO (RECHTS, LINKS)

4.3. *Lexical Entries with Specified Readings*

andere(cas(1)*(num(1)*(gen(2)*(ADJ(0.1)*(ANDER)))))
auszuführen(INF(3)*(AUSFÜHR))
beim(PRA(2)*(BEIM))
bogen(cas(0)*(num(1)*(gen(1)*(NOM(2)*(BOG)))))
ein(cas(0)*(num(1)*(gen(1)*(ART(2)*(DER)))))
einbiegen(cas(2)*(num(1)*(gen(3)*(NOM(0)*(EINBIEG)))))
eine(cas(1)*(num(1)*(gen(2)*(ART(2)*(DER)))))
enger(cas(0)*(num(1)*(gen(1)*(ADJ(0.1)*(HYPO(ANTO(ENG, WEIT), BOG)))))))
in(PRE(1)*(IN))
ist(pos(1)*(for(2)*(mod(3)*(tem(0)*(num(1)*(per(3)*(VEF(3)*(SEIN))))))))
links(ADV*(ANTO(LINKS, RECHTS)))
nach(PRE(2)*(NACH))
rechts(ADV*(ANTO(RECHTS, LINKS)))

straße(cas(1)*(num(1)*(gen(2)*(NOM(2)*(STRASS)))))
weiter(cas(0)*(num(1)*(gen(1)*(ADJ(0.1)*(ANTO(WEIT, ENG))))))

4.4. *An Applicability Condition for Rule* (*14)

Rule(*14) is a rule not usually contained in a PSG. Usually, a well-defined NOP[1]gen num cas is expanded into

ART(typ)[i]gen num cas
NOM(typ[i]gen num cas.

Because of rule 6 NOM(typ)[i]gen num cas can be recursively expanded into

ADJ(typ[i]gen num cas
NOM(typ[i]gen num cas.

The expansion of *NOP[k]gen num cas into

ART(typ)[k]gen num cas
ADJ(typ)[k]gen num cas

is permitted in the derivation (proof) of $\mathrm{SAT(typ)}_i^1$, iff

(1) corresponding rules of the form
NOP[i]gen num cas : ART(typ)[i]gen num cas
NOM(typ)[i]gen num cas
NOM(typ)[i]gen num cas: ADJ(typ)[i]gen num cas
NOM(typ)[i]gen num cas
have been used in the derivation of $\mathrm{SAT(typ)}_j^1$, *and*

(2) If the semanteme SEM_k assigned to ADJ(typ)[k] in the lexicon is marked as being hyperonymous to the semanteme SEM_i which is assigned to NOM(typ)[i]:

ADJ(typ[k]... (ADJ(typ)[k]*(HYPO(SEM_k, SEM_i))).

This applicability condition is neoessary for PSGs, because these grammars do not contain transformation such as nominslization, pronominalizaiion, deletion etc.

5. Some arguments for the delimitation of a sub-grammar $_j\mathrm{G}_{d_i}$ based on syntax and semantics, i.e. a grammar enumerating only sentences (norms, directives) belonging to the German language of jurisdiction

5.1. G_{di} generates the terminal string of $\mathrm{SAT[IMP](1)}_1^1$ (cf. Figure 1):

(1) *beim einbiegen in eine andere straße ist nach rechts ein enger nach links ein weiter bogen auszuführen*

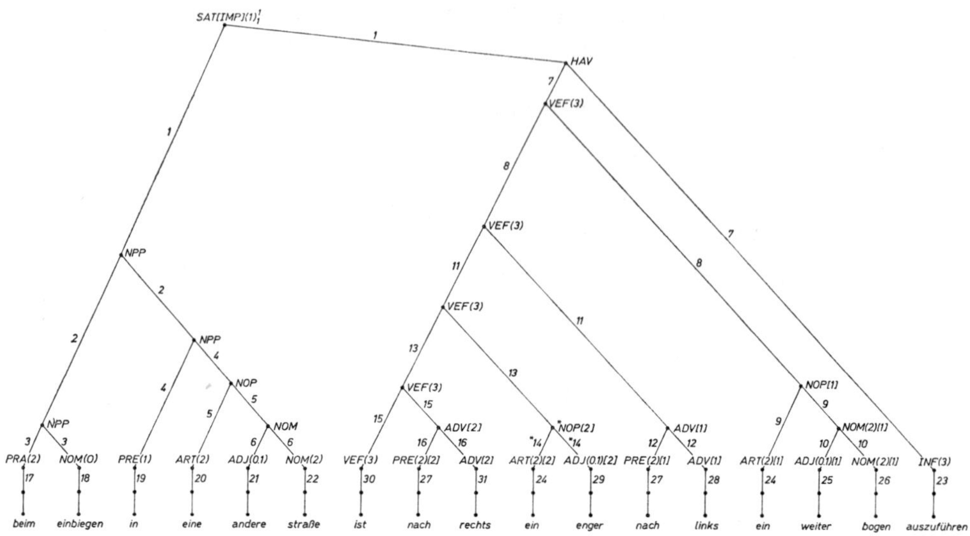

Fig. 1.

and the structural description belonging to this string. The application of the set of rules permits the construction of a finite directed graph, therefore subderivations (nonterminal sentences) and terminated derivations leading to the ultimate string (theorem) can be presented as a treediagram (cf. Figure 1).

SAT[IMP]$(1)_1^1$ counts as an element of the set of sentences L_d^1, which can be mapped into the set of utterances constituting L_d^0.

Because of the recursive rules 2, 6, 8, 10, 11, 13, *14, and 15 also a SAT [IMP]$(1)_1^1$ with the terminal string

(1) *beim einbiegen in eine andere straße in eine andere andere... andere straße in eine andere andere andere andere... andere straße ist nach rechts nach rechts nach rechts... ein enger enger enger... nach links nach links nach links nach links... ein weiter weiter weiter... bogen auszuführen*

can be derived.

Now, G_{d_i} *must contain* rules like 2, 6, 8, 10, 11, 13, *14, 15 if it is to account for the fact that the set of utterances constituting L_d^0 is infinite, i.e. that every utterance may contain an unlimited number of prepositional phrases, nominal phrases, adjectives in attributive position and adverbs and may therefore be of unbounded length (degree).

If only SAT[IMP] $(1)_1^1$ has to be derived, the property of recursiveness must be restricted or eliminated, i.e. rules 2, 6, 8, 10, 11, 13, *14, and 15 may apply not more than once. Because of this restriction in generality of G_{d_1} we get a formally delimitable proper subset of L^1_d which thus far contains only one element, namely ${}_j\mathrm{SAT[IMP](1)}^1_1$, a sentence belonging to the theoretically reconstructible language of jurisdiction ${}_jL^0_d$. This sentence is identical with the sentence (1) given above.

5.2. If L^1_d is to be enumerated one has to permit that the adjectives and adverbs introduced by the rules 10, 11, 12, 15, and 16 be permuted, because for the following sentences (i) and (k) $\mathrm{IS(SAT[IMP](1)}^1_i, \mathrm{SAT[IMP](1)}^0_i)$ and $\mathrm{IS(SAT[IMP](1)}^1_k, \mathrm{SAT[IMP](1)}^0_k)$ can be asserted:

(i) *beim einbiegen in eine andere straße ist nach links ein enger nach rechts ein weiter bogen auszuführen*

(k) *beim einbiegen in eine andere straße ist nach rechts ein weiter nach links ein enger bogen auszuführen.*

For the proper subset of L^1_d, ${}_jL^1_d$, however, (i) and (k) cannot be valid, because they clearly contradict (1). ((1) is valid by convention, i.e. as a directive or a norm set up by official institutions.) When G_{d_1} was set up, this fact had already been accounted for by the introduction of the selectional indices [1], [2]. The indices [1], [2] lead, if applied, to the result, that ADV[1], terminated as *links*, is only derivable together with ADJ(0.1)[1], terminated as *weit*, and that ADV[2], terminated as *rechts*, is only derivable together with ADJ(0.1)[2], terminated as *eng*. Therefore we can say that a further property of the sub-language ${}_jL^1_d$ is given by the fact that it must be delimited formally by the use of specific selectional indices.

5.3. Clearly this sub-language of L^1_d must be defined by an additional set of semantic properties. It must be mentioned, however, that even the selectional indices fulfil a semantic function; those indices have been integrated into the syntactic component for purely formal reasons, they are therefore regarded as syntactic indices, the separation of syntax and semantics within G_{d_1} being an arbitrary matter, i.e. a matter of convention.

In the lexicon of L^1_d only those semantic relations were listed which could be gained by a pre-theoretical, inductive analysis of the corresponding terms of L^0_d. The pragmatic context, i.e. the proper use of ${}_j\mathrm{SAT[IMP](1)}^0_1$ shows, however, that a term like *Straße* is applied only to the elements of a particular set of objects in the actual world. The objects which, according to the language of jurisdiction, can be labelled *Straße*, have to have particular properties or attributes.[6] Predicates denoting those attributes are given within

[6] The pragmatic context of the use of the term *Straße* is discussed in [23] and [28].

those paragraphs of ${}_{\mathrm{j}}L_{\mathrm{d}}^{0}$ which define *Straße* (if the term 'define' may be used here) somehow as an observational term.

If we therefore want to establish a lexicon for ${}_{\mathrm{j}}L_{\mathrm{d}}^{1}$, we have to regard the semanteme STRASS as a definiendum the definiens of which must contain the set of necessary and sufficient defining predicates. This set of defining predicates might guarantee that $\mathrm{SAT[IMP](1)}_{1}^{1}$ receives an adequate semantic interpretation matching the use of the utterance $\mathrm{SAT[IMP](1)}_{1}^{0} \in {}_{\mathrm{j}}L_{\mathrm{d}}^{0}$.

This result of more or less intuitive argumentation may be generalized without any serious difficulty: We can assume that the set of sentences belonging to the sub-language ${}_{\mathrm{j}}L_{\mathrm{d}}^{1}$ can be defined by means of a set of syntactic, semantic, and pragmatic features.

It has been mentioned above that the sublanguage ${}_{\mathrm{j}}L_{\mathrm{d}}^{1}$ may be regarded as the theoretical equivalent of ${}_{\mathrm{j}}L_{\mathrm{d}}^{0}$, the language of jurisdiction. ${}_{\mathrm{j}}L_{\mathrm{d}}^{0}$ is in this case the object language assigned to the theoretical language ${}_{\mathrm{j}}L_{\mathrm{d}}^{1}$ which in turn is enumerated by the grammar ${}_{\mathrm{j}}\mathrm{G}_{\mathrm{d}_1}$.

If the above argumentation is accepted we may lay down that ${}_{\mathrm{j}}L_{\mathrm{d}}^{1}$ is formally delimitable by:[7]

(1) a set of specific syntactic rules,

(2) a set of selectional indices assigned to the elements of *VNT* which are manipulated by the syntactic rules,

(3) a set of applicability conditions for a subset of the set of syntactic rules,

(4) a lexicon the elements of which contain

(a) a set of semantic features of an intensional nature, e.g. a complete list of synonyms, hyperonyms and antonyms related to the basic semantemes,[8]

(b) a set of reduction rules that explain how complex semantemes (theorems) are reduced to simple semantems (axioms),

(c) a set of semantic features of an extensional nature which guarantee that the semantemes (terms) used can be correctly applied to linguistic and non-linguistic events or states of affairs, i.e. a set of semantic features determining the referents of the terms in the actual world,

(5) a set of pragmatic conditions, i.e. hypotheses in the form of general laws, explaining that certain social institutions address certain people because of certain interests or motivations when using ${}_{\mathrm{j}}L_{\mathrm{d}}^{0}$.

We label a sub-grammar of $\mathrm{G}_{\mathrm{d}_1}$ which meets the conditions 1 to 5 with ${}_{\mathrm{j}}\mathrm{G}_{\mathrm{d}_1}$, where ${}_{\mathrm{j}}\mathrm{G}_{\mathrm{d}_1} \subset \mathrm{G}_{\mathrm{d}_1}$.

5.4. We regard L_{d}^{0} as the object language corresponding to L_{d}^{1}. Similarly ${}_{\mathrm{j}}L_{\mathrm{d}}^{1}$ is assigned a corresponding object language, called ${}_{\mathrm{j}}L_{\mathrm{d}}^{0}$. ${}_{\mathrm{j}}L_{\mathrm{d}}^{0}$ consists

[7] These arguments were presented and discussed first in [32] and [33].

[8] The problems of the treatment of semantics within a linguistic theory are discussed in [5], [17], [19], and [26]; the definitions of synonymy etc. are taken from [17], pp. 450–470.

of the set of all norms or directives belonging to the German language of jurisdiction. ${}_{\mathrm{j}}L_{\mathrm{d}}^{0}$ may be given an extensional or an intensional definition. The users of ${}_{\mathrm{j}}L_{\mathrm{d}}^{0}$ decide which utterances ${}_{\mathrm{j}}\mathrm{SAT}_{1}^{0},\ldots,{}_{\mathrm{j}}\mathrm{SAT}_{\mathrm{n}}^{0}$ belong to ${}_{\mathrm{j}}L_{\mathrm{d}}^{0}$ and which features distinguish $\mathrm{SAT}_{\mathrm{k}}^{0}$ from ${}_{\mathrm{j}}\mathrm{SAT}_{\mathrm{k}}^{0}$, given that both show an identical surface structure. The theoretical status of ${}_{\mathrm{j}}L_{\mathrm{d}}^{0}$, however, is still far from being clear.[9] If we assume that the use of norms, i.e. the application of the set of systematically interrelated sentences which constitute the language of jurisdiction, is directed by an appropriate theory, then ${}_{\mathrm{j}}L_{\mathrm{d}}^{0}$ would certainly have the status of a descriptional language.[10] This might imply that ${}_{\mathrm{j}}L_{\mathrm{d}}^{0}$ is a sort of technical and in principle formalizable language for which explicit and exhaustive syntactic, semantic, and pragmatic rules can be given. The primary function of such a ${}_{\mathrm{j}}L_{\mathrm{d}}^{0}$ would then be to permit the adequate and intersubjectively valid description of some states of affairs of the actual world.

One of the pre-conditions for the rational and theory-determined application of norms is that intersubjectively testable knowledge about events can be established. Consequently the descriptional or observational terms (predicates like *Straße, einbiegen, eng, weit* etc.) used to represent this knowledge must have precisely determined meanings (definitions). This of course cannot do the whole job. It must further be guaranteed that all people who use ${}_{\mathrm{j}}L_{\mathrm{d}}^{0}$ use the defined descriptional terms in the same way, i.e. the use of the terms of the language of jurisdiction has to follow certain (usage-) rules, agreed on by convention. The inconsistent use of such terms could be prevented if *operational definitions* for the terms in question are given. A term is said to be defined operationally if the user of ${}_{\mathrm{j}}L_{\mathrm{d}}^{0}$ gets objective and valid criteria by which he can decide for arbitrary states of affairs whether a given term does apply or not.

This operational definition provides a reasonable answer to the question: which sets of features must be given such that certain linguistic functions or relations (like *Straße*, *enger Bogen*, *weiter Bogen*, *einbiegen* etc.) can be assigned to the corresponding functions in the domain of objects constituting the actual world? To meet this purpose a test procedure T must be provided. This test procedure determines those sets of simple and complex states of affairs to which a term or the syntactically and semantically admissible combination of terms (expressions) applies. The result of the test procedure T serves as a criterion for the admissible applicability of a term or an expression. If the terms used in ${}_{\mathrm{j}}L_{\mathrm{d}}^{0}$ are defined operationally then it

9 The status of ${}_{\mathrm{j}}L_{\mathrm{d}}{}^{0}$ is discussed in [1], [22], [27], and [28].

10 The criteria for the operational set-up of descriptional languages were developed in [16], pp. 3–47 and pp. 137–155. The tasks of linguistically relevant descriptional languages are shown in [6], [7], and [26].

may be assumed with good reason that statements made by the users of ${}_{j}L_{d}^{0}$ meet the postulate of intersubjective testability: on the one hand it could be determined easily whether *one user* of ${}_{j}L_{d}^{0}$ applies a term in a consistent way if he has to classify identical states of affairs within *different* time intervals, on the other hand *one state of affairs* could be submitted to *different users* of ${}_{j}L_{d}^{0}$ in order to test whether they use the term according to the rules given. This operational definition leads to the delimitation/classification of those states of affairs (of functions and relations within the set of objects constituting the actual world) which belong to the domain of the theory of jurisdiction.

In addition to this the method of operational definition would permit that sets of features defining specific states of affairs or classes of specific states of affairs could be given, i.e. that a well-founded taxonomy could be established which would contain those events/phenomena/objects which belong to the universe of discourse of a theory of jurisdiction. A precise definition of the set of objects belonging to the theory of jurisdiction would only be one result of the use of operational definitions, although not an entirely unimportant one. It seems to be quite clear that this method would necessarily lead to a semantically (intensionally and extensionally) founded taxonomy of terms that can be assigned to objects etc. in the actual world; complex terms (definienda like *Straße, abbiegen* etc.) could be defined by the conjunction of simple terms (definientia). The simple terms (linguistic functions) can be assigned to those attributes or properties which uniquely characterize some given object/state of affairs. They are not regarded as definienda. Definienda are something like abbreviations standing for sets of simple terms (basic descriptions, axiomatic terms, axiomatic semantemes). The validity of the conjunction of simple terms is a necessary and sufficient condition for the validity of the complex term.[11]

It seems to be clear, however, that the taxonomy classifying the states of affairs cannot be set up in a 'natural way' (whatever this may mean). The decision therefore whether a specific state of affairs SVH_{i}^{0} belongs to the class SVH_{i}^{0} or SVH_{k}^{0} cannot possibly be given because of observable or reconstructible features alone, but, only because of theoretically motivated conventions. These conventions will depend on the classification of the set of defining properties into necessary and sufficient properties, i.e. on the construction of a detailed scale which permits to decide whether a given state of affairs belongs to a certain class.

5.5. L_{d}^{0} is regarded as the meta-language for the descriptional language ${}_{j}L_{d}^{0}$.

[11] The use of definitions within a specific linguistic theory is motivated and elaborated in [22] and [25].

A descriptional language is neither a theoretical language nor a theory. ${}_{\mathrm{j}}L_{\mathrm{d}}^{0}$ in the sense of 5.4 is simply one of the necessary preconditions for the construction of an empirically adequate ${}_{\mathrm{j}}\mathrm{G}_{\mathrm{d_i}}({}_{\mathrm{j}}L_{\mathrm{d}}^{0})$, i.e. for the construction of a theoretical language ${}_{\mathrm{j}}L_{\mathrm{d}}^{1}$, representing or corresponding to ${}_{\mathrm{j}}L_{\mathrm{d}}^{0}$, especially for the construction of an adequate lexicon containing all the necessary and sufficient definitions.

It is a deplorable fact that ${}_{\mathrm{j}}L_{\mathrm{d}}^{0}$ as used, at present, by official institutions, lawyers, judges etc. can certainly not be regarded as a proper descriptional language.[12] It is rather a mixture of every-day language, professional language and descriptional language. The development of a well-founded descriptional language ${}_{\mathrm{j}}L_{\mathrm{d}}^{0}$ is surely an urgent task. It could be well carried out with the aid of applied text linguistics. This of course would make text linguistics a socially relevant science.

It may be taken for granted that the power of an empirical theory is proved best if it can be shown to be elaborated and rich enough so as to be capable of solving practical problems. This implies that the successful application of a theory in an empirically given domain provides a good and obviously intersubjectively valid test for the power of a theory. We claim that theories which are held to be empirically valid or relevant should be evaluated relative to some specified task.

6. On the Derivation of Synonymous and Hyperonymous Sentences by Grammars of the Type ${}_{\mathrm{j}}\mathrm{G}_{\mathrm{d_i}}$

6.0. Although we are still unable to introduce into the derivation of ${}_{\mathrm{j}}$SAT (IMP)$(1)_1^1$ all those semantic (especially referential) and pragmatic features mentioned in § 5, we regard the PSG given on pp. 281–86 because of its rather strong syntactic restrictions (e.g. the elimination of recursive rules and the use of selectional indices) as a proper and well-founded subgrammar ${}_{\mathrm{j}}\mathrm{G}_{\mathrm{d_i}}({}_{\mathrm{j}}L_{\mathrm{d}}^{0})$.

6.1. If we extend $VNT({}_{\mathrm{j}}\mathrm{G}_{\mathrm{d_i}})$, $VT({}_{\mathrm{j}}\mathrm{G}_{\mathrm{d_i}})$, $R_{\mathrm{sy}}({}_{\mathrm{j}}\mathrm{G}_{\mathrm{d_i}})$, and $R_{\mathrm{se}}({}_{\mathrm{j}}\mathrm{G}_{\mathrm{d_i}})$, which is of course a rather trivial problem, we can easily generate the following synonymous sentences:

(2) *beim einbiegen in eine andere straße ist nach links ein weiter nach rechts ein enger bogen auszuführen (zu machen, zu fahren).*

(3) *nach links ist ein weiter nach rechts ist ein enger bogen beim einbiegen in eine andere straße auszuführen (zu machen, zu fahren).*

(4) *auszuführen (zu fahren, zu machen) ist beim einbiegen in eine*

[12] This is shown in [1], [27], and [28].

andere straße nach links ein weiter nach rechts ein enger bogen.

(5) *ein enger bogen ist beim einbiegen in eine ander straße nach rechts auszuführen (zu machen, zu fahren) ein weiter nach links.*

(6) *ein weiter bogen ist beim einbiegen in eine andere straße nach links auszuführen (zu machen, zu fahren) ein enger nach rechts.*

(7) *nach links ist beim einbiegen in eine andere straße ein weiter bogen auszuführen (zu machen, zu fahren) nach rechts ein enger.*

(8) *nach rechts ist beim einbiegen in eine andere straße ein enger bogen auszuführen (zu machen, zu fahren) nach links ein weiter.*

etc.

6.2. It follows from 6.1. that ${}_{j}G_{d_i}$ generates synonymous sentences if the following conditions are given:

(1) if a sentence ${}_{j}SAT_0^1$ is distinguished; we call ${}_{j}SAT_0^1$ a *distinguished sentence,* if ${}_{j}SAT_0^1 \in {}_{j}L_d^1$ can be proved and if ${}_{j}SAT_0^1$ is used as a theorem leading to the construction of a set of synonymous and/or hyperonymous sentences, i.e. if SYNO (${}_{j}SAT_0^1$, ${}_{j}SAT_1^1$), SYNO(${}_{j}SAT_1^1$, ${}_{j}SAT_2^1$), ..., SYNO (${}_{j}SAT_{n-1}^1$, ${}_{j}SAT_n^1$) or HYPO(${}_{j}SAT_0^1$, ${}_{j}SAT_1^1$), HYPO(${}_{j}SAT_1^1$, ${}_{j}SAT_2^1$), ..., HYPO(${}_{j}SAT_{n-1}^1$, ${}_{j}SAT_n^1$) is valid,

(2) if in all $\{{}_{j}SAT_0^1, \ldots, {}_{j}SAT_n^1\}$ the n-tuples of syntactic categories which receive a semantic interpretation are identical, i.e. if $VNT({}_{j}SAT_0^1) = VNT({}_{j}SAT_1^1) = \cdots = VNT({}_{j}SAT_{n-1}^1 = VNT$ $({}_{j}SAT_n^1)$.

(3) for all $\{{}_{j}SAT_i^1, \ldots {}_{j}SAT_{n}^1,\}$ a new terminal a_i can only be introduced, if the distinguished sentence ${}_{j}SAT_0^1$ contains a terminal a_k and if it is explicitly stated in the lexicon of ${}_{j}G_{d_i}$ that the semantemes SEM_i and SEM_k which are part of a_i and a_k, respectively, show the relation SYNO(SEM_i, SEM_k).

6.3. Due to the classification of the set $R_{sy}({}_{j}G_{d_i})$ into a subset of obligatory and a disjunctive subset of facultative rules, and by a proper extension of the set of $R_{se}({}_{j}G_{d_i})$ we can derive the following hyperonymous sentences:

(2) *beim einbiegen ist ein bogen auszuführen (zu machen, zu fahren).*

(3) *beim einbiegen in eine andere straße ist ein bogen auszuführen (zu machen, zu fahren).*

(4) *beim einbiegen in eine andere straße ist ein bogen auszuführen (zu machen, zu fahren).*

(5) *beim einbiegen in eine andere straße ist nach links ein bogen auszuführen (zu machen, zu fahren).*

(6) *beim einbiegen in eine ander straße ist nach rechts ein bogen auszuführen (zu machen, zu fahren).*
(7) *beim einbiegen in eine andere straße ist nach links ein weiter bogen auszuführen (zu machen, zu fahren).*
(8) *beim einbiegen in eine andere straße ist nach rechts ein enger bogen auszuführen(zu machen, zu fahren).*
etc.

6.4. For the enumeration of a set of hyperonymous sentences *relative to* a distinguished sentence (which may be regarded somehow as an auxiliary canonical form) the following derivability conditions must be observed:

(1) ${}_j\mathrm{SAT}_0^1$ may contain n obligatory rules only; if ${}_j\mathrm{SAT}_0^1$ contained $n-1$ obligatory rules, then ${}_j\mathrm{SAT}_0^1 \notin {}_jL_d^1$ and therefore *not* – IS(${}_j\mathrm{SAT}_0^1$, ${}_j\mathrm{SAT}_0^0$) would be the case; this means that ${}_j\mathrm{SAT}_0^1$ is a sentence of the sub-language ${}_jL_d^1$ *which cannot be reduced to any* ${}_j\mathrm{SAT}_{0-1}^1 \in {}_jL_d^1$,

(2) if ${}_j\mathrm{SAT}_0^1$ ${}_jL_d^1$ is derived by a set of n obligatory *and* facultative rules, then

(a) the application of the set k obligatory rules yields ${}_j\mathrm{SAT}_k^1 \in {}_jL_d^1$, such that HYPO (${}_j\mathrm{SAT}_k^1$, ${}_j\mathrm{SAT}_0^1$) is valid for $k<n$,

(b) the application of k obligatory rules plus one facultative rule yields ${}_j\mathrm{SAT}_l^1 \in {}_jL_d^1$, such that HYPO(${}_j\mathrm{SAT}_k^1$, ${}_j\mathrm{SAT}_l^1$) is valid for $(k+1)<n$,

⋮

(n – 1) the application of k obligatory plus r facultative rules yields ${}_j\mathrm{SAT}_r^1$, such that HYPO(${}_j\mathrm{SAT}_q^1$, ${}_j\mathrm{SAT}_r^1$) is valid for $(k+r)=n-1$,

(n) the application of k obligatory plus s facultative rules yields ${}_j\mathrm{SAT}_0^1$, such that HYPO(${}_j\mathrm{SAT}_r^1$, ${}_j\mathrm{SAT}_0^1$) is valid for $(k+s)=n$ and ${}_j\mathrm{SAT}_r^1 = {}_j\mathrm{SAT}_0^1$, i.e. SYNO(${}_j\mathrm{SAT}_r^1$, ${}_j\mathrm{SAT}_0^1$) is the case,

(3) for all ${}_j\mathrm{SAT}_i^1, \ldots, {}_j\mathrm{SAT}_n^1$ a new terminal a_i can be introduced only if the distinguished sentence ${}_j\mathrm{SAT}_0^1$ contains a_k and if the corresponding semantemes SEM_i, SEM_k show the semantic relation HYPO(SEM_i, SEM_k).

6.5. It follows from 6.1, 6.2, 6.3, and 6.4 that for every distinguished sentence ${}_j\mathrm{SAT}_i^1 \in {}_jL_d^1$ a sublanguage ${}_jL_d^{1\prime}$ can be generated consisting only of those sentences of ${}_jL_d^1$ which are synonyms of ${}_j\mathrm{SAT}_i^1$.

In analogy to this procedure, for every distinguished sentence ${}_j\mathrm{SAT}_i^1 \in {}_jL_d^1$ a sublanguage ${}_jL_d^{1\prime\prime}$ can be generated consisting only of those sentences which are hyperonyms of ${}_j\mathrm{SAT}_i^1$. Although ${}_jL_d^{1\prime}$ and ${}_jL_d^{1\prime\prime}$ show the property of decidability, they are certainly *not* complete sublanguages if compared with the corresponding sublanguages of ${}_{\mathrm{j}}L^0_{\mathrm{d}}$, i.e. $[{}_{\mathrm{j}}L^{1\prime}_{\mathrm{d}}]^0 \subset {}_{\mathrm{j}}L^{0\prime}_{\mathrm{d}}$ and $[{}_{\mathrm{j}}L^{1\prime\prime}_{\mathrm{d}}]^0 \subset$ $\subset {}_{\mathrm{j}}L^{0\prime\prime}_{\mathrm{d}}$ hold.

This incompleteness of the language ${}_{\mathrm{j}}L^1_{\mathrm{d}}$ is a decisive inadequacy which is due to a set of formal properties $\mathrm{R}({}_{\mathrm{j}}\mathrm{G}_{\mathrm{d_i}})$, i.e. an empirical shortcoming which is due to the formal set-up of PSG's. At the moment there does not seem to be any real chance to correct these inadequacies in a non-*ad-hoc* way.

The theoretical advantages of $\mathrm{G}_{\mathrm{d_i}}$, however, are obvious if we consider that

(1) a syntactically directed descriptional language can in principle be set up by automatizable procedures, i.e. part of the heuristic work leading to a grammatical theory on ${}_{\mathrm{j}}L^0_{\mathrm{d}}$ could be founded on a solid, non-intuitive basis,[13]

(2) grammars of the PSG-type can be used for recognition tests; they therefore permit the generation of decidable languages.

It is a matter of fact that, according to the intuitive competence of a speaker/user of ${}_{\mathrm{j}}L^0_{\mathrm{d}}$ and L^0_{d}, the sets of synonymous and hyperonymous sentences admissible in ${}_{\mathrm{j}}L^0_{\mathrm{d}}$ are far greater that the theoretically delimitable sublanguages ${}_{\mathrm{j}}L^{1\prime}$ and ${}_{\mathrm{j}}L^{1\prime\prime}_{\mathrm{d}}$.

Now if we adhered strictly to the theoretician's position, we could claim of course that all and only those sentences which constitute the sublanguages ${}_{\mathrm{j}}L^{1\prime}_{\mathrm{d}}$ and ${}_{\mathrm{j}}L^{1\prime\prime}_{\mathrm{d}}$ may count as theoretically admissible sets of synonymous and hyperonymous sentences respectively. This purely formalistic attitude would, however, lead us into serious difficulties: ${}_{\mathrm{j}}\mathrm{G}_{\mathrm{d_i}}$ would certainly lose the status of an empirically adequate theory, the criterion of testability would have to be restricted in such a way as to render it completely uninteresting, or, and this would even be worse, it would have to be abandoned altogether. It seems to be quite obvious, that such procedures are of no great use, if theories of natural languages or sublanguages are to be established.

According to the above argumentation, the present stage of development of ${}_{\mathrm{j}}\mathrm{G}_{\mathrm{d_i}}$ does not permit to relate the following two sentences ${}_{\mathrm{j}}\mathrm{SAT}^0_1$ and ${}_{\mathrm{j}}\mathrm{SAT}^0_{\mathrm{r}}$ to each other:

${}_{\mathrm{j}}\mathrm{SAT}^0_1$ *Beim Einbiegen in eine andere Straße ist nach rechts ein enger, nach links ein weiter Bogen auszuführen.*

${}_{\mathrm{j}}\mathrm{SAT}^0_{\mathrm{r}}$ *Jeder, der mit einem Fahrrad in eine andere Straße einbiegt, muß nach rechts einen engen, nach links dagegen einen weiten Bogen machen.*

More precisely: ${}_{\mathrm{j}}\mathrm{G}_{\mathrm{d_i}}$ is not strong enough to determine the syntactic and semantic relations between the corresponding theory-determined sentences

[13] A method for the approximative delimitation of a syntactical language is developed in [12], pp. 6–49.

${}_{j}SAT_{1}^{1}$ and ${}_{j}SAT_{r}^{1}$, although ${}_{j}G_{d_i}$ generates both sentences. Therefore analogous empirical inadequacies hold for any ${}_{j}TEG_{i}$ and for any TEG_{i} in general which shows the above-mentioned property a1′.

7. Some remarks on the evaluation of ${}_{j}G_{d_i}$

7.1. We now try to outline what a more promising grammar ${}_{j}G_{d_k}$ would have to look like. We assume further that this grammar can provide a model, or an integral part of a corresponding ${}_{j}TEG_{d_k}$. To reach this goal we shall try first to give an intuitive, logico-semantic analysis of ${}_{j}SAT[IMP](1)_{1}^{0}$: *Beim Einbiegen in eine andere Straße ist nach rechts ein enger, nach links ein weiter Bogen auszuführen.*

7.1.1. Explanation of the symbols used:

x	individual variable to which the predicate *adressat des gesetzes* may be assigned
y	individual variable to which the predicate *fahrzeug* in the sense of ${}_{j}L_{d}^{0}$ can be assigned
u, z	individual variables to which the predicate *straße* in the sense of ${}_{j}L_{d}^{0}$ can be assigned
v	individual variable to which the predicate *bogen* can be assigned

adressat, ausführen, bogen, einbiegen, fahren, fahrzeug, links, rechts, straße, eng, weit are predicates of the first order

T^0	time interval during which ${}_{j}SAT[IMP](1)_{1}^{0}$ is considered to be valid
T^1, T^2	arbitrary time intervals included in T^0, where $T^1 < T^2$
$\langle t_1^1 \ldots, t_n^1\rangle$	time intervals constituting T^1, where $t_1^1 < t_2^1 < \cdots < t_n^1$
$\langle t_1^2, \ldots, t_n^2\rangle$	time intervals constituting T^2, where $t_1^1 < t_2^2 < \cdots < t_n^2$
E	existential quantifier
(x)f(x)	the parentheses '( )' left from 'f' denote universal quantification
$\in$	element of
$\acute{\supset}$	entailment
$\subset$	class inclusion
$<$	earlier than
$\cdot$	logical conjunction
(,), [,]	parentheses
P	proposition (object-function)
P*	event (event-function)

7.1.2. According to the standard formation rules which need not be mentioned here, we derive the following well-formed formulae (preliminary or auxiliary propositions):

$$P1 = (E\ T^0)(T^1)(T^2)(E\ t_n^1)(E\ t_1^2)$$

$$[\mathit{adressat}(x) . \mathit{straße}(u) . \mathit{straße}(z) . (u \neq z) .$$
$$\mathit{fahrzeug}(y) . \mathit{fahren}(x, y, t_n^1, u) . \mathit{einbiegen}(x, y, t_1^2, z) .$$
$$\mathit{rechts}(z, x) . (t_n^1 < t_1^2) . (t_n^1 \subset T^1) . (t_1^2 \subset T^2) . (T^2 \subset T^0) . (T^1 \subset T^0)]$$

$$P2 = (E\ T^0)(T^2)$$

$$[\mathit{adressat}(x) . \mathit{fahrzeug}(y) . \mathit{bogen}(v) . \mathit{eng}(v) .$$
$$\mathit{ausführen}(x, y, v, T^2) . (T^2 \subset T^0)]$$

7.1.3. Then we re-formulate the expressions constituting $_j$SAT[IMP](1) in terms of events:

$$(k)P1^*(k) \overset{\prime}{\supset} (k)P2^*(k)$$

This expression is abbreviated as:

$$P1^* \overset{\prime}{\supset} P2^*$$

7.1.4. Two further auxiliary propositions are derived:

$$P3 = (E\ T^0)(T^1)(T^2)(E\ t_n^1)(E\ t_1^2)$$

$$[\mathit{adressat}(x) . \mathit{straße}(u) . \mathit{straße}(z) . (u \neq z) .$$
$$\mathit{fahrzeug}(y) . \mathit{fahren}(x, y, t_n^1, u) . \mathit{einbiegen}(x, y, t_1^2, z) .$$
$$\mathit{links}(z, x) . (t_n^1 < t_1^2) . (t_n^1 \subset T^1) . (t_1^2 \subset T^2) . (T^2 \subset T^0) .$$
$$(T^1 \subset T^0)]$$

$$P4 = (E\ T^0)(T^2)$$

$$[\mathit{adressat}(x) . \mathit{fahrzeug}(y) . \mathit{bogen}(v) . \mathit{weit}(v) .$$
$$\mathit{ausführen}(x, y, v, T^2) . (T^2 \subset T^0)]$$

7.1.5. These expressions constituting $_j$SAT[IMP]$(1)_1^0$ are also formulated in terms of events:

$$(k)P3^*(k) \overset{\prime}{\supset} (k)P4^*(k)$$

This expression is abbreviated as:

$$P3^* \acute{\supset} P4^*$$

7.1.6. The complete formalization of the norm ${}_j\mathrm{SAT[IMP](1)}_1^0$ is then:

$$[P1^* \acute{\supset} P2^*] . [P3^* \acute{\supset} P4^*].$$

7.2. A ${}_jG_{d_k}$ which permits to map the intuitive description given in 7.1. (more general: a descriptional language operating over logico-semantic structures) into a theoretical language is certainly powerful enough to explain the syntactic-semantic relations between ${}_j\mathrm{SAT}_1^0$ and ${}_j\mathrm{SAT}_r^0$. We have seen that ${}_jG_{d_i}$ is syntax-based, i.e. based on a syntactically founded descriptional language. The corresponding theoretical language (the strings of nonterminals generated by ${}_jG_{d_i}$) receive a semantic interpretation. We tried to show that ${}_jG_{d_i}$ is incapable of relating the sentences ${}_j\mathrm{SAT}_1^1$ and ${}_j\mathrm{SAT}_r^1$ to each other, a theoretical reconstruction of the syntactic-semantic relations between ${}_j\mathrm{SAT}_1^1$, ${}_j\mathrm{SAT}_r^1$, ${}_jL_d^{0\prime}$, and ${}_jL_d^{0\prime\prime}$ would therefore be quite impossible.

It is not known at present, how ${}_jG_{d_i}$ can be developed in such a way as to make it achieve the power of ${}_jG_{d_k}$ (and, as far as the problem of decidability is concerned, vice versa).

If, however, ${}_jG_{d_k}$ should be established as a general, consistent and empirically adequate theory of the sublanguage ${}_jL_d^0$, then the following tasks should be solved:

(1) the development of a transduction procedure which guarantees that expressions formulated in a logico-semantic descriptional language can be assigned to the corresponding expressions of the object language in a nonambiguous way, i.e. the development of a semantically founded taxonomy and of suitable transduction operations,

(2) the development of a transduction procedure which assigns expressions formulated in a logico-semantic descriptional language to expressions formulated in a theoretical language,

(3) the proof that ${}_jG_{d_k}$ generates a decidable language ${}_jL_d^1$. If those tasks can be accomplished, ${}_jG_{d_k}$ certainly provides a promising model for the construction of ${}_j\mathrm{TEG}_{d_k}$.

The discussion of the empirical adequacy of ${}_jG_{d_i}$ leads us to the view that there is probably no inclusive theory covering all interests and postulates, e.g. those of algebraic linguistics, semantic analysis, logic and the theory of science. It can be maintained further that a theory's supposed range of application determines its formal set-up as well as the heuristic steps producing this set-up. There seem to be thus good reasons for the assumption that a variety of complementary and probably even non-competetive theories can be developed over an identical range of objects, theories relative to the different interests which determine their empirical tasks.[14]

University of Constance
DFG-Projekt 'Textlinguistik'

BIBLIOGRAPHY

[1] Brinckmann, H.: 1972, 'Juristische Fachsprache und Umgangspsrache. Vorüberlegungen zu einer Formalisierung der Rechtssprache', *ÖVD* **2** (1972), 60–69.
[2] Brinckmann, H. and Rieser, H.: 1972, 'Paraphrasen juristischer Texte I', *Rechtstheorie*, 3. Bd., Heft 1 (1972), 83–89.
[3] Brinckmann, H., Petöfi, J. S., and Rieser, H.: 1972, 'Paraphrasen juristischer Texte II', *Angewandte Textlinguistik* (=*Papiere zur Textlinguistik* **2**) (ed. by P. Hartmann, and H. Rieser), Buske, Hamburg (forthcoming).
[4] Brockhaus, K.: 1971, *Automatische Übersetzung* (=*Schriften zur Linguistik* **2**), Vieweg, Braunschweig.
[5] Brockhaus, K. and v. Stechow, A.: 1971, 'Formal Semantics: A New Approach', *Linguistische Berichte* **11** (1971), 7–36.
[6] van Dijk, T. A.: 1972a, *Some Aspects of Text Grammars*, Mouton, The Hague.
[7] van Dijk, T. A.: 1972b, 'Text Grammar and Text Logic', contribution to this volume.
[8] van Dijk, T. A.; Ihwe, J., Petöfi, J. S., and Rieser, H.: 1971, 'Textgrammatische Grundlagen für eine Theorie Narrativer Strukturen', *Linguistische Berichte* **16** (1971), 1–38.
[9] van Dijk, T. A., Ihwe, J., Petöfi, J. S., and Rieser, H.: 1972a, *Zur Bestimmung narrativer Strukturen auf der Grundlage von Textgrammatiken* (=*Papiere zur Textlinguistik* **1**), Buske, Hamburg.
[10] van Dijk, T. A., Ihwe, J., Petöfi, J. S., and Rieser, H.: 1972b, 'Two Textgrammatical Models', *Foundations of Language* **VIII** (1972), 187–233.
[11] Gross, M. and Lentin, A.: 1970, *Introduction to Formal Grammars* (transl. by M. Salkoff), Springer, Berlin.
[12] Harris, Z. S.: 1968, *Mathematical Structures of Language*, John Wiley and Sons, New York.
[13] Hartmann, P.: 1968, 'Zum Begriff des sprachlichen Zeichens', *Zs. f. Phonetik, Sprachwiss. und Kommunikationsforschung*, Bd. 21 (1968), 205–222.
[14] Hartmann, P.: 1972, 'Zur Klassifikation und Abfolge textanalytischer Operationen', *Zur Grundlegung der Literaturwissenschaft* (ed. by S. J. Schmidt), Bayerischer Schulbuchverlag, München, pp. 124–143.
[15] Hartmann, P. and Rieser, H.: 1971, 'Paraphrasenbeziehungen in juristischen Texten', *Paraphrasen juristischer Texte* (ed. by D. Rave, H. Brinckmann and K. Grimmer), Deutsches Rechenzentrum, Darmstadt.

[14] It must be stated, however, that research done on grammars of the type $_{\mathrm{j}}\mathrm{G}_{\mathrm{d}_1}$ and $_{\mathrm{j}}\mathrm{TEG}_{\mathrm{d}_1}$ is by no means useless. On the contrary, we think that text grammars which are set up according to the models of different sentence grammars can be ranked in a hierarchy analogous to the hierarchy of finite state-grammars, context-free PSG's, context-sensitive PSG's and transformational grammars (as proposed e.g. by Harris, Chomsky, Seuren, Fillmore, Keenan, Petöfi and others). The foundation of such a hierarchy of text grammars by the specification of their formal set-up, their power and their empirical adequacy is one of the most urgent tasks still to be achieved. A preliminary discussion of such a hierarchy is given by J. S. Petöfi and H. Rieser in the introduction to this volume and by J. S. Petöfi in his contribution *Towards an Empirically Motivated Theory of Verbal Texts*.

[16] Hempel, C. G.: 1966, *Aspects of Scientific Explanation*, The Free Press, London.
[17] Lyons, J.: 1969, *Introduction to Theoretical Linguistics*, University Press, Cambridge:
[18] Mates, B.: 1969, *Elementare Logik*. Prädikatenlogik der ersten Stufe (transl. by A. Oberschelp), Vandenhoeck and Ruprecht, Göttingen.
[19] Petöfi, J. S.: 1971a, *Transformationsgrammatiken und eine kotextuelle Texttheorie*. Grundfragen und Konzeptionen (=*Linguistische Forschungen* Bd 3), Athenäum, Frankfurt.
[20] Petöfi, J. S.: 1971b, ''Generativity' and Textgrammar', *Gothenburg Papers in Theoretical Linguistics* **9** (1971), University of Gothenburg, Dept. of Linguistics.
[21] Petöfi, J. S.: 1971c, 'Zu einer grammatischen Theorie sprachlicher Texte', *Lili, Zs. für Literaturwissenschaft und Linguistik* **2** (1972), 31–58.
[22] Petöfi, J. S.: 1972b, 'Zum Aufbau eines 'Lexikons'', *Angewandte Textlinguistik* (=*Papiere zur Textlinguistik* **2**) (ed. by P. Hartmann and H. Rieser), Buske, Hamburg. (forthcoming).
[23] Petöfi, J. S.: 1973, 'Einige Probleme der Repräsentation der 'Argumente' im Rahmen einer Textgrammatik', *Konstanzer Textlinguistikkolloquium 1972* (=*Papiere zur Textlinguistik* **3**) (ed. by M. Rüttenauer,) Buske, Hamburg (forthcoming).
[24] Petöfi, J. S.: 1972c, 'Towards an Empirically Motivated Grammatical Theory of Verbal Texts, contribution to this volume.
[25] Petöfi, J. S.: 1972d, 'Juristische Texte und eine Textgrammatik mit 'linear nicht festgelegter 'Text-Basis'' ', *Angewandte Textlinguistik* (=*Papiere zur Textlinguistik* **2**) (ed. by P. Hartmann and H. Rieser), Buske, Hamburg (forthcoming).
[26] Petöfi, J. S. and Rieser, H.: 1973, 'Wissenschaftstheoretische Argumente für eine umfassende grammatische Theorie und eine logisch-semantische Beschreibungssprache', *Konstanzer Textlinguistikkolloquium 1972* (=*Papiere zur Textlinguistik* **3**) (ed. by M. Rüttenauer), Buske, Hamburg (forthcoming).
[27] Rave, D., Brinckmann, H. and Grimmer K. (eds.): 1971, *Paraphrasen juristischer Texte*. Referate und Protokolle der Arbeitstagung im Deutschen Rechenzentrum Darmstadt. 24.–26. Juni 1971. Deutsches Rechenzentrum, Darmstadt.
[28] Rave, D., Brinckmann, H., and Grimmer, K. (eds.): 1972, *Syntax und Semantik juristischer Texte* Referate und Protokolle der Arbeitstagung im Deutschen Rechenzentrum in Darmstadt. 11.–13. Mai 1972. Deutsches Rechenzentrum, Darmstadt.
[29] Reichenbach, H.: 1966, *Elements of Symbolic Logic*, The Free Press, New York.
[30] Rieser, H.: 1971, 'Allgemeine textlinguistische Ansätze zur Erklärung performativer Strukturen', *Poetics* **2**, pp. 91–118.
[31] Rieser, H.: 1972a, 'Probleme der Textgrammatik II: Zum Aufbau einer Textgrammatik (TEG)', *Folia Linguistica* **V** (1972), 55–73.
[32] Rieser, H.: 1972b, 'Zur syntaktisch-semantischen Analyse eines Rechtssatzes', *Syntax und Semantik juristischer Texte* (ed. by Rave, D. H. Brinckmann, and G. Grimmer), Deutsches Rechenzentrum, Darmstadt.
[33] Rieser, H.: 1973, 'Sprachwissenschaft und Rechtstheorie', *Rechtswissenschaft und Nachbarwissenschaften* (ed. by D. Grimm), Athenäum, Frankfurt (forthcoming).
[34] Strawson, P. F.: 1966, *Introduction to Logical Theory*, Methuen and Co Ltd, London.

JENS IHWE

ON THE VALIDATION OF TEXT-GRAMMARS IN THE 'STUDY OF LITERATURE'

ABSTRACT. Four contexts are specified in which the notion of 'text' is to be treated: text-grammars, text-typologies, text-processing, and text-didactics.

These four contexts, in this particular ordering, also imply the thesis that the introduction of this notion will only be of operational value if it has been sufficiently anchored both empirically and applicationally.

The paradigm chosen is that of the study of literature. Here it can be shown with all clarity, how motivations and aims both inherent in as well as external to linguistics are to be related to assure the empirical relevance of the basic data, of concept definition, and of theory construction.

The guiding point of view is that linguistics must develop the general frame within which explication and description of the complex phenomenon 'text-processing' may be pursued. Founded on an empirically anchored (i.e. heuristical-experimental) basis of specification ('text-grammar'), specific domains of research within all so-called language-centred disciplines may then be delimited ('text-typologies'). As guiding points of view, at least for the paradigm chosen here, perspectives of application, in particular those of a didactic nature, are outlined ('text-didactics').

0. PREFACE

The present paper claims to cover a very large area. It will touch on practically all aspects under which the notion of 'text' is being discussed at present. It does, however, differ in one essential point: I do not regard the notion of 'text' as a basic category of linguistics and the other language-centred disciplines (as, for instance, the study of literature). I am therefore not primarily interested in an explication – of whatever kind – of the notion of 'text' in itself; on the contrary, I think that it could only be meaningfully introduced *via* other primary contexts of research. I take the concept to be a purely operational one. The real task is to be faced elsewhere: I have attempted to indicate this task (and thus the primary contexts of research) in the four compound concepts mentioned above. At present we are far from a solution of all the problems implied. Still, I should like to regard my reflections as a first attempt, however tentative and provisional, to define these problems within a systematic context.

Due to the brevity of presentation, I have had to rely only too often on the capability of the reader to establish connections and to draw and follow conclusions all of which I could do no more than suggest. It was impossible to introduce all the concepts used at length, and with all desired unambiguity; very often their meaning will be laid down in the course of argumentation, or even considered presupposed by reference to existing works. I

J. S. Petöfi and H. Rieser (eds.), Studies in Text Grammar, 300–348.

hope to be able to eliminate these defects, as far as they are due only to the required brevity of presentation, in an extended version. Often, however, they are also indicative of a lack of data, or of conceptual obscurity, and last but not least, of my limited awareness of aspects which may be central to the questions discussed.

One such aspect which my presentation definitely does less than justice to is indicated by the following observation: if one adopts a notion such as 'text-processing' (as has been discussed principally by G. Wienold), it is exceptional that the actual processing of verbal utterances starts from 'original' products, it rather involves existing verbal utterances and transforms these in all sorts of ways in the process. A detailed and well-defined investigation of such processes will provide tangible concretisations of my abstract reflections. I do hope, on the other hand, to have clarified the prerequisites and the aims of such investigations to some extent.

In a certain sense I consider the present paper as a further elaboration of the 'Sketch of a Research Programme for the Study of Literature', published in 1972 (1972a, p. 12; completed in 1970). I should therefore like to present it again for discussion, in particular also because I think that essential points of such a programme have become clearer in the meantime and thus allow for better presentation with regard to their bases and implications. This applies particularly to the relationship between 'the' study of literature and linguistics together with the other 'language-centred' disciplines, and finally to all the conceptual consequences which, in part, have led to a considerable re-evaluation of the approaches presented there. This development would not have taken place, however, outside the community of researchers within which I have been able to work during the last two years.

I should therefore like to thank Wolfram Köck, Kurt Kohn, Uwe Mönnich, János S. Petöfi, Hannes Rieser, and Götz Wienold, though they are innocent of the form in which all our discussions and conversations appear here. Perhaps some of the blame must go to the members of my Amsterdam working-group whose difficulties and questions have often stimulated a different accentuation and orientation. I am grateful to them for their willingness to assimilate my thoughts, and for their patience.

1. THE VALIDATION OF TEXT-GRAMMARS IN THE STUDY OF LITERATURE

1.1. In the following I should like to offer some arguments in order to show that a certain type of work in the theory of grammar is *especially* acceptable to the study of literature. I should like to demonstrate why, and how, 'text-grammars' of a certain type are basic to the study of literature. This requires also a sufficient clarification of what is, in this context, to be understood by 'the study of literature'. My task is therefore a twofold one: to show (i) what motivations for 'text-grammars' will result from a specification of 'the' study of literature in one way or another, and (ii) how conclusions deducible from these motivations may be realised in the theory of grammar and the theory of literature. I shall deal mainly with question (i) and offer no more than scattered remarks on question (ii). This corresponds to the state of research in the last-named field.

1.2. 'Theory of Grammar' is, in this context, to be understood as

(iii) the formulation of a non-controversial set of statements about observable regularities of 'verbal utterances'.

These statements should, ideally, be arranged in such manner as to yield, by virtue of that arrangement, a hypothesis about relations between regularities among the range of objects studied. These objects were introduced by the neutral expression 'verbal utterances' as undefined primitives. However, it should be clear that if linguistics is understood as the discipline which aims at the *general* laws of verbal interaction, then this range of objects represents only part of the field of linguistics: the (physically) manifest products by means of which verbal interactions take place.

'Theory of Grammar' is also to mean

(iv) the elaboration of 'formal systems' which coordinate definite structures with those regularities which are formulated and represented by the respective observational statements.

By 'formal systems' are understood such structures as are investigated by the fields concerned with the foundations of mathematics and logic, and by various other fields interested in their application ('calculi', 'formal languages'). The notion of 'structure' is thus restricted to specific contexts of use w thin which it could be given unequivocal meaning. If the formal systems considered are limited to those which contain at least one recursive element, there is another essential implication of (iv): the regularities established in the range of objects are projected onto the infinite. As the assignment of a definite structure already implies a very strong hypothesis about *law-like regularities* within the range of objects, the introduction of a recursive element has the far-reaching consequence that the hypothesis is no longer made to refer to finite sets only (given corpora of verbal utterances) but to infinite sets. The grammar of a natural language thus automatically, specifies this language as an infinite set of 'verbal utterances' with a definite structure.

1.3. The question as to *what* regularities of 'verbal utterances' one observes, wants to observe, or is able to observe, is an entirely different one, and so is the way in which the phenomena subsumed under this expression are to be reconstructed by the theory. This is an *empirical* question. Speaking therefore of 'sentence-grammars', 'text-grammars', etc., links up with differing interests or conceptions of the field, and does not touch the *notion* of grammar itself. This does not mean, however, that different answers to the empirical question will have no bearing on the choice, and the evaluation, of formal systems. On the contrary: it will be a sign of continuity in linguistics that 'new' facts, or a re-evaluation of facts, will produce evidence against one kind of formalisation and 'demand' another. This applies particularly to the implementation of formal systems which have, expressly, *not* (or not primarily) been developed for the structuring of linguistic facts (e.g. from the theory of formal languages, or also the theory of logical calculi; cf. the respective difficulties in the schools of Chomsky and Lakoff). It is important here to be aware that a specific formalisation may exert strong regulative, and often inhibiting, influence upon what is, or may be, taken to be relevant knowledge. It has to be emphasised, in any event, that what was said in (iii) and (iv) represents the ideal pattern of linguistics and the theory of grammar, respectively, but that its implementation – both as to (iii), i.e. as to its heuristics, and as to (iv), i.e. the *range* of eligible formal systems and their *linguistic* implications – is still in its infancy.

1.4. What is being discussed at present under the heading of the opposition 'sentence-grammar vs text-grammar' amounts predominantly to an empirical question. The answers to this question form the basis, as well as the point of orientation, of all formal investigation. Its topicality is not accidental: it concerns the central linguistic question, i.e. the observation of verbal utterances with regard to the extent, and the nature (the status), of statable regularities.

The formalisations of the type presented by Chomsky's *Aspects* (1965) postulated regularities between 'words' within the domain of the 'sentence' as the basis of all structuring (i.e. the grammar was supposed to be the formal explication of the notion of 'sentence'). This basis had been partly pre-established intuitively, partly justified distributionally (mainly on the assumption of the general validity of the procedures developed by Harris). Regularities 'beyond the sentence' were viewed as occasional, as reducible to the sentence format, or as phenomena that could only be structured by a theory of situative context (Katz-Fodor). All argumentation remained 'intrinsically' linguistic (i.e. restricted to the theory of grammar) and relegated the relevant adjoining disciplines (or sub-'theories') required to the field of 'performance' as given in some statable sense (Chomsky).

Against these (and similar) positions, two strands of argumentation may be singled out which I shall briefly summarise in the following (disregarding their respective histories). It has been argued, on the one hand, that the regularities within the domain of the sentence can only be explained (satisfactorily structured) if at least the linear sequence of the 'sentences', which represents a given 'verbal utterance' linguistically, is taken into account. The development of adjoining disciplines has, on the other hand, yielded arguments for the specification of the 'connecting points' to linguistics in such a way as to have linguistics investigate the *general* law-like regularities in the range of objects called 'verbal utterances' (which is under discussion here), whereas the adjoining disciplines (for this field) are defined by their investigations of *specific* law-like regularities. This means in practice that all such investigations have a common core which is referred to, in one way or another, by all their more general statements (cf. 'narrative' analysis in its varying forms, in the study of literature, in anthropology, in the study of religions: I shall come back to all this in §3.4.). Uniting both these strands of argumentation, one may speak of 'internal' and 'external' motivations for postulating, as the basis of structuring, the regularities between 'words' *and* 'sentences' within the domain of 'text'. The consequence seems obvious: the grammar is to be the formal explication of the notion of text. Whether it is possible to accept this consequence will depend on the strength of the justifications provided by both the 'internal' and 'external' motivations.

I shall only briefly comment on the 'internal' justification here. It also involves the formal aspect of the opposition 'sentence-grammar vs text-grammar'. The observations made so far (e.g. regarding stress distribution and intonation patterns, selection of articles, quantification, word order, embedding of relative clauses, distribution of personal pronouns, distribution of temporal expressions, etc.) have been regarded as unamenable to the grammatical models available at the time. Various proposals have been made: they must, however, on the whole be criticised on two essential points.

First of all, it is in no sense clear what the function of the facts quoted is. Ewald Lang (1972) has made this clear by an analysis of the suggestions presented by Horst Isenberg (1968a and b): the analysis of the data is, in general, much too superficial to allow for any conclusions as to whether their function will seriously affect (modify and falsify, respectively) the construction of the grammar. As far the case quoted, it can be shown that the grammar *can* supply means for a non-problematic integration of Isenberg's data[1]. This serves to underline once more how little we know about the properties even of those systems which have been discussed some time in the theory of grammar (cf. the presentation in Brainerd, 1971). In view of this fact, attempts to introduce a 'text-level' into grammars must be considered untestable as long as it has not been shown, by a *detailed* analysis of the data, which part of the data would require a *systematic* modification of the underlying formalism or, conversely, in which respect the alternative *formalism* presented differs *systematically* from the rejected one. This means that a discussion of such proposals will only make sense if it is a discussion of facts (in the majority of cases), or if it is going to face the complex question of the linguistic relevance of formal systems – an enterprise which, in general, leads far beyond the limits of such proposals (as they usually rest on intuitive ideas). A simple introduction of 'text'-elements can by no means be accepted as an answer to the empirical question of the structuring of regularities in the range of objects.

Only after an analysis of the facts which is of sufficient depth, i.e. an analysis which yields a satisfactory, non-controversial set of observations in the range of objects, and furthermore shows what elements we consider recurrent in the range of 'verbal utterances' and how we may relate these elements with each other – only after all this has been achieved, will it prove meaningful to discuss the question of how to construct the grammar which will structure the specifications resulting from these analyses in the best way. I should also like to point out that one of the most difficult questions to be solved by this analysis has barely ever been examined, i.e. the question of whether the relationships between the 'words in the sentence' and the 'words, or sentences, within the text' are of the same nature, and if not where, and how, they differ. Previous explorations of this question (cf. e.g. the grammatical models by Petöfi and Kummer) seem to suggest delimiting criteria of a 'pragmatic' (and not distributional) kind for 'sentences' and 'texts', and thus a network of 'pragmatic' relationships into which 'verbal utterances' are integrated. This implies a far-reaching extension of the range of objects. It is, on the whole, obscure as to how this extension, which is here (and also in other writings) intimated by the expression 'pragmatic', can be controlled, and thus too, what kind of empirical justification can be supplied for the modified

[1] Isenberg had investigated the distribution of the preposition *a* preceding an indirect object in Spanish; he concluded from the fact that the use, or omission of the preposition in a sentence determined its use, or omission in the sentence immediately following, that a grammar which derives the one sentence independently of the other was unsatisfactory. Lang was able to show that here a special case of coordination was involved which could/can in no way be taken to be an indication of a genuine 'textual feature'. Lang then outlined genuine 'textual features', as belonging to the domain of linguistics, on the level of semantics.

basis of structuring if we do nothing but postulate it intuitively or rely on some global phenomenological (Hartmann) and/or language-philosophical (Schmidt) 'foundation'. (I shall treat the question of a 'formal' and 'empirical' pragmatics for linguistics more extensively in §2.3.)

Secondly, the status of the facts remains obscure, especially when facts of a 'pragmatic' nature are confronted with a grammatical model that apparently cannot deal with them in an adequate way. Again Lang has shown the shortcomings of this approach by his analysis of Isenberg's (1970) examples. First there is the triviality that not just any fact from the range of verbal interactions is an admissible (negative) instance to test a grammatical theory whose range of objects is more narrowly delimited. It would have to be shown either that the respective fact is a genuinely admissible text-instance for the limited range of objects, or that it is apt to challenge that very delimitation itself. This can, however, only be done on the assumption that there is sufficient clarity as to the domain of linguistics as well as to the actual (or potential) relations of linguistics with other language-centred disciplines – i.e. as to how the range of verbal interactions may be made transparent through different activities, and how such counter-arguments can be developed into a rational (controlled) strategy of research.

This point has already been mentioned and will be dealt with more extensively in the following, in connection with the possible justification of the 'external' motivation. (In the course of his attempt to develop a constructive alternative to Isenberg's proposals, Lang sketches a scheme which I should like to consider as one of those rare instances to determine,inside linguistics, the function of linguistics within all the other language-centred disciplines. Cf. the following.)

1.5. The 'external' justification is directly related to the definition of the function of grammatical theory within linguistics, and furthermore to the definition of the function of linguistics in the domain of all language-centred disciplines. The common feature of both definitions was that grammatical theory and linguistics respectively aim at establishing *general* laws (§1.2 and §1.4). In principle, the position of linguistics among the language-centred disciplines, as well as the relationship between the latter and linguistics, could be indicated *more geometrico:* linguistics is, in all events, the 'preceding discipline', whereas the respective individual discipline is defined by the investigation of specific characteristics of 'verbal utterances', by specific questions and aims within the wider (more inclusive) range of objects which I have circumscribed as 'verbal interactions'.

The attempt to fathom the implications of this rather evocative synthesis of all language-centred disciplines yields rigorous conditions for a mutually-conditioned heuristics as well as theory construction, and thus binding obligations for a coordinated research procedure. It remains to be proved, however, that this synthesis is required by at least one of the disciplines mentioned, in our case, by the study of literature. To anticipate the consequences for linguistics: the difficulties, becoming increasingly manifest at present, in achieving a consensus as to whether, and as to how, linguistics may be built up as an empirical theoretical science, are, in our view, to be explained by the insufficient clarification of its function in the ensemble of all language-centred disciplines. Linguistics will be an empirical discipline in such measure as it describes, and explains, observable regularities (i.e. structures them in the manner indicated). It is, however, not an empirical discipline in the usual sense in that it attempts to grasp the phenomenon of *one* specific area of experience in an *exhaustive* way – not even if the notion of exhaustivity is restricted to specific aspects or to specific *corpora*. The picture which presents itself is not the picture of a uni-dimensional segmentation of all language phenomena, implying the corresponding segmentation of language disciplines. It is much rather the picture of a controlled, multi-dimensional, 'stage-by-stage'-approximation of one complex phenomenon (as this is, if I am not mistaken, also prevalent in the natural and the social sciences): the general law-like regularities of verbal interactions which linguistics aims at are of a 'deeper' level, as it were, than the general law-like regularities aimed at by the study of literature, for instance. The latter field can, and must, in order to be able to formulate its own laws, take recourse to the statements of linguistics, or reformulate these in its own terms. Conversely, the former regularities can only be established on the basis of an extensive heuristics for the domain of all language-centred disciplines. The simple (and often naive) appeal to 'intuition' is thus to be excluded.

1.6. All this implies an immediate criticism of current linguistics, as well as (in our case) of the procedures of literary study. I have already suggested the kind of criticism to be levelled at linguistic procedures in § 1.4.: it is not only that 'pragmatic' factors are advanced against a model of grammar whose properties (and, in particular, whose 'pragmatic extendability') are far from clear, but there is also no differentiation between *basic* 'pragmatic' elements and relations (from the observation of general regularities of 'verbal interactions') and *secondary* ones. (This remains true also when a set, even an ordered set, of pragmatic factors is postulated as a representation of 'communication situations': in the transcription of these factors precisely the above differentiation, which is central for us, is lost; cf. for instance Wunderlich, 1970). The immediate result of all this is the current proliferation of conceptualities from all those fields which may, or can, purportedly be subsumed under 'pragmatics' (or under a concept of 'text' defined 'semiotically'). Such conceptualities remain irrelevant to linguistics as long as they are not connected with some controlled technique which would help to explicate the suggested *systematic* relationship between linguistics and the language-centred disciplines in a rational way.

As for the procedures within the study of literature, the criticism concerns the discussion of the topic 'linguistics and the study of literature' in the widest possible sense. As far as I can see, this discussion has been, and is being, conducted on two levels.

The first level is the level of the *description* of 'verbal works of art', or of the 'verbal nature' of the object of the study of literature, of 'literature'. The controversy is essentially about what function is to be ascribed to linguistics more or less between the following two poles: linguistics supplies instruments which permit a better (or only easier) analysis of the 'literary content' (whatever that may be) of 'verbal works of art'; and linguistics alone provides structuring means which may help to illuminate the specific processes of the constitution of such 'verbal utterances' as belong to the class of 'literary texts'.

The second level is the level of the *methodology* of the study of literature. The two points of departure are the *differentiae specificae* of 'literature', on the one hand, and the possibilities of developing the 'scientificness' of critical statements about literature, on the other. The controversy here is essentially about the way in which the study of literature may be built up as a 'science' in analogy to linguistics, or about whether the nature of the data of literary study would require the development of 'another' type of science. (This sometimes leads on to the consequence that linguistics, too, is to be subsumed under this different notion of science.) Topical oppositions (which often merely represent more modern formulations of the 'classical' opposition of 'sciences' vs 'arts', 'Natur- vs Geisteswissenschaften', etc.) are 'hermeneutics' vs 'structuralism', or 'structuralism' or 'pragmatics' or 'communicative theory of action' vs 'generativism' – where the shifting of the elements of the oppositions indicate clearly how blurred and unstable such delimitations are.

The discussion on both these levels (for an extensive presentation cf. Ihwe, 1972a) exhibits, I think, two fundamental defects. The first involves the inability to conceive of the problem of the relations between linguistics and literary study in any other way than as summarising procedures (level of description), or superficial analogies, or global designs (level of methodology). The second defect, by which, I think, the first is necessarily entailed, concerns the status of the conceptual matter itself as it is used in the discussion of the topic "linguistics and literary study". On both sides it is – implicitly or explicitly – assumed that the respective conceptualities are ultimate instances (something which normally kills communication quickly), or that the conceptual matter of the other may be reduced to one's own (which normally creates something like an 'imperialism' of a conceptual terminology, which is then accepted or rejected).

In contradistinction to all this, I am of the opinion that the meaning of the topic "linguistics and literary study" can only be realised fully, if it is understood as a challange to reconstruct at least the two disciplines involved (in principle, however, the ensemble of all language-centred disciplines) from the mutually-conditioned, and in some sense common, definition of their object. Historically viewed, this may sound extremely trivial. What stands in need of discussion, however, is the question of the empirical content of the language-centred disciplines. As for linguistics, an outline of its development has come into view which takes this question – at least for part of its domain – seriously. I have been trying to make the essence of this development clear in the preceding paragraphs (cf. also §3.2.). As for literary study, there have only been provisional attempts to elucidate the nature of this question and to intimate some of the possible consequences. One thing, however, has become clear: what has become institutionalised as "the study of literature" is as far away from an empirical and theoretical science as, in another area of human superstition, astrology is from astronomy.

1.7. I have now reached the point at which a more extensive discussion of the study of literature becomes necessary. To summarise what has been said so far: first, a specification of the object of literary study will only be of interest once it is conceived of as a constitutive sub-process within the frame of all language-centred disciplines, and also in a definite relation to linguistics. Secondly, this does in no way advocate a 'linguistisation' of the study of literature; point one is, rather, necessarily entailed by the question of the empirical content of both the study of literature and linguistics (as well as all the other language-centred disciplines). Thirdly, literary study (like all the other language-centred disciplines) is tied to a certain conception of linguistics; this conception in itself, however, can only be realised if it is informed by converging conceptions from, ideally, all the language-centred disciplines.

The mutual relationship to be noticed here is undoubtedly a product of the assumption that the anthropological and/or social sciences concerned are to be conceived of as *empirical and theoretical sciences*; it is on the other hand also convincing evidence for the validity of this assumption. This evidence is the more convincing as it is given by scientific practice, by the sucesses or failures in the course of the construction of these disciplines. (I have therefore deliberately excluded a more extensive discussion of the problems of the "theory of knowledge".) By "successes in scientific practice" I mean the actual elaboration of strategies of research capable of being put into practice, together with an indication of the functions which may or may not be served by such strategies of research with regard to specific applications. The latter point of view is the superordinated one, it raises the further task of formulating corresponding perspectives of application, to assess their relative importance, and to establish priorities. The fact that the criteria involved will be of a social (or of a society-critical) nature may merely be mentioned here. I shall return to this question at greater length in Section 2 (§2.8 and §2.9.) and Section 3 (§3.5.).

2. THE EMPIRICAL CONTENT OF THE STUDY OF LITERATURE

2.1. The question of the empirical content of the study of literature could be answered by pointing to its existing practice and saying it has to do with the description and evaluation ('interpretation') of given objects – of 'verbal works of art' or 'literary texts', or however one cares to name these objects. (The perspectives, too, in which such objects are treated may differ greatly: e.g. directed more at the 'intrinsic' or the 'extrinsic' aspects, to use Wellek and Warren's terminology.)

This type of answer seems to be generally accepted today – even though individual practice may follow widely different paths according to different approaches and schools. The point of departure is something like 'literature' (to use a general term), and one attempts either to explain this 'phenomenon' from a philosophical foundation (in an 'aesthetics' based on one of the many diverse '-isms') or/and to develop specific techniques to describe or, better, to appropriate 'literature'. What happens is basically very simple: the set of 'verbal utterances' is, in this perspective, divided up into two complementary subsets: 'literature' and 'non-literature'. What counts as 'literature' is laid down by the very categories (criteria) that were used in the delimitation of the phenomenon 'literature' itself. Such 'essentialist definitions' (because that is what they are) necessarily characterise 'literature' as an infinite set (though I would doubt whether the advocates of such essentialist definitions would be prepared to accept this conclusion with all its consequences): every verbal utterance exhibiting such and such attributes ('qualities') *is*, or must be, by definition, an instance of 'literature'. This is logically connected with the profoundly normative character of such 'essentialist definitions': what is to be counted as 'literature' is – at least in principle – laid down once and for all. A certain measure of 'literariness' is given, then, to the extent that 'literature' is ordered hierarchically by virtue of value judgements: some 'literary works of art' are assigned a paradigmatic value, others which resemble them only to a limited extent are ranged as 'deviations' range among the lowly-valued regions of 'literature'. In principle there will then be as many conceptions of literature as there are schools and opinions. And the field of literary study will present itself as a field of competing schools and opinions, each of which will be eager to have its own conception of literature spread and accepted as widely as possible.

It might be objected that this is a gross overstatement of the case: it will always be possible to establish a common class of what counts as 'literature', however small it may be: one will at least be able to reach some agreement over a handful of 'great works of art'. This way is illusory, however. For if one examines the arguments for the 'greatness' of a 'work of art', the differing conceptions of literature become apparent with all forcefulness: they are essentially based upon *value-statements*. (Such and such an attribute of a 'work of art' is made responsible for its 'greatness' by *X*, i.e. is valued more highly than other attributes, which in turn, however, are made responsible for its 'greatness' by *Y*, etc.) Value-statements are statements related to points of view. And as schools and opinions develop precisely because of differing points of view, value-assignments will rarely coincide – quite apart from the fact that the same values (as for instance 'great') have a different function for each point of view, and that normally no complete and well-ordered system of values has been developed to guarantee that value-assignments can be made in an unambiguous consistent, or predictable way. The procedure quite obviously involved in all this is individualistic and authoritarian, and largely determined by accidentals, reproducing more or less directly the prejudices and pressures of the political and socio-cultural context of the individual and his group.

It may have become clear what type of 'literary study' this answer to the question of the empirical content of the study of literature is related to.[2]

It must, however, be stressed that the critical analysis just given does not

[2] It is a different matter to ascribe to activities of this type another function, i.e. to assign tasks to them which are usually subsumed under 'literary criticism'. *Here* we have to do with activities which exhibit their socio-cultural commitments quite openly: they seek to direct 'literary' production and reception on the basis of certain norms (systems of values) which may derive from the most diverse needs. But even on this level all is not arbitrary; from the conception of the study of literature to be developed in the following, both a programme of 'literary didactics' and a programme of 'literary criticism' may be developed, and the latter will at least commit the 'critic' to a way of behaviour which is critically reflected with regard to his society (something which, in principle, should result from his insight into the processes of the 'attainment of literary status' of a verbal utterance, processes which he himself co-determines as an essential factor; cf. infra). The practice of the 'literary scholar' as I have described it thus in its totality invites severest critical attack in this perspective also – it is neither literary study, nor literary criticism, nor literary didactics, in this sense.

employ oppositions like 'modern vs traditional'. On the contrary: the majority of those activities which claim to be entitled to the designation 'modern literary study' are naturally included in this analysis in its entirety (cf. also above §1.6.). Thus the introduction of the methodology of (Chomsky's) generative grammar into literary study does not change the given picture in a *qualitative* way: rather it adds some new aspects and makes for a consolidation of certain positions (for example, by taking concepts, and distinctions related to them, which by their very nature are nothing but *constructs*, to be empirical objects; a case in point is the adaptation of the famous distinction between 'competence' and 'performance', especially the introduction of a 'poetic competence' in order to give a more 'comprehensive' and 'systematic' account of the 'infiniteness' of 'literature' just discussed, by setting up a 'generative poetics' as a formal analogue to a 'generative grammar'; cf. on this also §3.2. infra). The same applies generally to all the various kinds of attempts to 'improve' the character of literary study by propagating the introduction of formal means and techniques (whether of a statistical or structural nature): it is a triviality that the use of formal means and techniques in the empirical sciences can only be made meaningful and effective after a definition of the *empirical* task has been given which is specified precisely and is a direct result of the delimitation of the object of investigation. As long as this requirement is not met with, the 'results' yielded by the application of formal means and techniques in literary study can only be checked as to whether they 'are correct', i.e. as to whether the means have been employed correctly (essentially a most primitive requirement, but still not met with in most cases). What sense they make for the study of literature, however, is impossible to ascertain. One might perhaps, if anything, infer which parts of the quasi-study of literature, as sketched above, they perpetuate in what form.

2.2. The picture just presented here of what I have called the 'quasi-study of literature', as I cannot see in what sense it might claim to be 'scientific', is at the same time meant to be a first circumscription of a certain *partial* area of the *observational range* of the study of literature, when I pose the question of the empirical content of the study of literature in the following way: I understand this question to ask precisely after that which so far has always been presupposed as 'given' and posited as 'phenomenon *per se*', respectively; as the question of how it comes to be that a 'verbal utterance' *has the* (*valid, accepted*) *status* of an instance of 'literature'. I take the central phrase of my answer, "to have the (valid, accepted) status" to be the central, if one will, 'pragmatic' notion of the study of literature: it implies, in my analysis, that we have to indicate *for whom* a 'verbal utterance' counts as 'literature', and furthermore that this is true at a *certain point in time* and *in a certain situation* (more precisely: at a certain place, in a certain physio-psychological condition, in certain political and socio-culturally conditioned circumstances).

I thus delimit a *field of observation* which is not solely determined by the occurrence of a 'verbal utterance' of such and such a kind. I am rather observing processes within which 'verbal utterances' function as components and products: my explication of the expression "to have [a] (valid, accepted) status" presupposes that a 'verbal utterance' *exists* as the result of human activity, and in my description of the components I also suggested that it was the concurrence of certain factors which led to a 'verbal utterance' becoming marked in a certain respect.[3] I have so far used the expression 'literature' for that. It must have become apparent by now, however, that this expression, if it is to be given empirical content *in this context*, must be examined critically. It can no longer serve to classify phenomena, it rather represents an object to be investigated: in what contexts is the expression 'literature' used? One such context comprises the activities of the quasi-study of literature or of 'literary criticism', as they were analysed in §2.1. But it must also have become clear that this cannot yet be the primary object of investigation: the expression 'literature' usually appears in contexts in which persons act under the pressure of cultural instances, institutions of society, and are thus obliged to process 'verbal utterances' in a certain way.

Hence it seems natural to claim that all this must be preceded by an investigation of those processes in which a notion of literature is not introduced, established and conserved, but in which the "original, ordinary functions" of verbal utterances are of primary importance. On this level of inquiry it is in no way obvious that something like the 'literary status' of a 'verbal utterance' does exist at all. We can only, and this is actually all we are allowed to do, formulate our 'prior knowledge' (or in terms of ideological criticism, our socio-culturally conditioned pre-conceptions) as a working hypothesis. This hypothesis might be worded as follows:

(v) if we conceive of the whole area of verbal interactions as a field of social processes within which verbal utterances fulfil certain functions as components of (partly verbal, partly extra-verbal) behaviour, then one may delimit a *specific set of (psycho-social) functions* all of which are fulfilled by a *specific type of verbal utterance*, and only by this type.

[3] Which clearly does not mean that there are no other effects resulting these processes; on the contrary, I would claim that every component is subject to influences of the other components in a certain way; I am restricting myself to the previously mentioned effect on 'verbal utterances' only in order to clarify the concept of 'literature', cf. also §§2.5 and 3.5.

In other words we postulate some delimitable '(re-)action' (in the widest possible sense) against a delimitable set of verbal utterances. The only posits introduced are the concepts of 'verbal utterance' and 'verbal interaction' as introduced above in §1.2 as undefined primitives. The hypothesis itself is therefore formulated essentially with the help of fundamental notions of linguistics, its contents, however, define specific problems in the manner indicated, which in turn have to be filled with content by appropriate problem-definitions in the disciplines concerned with language. (In the following I shall only be concerned with the study of literature.) On the other hand, the hypothesis rests on the notion of 'social processes' and 'psycho-social functions'. The introduction of these concepts is justified by the assumption that the study of literature is an empirical and theoretical science, more precisely that it belongs, together with all the other "language-centred disciplines", to the range of the 'social sciences'. I shall not attempt any further justification of this here, and thus posit the two concepts introduced as fundamental notions of social science. The elaboration and verification of the hypothesis will then require a series of observations and experiments which can only be devised in an interdisciplinary way. Practically no work of any kind has been done on this within the study of literature. The next task of the study of literature will therefore be to elaborate heuristic programmes and to examine the instrumentarium of all the pertinent anthropological and social sciences (for instance of empirical and theoretical psychology, empirical and theoretical anthropology and sociology), to develop the hypothesis in this process, and, finally, to find forms of (cooperative) empirical research. To emphasise it once more: this will only be possible if linguistics investigates the fundamental and, in this sense, 'more general' functions of 'verbal utterances' in human behaviour according to the constitutive mutual relationship as it was developed in §1.5. and §1.7.

2.3. Now our considerations begin to come full circle. To come back to the question of a formal and empirical pragmatics (§1.4.): from our 'external' perspective we may derive arguments to secure the transition from the narrower range of objects 'verbal utterance' to the wider range 'verbal interaction' by attempting to structure the fields of observation of all language-centred disciplines in a unified and coherent way. At the same time we must ask ourselves whether our analysis of the expression "to have [a] (valid, accepted) status" in §2.2. was exhaustive. Here the use of one of the many 'communication models', as they appear to thrive all about the place today, seems to suggest itself as a possible framework for an answer. I should prefer not to pursue this course. It is completely obscure to me what kind, and what degree, of structuring can be achieved in the context under discussion by such 'models'. First of all, the formal systems on which such attempts are based have been created for quite different fields of application, i.e. mainly with respect to technical realisability. The analysis of the regularities to be structured, has shown on the other hand, that, if it tries to give more than a superficial account or some 'philosophical' discussion the strategies of verbal interaction follow patterns quite different from those invented by the communication engineers (cf. e.g. the analyses of rather simple 'speech acts' in the "ordinary language philosophy" tradition).

The field of observation of the study of literature is – according to hypothesis (v) – a very complex social sub-process. Its essential components are persons *P* who 'process' the verbal utterances of a specific type *A* in a specific way. The expression 'process' is to suggest that the field of observation will be distorted if it is forced into a 'communication model' in which the 'transmission' of a 'message' is central, i.e. for which an immediate principle of success is postulated (the correct 'decoding' of the content of the 'message'). What we are observing, however, are such activities of persons *P* as can be called 'decoding' of a 'message' only in a very forced interpretation. The issue here is not (or not primarily) how objectifiable contents are established and transmitted; it is rather the *appropriation* and the *use* of 'verbal utterances' according to their suitability to play a certain role in specific contexts or strategies of behaviour – a role which can hardly ever be analysed in terms of the objectifiable content. (It remains to be determined whether, and how, the differing aspects of 'verbal utterances' come to bear on this, but the question will have to be dealt with more extensively below, cf. especially §3.3.)

An empirical pragmatics of the language-centred disciplines thus comprises the analysis and description of precisely these constitutive elements of complex sub-component processes. It aims first of all at the fundamental regularities of the different fields of observation. It attempts further to be exhaustive in the sense that it seeks to take into account *all* regularities that are actually observable. This implies on the one hand that it is not enough to enumerate a handful of 'pragmatic factors' (cf. §1.6.), and on the other, that correspondences and differences are expressed *systematically*. I have tried to show on what general methodological assumptions this is possible. An empirical pragmatics of the language-centred disciplines (including linguistics) thus no longer appears to be the programme of a modern super-science or just a beautiful promise, in brief an unattainable Utopia, but a working programme which is quite within the bounds of our present possibilities only, however, if the attribute 'empirical' is taken seriously. As to the relationship between empirical pragmatics and formal pragmatics, what I have said in §1.2.–§1.3. about the theory of grammar, in principle holds good here also. I therefore do not share the view either of those who quote the state of research in formal pragmatics as an alibi for their ignorance or their scepticism with regard to the postulate of exhaustivity just introduced (a postulate which is essentially concerned with empirical matters), or of those who, conversely, think that the only admissible 'scientific' foundation of such activities as are currently summarised by 'pragmatics' can be expected from an elaboration of formal pragmatics. In both cases the expression seems to me to be unnecessarily mystified.

In the preceding I had used the expression 'processing' as a general concept for the characterisation of all those individual processes which form the fields of observation of the language-centred disciplines. It is more neutral, for a start, than the notion of 'text-processing' which was introduced by G. Wienold (cf. now 1972, especially Chapter III, §3.2). The latter expression attributes a specific quality to verbal expressions A, i.e. a 'text-quality'. Though this postulate may have already become evident from the characterisations of that component process which is of particular interst to us, I should like to set this question aside for the time being. The answer to it may become amenable to more rigorous formulation in two respects: on the one hand, from an applicational point of view (§2.8.), and on the other, from a structural-functional point of view (§3.2.ff). In both perspectives, hypothesis (v) thus receives its 'literary' content proper.

2.4. What then is to be the meaning of statement

(vi) Person P processes a verbal utterance A

in terms of the study of literature? In my analysis of the expression "to have [a] (valid, accepted) status" (§2.2.) I had isolated the following components:

(vii) a verbal utterance
for whom?
at a specific point in time
in a specific situation.

If we take into account the further specifications of the last-named component, we may establish the following objects in our field of observation:

(viii) Persons P, who are distributed in sub-groups P^1, P^2, P^3,...

relative to

(ix) time intervals $T^1, T^2, T^3, \ldots$
(x) spaces $R^1, R^2, R^3, \ldots$
(xi) (socio-cultural) contexts $K^1, K^2, K^3, \ldots$
(xii) (psycho-physical) conditions $Z^1, Z^2, Z^3, \ldots$
(xiii) verbal utterances $A^1, A^2, A^3, \ldots$

(The capitals with superscripts indicate distinct sets. Like the corresponding small letters with subscripts in (xiv), they designate constructs, whereas the capital letters P and A are used as abbreviations for some 'immediately given' observational entities throughout the text.)

An *elementary observational situation* may then be characterised by an ordered pair of data,

(xiv) $\langle p_i; \{t_i, r_i, k_i, z_i, a_i\}\rangle$,

such that

$$p_i \in P,$$
$$t_i \in T^i,$$
$$r_i \in R^i,$$
$$k_i \in K^i,$$
$$z_i \in Z^i,$$
$$a_i \in A^i.$$

t_i designates a point in time; r_i a point in space; k_i an instance of a socio-cultural context; z_i an instance of a psycho-physical condition; a_i an instance of a type of verbal utterance. These assigments take for granted that there are mechanisms of analysis such that it is possible, in principle, to decide unambiguously whether a datum belongs to a determined class. It is thus taken for granted (a presupposition which implies rather strong empirical assumptions) that it is also possible to form classes over socio-cultural contexts, psycho-physical conditions, and verbal utterances. It is therefore necessary to add a supplement: in all three cases, the time-space coordinate will form the natural basis for the distinction of (sub-)classes. I therefore do not postulate sets of contexts, conditions, and utterances by virtue of specific, and constant, attributes but assume that particular contexts, conditions, and utterances, may be distinguished temporally (and spatially). It must be emphasised that the question of variability and constancy, respectively, is characterised as an empirical question. This question appears in linguistics in such a form that it is not only the relations between the underlying linguistic system and the actual use of language which are treated in an abstract way, but equally the spatial and temporal dimensions of the language-system; one asks what, in the system of a language, is subject to change, or what breadth of variation is exhibited by a system of language in space and time.

In the case of a_i in (xiv), the mechanism of analysis would be a grammar which is time-space sensitive and which would assign to verbal utterances a structural description and a spatio-temporal index. Within an A^i one may make further divisions on the basis of different *types of structure* (cf. §2.7., and Section 3). The weaker condition for p_i is explained by the fact that the group P^i to which p_i – in this context – belongs can only be determined on the basis of specific 'functional' relations which are established between the elements of the second member of the ordered pair in (xiv). This is to characterise the expression 'processing' in (vi) as an evaluative concept (or an evaluative function):

(xv) Person p_i *is prepared to assign* the verbal utterance a_i, at a specific point in time t_i, at a specific point in space r_i, within the socio-cultural context k_i, and in the psycho-physical condition z_i, *a determined value f.*

We must now ask ourselves whether the delimitation of the *elementary situation of observation* is sufficient to describe systematically how these 'functional' relations are established, how further structuring of P can be achieved, and, finally, how those properties of the value-assignment, which are characteristic of *literary* study, can be distinguished. Obviously this is not the case: it makes it possible for us to state *that* there are such processes in the field of observation, but not *how* they originate and of what nature they are. We must therefore extend the delimitation more specifically in the direction of the datum p_i, which has remained unanalysed so far.

2.5. Before going on, we must mention a few more observational facts. The assignment of a value can obviously not be understood as a momentary event. We can observe that a verbal utterance, once marked in this way, will retain this evaluation for shorter or longer time-intervals. This does not mean, on the other hand, that it will forever retain the 'original' value: as person p_i varies, the value will vary with the variations in K^i and Z^i, or the transitions between K^i and K^{i+1}, and Z^i and Z^{i+1}, etc.... It may thus be 'shifted', enter new relations, be adapted, corrected, and rejected. We can also observe that the assignment of a value may be objectified by the evaluating person p_i, but that, in most cases, the process proper is usually abbreviated or even re-interpreted. The subject reflecting on his use of 'verbal utterances' is, in general, incapable of reconstructing in an objective way the *systematic* connections between all those factors which govern his evaluations – and thus the course of his processing of 'verbal utterances'. This is impossible not only because of the large and varied number of such processes a person is continually required to perform (biological-psychological limitations), but also because of his orientation according to the existing conventions of his group, i.e. the channeling patterns which are accepted as processing procedures by the society (socio-cultural limitations). With these limitations, some of the factors have already been named which govern his *actual* behaviour. The assignment of a value must thus not be seen as a spontaneous – conscious or unconscious – act of the will of a hypothetically-free individual, it is much rather the resultant of a multiplicity of interacting processes which take place simultaneously, are interconnected in specific ways, and are determined biologically, psychologically, and socio-culturally (and thus, in large measure, group-specifically), i.e. are part of a continuum. On this basis we may now reconnect our argument with the observations introduced earlier in order to create a uniform picture: every attempt to establish something like the 'original' value is doomed to failure in view of the fact that the value under discussion is of the kind of a vector. This is also true of all persons *P*: it would be meaningless to differentiate on this level between 'producers' ('authors' etc.) and 'recipients' (readers' etc.) – one more reason to reject the scheme o fthe various 'communication models', which are essentially based on the differentiation between 'sender' and 'receiver'.

2.6. This extension of the elementary situation of observation thus requires us to look for regularities which may be observed in the course of evolution of such values. My considerations converge here, and as it seems to me not at all accidentally, with the approach of Russian Formalism, in particularly with its elaboration by Tynyanov. The approach of Russian Formalism is directed at the discovery of "inner-, and extra-, literary" regularities which make for the 'literary status' of a verbal utterance and cause it to function as a 'literary fact' (Tynyanov's expression). The emphasis here was on the 'inner-literary' regularities. I need not reiterate here my interpretation of Russian Formalism, which centres in the contention that Russian Formalism marks the central turning point in the history of literary study and represents the first elaborated sketch of a study of literature as an empirical and theoretical science (cf. Ihwe, 1972a; especially Ch. III).

A critical perusal, for example, of Tynyanov (1924/1969), from this point of view, shows how radically and consistently the accepted 'essentialist' (or 'static') notions of literature are called in question, and how in their stead an instrumentarium of operational concepts is introduced which delimits a field of observation in our sense (a 'dynamic' concept of literature, to quote Tynyanov's pair of opposites). The central notion is the notion of 'evolution'. (The observations to be subsumed under 'evolution' are based both on the theory of perception and on epistemology, neither of which I shall consider here.) 'Literature' is conceived of as an 'evolving series' whose guiding principle is the principle of significant opposition to "other verbal series", i.e. to other types of verbal utterances and thus verbal behaviour. Only inasmuch as this difference is maintained may it fulfil its specific function, which consists in the "disautomating of perception". Insofar as it is itself subject to the "laws governing the automation of perception" – as the linguistic means which it employs to fulfil its functions are 'worn down' – it is forced to search continually for new forms to re-establish the difference or to maintain it. The means used at a specific point in time will depend, on the one hand, on the means used at the same time in other verbal series ('extra-literary'), and will be determined negatively, on the other, by those which have been used previously and have thus become 'automated' ('inner-literary'). The problem, then, consists in positively determining the 'direction' in which the evolution of the 'literary series' will take place. In Russian Formalism, three principal possibilities were envisaged: (a) the reactivation of means available in earlier periods ('grandparents' or 'uncle'), which thus do not (any longer) belong to the range of the automated means; or the adoption of means from other 'national literatures'; (b) the elevation to the status of literary facts' of phenomena which had been "outside the literary series" before (or for a sufficiently long time so as not to be automated (any longer)) (cf. Tynyanov's 1924/1969-illustration by the 'letter'; this also includes the purposeful use of dialectal and/or diastratal differentiations, in contradistinction to 'standard' or 'educated language'); (c) operations within the system itself.

These *principal* possibilities may also co-occur; their concrete manifestations will depend, on the one hand, on the stage of development of the respective natural language at a specific point in time (as to the concept of 'stage', cf. Lieb (1970) and the review by Heger (1972)) and, on the other hand, on the state of the respective 'national literature' at the same time. The notion of the "state of the national literature" does not comprise only verbal utterances of the natural language involved which at that time possess the status of 'literary fact', but also all those verbal utterances from other natural languages which are at that very same point in time (in translations, or in the original) constitutive elements of the set of verbal utterances marked in such a way (cf. (b) supra).

The Russian Formalists had emphasised specifically the 'intrinsic dynamics' of the 'literary series' in order to work out its specific character – and thus the specific character of the study of literature. They were, first of all, interested in the 'inner-literary' regularities and held the opinion that only after these had been clarified could the complex interaction of 'inner-' and 'extra-literary' regularities be discovered, without precipitately relating the former causally with the latter (cf. for instance Tynyanov (1927/1969)). Some central concepts to denote 'inner-literary' regularities are "the work as system", "the genre as system", "the epoch as system". The term 'system' is used to mean that the elements – on the various levels indicated, cf. the following – can only be made out in their positional values, in relation to each other and to the whole. They may nevertheless be considered in isolation, but an examination of this kind remains restricted to the 'form' of the element and does not grasp its 'function'. It thus misses precisely those functional relationships which make a verbal utterance a 'literary fact', or coordinate it to a 'genre'. Elements of the same 'form' can have very different 'functions' in different systems, and it is, in fact, only the functional approach which takes the evolutionary connections into account, allowing for the recognition of different systems on the basis of functional differences. As already suggested, the evolutionary connection is represented by an ascending hierarchy of concepts (work-element, work; work as genre-element, genre; genre as epoch-element, epoch). It is only by passing through these levels, that verbal utterances of the same, and of different, 'epochs' become, in principle, comparable with each other. And only on the level of the 'epoch' may the differential function for the respective 'extra-literary life', as fulfilled by the 'literary' series, be identified, as it is a function of the whole 'literary series' at a specific point in time, and not of only one of its elements. It is of such differential functions, as they emerge in the course of the 'epochs', that the function of the 'literary series' in its totality, as an 'evolving series', is composed (cf. Tynyanov (1927/1969), pp. 449–451).

If one inquires into the nature of these concepts, it becomes apparent immediately that they are conceived of as pragmatic concepts. Their essential components are the 'carriers' of these functions, i.e. they do not designate 'objective' facts, but facts relative to persons *P*. This is particularly true for the notion of 'national literature', or the "state of a national literature", whose meaning is explicated by the pragmatic notion of 'epoch': from the multiplicity of activities directed at 'literature', the traits of an epoch will emerge from the recurrent coincidence of coordination (especially of 'works' and 'genres') and evaluation ('dominants' in works, 'dominants' in genres) with regard to those groups which determine the 'literary life' (in 'production' and/or 'reception': here these concepts are quite appropriate as they refer essentially to the different manipulative strategies at work in the actual processing of verbal utterances; see the following). And the 'objective' features of 'literature', in particular, on which most essentialist definitions are based (as for example metre, rhythm, semantic figures, etc.), are interpreted by Russian Formalism quite consciously relative to this point of view (cf. our remarks on the differentiation between 'form' and 'function').

Here, however, a fundamental limitation of Russian Formalism becomes manifest. Its reconstruction of the study of literature as the theory of the evolving 'literary series' is essentially grounded on the role of specific groups. It foreshortens the actual processes to the retracing of the antagonism between various conceptions of literature. The hierarchical ordering of works, the hierarchical ordering of genres on the basis of their functional meaning (cf. the central notion of 'dominant') reproduce the values of the dominating stratum of the groups which, in a more or less institutionalised way, govern the handling of the cultural products of society. The observed 'struggles' and 'changing of systems', which are viewed as the significant features of 'literary evolution' (cf. the two cited articles by Tynyanov) thus prove to be substitutes from precisely those 'social series' whose interference had first been excluded programmatically (one of the most telling examples in this respect is Jakobson's analysis of the notion of 'realism' of 1921, cf. Jakobson (1921/1969)).

I should like to give these findings a positive interpretation by connecting them with the distinction between the primary and secondary object of investigation, as it was introduced in §2.2. However much we must be on our guard to accept, in the delimintation of the object of our investigation, proposals amounting to the conscious or unconscious reproduction (and thus 'scientific' camouflageing) of an ideological manipulation of the data, we must be equally careful to avoid the construction of a 'pure' object of investigation. 'Pure' characterises an object of research which is won through the restriction of the field of observation to directly amenable regularities (in some 'physical' or 'phenomenological' sense). Thus the activities criticised in §2.1. form an integral part of the field of observation as suggested above, which might be further analysed using the concepts developed by the Russian Formalists. I have therefore introduced the *elementary* situation of observation as a situation of observation that is basically capable of extension in this direction.

2.7. This extension implies that the primary and secondary objects of investigation are connected in such a way as to yield a *complex* object of research. And this is, in fact, what the facts demand. All the observational facts quoted in §2.5. suggest that the evaluations of a person P_i are governed by a set of complex interrelated factors from among which I should now like to isolate those which are responsible for the more or less institutionalised dealing with cultural products, as they are the most essential in this context: close analysis would have to show how these institutions evolve, how they are constituted, how they are interrelated, how they mutate, what antagonistic relationships there are between them, how they exercise progressive stabilisation or regressive effects, and also whether they exert unimedial or multi-medial effects (cf. §3.1.) – in short, it would have to show how mind and behaviour in this social domain are *manipulated*, and investigate whether, and how, a common denominator could be found for all this.

The expression 'manipulation', which is introduced here as a keyword, will be dealt with preliminarily in the next section, where I shall also present fragments of such a close analysis from a specific point of view. It immediately follows from §2.6., however, that, depending on what aspect of the *complex* object is emphasised one is bound to focus on different verbal activities of persons P_i. It should be possible, at least in principle, to establish exhaustively the 'spheres of action' of a person P_i this way, depending on what functionally, determined contexts a person P_i is related to. This is an empirical task and cannot be solved by a pre-established classification of 'roles' (or similar entities). (The most sterile of these I take to be the schema of the 'communication model', cf. §2.5[4]).

The P^1, P^2, P^3,... in (viii), however, refer to the actual, temporarily changing, group-formations (according to our characterisation of all other objects): using the terminology of Russian Formalism, the time-space coordinate would, in this case, coincide with the spatio-temporal extensions of the epoch-concept. The reason for characterising p_i in (xiv) as simply an element of P (i.e. in the weakest possible way) may now be clear: p_i *may* be an element of various P^{11}, P^{12},..., P^{1n}, at the same time. The value-assignment will then depend upon what group-specifically concretised 'action-sphere' p_i acts in.[5] That is, it will be done in a form specific for this 'sphere of action' and appropriately characterising the 'sphere of action' with regard to the momentary socio-cultural determinants, on the one hand, and the ability of p_i to 'employ' the following objects, on the other:

(xvi) (1) the linguistic system of the languages $\{..., L_i, L_{i+1}, ...\}$ with $\infty > n \geqslant 1$, whereby, if $n = 1$, L_N is maximally *distinguished*, otherwise some L_i is *relatively distinguished* (the language of the linguistic community in which most processing actions of p_i take place).

(2) stages of the languages $\{..., L_i, L_{i+1}, ...\}$ (with the characterisations as in (1)).

(xvii) (1) types of verbal utterances in the languages $\{..., L_i, L_{i+1}, ...\}$ (with the characterisations as in (xvi) (1)).

[4] While revising this paper, I came upon Leo Apostel's considerations (1972) which, first of all, seem to justify particularly my scepticism towards the prevalent 'communication models', as he rejects forcefully the current procedure of simply postulating the conceptual dichotomy 'speaker-hearer' and then formalising it. It seems to me, furthermore, that the step-by-step development of an 'M-pragmatics' for natural languages (as sketched pp. 9–12) offers many parallels to my present, and subsequent, considerations here (cf. especially Apostel's point 7, p. 11).

[5] This is to do justice to the observation that one and the same person may assign several values to the same 'verbal utterance', though of a different kind, and that these values exist side by side even when they – 'objectively' – ought to exclude each other. The only restricting explanation of mine is that p_i will never act in more than one action-sphere at one and the same time, i.e. that the observation situation as described in (xiv) must be unambiguous; cf. also the following remarks.

(2) means of forming types of verbal utterances in the languages $\{..., L_i, L_{i+1}, ...\}$ (with the characterisations as in (xvi) (1)).

(xviii) (1) types of socio-cultural contexts.
(2) types of psycho-physical conditions.

I shall return to a detailed discussion of (xvi)–(xviii) below. I can now write out the *complex situation of observation* as an ordered pair of ordered data:

(xix) $\langle(p_i, a_i, t_i, r_i, k_i, z_i); (AR_i, V_i)\rangle$,

such that

(1) for a_i, t_i, r_i, k_i, z_i the same conditions hold as in (xiv).
(2) $p_i \in P^{ij}$, with $j = f(AR_j)$.

And (xv) may be rewritten as:

(xx) The value *f*, which a person p_i is prepared to assign to an utterance a_i, at a point in time t_i, at a point in space r_i, in the socio-cultural context k_i, and in the psycho-physical condition z_i, depends on the sphere of action AR_i in which p_i is acting and on his ability V_i to employ the objects named in (xvi)–(xviii).

Condition (2) in (xix) lays down that p_i's belonging to the sub-group P^{ij} of P^i is determined by the action-sphere AR_j in which p_i is situated. The complex relation of possible employment as introduced by (xvi)–(xviii) may be viewed as representing the 'active' part of a person P_i, after I had emphasised its 'passive' part, as it were, in §2.6. Such oppositions, however, similar to those which would attempt to differentiate between 'conscious' vs 'unconscious' with regard to *V*, miss the essential point by postulating pseudo-empirical 'problems'. As has become manifest from the repeated misunderstandings of the methodology of Chomsky's generative grammar, there is no point in asking for the extent to which a speaker is 'aware' of his linguistic competence – including all derivable conclusions for linguistic techniques of testing (cf. my presentation in Ihwe (1972a), §1.6.). In a certain sense, however, even p_i's possible employment of the objects named in (xvi)–(xviii) is determined, of course: his 'knowledge' of the linguistic system of L_i (any natural language), of the stage of L_i, etc., depends on the primary socialisation-processes he has gone through, on the education or non-education he has received, on the chances of his developing systematic and historical interests and of realising these (studying one or more natural languages, etc.). This becomes particularly obvious with regard to his ability to 'employ' socio-cultural contexts and psycho-physical conditions: discussing (xiv), I have already pointed out that the assumption of the existence of classes (or types) in this domain, which uses criteria other than the space-time coordinate, implies far-reaching empirical assumptions. How this kind of classification takes place is a question which can only be answered inter-disciplinarily (in the sense of our remarks on hypothesis (v)). In this context I can only state *that* such processes take place in the field of observation, as it is only on the basis of this socio-cultural assumption that I can describe the fact that persons P are capable of differentiating, controlling, and correcting their behaviour (by taking into account other contexts and experiencing other psycho-physical conditions: I shall come back to this in §§2.8.ff; cf. also §3.5). What effect this may have on the concepts of explanation and prediction of the 'classical' philosophy of science as applied to the anthropological and social sciences would have to be examined carefully. As my attempt to review this particular field of social science has shown, not enough suitable material for this kind of rigorous examination is at our disposal yet.

With the characterisations of (xvii), I am resuming occasional remarks (cf. §2.4. on A^{i} and §2.6. on the notion of '(verbal) mean' in Russian Formalism) which are to supplement classification along the temporal dimension by classification of a structural kind. Every grammar (in the more rigorous sense of §1.2.) contains a classification of types of strings of symbols. This would represent a type-forming (structural) constant for this area. It is one of the current empirical questions (cf. §1.4.) how such a classification could be extended from 'sentence'-types to 'text'-types. Proposals include 'technical' ploys within existing 'sentence-grammars' as well as an extension of the criteria for 'sentence'-types – an extension which would or would not include the 'sentence'-types established so far (for instance, specified derivational identity, indicated by a common prefix of sentence operators) – and, finally also 'qualitatively' differentiated, *additional*, classification. The last-named seems to be suggested by the fact that diverse 'sentence'-types occur side by side in 'verbal utterances'. Here however the question arises in what way 'text'-types postulated in such a manner can be mapped onto 'sentence'-types: is it possible and meaningful to postulate that the realisation of a specific 'text'-type requires a specific distribution of specific 'sentence'-types? Or would the introduction of 'text'-types necessarily imply a thorough modification of the notion of 'sentence'-types?

Previous explorations of these questions are defective either because they foreshorten the empirical investigations (which observable regularities in 'verbal utterances' suggest the introduction of 'text-types', and which do not?) in such a way as to base their approach on available typologies, or because they use formal properties of grammars as the base of typologies. In the first case the result is a proliferation of 'text-typologies' of the most diverse origins, all drawing their life more or less from the appeal to intuition or advancing normative claims (cf. also §3.4.); in the second case there is nothing but pure combinatorics, and it is impossible to decide which of the *infinitely* many possible variants (infinite in the case of grammars with only one recursive element!) is to be valid. The conclusion is very simple: only empirical analysis can decide about the direction in which a typology is to be looked for, and thus also about the selection of the appropriate grammatical model (cf. Ihwe and Petöfi and Rieser (1972)).

The elaboration of a *complete empirical* text-typology would first have to start with an investigation of the origins of such available 'text-typologies'. Here too we may go back to Russian Formalism whose notion of 'genre' covers precisely these (socio-culturally conditioned) processes of typology-formation: the function-determined reconstruction of characteristics of verbal utterances into class indices, or, in other words, the coordination, by *functional* criteria, of verbal utterances to a set of classes ordered hierarchically according to value.

The *primary* object of investigation is then delimited by the question whether and how we may correlate specific 'formal' (or structural) characteristics of verbal utterances (such as the 'length' of verbal utterances, made explicit in structural and also qualitative terms, and the kind of phonological, syntactic, and semantic construction) with certain psycho-social functions in specific behavioural contexts or strategies. The answer to this question can only be given by *empirical* research. Only on this basis will it then also be possible to distinguish the specific object of linguistics from the specific objects of all language-centred disciplines (cf. §1.4.–§1.5.): we will then be able to indicate what the *fundamental* general regularities of verbal utterances are, and what the *specific* general regularities are, *by virtue of the fact that the latter provide the foundation for the differentiation of empirical "text"-types.* In some of my own programmatic writings I have tried to illustrate the *schema* which can be derived from this formulation of the problem of the specific range of objects, in the context of 'metrics' and 'narrative theory' (cf. Ihwe (1972b, c, d)):

(xxi) the theory of grammar specifies how verbal utterances may, in general, be organised as 'texts'; literary theory specifies – in the case under discussion – how verbal utterances may be organised as 'texts' of a specific type (or of specific sub-types).

The implications for grammatical theory to be derived from (xxi) were dealt with in Section 1, the implications for 'literary theory' (I am using the term in analogy to grammatical theory) will be discussed in Section 3 (cf. particularly §3.4.). As for the relation of possible employment, the distinction made in (xvii) between (1) and (2) is important. (1) and (2) require that 'literary theory' organise, in one way or another, the 'means' which, according to hypothesis (v), characterise the verbal utterances allotted to the domain of the study of literature. (1) is to account for the fact *that* 'text'-types as singled out by (xxi) are of importance to the kind of processing of verbal utterances as well as to its actual taking place, whereas (2) aims at the 'productive' aspect of the processing of verbal utterances. Here again I can take up some of the research results of Russian Formalism, as concerns the regularities observable (cf. (a) in §2.6.). It is, however, necessary to introduce a qualification, as the observations of Russian Formalism aim essentially at the establishing of 'genres'. They do, though, also accept certain 'secondary' means of type-formation as constants (for instance the 'verbal extension' of a verbal utterance, i.e. its 'length', cf. supra the cited articles by Tynyanov). Thus it becomes understandable that Tynyanov finally names the question of 'contingency' in the "combination of function and form" as the central question in all research on the 'literary evolution' (1927/1969, p. 449). I shall not deal with this question here (cf. my discussion, Ihwe (1972a), §3.3.3.). It requires, in any event, a deeper analysis of both elements of the opposition. I have suggested the direction to be taken in my criticism of Russian Formalism for the conception of function. As to the concept of form, the direction is clear from my definition of grammatical theory and from (xxi) (cf. also §3.4.).

2.8. I should like to conclude my reflections on the question of the empirical content of the study of literature in the sense of the suggestion under §1.7. In my development of the concept of the *complex* situation of observation, I have tried to make *systematically* explicit the presence of manipulative strategies within the field of observation. Now, there is a domain in which we may isolate these manipulative strategies very nicely, it is "the teaching of literature" at school. There are several reasons for this: the domain is, first of all, somewhat surveyable. The institutions and their inferences can be identified. The 'learning processes' of a pupil are long-term processes and may be followed up continually. On the other hand, the interests of the institutions are established and reinforced in such massive measure that it is not difficult to make them explicit, even where they are not formulated directly.

What, then, does the pupil 'learn'? To give a 'neutral' answer: he learns how to handle 'literature'. That which is to count as 'literature' has already been pre-determined. Starting out from the teacher, a chain of selection and valuation processes may be observed which all follow an accepted concept of literature. The extent to which the material carriers of these processes, i.e. the hierarchy of school officials, are committed to this notion of literature, depends on the extent to which it conforms to their interests. (Here the phenomenon of the 'convergence' of 'useful' concepts of literature and its 'uses' ought to be analysed further: this analysis would demonstrate once more to what extent the development and the enforcement of a notion of literature can only be understood from the point of view of ideological criticism). These interests are of a complex nature; they tend, in any case, to stabilise the system, and they conform to the self-interpretation of the groups in power and the objective needs of their ideology. The concrete implementation of these interests take shape in the definition of a 'canon' of 'literature' whose 'appropriation' will decide about the measure of the 'education' of the pupil. The methods of such appropriation can less readily be fixed; they derive, however, in one way or another, from the points of view (socio-cultural norms) which were – explicitly or implicitly – at work in the definition of the canon. (This explains the virulence of all "discussion of method" whenever a specific method seems to threaten to restrict or disrupt the – as much as possible – direct re-working of such norms, realised as 'values', into learning material). Both variability of the canon and as its extension – in particular so as to include 'modernity' – will be tolerated (in varying measure, according to the concrete case) as long as the functioning of this type of "teaching of literature" (which is certainly not restricted to any one country) remains unaffected. What is happening may be stated in very simple terms. The capacity of processing verbal utterances is steered into a certain direction, otherwise blocked, and thus activated only so much as to make it guarantee the reproduction of the cultural values of a certain group. It is an essentialist definition of 'literature' which is learnt from a narrow sample of verbal utterances, to which all the other occurrences are related as far as their value is concerned.

It seems easy to me to explain the much-deplored 'literary fatigue' as an immediate consequence of this type of "teaching of literature". This fatigue springs from the fact that instances of 'literature' play no role, or at most a subordinate one – excluding, clearly, privileged and/or institutionally interested groups – in the daily processing of verbal utterances, as long as they are not enforced more or less strongly. Another closely connected consequence is the observable inability to derive from utterances of higher complexity information going beyond the immediate surface information. This is true at least for the average case, in contrast to which there is the training in the art of 'interpreting texts' for privileged groups, which is becoming more and more sophistical. A further relevant consequence is the increasing popularity of specific types of multimedial 'texts' with easily accessible information content (comics).

Despite the differences in the types of school and the social barriers built into advanced school education ('higher' education) the type of language and literature teaching described is, nevertheless, of so uniform a kind that one may generalise these consequences (though they have only been stated very crudely): they imply maximal manipulability in all aspects of everyday life, exploiting the inability to react in any other way than superficially to the mass of processing actions of verbal utterances required every day; and they demand conformity to the behavioural patterns which are offered (or prescribed) and which take up the space which was left untrained by the school, or which have already become firmly established *via* the canon as intellectual and emotional attitudes. (Here, however, there may be conflict whenever the distance between the required behavioural pattern and the value-bound intellectual emotional attitude is (or has become) great: this is the well-known phenomenon which has only been analysed by Brecht in some depth for the cultural domain, the phenomenon that the 'basis' develops faster than the 'super-structure').

2.9. I should like to draw three conclusions from this (still very crude) analysis.

It is first of all obvious that in this concrete area of verbal interaction only the delimitation of a complex situation of observation (with all its prerequisites) will open up a field of observation which is of social relevance. (The reconstruction of 'teaching situations', for instance, within the 'communication model' as one encounters it in various reform proposals is thus far from adequate.)

Secondly, the need to develop an alternative type of 'teaching' in this area is also a main motivation for my strategy of research as sketched above. From what has been said so far, the 'ideology-critical' intention of various alternative proposals (cf. for instance Ide (1971, 1972); as well as the references cited by Wienold (1972), especially in § 19–§34) may be accounted for systematically. To formulate this succinctly: instead of the passive appropriation of a 'canon' there will have to be directed training of the ability to process verbal utterances. The definition of teaching aims, teaching matter, and teaching methods may be derived directly from my previous reflections. By 'directed training' I mean that the 'learner' is given the chance to appropriate consciously those types of verbal utterances which play a central role in his sphere of existence and experience. And further that he is given the chance both to recognise the manipulative strategies connected with types of verbal utterances and to take an active part in the processing actions of his environment. 'Directed training' thus covers more than the training for effective behaviour in verbal interactions. It is aimed particularly at the discovery of manipulative strategies and effects of the dominant cultural institutions. It thus is directly opposed to the traditional "teaching of literature" which I have characterised above as precisely the excercise of such manipulative strategies (including the effects or 'consequences', which were crudely sketched). The corresponding approach consequently demands a radical restructuring of the whole of the teaching of language and literature. From my considerations it will be obvious that linguistic and literary teaching are to be seen as a unity; thus there was no need to stress this point in the foregoing (just as it is basically impossible to separate the teaching of language and literature in schools from their teaching in the universities): insight into differentiations and possibilities of differentiating (according to specific 'types', 'manipulative strategies', 'effects') obviously require insight into their common basis. The central object of research for a *didactics* would then be the way in which this insight is transmitted, the way, furthermore, in which insight into differentiations and possibilities of differentiating ought to be transmitted. This kind of didactics would, on the one hand, have to run parallel to the sketched construction (and thus the interconnectedness) of linguistics and all language-centred disciplines, and on the other, have to define the criteria for "success in scientific practice", as barely suggested here, one of its special topics in the perspective of application (cf. § 1.7.). I consider the construction of such a didactics to be the most important task of the study of literature in the future: it will quite evidently imply close collaboration of 'theory' and 'practice', and actually take this union for granted. The fulfilment of this programme will create the criteria for a study of literature as a 'successful' empirical and theoretical science, in the long run. These criteria will have to be met with by every kind of literary activity. As we, however, find ourselves still at the very beginning of all this, I shall not go beyond these very general remarks, and only indicate a few points of view in the following which seem to me to be of interest in this connection.

The aim "to participate actively in the processing actions of one's environment" could be stated more precisely in the light of the relation of possible employment, described in 2.7. (xvi)–(xviii) thus delimit determinable teaching matter. The organisation of this teaching matter will depend on the addressees in question and the specification of the teaching target relative to them. This specification will include, in particular, what spheres of action the addressees (will) move in and what specific groups they belong to. A classification according to primary and secondary spheres of action might also be introduced here, possibly in view of the repeatedly made distinction between primary and secondary objects of investigation. The meaning of 'acting in' relative to a given sphere of action would have to be clarified, in particular. The problems of 'language barriers', of linguistic, actional, and perceptual disturbances in this area would have to be taken up here. The question of the therapeutic strategies would thus acquire a new place: such strategies do in no way aim at the (re-)construction of 'normal' behaviour, because this kind of 'normal' behaviour can, with regard to the previous considerations, be no other behaviour than that conforming to the norms (values) of the groups in power – the therapy would thus, in the last resort, result in an adaptation to precisely that which in most cases caused the 'disturbances', i.e. the inability to conform to these norms. The construction of therapies would rather, in contrast to what is generally happening today, contain, as an essential component, the central principle of all methodological teaching: the ability to act in a specific sphere of action is essentially a *constructive* ability, not a reproductive one, an ability which, in the last report, aims at the construction of a better reality for Man and society within the spheres of the development of mind and interaction, which are under discussion here (cf. also §3.5.).

This kind of specification of teaching matter and teaching targets is of fundamental consequence for the type and the status of the 'material' which is used in 'teaching'. The material will first of all consist of verbal utterances or, more generally, of 'texts'. (What is meant by 'texts' here will be dealt with in the following.) These 'texts' will not be assigned values 'in themselves', which are to be grasped (as in traditional 'teaching of literature'): they will much rather serve as objects of demonstration with respect to a specific target. The 'formal' (or 'structural') means of organising a text do not constitute independent teaching matter (as I had still formulated it in my programmatic reflections 1972c). Their presentation must *in this connection* be subordinated to their 'functional' role in the primary 'text'-processing actions of the addressees (the notion of 'text'-processing will also be dealt with in the following).

It is quite another thing to devise a *heuristics* which would have to investigate *which* of these means may *at all* assume a 'functional' role in such processes: such a heuristics would be an essential component of the research required by hypothesis (v) and the remarks appended to (xvii) in §2.7. Such research may (and must) cover areas of differing extent and nature, according to the way the task of confirming hypothesis (v) has been divided up into sub-tasks. To what extent the results of these investigations (and not other investigations) are to be interpreted as partly confirming (or falsifying) hypothesis (v) can undoubtedly be only a question of consensus, a consensus, however, derived precisely from "success in scientific practice" (cf. supra). The same holds, in principle, for the more wide-ranging question as to when the confirmation of hypothesis (v) or *its concretisations as a set of mutually related partial hypotheses* (cf. Section 3,

§3.4.) may be considered concluded. (Here, too, the assimilation of all pertinent literature in the philosophy of science and theory of knowledge is an urgent desideratum, and I shall therefore not say any more about it here.) Whether this kind of activity is still to be called 'literary history' remains an open question. (It will certainly not be the kind of 'literary history' that is coming into fashion at the present time; I shall return to the question of the possibility of a 'theory of change' within the context of the approach developed here in §3.4.). It would, amongst other things, have to be clarified in what stage of 'teaching', and how, the 'learners' may (and ought to) participate in these activites. The answer to this question will depend upon how far it is possible and meaningful (in view of the immediate teaching targets) to go beyond the primary spheres of action of the addressees within their groups. (Here at last, if not before, the 'ideal' of "the same education for all" reveals itself as a fiction, to put it mildly.) This would require a more precise definition of the notion of 'environment', as I have so far taken its meaning to be evident.

I shall not continue the discussion of these points here. It will, by the way, not be too difficult to derive from them the guiding principles for the discussion of those activities which are subsumed under the expression literary criticism (cf. §2.4.).

3. Reconstruction of the Text Concept

3.1. In a third conclusion which can be drawn from the results of §2.8., I here take up the concept of 'text-processing', which was first referred to at the end of §2.3 (and was dealt with again in §2.9.).

In §2.9. I used the expression 'common basis'. This would require clarification as to how the approach sketched can lead to a 'crossing' of medial borderlines. I have so far restricted my reflections to the medium 'natural language'. There is, however, evidence for the fact that the differentiation of processing actions relative to media proceeds in too abstract a way and foreshortens the object of investigation in an unjustifiable manner. This does not only hold for the case of 'multimedial texts', but also for 'translations' from one medium into another, as they can constantly be observed in 'text'-processing actions. Here we come across another 'external' motivation for extending the basis of the theory of grammar as it stands (cf. §1.4.). The consequence is, namely, that a 'text-quality' must be postulated for verbal utterances, too, in order to account for observable correspondences between processing actions of multimedial 'texts' and of 'texts' in other media. These correspondences are grounded in precisely the specific functionality of semiotic structures (or 'texts'), which we have tried to demonstrate as given in verbal utterances. And it is by virtue of the qualities of their overall organisation, involving all of their parts and none of them in isolation, that semiotic structures may fulfil precisely these specific functions. I shall say no more about this as I cannot go into the question of a 'semiotic' foundation here (cf. the first explorations by Wienold (1972)). I shall restrict the discussion in the following to the medium 'natural language', though the 'semiotic' level of argumentation would undoubtedly be 'more natural' with respect to the approach sketched. I thus also, and deliberately, set aside the question to what extent differences in medium may be correlated with differences in functions fulfilled in behaviour by semiotic structures, and what specific role is played, in this context, by 'multimedial texts'. (The attempt to answer the latter question will, on the one hand, have to fall back on investigations of the biological-physiological prerequisites of complex perceptions, and on the other, to investigate on this basis in what way 'multimedial texts' are especially suited to manipulate information or to transmit 'surface content', cf. my remarks in §2.8.).

I should like to develop my argument from the remarks made on (xvii) in §2.7. They amount to saying that, as regards verbal utterances, the study of literature can only be interested in those 'formal' (or structural) 'means' which make for types (and can thus be correlated). These means cannot, as I would like to show in the following section, be represented in the framework of a linguistic basis, which is restricted to the structuring of regularities between "words in the sentence". The results of §2.9. offer – from the point of view of application involved – further evidence for this assumption, determining the relationship between linguistics and literary study (which I have anticipated in §2.7. by (xxi).)

But something else has to be mentioned first. The specification of the teaching target and the teaching method as well as the resulting preparation of teaching matter (cf. §2.9.) must, in any case, also involve the analysis of both the *basic* and the *actual* linguistic competence of the addressees (cf. §2.7. on (xvi) and (xviii)). Without this prerequisite the programme sketched would remain quasi-'idealist' and Utopian. This analysis will, on the other hand, always depend on the assumptions and aims connected with it, and therefore does not create an 'autonomous' space for linguistics (as has been falsely suggested by Chomsky's use of the expression 'competence'). This applies both to the investigation of the ontogenetical determinants of verbal interactions and the processes and stages through which a *basic* linguistic competence develops into *actual* competence: this development will always take place in and through complex processing actions, and is thus connected with the 'text-quality' of the verbal utterances involved (cf. §3.5.). I have already pointed out in §2.9. that 'disturbances' observable in this respect can only be countered by strategies which are themselves essentially related to the (functionally determined) 'text-qualities' of verbal utterances. The concept of 'linguistic competence' is thus characterised unambiguously as an empirical, operational concept: this must be emphasised in view of its philosophical misinterpretation (in particular in the Chomskyan tradition) as well as in view of its communication-theoretical re-interpretation (by Habermas and others), which both amount to an ontologisation of an operational term.

It remains to be asked what precisely is to be understood by such 'text-qualities' of verbal utterances, and furthermore whether and how we will be able to isolate a specifically 'literary' aspect of 'text-processing' on the basis of such 'text-qualities'.

3.2. In §2.3. I characterised the 'text-quality' of a verbal utterance by its ability to play a specific role in specific behavioural contexts or strategies. I also pointed out there, that it is not possible to declare aspects of verbal utterances which have been worked out 'deductively', as it were, to be carriers of their functionality. It is for this reason that I have so far left the expression 'text-quality' deliberately vague: nothing more is postulated than that the functionality of verbal utterances has to do with their overall organisation (§3.1.). This postulate seems to me to be a natural point of departure for the more wide-ranging question of what specific aspects of their overall organisation the various specific functions fulfilled by verbal utterances can be related to.

But this takes for granted *that* verbal utterances show overall organisation in one way or another – a presupposition which is confirmed both by the immediate evidence of intuition and by experimental results: the latter involve the possibility of quoting, for one verbal utterance, other verbal utterances which will be taken to be paraphrases (of each other), by more than one informant, and in differing situations, even though they may differ considerably as to their formal (structural) organisation; furthermore, the possibility of storing verbal utterances in such a way as to guarantee their recognition, on recall, by more than one informant, as well as their reproducibility in a way adequate to the situation, etc. We may thus assume specific organising principles of verbal utterances to be operating in this area, principles which in one way or another make it possible to transform the 'extension' of a verbal utterance, which as such can only be perceived and reproduced in especially favourable circumstances (and not always even then) into essential features characterising it as a whole. I am quite deliberately choosing the neutral expression 'essential features' to avoid premature determinations. In experiments of this kind, it is always possible that the experimental set-up predetermines the possible results and that thus the direct interpretation of the results with regard to the initial assumptions may easily lead into circular conclusions. It is also true that such experiments have so far yielded only very diffuse impressions of organising principles as they have only very rarely, and in the given cases only very superficially, reflected on the actual differences between processing actions as the result of differing behavioural contexts and strategies. This has not only to do, on the one hand, with the set-up, but also with the execution of the experiments, which transformed the natural processes into stylised ones (cf. the comments by Labov (1970)), and, on the other, with the fact that so far the only aspect considered interesting – explicitly or implicitly – has been the cognitive aspect. This spotlighting of the cognitive aspect has falsely suggested the existence of a constant which was advanced to justify attempts to make the construction of the grammar reflect the processes of production and perception of verbal utterances (cf. e.g. Fodor and Garret (1966)). These attempts were bound to fail merely because they relied on an *abstract* notion of 'sentence'. It would thus be misguided to expect results of better quality solely from the introduction of the notion of 'texts', even if the 'text'-concept used represented more than a 'technical' re-interpretation of the concept of 'sentence'.

These problems cannot be solved on the level of constructs. It is quite another matter, however, *that* we need constructs in order to solve them. Allotting part of the means of organisation of verbal utterances to the theory of grammar and to literary theory, respectively, is a first step in this direction. I have pointed out at the end of §1.5. and §2.9. that the realisation of such a division of labour can only be the result of a comprehensive heuristics. Here, however, I am interested in the guiding hypothesis on the basis of which this kind of heuristics has to be organised for the study of literature. (This applies in principle to all language-centred disciplines). It postulates, on the one hand, a set of specific 'means', and on the other specific 'organising principles' which constitute verbal utterances as 'texts' of a specific type. (Earlier, I had characterised this set of 'means' as type-forming means.) The hypothesis thus presupposes a further set of 'means' as fundamental. What then is the type-forming function of these means, and what particular means are there?

Grammatical theory organises, in principle, the totality of means for the construction of verbal utterances. Its guiding point of view is the discovery of the most general regularities. That does not preclude the possibility of introducing different levels of generality (a point which seems trivial, but often raises confusion, cf. e.g. the discussion following Van Dijk *et al.* (1972b), pp. 14–24, in Gülich and Raible, (eds.), (1972)). Linguistics chooses different levels of generality according to the nature of its object. What will thus emerge is a complicated structure which includes both the structuring of universals and the structuring of specific sub-systems of a natural language, together with an account of the relationship of these structural dimensions. This structuring is certainly of three dimensions (cf. the cited works by Labov, Lieb and Heger). It tries to integrate naturally the factors of time, space, and social stratification, respectively. The theory of grammar thus also forms the foundation for a general explication (and re-evaluation) of concepts such as 'dialect', 'style', etc. (cf. here in particular Labov's comments, (1970)).

The construction of a theory of grammar can thus be viewed as a filter which will admit – with respect to each structural dimension – only those results of the complex heuristics and pre-analyses of the language-centred disciplines which are in accord with specific criteria of generality (e.g. pervasive recurrence). What is not allowed to pass through this filter will belong to the domain of the other language-centred disciplines: of course effective criteria will have to be defined here, which will derive from the specification of the questions to be asked and the definitions of aims. Literary theory has then to relate the results of its attempt to impose further structuring upon a special class of phenomena to these structurings. It is possible to indicate various points at which these results affect the basic structurings offered by grammatical theory. This means that they have to be transduced into statements which move on differing levels of generality and apply to differing areas. Inasmuch as these attempts have a certain inductive power, they will lead to meta-statements about the relationship between grammatical theory and literary theory.

In the following I should like to give something like a synthesis of the different directions of the modern study of literature *from this point of view*. I shall do no more than make use of results capable of generalisation and leave out all presentation as well as critical appraisal (as for the latter, cf. my remarks on Russian Formalism and the works cited there).

One of the most striking findings is that the question of 'literarity', ('poeticity', etc.) of verbal utterances cannot be answered on the level of linguistic structuring: it has been proved impossible to derive, in any systematic way, differentiating criteria in terms of any of the fields discussed in this connection (e.g. in terms of different 'styles' or '(sub-)languages' within a natural language: cf. Ihwe (1971)). Positively viewed, this means that 'textqualities' as they are postulated by such expressions can only be established adequately if their origination *with regard to the whole area of linguistic structuring* is illuminated.

A further result implies – in connection with this – a more rigorous formulation of the question of the 'means', which are responsible for the 'literarity' ('poeticity', etc.) of verbal utterances. Two directions, not mutually exclusive, may be distinguished here. It becomes clear, first of all, that such means may essentially be characterised as *exploiting* linguistic structures: both 'metrical' and 'narrative' theory may be built up in such a manner that throughout, those points of linguistic structures are marked at which additional, extending or weakening, conditions operate. The attempts to systematise these conditions make apparent the outline of a 'hyper-structuring' of verbal utterances. It is, however, necessary to make various qualifications. They all have to do with the possible interpretation of such a procedure. The introduction of such a concept of 'hyper-structuring' can only then be justified if it is related to a corresponding empirical hypothesis. The main difficulty is, however, that, on the one hand, we are forced to delimit definite sets of verbal utterances through such hyper-structuring (otherwise it will be ineffective), and that on the other we cannot delimit more than *one*. But this involves an extremely strong empirical assumption, against which the characteristic asymmetry between constructs and data must immediately be quoted: means to characterise one type unambiguously will also become necessary for the characterisation of the other types. (Cf. in this context the comments by Jakobson on the 'poetic function' as an equivalence notion: 1960, p. 356.) On the level of constructs, on which we are moving here, it cannot be decided what the range of this hyper-structuring is to be, of what kind it is to be, or what implications for grammatical theory have to be derived from it (cf. the remarks on 'text'-types in §2.7.).

This is also where the second approach starts out from, the approach which aims at the definition of the functionality of the means applied. And though it accepts, in principle, the idea of a closed repertoire of such means, it focuses on the investigation of the distribution of these means on the basis of the requirements of 'literature' as an 'evolving series' (cf. §2.6.). It is to be emphasised that here another point of view comes into play (though only by way of suggestion). Such a repertoire must be positioned at a definite point in the most basic linguistic structuring: in the theory of grammar (or of universals), whereas the grammar of a natural language is only important in its specifying function (cf. for instance the 'correspondence rules' in the metrical theory by Halle-Kayser, (1971). 'Literarity' cannot be reconstructed in this abstract way only; it must also be described with respect to the 'three-dimensional' nature of the basic linguistic structuring: Tynyanov has already pointed out very clearly that the 'literarity' of a verbal utterance is essentially the result of continual "mixing of languages" ('dialects', 'styles') taking place within the 'series' and between 'series' (cf. for instance his comments on the 'letter', 1924/1969). And he had to ask himself to what extent the range of such "mixing of languages" could be covered by a complete theory (cf. the comments at the end of §2.7.) without advocating an 'essentialist' notion of literature. His answer, however, is still too dependent on the point of view of the evolution of the notion of literature within a privileged group (cf. §2.6.). The question of the *primary* object of investigation must therefore be raised again. To answer it once more throws into relief the ideological character of accepted notions of literature: taking into account the parameters established by 'socio-linguistics' and social anthropology, we find that verbal utterances within natural languages are very strongly dispersed, and layered, respectively, according to class (cf. Labov (1970)); on the other had, such notions of literature postulate only a few substantial features of differentiation of verbal utterances which are not related to the standard of privileged groups, or attempt to stabilise it, in this sense. They thus postulate a context for the perception and the use of verbal utterances which is one-sided and distorted (cf. also §2.8.), taking a specifically reductionist position. They represent the instance which, as it were, lends the very manifest, that is to say, class-conditioned, usurping of linguistic means the light of eternal values. Contrastively, we would have to investigate the actual processing of verbal utterances in their 'natural' contexts, which themselves would have to be reconstructed. As far as the results of 'socio-linguistics' and anthropology will take us in this respect, there is also, on this level of differentiation, evidence for specific 'text-qualities' of verbal utterances, evidence, that is, for the presence of specific 'organising principles' in their total organisation (cf. for instance Labov and Waletzky (1967/1972)).

If, therefore, despite all differentiation, constants emerge in verbal behaviour, it seems reasonable to look for them on the level of 'organising principles'. It is not the means in themselves, however one will determine them, which determine the 'text-quality' of a verbal utterance, nor is it the ('arbitrary') decisions of persons *P*. The type-forming (or better, type-characteristic) specificity of a verbal utterance much rather takes effect in the specific manner in which formal (structural) means are organised, which may be encountered in the correspondings pecificity of processing actions. This specificity serves to constitute verbal utterances, *qua* possibility of specific organisation of their means in certain behavioural contexts and strategies, *effectively* as 'texts'. The criterion of effectivity is used to mean that it can only be guaranteed through the constitution of verbal utterances as 'texts' in this way, so that they may fulfil specific psycho-social functions in social processes.

3.3. I should like to gather the various threads of my argument together now and try to characterise these functions first in their most abstract form:

(xxii) The metric of the value f in (xx), that is, for every concrete case under (xx), consists in the satisfaction of an ordering relation over the 'world' of p_i.

This is to continue my consideration of §2.7. in the sense of a deeper analysis of the complex situation of observation. The notion of 'metric' is used to represent the fact that an evaluation for a person P_i does not take place in isolation but corresponds to a *definable value on a scale* (the values that f can take for an ordered 'metrical space'). This, on the other hand, does not mean that such values are in some way immediately accessible to us. On the contrary, according to my argument so far, they are completely beyond the reach of immediate observation, but may be derived from such complex objects as *AR*, *V* and *P* in (xix), which are observable indirectly.

The second part of (xxii) postulates a 'world' for every person P_i. By 'world' I understand the comprehension of physical, social, historical, and psychological states, processes and relationships which are accepted and practised respectively by p_i in the corresponding verbal and non-verbal contexts. This characterisation does not exclude the fact that the 'world' of p_i may overlap the 'world' of (co-existent) p_j. In particular, it does not exclude the fact that the 'world' of p_i may change and that it is in essential components a product of complex socio-cultural determinants. (I shall come back to this in §3.5.)

The phrase "satisfaction of an ordering relation over the world of p_i" is used to represent a material interpretation of the expression 'organising principles' of §3.2. I am taking up the assertion which has been made very often, and in the most diverse contexts, that 'literary texts' etc. do not designate directly (with respect to a 'physical world' $\mathbf{W}_0$, which is in some way given or determined in a wider or a narrower sense by a set of statements about physical, social, historical, and psychological states, processes, and relationships, which function as a conventional base of reference in speaking of 'the world'), but that they much rather constitute a kind of fictive 'autonomous world' which may be distinguished from the other constitutive achievements of language. Two things are important about this assertion: first, it relates this constitutive achievement to the overall organisation of verbal utterances, and second, the 'referential function' (to use Jakobson's terminology) of 'literary texts' etc. is not completely excluded. On the contrary: the formulation of the assertion to which I am referring here in particular (predominant in the structuralism of Prague and Tartu, cf. Ihwe, §2.3., §2.4., *passim* and §3.4.) implies precisely the attempt to introduce 'literary texts' *via* peculiarities in the reference of linguistic expressions in verbal utterances. These peculiarities concern, in brief, the fact that immediate reference to given particularised 'contexts' (segments of W_0) is blocked in favour of a systematic and continuous 'attributive' use of linguistic expressions (in the sense of the distinction as indicated e.g. by Donnellan (1966), Stalnaker (1972), pp. 389–394, and others), and hence in favour of a mediated kind of reference to 'possible' states, processes, and relationships not necessarily compatible with those accepted for W_0. The term 'mediated' is used to exclude the possibility of 'contexts' being built up through the succession of sentence meanings, as for instance in the case of deductive reasoning. The elements capable of referring are much rather organised is such a way as to introduce, at first, only objects with their attributes into the succession, without allowing for the reconstruction of a context (mediately or immediately, 'in the text' or 'outside the text') within which one talks about them. (A crucial test would be the impossibility of assigning a definite truth-value to the sentences in the sucession: only after the end of the 'text' is reached can the distribution of the truth-values be ascertained *via* the 'possible world' created by this particular verbal utterance.) What is built up is rather an internal system of cross-references, and the stages of this process are determined by specific formal (structural) means such as mark beginning and end and complexity of the process of structuring (I am extrapolating here from the little knowledge we have about 'organising principles').

Only the internal system of reference in its totality yields the 'possible world' which is *introduced* – not the one *about* which one talks (cf. the analogy to 'use' and 'mention' in logic). It consists of a network of relations between a set of objects. Once there is no obligation any longer to look for these objects in an immediate referential way, once there is in particular no obligation to account for their relationships by – inductive or deductive – argument (i.e. with regard to valid laws and rules in W_0), the only obligation left is to postulate such relationships, states, and processes between those objects of all kinds which introduce a '(humanly) interesting' 'possible world'. The expression 'interesting' is *not* determined materially (as to the selection of objects and the relations between them): this is to be read as a two-place, not a one-place, predicate, and relates a process of structuring to the 'world' of persons *P* (which is made clear by the added word 'human'). This means that the value which is assigned by a person P_i to a verbal utterance depends essentially upon the measure in which this person is capable of constituting it as 'text', and also on the measure in which this 'text' is relatable to its 'world'. Under 'relatable' diverse functions may be subsumed, all of which are fulfilled by verbal utterances, according to extant observation (experimental observations as well as intuitive ones, cf. the survey in

Wienold (1972), Ch. II of Maranda and Maranda (1971), as well as §3.5., infra):

(xxiii) (1) the confirmation of elementary (fundamental) assumptions on which the 'world' of p_i rests (the phenomenon of 'identification' is to be included here, often in the sense of a 'sentimental', 'heroic', etc., stylisation),
(2) the mediation of conflicts of the most diverse kinds, but always of social relevance, in the 'world' of p_i,
(3) the extension, restructuring, and orientation (direction) of the relations valid in the 'world' of p_i.

These are only a few of the functions which can be stated immediately, they are still formulated in too general a way and appeal to the intuition of the reader. This should, however, not lead to the misunderstanding that the processes related to them always (or completely) take place on the level of consciousness or consciousreflection. I have tried to show in Section 2 of what nature these processes are. (To attempt to make them the subject matter of a didactics is an entirely different thing. I shall come back to this in §3.5.).

It is thus possible to formulate a category of verbal interactions with the help of the expression '(humanly) interesting' which in principle allows for the isolation of a specifically 'literary' aspect of 'text processing'. Though it is true that the expression 'literary' will not remain unaffected by this characterisation (cf. §3.4.), just as the expression '(humanly) interesting' receives a very different context of meaning from various 'aesthetics' in which this (or a similar) expression often appears also as a fundamental category (cf. for instance the *Poetics* by Aristotle).

Inasmuch as 'texts' are, in this way, uniquely related to the 'world' of persons P, the (transformation) effect of 'organising principles' may be conceived of as the construction of a 'possible' world w_i (with $i=f(p_i, a_i, t_i, r_i, k_i, z_i)$. Without wanting to enlarge on this point any further, we have thus discovered a reason for my belief that it is misguided to try to analyse the 'essential features' (cf. §3.2.) of verbal utterances on the 'semantic' level of verbal utterances, if this is conceived of as an (autonomous) aspect of their linguistic structure. An analysis which aims only at objectifiable contents (cf. §2.3.) cuts its task short; it must even appear, and especially when it has 'texts' as its objects, as nothing but a technicalised continuation or reproduction of the quasi-scientific interpretive procedures of all language-centred disciplines (cf. §2.1.–§2.2.). It is quite another matter to attempt to build up a unified descriptive language for the language-centred disciplines, and hence to develop a categorical framework (oriented towards an extended standard logic) for the investigation of the principles governing the referential mechanisms in various types of verbal utterances.

The foregoing thus represents a strong 'external' motivation for a theory of grammar which necessarily connects the introduction of the 'text'-concept in a controlled way with a structuring of the transition from the narrow range of objects, 'verbal utterance', to the wider range of objects, 'verbal interaction', within the framework of all language-centred disciplines; cf. §2.3. If it is possible to find a way of structuring to which the structurings of all the other language-centred disciplines may be related in a natural way, then also a central criterion for the evaluation of grammars will be formulated, and it can be shown with all desirable clarity that – apart from questions of internal correctness – every criterion of evaluation, in this area, is of an empirical (that is, in the last resort, applicational) nature. It remains to be seen however, to what extent a certain variability of grammatical models may be demanded by differing needs of the language-centred disciplines (and of course, what kind of variability this might be). Given the present state of research in linguistics (or 'text'-grammar), it seems plausible to demand a grammatical theory for the study of literature which is compatible with certain procedures and developments of modern logic. It may be expected that essential points of view of my argumentation could be systematised within a logical, language-analytical framework, and it is also beyond doubt that specific sub-areas can only be successfully treated with the help of specific logical, or logic-analogical, means. This is, for instance, true of the analysis of narrative structures using means from (or analogous to) modal predicate logic (cf. van Dijk *et al.* (1972a), parts I and III; I shall come back to the analysis of narrative structures in the following section). I shall say no more about this here as I have been concentrating principally on the formulation of the approach to literary study itself, as well as its connection with the development to linguistics under the key-word 'sentence grammar vs. text-grammar'.

3.4. I have abstracted from a number of factors in the preceding sections in order to be able to present as clear a picture as possible. I have, in particular, paid no attention to the question whether or not the 'organising principles' in the domain of a 'type' are uniform. From this point of view, the whole question of a complete and empirical text-typology would have to be discussed. The discussion in §2.7. was far too abstract in this respect, as it did not take into account the relationships between types and sub-types. The question for the study of literature is a two-fold one. First it is evident that, within its proper sphere, strongly varying ways of organising the means may be operative. We have to show that the given characterisation of the 'organising principles' does indeed cover them all, otherwise the objection would be valid that this construction achieves no more than the introduction, in an uncontrollable way, of the postulate of a unified concept of literature. On the other hand, it is in no way clear what actually is to be understood by "strongly varying ways of organising the means" in this domain. Typologies that have been presented on this basis quickly prove to be no more than a mixture of 'formal' (structural) categories and all sorts of 'functional' points of view. The variance of the points of view which have led to the unique abundance of 'literary' typologies is due to the obscurity of the underlying basis of interpretation: it can only be stated in a very vague way that the basis of reference chosen is in some way psychologising – 'phenomenological', psychologising-'behaviouristic', 'characterological', or something similar. (Presently the psychologising approach is losing ground in favour of the sociologising approach, but the basic procedure remains the same.)

In the preceding I have tried to make the basis of my interpretation clear. What is to be discussed now is the unity or diversity of the 'organising principles' themselves. I should like to answer this question in keeping with what was said in §3.3., less with regard to structural points of view than to the organisation of the means. The variability of the 'organising principles' can be explained in a natural way by saying that it is different aspects of the 'world' of persons *P* which are affected. The characterisations of (xxiii) would in this respect have to be differentiated more finely. The constancy of the 'organising principles' is due to the fact *that* verbal utterances of this type are constituted into 'texts' which are related to the 'world' of persons *P*; in this way, however, it might be further differentiated. If we then add the structural aspect, it is possible to make plausible a corresponding working hypothesis. The investigation of 'narrative structures' in varying media, cultures, and social organisations, has made apparent that specific basic elements of 'narration' may be reduced to a common basis despite the most diverse manners of organisation. It has also been shown how the observable formation of types and sub-types (even across the 'boundaries' of media) can in each case be related to diverse psycho-social functions in social processes of a certain type (cf. especially Maranda and Maranda (1971), Ch. II). These results, which may find an analogy within the 'classical' study of literature in the investigations of Russian Formalism with respect to the notion of 'genre', provide the foundation for a generalisation over the constants in the correlation of type-forming means and specific functions. All this implies at the same time the formulation of a very complex empirical task. The search for such constants is one face of this task, the structuring of the variable factors the other. It has to be explained how these constants, which have after all to be posited on a very high level of abstraction, are realised in a concrete case. This is the genuine point of departure for a 'theory of change' (cf. §2.9.); it could take up the suggestions of Russian Formalism to the extent that the notion of 'genre' focuses on the expression of a variable system of 'text sub-types' in time which in itself is socio-culturally determined. An important qualification has again to be made concerning the underlying notion of literature, which in this case has prevented an integral conception and treatment of the total process – though Russian Formalism was in the possession of some of the best basic material for it (Propp! cf. however an analogous criticism by Lévi-Strauss (1960), as to Propp). This applies in particular to the separation of 'verse' from 'prose' ('the' drama plays no more than a peripheral role). 'Verse' and 'prose' were conceived of as two functionally related 'series', and their specific 'means' as variable expressions of the same 'procedure', the same kind of organisation of verbal utterances in this area. The practical and theoretical consequences of these assumptions were, however, not followed up systematically.

It seems the obvious thing to posit the category of 'narration' as one of the most fundamental categories of all language-centred disciplines (this is immediately evident for journalism and historical, religious, and mythical research, possibly also for theology). The differentiation into types and sub-types (according to the constants established on various levels of generality) will then lead to a corresponding organisation of the objects and procedures of description for each domain.

In the case of the study of literature this means that literary theory would have to represent the techniques of formation, combination, and transformation of narrative structures and their realisation in sub-types, of those procedures, that is, which make up its specific domain. The concept of 'hyper-structuring' and its further differentiation is involved here in one way or another (cf. van Dijk *et al.* (1972a), Part I). The question of 'hyper-structuring' (cf. §3.2.) has, however, rarely been viewed from this angle of vision, so that I cannot go beyond these suggestions. This is particularly true for the emerging possibilities to indicate a *continuous transition* from 'narrative theory' to the theory of 'drama' and 'verse' on the basis of a specified 'literary' notion of 'narration'. The complete structuring of the notion of 'narration' thus specified would prove many problems of traditional 'genre theory' to be pseudo-problems (for instance the problem of 'mixed form', the search for 'pure' or 'basic forms', etc.). It would, on the other hand, bring many problems to light which have so far rarely moved into the field of vision, or have – especially in more modern times – remained taboo, thus, for instance, the hypothesis, related to this kind of structuring, "that also poems narrate", or "that one may view a drama as the staging of a narration". It must, however, be emphasised expressly that I have introduced 'narration' as a complex empirical concept (i.e. founded on an extensive and complex heuristics, including crucial experiments, cf. §3.2.), and that at this point (in literary theory) I am working with a construct which has connections with a specifically empirical analysis of this notion and will thus, most probably, receive a meaning very different from its meaning in other contexts, both those of everday life and 'literary study' (cf. also §3.3, the analysis of the *relata* of '(humanly) interesting).

On the structural side, constancy would thus be contained in the notion of 'narration' (as specified, in our case, by "the study of literature"), whereas variability would be connected with the means forming the sub-types and their realisation in time and space.

Again these assertions do not contain a normative component: they postulate nothing but an area in which certain processes take place. The structuring of this area as I have developed it in the preceding is, in addition, devised in such a way as to make it possible to include interferences between processes, transitions, and changes, in a natural way. This, however, presupposes that the notion of 'language-centred discipline' whose meaning I have so far taken for granted must be subjected to deeper analysis: my explication of the concept of 'study of literature' is emphatically declared to be a first exploration in this direction. Basically such a notion can only be introduced in a meaningful way after this kind of comprehensive work has been done.

3.5. Another abstraction concerns factors which are of an entirely different nature from those which were discussed in §3.4. The concepts introduced in the preceding sections represent a first and provisional systematics of the areas of investigation. This systematics aims essentially at the reconstruction of dynamic processes; it does not, however, contain information about the actual mediation of these processes in the actual processing. I have so far only touched upon this point of view very lightly, as we will need more wide-ranging reflections and, in particular, concrete analyses in order to achieve defensible systematic assertions.

That the analysis of the actual processing actions will require additional factors becomes immediately evident from my discussion of the approach and the aims of a specific didactics (cf. §2.8. and §2.9.). Its actual development requires a systematising of these factors even though as to their interrelationship they may be diffuse and very difficult to elucidate. Earlier I subsumed them under the key-word of the presence of 'manipulative strategies' and characterised them as to their effects by saying that these strategies were to block central functions in linguistic interaction in favour of peripheral ones, to neutralise and to distort them in this way. This must lead to profound 'disturbances' in the development of the ability of processing 'texts' (the recognition of 'types', the constitution and application of 'texts').

In this respect, the concepts introduced in §3.3. immediately assume a corrective function: their further elucidation must be directed at the establishing of criteria for a 'natural' development as well as the breaking down of 'distortions' of varying kinds. This is true, in particular, for the *relata* of the expression '(humanly) interesting', the 'text' of a_i, and the 'world' of p_i. Both *relata* are to be conceived of as complex social processes. Both processes are necessarily interrelated: the 'world' of p_i evolves through, and in, processing actions of verbal utterances of varying types. If verbal utterances of a specific type assume a particular role here, as my analysis of the expression '(humanly) interesting' suggests, the 'extension' of the 'world' of p_i, its 'direction', and thus, in the last resort, its 'effectivity' with regard to the mediate and immediate needs of persons *P*, will essentially depend on an as comprehensive and 'undisturbed' development as possible of f_i's ability to select such verbal utterances, to constitute these into 'texts', and to relate them to his 'world' and the 'world' of (co-existent) p_j's. The term 'effectivity' thus postulates a still more extended kind of activity of persons *P* than was demanded by the criterion of effectivity in §3.2. (which referred, in a less differentiated way, to the corrective function of the notions of §3.3). The expression implies further material characterisation of the aim of a specific didactics; if this didactics, in the present context, aims at putting persons *P* into a position to gain a certain amount of insight into, and control over, the factors which are operative in building up their 'world', this expression postulates, in addition, that the insight and control may be, at least partly, transformed into a purposive governing of the two processes of text-constitution and world-formation, and may thus, in fact, do justice to the social nature of these processes: independence of justified general and specific requirements and needs of the social space, as it is delimited by the expression 'verbal interaction', if this expression is to be more than a fashionable slogan.

In such a context it would then also be meaningful and necessary to investigate the specific functions which are fulfilled by 'text producers' of all kinds: it may have become clear that the idea of a freely acting 'author' will find no acceptance here but is to be analysed as a fiction or as a surrogate of certain ideologies. (This does not mean that 'text-producers' – consciously or unconsciously, explicitly or implicitly – will not aim at a perpetuation of this fiction: as to my own case, I hope not to have done that.)

I cannot go beyond these preliminary remarks. I hope, however, that I have made clear how the research strategy developed here results naturally from "applicational points of view", and, conversely, how such a strategy of research may make it possible to transform these points of view in a controlled way into socially-relevant practice (cf. § 1.7.).

University of Amsterdam

BIBLIOGRAPHY

Apostel, L.: 1972, 'Further Remarks on the Pragmatics of Natural Languages', in Y. Bar-Hillel (ed.), *Pragmatics of Natural Languages*, Reidel, Dordrecht, pp. 1–34.

Brainerd, B.: 1971, *Introduction to the Mathematics of Language Study* (= *Mathematical Linguistics and Automated Language Processing* **8**), Elsevier, New York.

van Dijk, T. A., Ihwe, J., Petöfi, J. S., Rieser, H.: 1972a, 'Zur Bestimmung narrativer Strukturen auf der Grundlage von Textgrammatiker', *Papiere zur Textlinguistik* = *Papers in Text-Linguistics* **1**, Buske, Hamburg.

van Dijk, T. A., Ihwe, J., Petöfi, J. S., Rieser, H.: 1972b, 'Thesen', in E. Gülich and W. Raible (eds.), 1972, pp. 7–8.

Donnellan, K.: 1966, 'Reference and Definite Descriptions', in *Philosophical Review* **75**, 281–304.

Fodor, J. and Garrett, M.: 1966, 'Some Reflections on Competence and Performance', in J. Lyons and R. J. Wales (eds.), *Psycholinguistic Papers*, University Press, Edinburgh, pp. 135–179.

Gülich, E. and Raible, W.: eds. 1972, *Textsorten*, Athenäum, Frankfurt/M.

Halle, M. and Keyser, J. S.: 1971, *English Stress. Its Form, Its Growth, and Its Role in Verse*, Harper and Row, New York.

Heger, K.: 1972, 'Rezension von H. H. Lieb 1970', *Zeitschrift für Romanische Philologie* **88**, 550–560.

Ide, H. (ed.): 1971, *Bestandsaufnahme Deutschunterricht. Ein Fach in der Krise*, Metzler, Stuttgart.

Ide, H. (ed.): 1972, *Ideologiekritik im Deutschunterricht* (= *Diskussion Deutsch*, Sonderband), Diesterweg, Frankfurt/M.

Ihwe, J. (ed.): 1971, *Literaturwissenschaft und Linguistik: Ergebnisse und Perspektiven*, 3 vols., Athenäum, Frankfurt/M. etc.

Ihwe, J. (ed.): 1972, *Literaturwissenschaft und Linguistik: eine Auswahl, Texte zur Theorie der Literaturwissenschaft*, 2 vols., Athenäum-Fischer Taschenbuchverlag, Frankfurt/M.

Ihwe, J.: 1971, *Das Problem der poetischen Sprache: ein Scheinproblem*, in J. Ihwe (ed.), 1971, vol. II, pp. 603–616.

Ihwe, J.: 1972a, 'Linguistik in der Literaturwissenschaft: Zur Entwicklung einer modernen Theorie der Literaturwissenschaft' (= *Grundfragen der Literaturwissenschaft* **4**), BSV, München.

Ihwe, J.: 1972b, 'Aspects empiriques et aspects théoriques d'un modèle de littérarité basé sur un modèle de la communication verbale', in Ch. Bouazis (ed.), *Essais de la théorie du texte*, Galilée, Paris, pp. 51–78.

Ihwe, J.: 1972c, 'What's Wrong with the 'Theory of Literature'? On the Role of Linguistics in the Study of Literature', in: *Linguistische Berichte* **23**.

Ihwe, J.: 1972d, 'Aspekte der Literaturwissenschaft. Ein Arbeitsprogramm', in J. Ihwe (ed.), pp. 7–16.

Ihwe, J., Petöfi, J. S., Rieser, H.: 1972, 'Möglichkeiten der Texttypologie auf der Grundlage expliziter Textgrammatiken' in E. Gülich and W. Raible (eds.), 1972, pp. 9–13.

Isenberg, H.: 1968a, 'Das direkte Objekt im Spanischen' (= *Studia Grammatica* **IX**), Akademie Vlg., Berlin.

Isenberg, H.: 1968b, 'Überlegungen zur Texttheorie', in *ASG-Bericht* **2**, August 1968, 17 p. (Revised version in J. Ihwe (ed.), 1971, **I**, 150–172.)

Isenberg, H.: 1970, 'Der Begriff 'Text' in der Sprachtheorie', in *ASG-Bericht* **8**, 21 p.

Jakobson, R.: 1921/1929, *Über den Realismus in der Kunst*, in Ju. Striedter (ed.), 1969, pp. 372–391 [vid. s.v. Tynyanov].

Jakobson, R.: 1960, 'Closing Statement: Linguistics and Poetics', in T. A. Sebeok (ed.), *Style in Language*, MIT Press, Cambridge Mass., pp. 350–377.

Labov, W.: 1970, 'The Study of Language in Its Social Context', *Studium Generale* **23**, 30–87.

Labov, W., and Waletzky, J.: 1967, 'Narrative Analysis: Oral Versions of Personal Experience', in J. Helm (ed.), *Essays on the Verbal and Visual Arts*, Am. Ethnological Soc., Seattle/London, pp. 12–14.

Lang, E.: 1972, *Über einige Schwierigkeiten beim Postulieren einer Textgrammatik*, in J. Ihwe (ed.), vol. **II**, pp. 17–50.

Lévi-Strauss, Cl.: 1960, 'L'analyse morphologique des contes russes', in *International Journal of Slavic Linguistics and Poetics* **III**, 122–149.

Lieb, H. H.: 1970, *Sprachstadium und Sprachsystem*, Kohlhammer, Stuttgart.

Maranda, E. K., and Maranda, P.: 1971, 'Structural Models in Folklore and Transformational Essays', *Approaches to Semiotics* **10**, Mouton, The Hague.

Stalnaker, R.: 1972, 'Pragmatics', in D. Davidson and G. Harman (eds.), *Semantics of Natural Language*, Reidel, Dordrecht, pp. 380–397.

Tynyanov, Ju.: 1924/1969, 'Das literarische Faktum', in, Ju. Striedter (ed.), 1969, *Texte der Russischen Formalisten I: Texte zur allgemeinen Literaturtheorie und zur Theorie der Prosa* (= *Theorie und Geschichte der Literatur und der schönen Künste* **6**/I), Fink, München, pp. 392–431.

Tynyanov, Ju.: 1927/1969, *Über die literarische Evolution*, in Ju. Striedter (ed.), 1969 (op. cit.), pp. 433–461.

Wienold, G.: 1972, *Semiotik der Literatur*, Athenäum, Frankfurt/M.

Wunderlich, D.: 1970, 'Die Rolle der Pragmatik in der Linguistik', in *Der Deutschunterricht*, Heft 4, pp. 5–41.

FOUNDATIONS OF LANGUAGE

SUPPLEMENTARY SERIES

Edited by Morris Halle, Peter Hartmann,
K. Kunjunni Raja, Benson Mates, J. F. Staal,
Pieter A. Verburg, and John W. M. Verhaar

1. John W. M. Verhaar (ed.), *The Verb 'Be' and its Synonyms. Philosophical and Grammatical Studies.* Part I: *Classical Chinese. Athapaskan. Mundari* 1967, VIII + 100 pp.
2. Nicholas Rescher, *Temporal Modalities in Arabic Logic.* 1967, IX + 50 pp.
3. Tullio de Mauro, *Ludwig Wittgenstein. His Place in the Development of Semantics,* 1967, VIII + 62 pp.
4. Karl-Otto Apel, *Analytic Philosophy of Language and the Geisteswissenschaften.* 1967. X + 63 pp.
5. J. F. Staal, *World Order in Sanskrit and Universal Grammar.* 1967, XI + 98 pp.
6. John W. M. Verhaar (ed.), *The Verb 'Be' and its Synonyms. Philosophical and Grammatical Studies.* Part II: *Eskimo Hindi. Zuni. Modern Greek. Malayalam. Kurukh.* 1968, IX + 148 pp.
7. Hugo Brandt Corstius (ed.), *Grammars for Number Names.* 1968, VII + 123 pp.
8. John W. M. Verhaar (ed.), *The Verb 'Be' and its Synonyms. Philosophical and Grammatical Studies.* Part III: *Japanese. Kashmiri. Armenian. Hungarian. Sumerian. Shona.* 1968, VIII + 125 pp.
9. John W. M. Verhaar (ed.), *The Verb 'Be' and its Synonyms. Philosophical and Grammatical Studies.* Part IV: *Twi. Modern Chinese. Arabic.* 1969, VIII + 125 pp.
10. F. Kiefer (ed.), *Studies in Syntax and Semantics,* 1969, IX + 242 pp.
11. A. C. Senape McDermott, *An Eleventh-Century Buddhist Logic of 'Exists'.* 1969, X + 88 pp.
12. Karl Aschenbrenner, *The Concepts of Value. Foundations of Value Theory.* 1971, XVII + 462 pp.
13. F. Kiefer and N. Ruwet (eds.), *Generative Grammar in Europe.* 1973, VIII + 690 pp.
14. J. W. M. Verhaar (ed.), *The Verb 'Be' and its Synonyms.* Part 5. 1972, VII + 232 pp.
15. H. J. Verkuyl, *On the Compositional Nature of the Aspects.* 1972, XIII + 185 pp.
16. Charles H. Kahn, *The Verb 'Be' in Ancient Greek.* 1973, XXXIII + 486 pp.
17. W. G. Klooster, *The Structure Underlying Measure Phrase Sentences.* 1972, XII + 264 pp.

In Preparation:

18. F. Kiefer (ed.), *Trends in Soviet Theoretical Linguistics*

SOLE DISTRIBUTORS IN THE U.S.A. AND CANADA:
Volumes 1–12 Humanities Press / New York

FOUNDATIONS OF LANGUAGE

SUPPLEMENTARY SERIES

Edited by Morris Halle, Peter Hartmann,
K. Kunjunni Raja, Benson Mates, J. F. Staal,
Pieter A. Verburg, and John W. M. Verhaar

1. John W. M. Verhaar (ed.), *The Verb 'Be' and its Synonyms. Philosophical and Grammatical Studies*. Part I: *Classical Chinese. Athapaskan. Mundari* 1967, VIII + 100 pp.
2. Nicholas Rescher, *Temporal Modalities in Arabic Logic*. 1967, IX + 50 pp.
3. Tullio de Mauro, *Ludwig Wittgenstein. His Place in the Development of Semantics*, 1967, VIII + 62 pp.
4. Karl-Otto Apel, *Analytic Philosophy of Language and the Geisteswissenschaften*. 1967. X + 63 pp.
5. J. F. Staal, *World Order in Sanskrit and Universal Grammar*. 1967, XI + 98 pp.
6. John W. M. Verhaar (ed.), *The Verb 'Be' and its Synonyms. Philosophical and Grammatical Studies*. Part II: *Eskimo Hindi. Zuni. Modern Greek. Malayalam. Kurukh*. 1968, IX + 148 pp.
7. Hugo Brandt Corstius (ed.), *Grammars for Number Names*. 1968, VII + 123 pp.
8. John W. M. Verhaar (ed.), *The Verb 'Be' and its Synonyms. Philosophical and Grammatical Studies*. Part III: *Japanese. Kashmiri. Armenian. Hungarian. Sumerian. Shona*. 1968, VIII + 125 pp.
9. John W. M. Verhaar (ed.), *The Verb 'Be' and its Synonyms. Philosophical and Grammatical Studies*. Part IV: *Twi. Modern Chinese. Arabic*. 1969, VIII + 125 pp.
10. F. Kiefer (ed.), *Studies in Syntax and Semantics*, 1969, IX + 242 pp.
11. A. C. Senape McDermott, *An Eleventh-Century Buddhist Logic of 'Exists'*. 1969, X + 88 pp.
12. Karl Aschenbrenner, *The Concepts of Value. Foundations of Value Theory*. 1971, XVII + 462 pp.
13. F. Kiefer and N. Ruwet (eds.), *Generative Grammar in Europe*. 1973, VIII + 690 pp.
14. J. W. M. Verhaar (ed.), *The Verb 'Be' and its Synonyms*. Part 5. 1972, VII + 232 pp.
15. H. J. Verkuyl, *On the Compositional Nature of the Aspects*. 1972, XIII + 185 pp.
16. Charles H. Kahn, *The Verb 'Be' in Ancient Greek*. 1973, XXXIII + 486 pp.
17. W. G. Klooster, *The Structure Underlying Measure Phrase Sentences*. 1972, XII + 264 pp.

In Preparation:

18. F. Kiefer (ed.), *Trends in Soviet Theoretical Linguistics*

SOLE DISTRIBUTORS IN THE U.S.A. AND CANADA:
Volumes 1–12 Humanities Press / New York